ENGLISH POETS
BRITISH ACADEMY CHATTERTON LECTURES

ENGLISH POETS

BRITISH ACADEMY CHATTERTON LECTURES

CLARENDON PRESS · OXFORD
1988

Oxford University Press, Walton Street, Oxford OX2 6DP

Oxford New York Toronto
Delhi Bombay Calcutta Madras Karachi
Petaling Jaya Singapore Hong Kong Tokyo
Nairobi Dar es Salaam Cape Town
Melbourne Auckland

and associated companies in
Berlin Ibadan

Oxford is a trade mark of Oxford University Press

Published in the United States
by Oxford University Press, New York

British Library Cataloguing in Publication Data
English poets: British Academy Chatterton
lectures.
1. Poetry in English, ca. 1500–1969—
Critical studies
I. Title
821'.009
ISBN 0-19-812842-8

Library of Congress Cataloging in Publication Data
English poets: British Academy Chatterton lectures.
p. cm.
"Lectures collected in this volume were first delivered in the
British Academy's series of Chatterton Lectures on an English Poet,
and subsequently published in the 'Proceedings of the British
Academy' and separately thereafter"—Foreword.
Includes bibliographical references and index.
1. English poetry—History and criticism. I. British Academy.
II. Title: British Academy Chatterton lectures.
821'.009—dc 19   PR503.E54 1988   88–9853
ISBN 0–19–812842–8

Set by Rowland Phototypesetting Ltd.
Printed in Great Britain by
Biddles Ltd.
Guildford and King's Lynn

FOREWORD

THE lectures collected in this volume were first delivered in the British Academy's series of Chatterton Lectures on an English Poet, and subsequently published in the *Proceedings of the British Academy* and separately thereafter. The series was established under the will of E. H. W. Meyerstein, which made provision for an annual lecture, to be given by a lecturer under the age of 40, on the life and works of a deceased English poet. (This last term is interpreted as 'a deceased poet writing in the English language'.) Between 1955 and 1987 thirty-three Chatterton Lectures have been delivered by suitably youthful scholars, and the present selection of thirteen thus represents approximately two-fifths of the whole series.

Chatterton and poetry were the principal abiding passions of Meyerstein's life. Of poetry he was both learned student and eager practitioner. Thirty-four volumes of poems appear in the list of his published works (nearly all printed at his own expense). It was no mere conceit that the first Chatterton lecture should have been on the subject of Meyerstein himself, delivered by his friend, executor, and trustee, Dr Lionel Butler, then a Fellow of All Souls College, Oxford.[1] It offers an eloquent, generous, but also judicious, summing up of a scholarly eccentric of remarkable accomplishment—poet, novelist, biographer, dramatist, and critic. There exists also a volume of Meyerstein's autobiographical writing, *Of my Early Life*, published posthumously[2] (which bears the curious epigraph 'I suspect but you mustn't tell anybody—that I was born out of Jane Austen by Apuleius'). And Mr John Wain (himself a distinguished Chatterton Lecturer) has written memorably of Meyerstein in his volume of autobiography, *Sprightly Running.*[3]

E. H. W. Meyerstein (1889–1952) was the only son of a wealthy London financier and philanthropist. After taking his

---

[1] *Proceedings of the British Academy* xli (1955).
[2] Neville Spearman Ltd., London (1957).   [3] Macmillan, London (1962).

degree at Oxford, he served from 1913 to 1918 in the Department of Manuscripts of the British Museum, with a brief interlude for war service in 1914. Thereafter he lived the life of an independent man of letters in London, save that between 1941 and 1946, displaced by bomb damage suffered in the blitz, he took up residence in Oxford. In 1930 his *Life of Chatterton* was published, a work that has not been superseded. To quote Dr Butler:

Marked by small attention to 'readability', and by no deftness in apportioning material between text and footnotes, it is nevertheless of a quality and insight far beyond those of the average standard biography. A reader who had not met the author might rightly suppose this book to have come from a scholarly, clever, and tireless mind. Meyerstein's friends knew that it was also a work inspired by passion . . . For Meyerstein was absorbed, indeed, obsessed, by Chatterton. He described him in poetry as his guardian angel, and he saw him in dreams . . .

Butler goes on to record:

One summer's morning, in Magdalen Grove, when I had thoughtlessly spoken to him of Chatterton in loose connexion with literary 'forgers' (I could have bitten out my tongue), Meyerstein turned on me in a sublime fury, the fury of one poet vindicating the fame of another: I never heard him defend a *living* person with such spirit or righteous anger.

And he speaks of Meyerstein's 'ambition for poetic renown' and 'his natural impulse to turn into poetry whatever he touched'. The following sentences read more sadly now, even than when they were first delivered:

His spirits often sank for lack of recognition, though he consoled himself that posterity would find in him the poetic stature to which contemporaries had been blind. The example of Chatterton strongly suggested to him that publicity is not fame, that fame roots itself most firmly in the grave. Yes, he had some faith in a posthumous laurel.

In conclusion, something should be said about the lectures here presented. When this volume was first proposed, the Academy invited Dame Helen Gardner to make the selection and write an introduction. She had for a good many years taken a close interest in the Chatterton series (and in the choice of lecturers), and regularly presided in the Academy on the evenings when the lectures were delivered. She accepted the invitation, called for a complete set of the papers, and reread them with evident care. Letters written while she was at work provide an enjoyable commentary, usually appreciative, sometimes caustic, on her task. The selection here presented is hers, and she was confident that it made 'a nicely balanced and lively volume'. The Academy is grateful to the lecturers for allowing their work to be reprinted in this form. When Dame Helen turned her thoughts to the introduction, she concluded that it ought mainly to be concerned with Meyerstein, 'as a sort of tribute to the memory of a remarkable and gifted eccentric . . .'. She had known him in the war years in Oxford, when both of them had worked in the New Bodleian on the Red Cross scheme for books for prisoners of war. She concluded, 'I do think the learned world owes some reparation to Meyerstein for neglect.' It is cause for great sadness that she died without being able to write her introduction. This Foreword is written in appreciation and respectful memory of Dame Helen Gardner and E. H. W. Meyerstein.

P. W. H. BROWN
Secretary
The British Academy

CONTENTS

CONTRIBUTORS

John Holloway Emeritus Professor of Modern English, University of Cambridge

Barbara Everett Senior Research Fellow, Somerville College, and Lecturer in English, University of Oxford

Anne Barton Professor of English, University of Cambridge

John Fuller Fellow and Tutor in English, Magdalen College, University of Oxford

Emrys Jones Goldsmiths' Professor of English Literature, University of Oxford

Roger Lonsdale Fellow and Tutor in English, Balliol College, University of Oxford

Claire Lamont Senior Lecturer in English Literature, University of Newcastle upon Tyne

John Bayley Warton Professor of English, University of Oxford

Christopher Ricks Professor of English, Boston University

Seamus Heaney Boylston Professor of Rhetoric and Oratory, Harvard University; poet

Jacqueline S. Bratton Reader in Theatre and Cultural Studies, Royal Holloway and Bedford New College, University of London

Laurence Lerner William R. Kenan Professor of English, Vanderbilt University, Tennessee

G. S. Fraser (1918–1980) Poet, critic, and university teacher

1. SKELTON

BY JOHN HOLLOWAY

To discuss Skelton effectively is to do more than elucidate the past on its own terms, and for its own sake. There is no constraint on anyone to do more than this, and to think that there is, is to think like a barbarian. But if a critic finds that his subject empowers him to do more, he ought to say so. Although Skelton was writing more than 450 years ago, there are certain respects in which his poetry offers us enlightenment and guidance in the literary and cultural problems which confront us today. To seize on the essence of his poetry is to be wiser for our own time. Were that not so, I should perhaps have left the subject of Skelton to others, because I find it congenial but do not find it reassuringly easy.

The problems of today upon which this poet casts light may be indicated by two quotations: one from Mr Robert Graves and one from Bernard Berenson. Mr Graves, writing in 1943 on the development of modern prose, referred to the 'eccentrically individual styles' of Meredith, Doughty, James, and others and added, 'many more styles were invented as the twentieth century advanced and since there was keen competition among writers as to who should be "great" and since it was admitted that "greatness" was achieved only by a highly individual style, new tricks and new devices multiplied'.[1] Forty years before this, Berenson in his essay on the decline of art pointed out how modern European culture, 'mad for newness' as he put it, has committed itself to a ritual of unremitting dynamism. 'We are thus perpetually changing: and our art cycles, compared to those of Egypt or China, are of short duration, not three centuries at the longest; and our genius is as frequently destructive as constructive.'[2]

Modern English literature surely illustrates what Berenson

[1] *The Reader over Your Shoulder* (1943), p. 120.
[2] *Italian Painters of the Renaissance* (1938 edn), p. 331.

referred to. The unremitting search for a new way with words, a
new kind of hero, a new device for carrying poetry a stage
further, a new model from some past writer or some foreign
literature—these features of the scene are familiar. The search
for newness is not itself new, and probably no age has been
quite without it. Naturalizing foreign models was an integral
part of Chaucer's achievement (though very far, of course, from
the whole of it). But the question is not one merely of innovation; it is of a growing need for constant innovation, and a
sense that however often the game of change is played, we are
always soon back with what is played out and old-fashioned.

This attitude to writing seems to have become established in
England in the course of the sixteenth century. There is a
well-known passage in Bacon's *De augmentis scientiarum*, written
towards the close of his life, in which he hints at the playing-out
first of the vogue for Cicero, then of the vogue for Seneca,
shortly before, and shortly after, 1600. More to our immediate
purpose is a passage from Puttenham's *Art of English Poetry* of
1589. Puttenham was himself the author of the best and
best-known manual of a new poetry, which was learning amply
from ancient and from foreign models, and which had for many
years been coming to dominate the English literary scene. The
following passage not only illustrates how Puttenham saw
Skelton as the last of the bad old days, and Skelton's immediate
successors as those who laid the foundations for the new and
stylish; it also points unconsciously forward, in several turns of
phrase, to the derivativeness, or the vacuous grandiosity, or the
empty ingenuity, which have plagued us intermittently ever
since:

Skelton [was] a sharp satirist, but with more rayling and scoffery than
became a Poet Lawreat, such among the Greeks were called Panto-
mimi, with us Buffons, altogether applying their wits to scurrilities
and other ridiculous matters. *Henry* Earle of Surrey and Sir *Thomas
Wyat*, betweene whom I find very littel difference, I repute them . . .
for the two chief lanternes of light to all others that have since
employed their pennes upon English Poesie, their conceits were loftie,
their stiles stately, their conveyance cleanly, their termes proper,
their meetre sweete and well proportioned, in all imitating very
naturally and studiously their Maister *Francis Petrarcha*.[3]

[3] *Art of English Poetry* (1589), i. 31, ed. G. D. Willcock and A. Walker (1936), p. 62.

Ever since the time of these two allegedly indistinguishable lanterns of light, imitating one's master naturally and studiously, or finding a new master, or going one better than the old master, have figured prominently in English verse; and whether the end sought has been stateliness and loftiness, or cleanness and propriety, or sweetness and naturalness, the underlying ideas of a regulation of poetry, or a reform of poetry, have seldom been far distant.

To take Skelton as representative of something different from this tradition, and as instructive on account of the difference, is not to see him merely as an illiterate extemporizing buffoon. He has been seen in these terms in the past, but modern scholarship has made the view quite untenable. Skelton was one of a group of Latinists—the proto-humanists we might call them —whom Henry VII drew into his service, and of whom Polydore Vergil is perhaps the best known.[4] He was an accomplished rhetorician, and his employment of the figures of rhetoric is as deliberate (if somewhat more intelligent) as that of his contemporary Stephen Hawes.[5] His best-known poem, *Phyllyp Sparowe*, is a kind of reverent burlesque of the ritual of the Mass, and certain attendant offices, in accordance with established medieval convention;[6] and in the description of his heroine in this poem, we can recognize the two places, and no more, where Skelton the poet abandoned the literary model, for the sake one supposes of the real girl.[7] That model was the first specimen *descriptio* in Geoffrey de Vinsauf's *Poetria nova*, and this work was as much the medieval poetic handbook as Puttenham's work was the Elizabethan one. Skelton's own disclaimer, 'though my rhyme be ragged',[8] is itself something of a literary convention: his first modern editor, in 1843, pointed out that Sir David Lindsay and Spenser say the same of their own verse. William Caxton notices that in his translation of Diodorus Siculus Skelton wrote, 'not in rude and old language

---

[4] W. Nelson, *John Skelton* (1939), pp. 4–59.

[5] V. L. Rubel, *Poetic Diction in the English Renaissance* (1941), pp. 37–9.

[6] See, e.g., Ian A. Gordon, *John Skelton* (1943), pp. 122 f.

[7] See the Introduction to Skelton's translation of the *Bibliotheca historica* of Diodorus Siculus (ed. F. M. Salter and H. H. L. Edwards, 1956; EETS, original series 229, p. xxxix).

[8] *Colyn Cloute*, l. 83.

but in polished and ornate terms craftily', and it is essentially the same kind of compliment as Caxton pays elsewhere, justly, to Chaucer ('crafty and sugared eloquence') and as Spenser's spokesman E.K. was later to pay to the 'well grounded, finely framed' verse of Spenser. Skelton was a learned, a professional writer, conversant with his craft and art, an aureate poet as well as a laureate one.

There is always a danger, however, that in registering the qualities of a poem which have been laboriously and scrupulously brought into focus by scholarship, we become blind to the qualities which were never in need of such focusing, because they sprang off the page at us. This is a vital point for Skelton. One of his shorter poems, which begins: 'Knolege, aquayntance, resort, fauour with grace', has been described as 'an ecphrasis in the aureate manner of Lydgate'.[9] So it is: we can easily see that it conforms to a literary recipe, and there is little to see in it besides. A companion piece is in part very similar. Also an address to a woman, it closes with an appeal to her to observe the conventional courtly code. It opens with the literary convention at its limpest and most stilted:

> The auncient acquaintance, madam, betwen vs twayn,
>   The famylyaryte, the formar dalyaunce,
> Causyth me that I can not myself refrayne
>   But that I must wryte for my plesaunt pastaunce . . .

But Skelton's tongue is in his cheek; this poem is rapidly transformed; its subject—a wife who has been playing fast and loose with her husband—turns into a hectic stable-yard scene, and a horseman struggling with a mare that has the devil in her: 'ware, ware, the mare wynsyth wyth her wanton hele!', 'Haue in sergeaunt ferrour [farrier]'. The violence and confusion veritably explode what was only a mock-decorous poem. It is not, of course, the first English poem to explode the convention in which it is ostensibly written; but to explode a literary convention, it is necessary to obtain a powerful charge drawn from outside convention.

What this charge is, may be seen, perhaps, by turning to the most misjudged of all Skelton's poems, *The Tunnyng of Elynour*

[9] Salter and Edwards, edn cit., p. xxxvii.

Rummyng. To say that the tradition of this rough, vernacular poetry has been lost, is not to say everything about it; but is certainly to point towards the difficulty which this poem has created for one critic after another. Henry Morley saw it as 'a very humble rendering to simple wits of the repulsive aspects of intemperance in women';[10] Miss E. P. Hammond refers to its 'wallowing coarseness';[11] even Professor Lewis seems to see the problem as one of tolerating ugliness for the sake of liveliness, and expresses his preference for the Scottish poem *Christis Kirk on the Grene*, which he praises for melody, gaiety, and orderliness, and which attracts him through its occasional underlying lyricism.[12]

To experience these feelings about *Elynour Rummyng* is to wish that it were different in kind from what it is, rather than better in quality. This picture of a morning in a low, country ale-house is if anything less coarse than Langland's superb account of Gluttony in the ale-house in *Piers Plowman*,[13] and melody and gaiety are as far from Skelton's purpose as they were from Langland's. Indeed, to mention Langland is to become aware that Skelton's piece is no thoughtless extemporization, but has its literary antecedents. Its subject, and its attitude to that subject, were both recurrent in medieval writing;[14] and it is possible that Skelton's poem, with its old and ugly ale-wife whose customers are all old and ugly women, is even a kind of calculated counterpart to a poem by Lydgate, the 'Ballade on an Ale-Seller', in which (to express oneself in modern terms) a bold and handsome barmaid attracts an exclusively male clientele. In Lydgate's poem, we certainly have orderliness, the order of the ballade; and we have a literary, even sometimes a lofty, diction. But they are quite out of key with the subject; and

> With your kissyng thouh that ye do plesaunce
>   It shall be derrer, er thei go ther way
>   Than al ther ale, to them I dar wel say

[10] *English Writers*, vol. vii (1891), p. 190.
[11] *English Verse between Chaucer and Surrey* (1927), p. 337.
[12] C. S. Lewis, *English Literature in the Sixteenth Century* (1954), p. 138; p. 106.
[13] C Text, Passus vii, ll. 349–441.
[14] Cf. R. L. Greene, *Early English Carols* (1935), no. 419 ('The Gossips' Meeting'); Greene compares this with the 'Good Gossippes Songe' in the Chester play of the Deluge, but this is too short and slight to have much in common with Skelton's poem.

that is the best that Lydgate's poem can do: a hasty glimpse of fact, a trite moral, a reader nonplussed with tedium.

The ugly side of *Elynour Rummyng* is simply an honest reflection of the poverty and primitiveness which were the staple of life for a rural peasantry in England at that time, as they doubtless are still for rural peasants over most of the planet. If we find coarseness, it is not through identifying what Skelton is trying to make of his material, but through plain unfamiliarity with the material itself. In a now almost unknown poem of just after Skelton's time (happily almost unknown, for in the main it is very bad), we can glimpse those same conditions, but they peer through despite the poet's almost admitted inability to render them. The poem is Copland's *Hie Waie to the Spitale Hous*, and the passage is that which describes the beggars and vagrants as the Watch sees them at night:

> But surely, every night here is found
>   One or other lying by the pound
> In the sheep cotes or in the hay loft
> And at Saint Bartholomew's church door full oft
> And even here alway by this brick wall
>   We do them find, that do both chide and brawl
> And like as beasts together they be throng
>   Both lame and sick and whole them among,
> And in many corners where that we go,
>   Whereof I greatly wonder that they do so.[15]

Copland virtually confesses, with that disastrous last line, how his facts defeat him. Skelton's poem is in another world; or rather, his ale-wife with her skin that is 'grained lyke a sacke', her customers who tie their hair up in a shoe-rag when they come to pawn their crocks for ale, her pigs that wander in and out of the bar and scratch themselves on the furniture, take us back with exuberant vitality into the real world.

This extraordinary vividness, where many find vividness an embarrassment, has prevented readers from grasping the full range of the poem as a record of fact. *Elynour Rummyng* is not, as it has been called, a 'purely objective' record of peasant reality.[16] It is not a moralizing poem, but it is full of an

---

[15] Quoted from A. V. Judges, *The Elizabethan Underworld* (1930), pp. 4–5.
[16] W. L. Renwick and H. Orton, *The Beginnings of English Literature to Skelton* (2nd edn, 1952), p. 114.

awareness of the essential humanity of the scene it depicts, and of such a comprehension of this (a comprehension neither harsh, nor slack and casual) as is the only foundation for significant moralizing. It is easy to miss this subtler side to the poem; but it is there, in the customers who

> lothe to be espyde,
> Start in at the backe syde,
> Ouer the hedge and pale,
> And all for the good ale.

It is there in those who sit glumly because they have nothing to barter, and can only drink as much as they can chalk up on the beam. It shows in the differences among what customers bring to barter: some the reasonable merchandise of the prosperous peasant, some the last thing in the house or the last thing that they ought to part with. Once we are conscious of these aspects of the poem, even the character of Elynour herself takes on a new light. Her shocked indignation when one of the customers falls over and lets her skirts fly up is a genuine and convincing turn of peasant humanity. Some of the customers ask for drink and have no money. Skelton writes:

> Elynour swered, Nay,
> Ye shall not beare away
> My ale for nought,
> *By hym that me bought*!

This does not merely contrast the bargains which men and women strike, with that which Christ struck: it brings them disquietingly, revealingly together. With these things in mind, one can see that the opening description of Elynour herself has a similar deeper significance. In general idea it clearly resembles one of the most humane and moving passages in the whole of Chaucer's writings, the 'Prologe of the Reves Tale':

> For sikerly, whan I was bore, anon
> Deeth drough the tappe of lyf and leet it gon;
> And ever sithe hath so the tappe yronne
> Til that almoost al empty is the tonne.

Incidentally, the elderly Reeve's 'grene tayl' may have its connection with 'Parot hath a blacke beard and a fayre grene

tale' in Skelton's *Speke, Parot*, a poem which I shall discuss later.
But there is a clear detailed link with *Elynour Rummyng* too.
Chaucer's Reeve says:

> But ik am oold, me list not for pley for age;
> *Gras* tyme is doon, my *fodder* is now forage;
> This white top writeth myne olde yeris.

Skelton uses just this idea of fresh plants and dead forage; and
when he does so, it is difficult not to see both Chaucer's direct
influence, and the general quality of his insight into human
transience:

> Her eyen . . .
> . . . are blered
> And she gray hered . . .
> Her youth is farre past:
> Foted lyke a plane
> Leged lyke a crane;
> And yet she wyll iet,
> Lyke a jolly fet . . .
> Her huke of Lyncole grene,   [hood
> It had been hers, I wene,
> More then fourty ycre;
> And so doth it apere,
> For the grene bare thredes
> Loke lyke sere *wedes*,
> Wyddered lyke *hay* . . .

As against this poem, *Christis Kirk on the Grene* is gay, boisterous
comedy with something even of slapstick; and to compare it
with Skelton's poem is to bring out not the defects, but the
distinctiveness, and the depth, of the latter.

Miss M. M. Gray has pointed out that the spirit of poems like
Christis Kirk on the Grene is not typical of the Scottish poetry of its
period.[17] If *The Tunnyng of Elynour Rummyng* is related instead to
such poems as *Tydingis fra the Sessioun*, which is by Dunbar, or
The Devillis Inquest, which is almost certainly not so, a quite new
kind of difference emerges. In *The Devillis Inquest* we find:

[17] M. M. Gray, *Scottish Poetry from Barbour to James VI*, Introduction (1935 edn,
p. xvii); these remarks relate specifically to another similar work, *Peblis to the Play*, but
also generally to the humorous poems in the Bannatyne and Maitland MSS which
stand out (like *Christis Kirk on the Grene*) for their 'boisterous merriment and rough-and-
tumble'.

'Be Goddis blud', quod the taverneir,
'Thair is sic wyine in my selleir
Hes never come in this cuntrie.'
'Yit,' quod the Devill, 'thou sellis our deir,
With thy fals met cum downe to me.'   [measure

This is not a Chaucerian movement of thought; it is a vision which concentrates on the evil in the fact, sees it intensely, and is directed by uncompromising though sternly controlled indignation. One side of reality is brought into a clear focus by a cold and masterly economy of language. This is still a link with Chaucer, but it is not Skelton's kind of link. With rare exceptions, Chaucer's firm linguistic line, his masterly economy, do not serve purposes like these, but less severe ones. Dr Edwards, discussing Skelton's lyrics, wrote, 'He possessed none of Chaucer's smiling acceptance of men and women as they are.'[18] Even as an account of Chaucer, that might need a little amendment; but what is relevant for the moment is that it distinguishes too sharply between Chaucer and Skelton.

In my view, *Elynour Rummyng* is the most significant of the poems which Skelton wrote in the short metre which has been named after him. *Phyllyp Sparowe* has great grace and charm, but its chief character is to be an endearing poem, and one which deserves a rather higher place in our affections than it does in our minds as a whole. What may be found in it is not far from what may readily be found elsewhere, and its principle of organization lacks the vitality and distinctiveness of what integrates *Elynour Rummyng*, the single scene of the poem itself as that is brought progressively into focus.

Colyn Cloute and *Why Come Ye Nat to Courte* can by no means be passed over altogether, and if I pass them over for the moment, it is in order to give emphasis to a more general point. The poems which Skelton wrote in short lines, rhyming consecutively—in 'Skeltonics'—are usually thought of as his most distinctive and most interesting ones. Long ago, this idea supplied Isaac D'Israeli with a cumbrous joke and a mixed metaphor: 'Whenever [Skelton's] muse plunges into the long measure of heroic verse, she is drowned in no Heliconian stream.'[19] The idea reappears implicitly in what has surely

---

[18] H. L. R. Edwards, *Skelton* (1949), p. 53.   [19] *Amenities of Literature* (1841), ii. 69.

been the most influential of recent pronouncements on Skelton,
Mr Graves's poem 'John Skelton';[20] which is itself written in a
kind of Skeltonics, and which catalogues most of 'helter-skelter
John's' short-line poems, without any reference to his other
works. And when Professor Lewis writes[21] 'the things that Mr
Graves gets out of Skelton's work are much better than anything Skelton put in', he is clearly not taking issue with this
conception of Skelton, even if it is not entirely clear that he is
endorsing it.

This notion of what most distinguishes Skelton is erroneous.
The Skeltonics are what stand out if we survey only the
externals of his work, if our findings are a little too much like
what a computer could find if Skelton's poems were fed into it.
Some of the most remarkable qualities of Skelton's work are
obscured and concealed by his short line. It is in what D'Israeli
misleadingly called 'the long measure of his heroic verse' that
these qualities are most abundantly manifested; and when this
is realized, Mr Graves's

> What could be *dafter*
> Than John Skelton's laughter?
> What sound more *tenderly*
> Than his *pretty* poetry?[22]

falls short of adequacy.

Skelton's *The Bouge of Court* is widely recognized as a poem
which gives a new individuality to a conventional form, that of
the dream-poem; but this is perhaps to praise that work on too
easy terms. References to Skelton's avoidance of 'the conventional arbor',[23] or statements like 'for the first time the medieval
vision is given a strictly local habitat',[24] ignore such things as
the opening of *The Kingis Quair*: King James of Scotland's
sleepless night, with his book at his bedside and the matins bell
to disturb him. With this, one might take Henryson in his study
mending the fire and taking strong drink to keep out the cold
before he settles down to write *The Testament of Cresseid*. The
distinction of Skelton's poem lies less in any simple change in its
mechanical organization than in something which is woven
intimately into its texture. Among the various allegorical

---

[20] *Poems (1914–26)*, pp. 6–8.   [21] Op. cit., p. 143.   [22] The italics are mine.
[23] Nelson, op. cit., p. 78.   [24] Edwards, op. cit., p. 62.

figures whom Skelton meets as passengers when he boards the
ship from which the poem takes its title, that of *Riot* is perhaps
the best known.

> Wyth that came Ryotte, russhynge all at onces,
>   A rusty gallande, to-ragged and to-rente;
> And on the borde he whyrled a payre of bones,   [dice
>   Quater treye dews he clatered as he wente;
>   Now haue at all, by saynte Thomas of Kente!
> And euer he threwe and kyst I wote nere what: [cast
> His here was growen thorowe oute his hat.
>
> Thenne I behelde how he dysgysed was:
>   His hede was heuy for watchynge ouer nyghte;
> His eyen blereed, his face shone lyke a glas;
>   His gowne so shorte that it ne couer myghte
>   His rumpe, he wente so all for somer lyghte;
> His hose was garded wyth a lyste of grene,
> Yet at the knee they were broken, I wene.

The whole account is more than 'a brilliant sketch of the
seedy jazz-humming early Tudor roué' as it has been called;[25]
and it displays more than 'a genius for satirical portraiture'[26]
tout court. The affinity with Chaucer's *Pardoner's Tale* may be
partial, but it is unmistakable. The note of pathos, of tragedy, in
Riot's high spirits and gay tatters is surely not the mere inter-
polation of a modern mind. 'Counter he coude *O lux* vpon a
potte', Skelton writes: it is the medieval hymn *O lux beata trinitas*
that Riot counters. We are never—even if only through the
oaths that come incessantly throughout this poem—allowed to
forget the religious dimension in which all these essentially
human and mortal figures have their being: '. . . by that Lorde
that bought dere all mankynde, I can not flater, I muste be
playne to thē'; 'by that Lorde that is one, two, and thre, I haue
an errande to rounde in your ere' (an echo of Chaucer echoing
Dante). This note might not be clear as irony, were it not for the
constantly scriptural note, also sounding ironically, of the rest:

> Loo, what it is a man to haue connynge!
> All erthly tresoure it is surmountynge.

and

[25] Edwards, op. cit., p. 63.   [26] Nelson, op. cit., p. 82.

> Nay, naye, be sure, whyles I am on your syde,
> Ye may not fall, truste me, ye may not fayle

and

> Maystress, quod I, I haue none aquentaunce,
> That wyll for me be medyatoure and mene

All these illustrate something which is sustained so much without intermission through the poem, that in the end it is quite inescapable. Skelton is leading us to see these figures —figures 'for whome Tyborne groneth both daye and nyghte' —as erring mortal creatures in the fullest sense. In fact, his compassionate comprehension is if anything more in evidence here, and more sombrely and solemnly in evidence, than it is in *Elynour Rummyng*.

Something else is in evidence also. Skelton's insight into men's behaviour, exact and humane as it was, could not but equip him with real power for dramatization. English literature seems to have reached fully dramatic writing only with difficulty: perhaps because this demands a sense of realistic detail, a power of comprehension and selection which is more than realism, and also (if it is to be in verse) an appropriately developed metrical vehicle. Chaucer mastered it even as early as the *Hous of Fame*; most English medieval plays only strive towards it. In *The Bouge of Court* it is otherwise. Dyssymulation, for example, tells the poet that the people in the court are all malicious gossips. Then he makes an exception of himself:

> For all be it that this longe not to me,
>   Yet on my backe I bere suche lewde delynge:
> Ryghte now I spake with one, I trowe, I see;
>   But, what, a strawe! I maye not tell all thynge.
>   By God, I saye there is grete herte brennynge
> Betwene the persone ye wote of, [and] you.

These lines are typical; and to read them is to find oneself in almost total contact with the movement of a living mind, as it works its way from word to word.

Contrast that moment in Stephen Hawes's *Example of Vertue* when the poet meets Dame Sensuality riding on a goat. If we have any hopes that her arrival will infuse a little vitality into the poem, the poet extinguishes those hopes with stunning celerity:

'Nay' said Discretion, 'that may nat be'
'No' said I 'in no maner of wise
To her request will I now agree
But evermore her foul Lust despise . . .'

'So forth I went . . .', Hawes's next stanza baldly opens. That is
a phrase which recurs throughout his poem: each time it marks
an evasion of reality, a giving up by the poet before material he
cannot handle.

By contrast, the personifications of *The Bouge of Court* have a
vivid vernacular life. So have those in *Magnyfycence*. Among
Skelton's works for acting, this is the only one (apart, probably,
from a recently discovered and uninspired fragment) which
survives.[27] For all that it is too intricate and much too long,
some of the dialogue of this play is remarkable for the period in
which it was written or indeed for long after. One example is the
scene in which three of the characters in the play recognize a
fourth through his disguise, and then pretend that he is a priest
and maul at his clothes:

CLOKED COLUSYON. Knowe they not me, they are to blame.
    Knowe you not me, syrs?
FANCY.   No, in dede.
CRAFTY CONVEYAUNCE. Abyde, lette me se, take better hede:
    Cockes harte, it is Cloked Colusyon.
CL. COL. A, syr, I pray God gyve you confusyon!
FAN. Cockes armes, is that your name?
COUNTERFEIT COUNTENAUNCE. Ye, by the masse, this is euen the
    same,
    That all this matter must vnder grope.   [spy out
CR. CON. What is this he wereth, a cope?
CL. COL. Cappe, syr; I say you be to bolde.
FAN. Se, howe he is wrapped for the colde:
    Is it not a vestment?
CL. COL.   A, ye wante a rope.
C. COUNT. Tushe, it is Syr Johnn Double cloke
FAN. Syr, and yf ye wolde not be wrothe—
CL. COL. What sayst?
FAN.   Here was to lytell clothe.

[27] See G. L. Frost and Ray Nash, ' "Good Order": a Morality Fragment', *Studies in
Philology* (1944), 483.

This is essentially—a point to which my argument will revert
—a colloquial, a vernacular kind of drama. But it is written
with a fine sense of action upon the stage, and with real
shrewdness and insight into how men can behave.

Yet vivid dialogue is not what gives *Magnyfycence* its essential
significance. After all, the most that can be said of it on that
score is that it points forward, hesitantly and intermittently, to
the comic dialogue of Shakespeare. In some other qualities also
(its overtly political setting, and perhaps its emphasis on
Aristotelian ideas of the good ruler and of virtue) this work
looks forward; but in its most deeply significant qualities it does
not. Miss Dodds has pointed out that although the moral of the
play for Magnyfycence himself is Measure, the Aristotelian
Golden Mean, it is not that for the audience.[28] For the audience
the moral is the more deeply traditional idea of universal
Mutability:

> A myrrour incleryd is this interlude,
> This lyfe inconstant for to beholde and se;
> Sodenly riches, and sodenly pouerty,
> Sodenly comfort, and sodenly adversyte . . .

With these lines, and the quite new note that they strike, we
reach the core of Skelton's achievement. The idea is that upon
which Chaucer ends his *Troilus and Criseyde*, and the lines are
from a rhyme-royal stanza, which is Chaucer's metre in *Troilus*
also. But what Skelton writes in the two whole stanzas which
follow is a collection of gnomic sayings, having the structure of
thought and the rhythm of language of an essentially proverbial
wisdom—in this case, the basic idea that life is suddenly one
thing, and then suddenly its opposite.

I have not seen any explicit recognition of how much
Skelton's work owes to proverbial language and, in doing so, to
the whole way of life and cast of mind which finds its expression
in proverbial language; although the first modern edition of his
work is full of information on this very subject. Here the
short-line poems are relevant once again. 'Such apple-tree,
such fruit'; 'loth to hang the bell / About the cattes neck';
'hearted like an hen'; 'not worth a leek'; 'as wise as Waltham's

---

[28] Madelaine Hope Dodds, 'Early Political Plays', *Library*, Series III, iv. 393.

calfe'; 'all is fish that cometh to net'; 'we may blow at the coal';
'Mock hath lost her shoe'; '. . . it is a wily mouse / That can
build hys dwellyng house / Within the cat's ear'. It is not a
matter merely of Skelton's using proverbial wise sayings. His
verse draws on the proverbial kind of expression for a good deal
of its vivid metaphorical wealth, and for something of its whole
attitude to its subject—bold yet unassuming, essentially down-
to-earth. It uses the clichés of ordinary people (which are not
clichés at all, because instead of making the mind gloss over the
plain facts, they bring it abruptly up against them), but it is
using these in order to assimilate the whole idea which ordinary
people form of reality. To notice Skelton's reliance on the
proverbial expression is not to notice a literary trick or a literary
routine, but to notice, at its most easily recognizable point, the
essential quality of what was creative in his mind. It is the same
quality which shows, if we consider the use that he made of the
authors on whose work he draws. Juvenal in his Eighth Satire,
for example, had written:

> quo, si nocturnus adulter
> Tempora Santonico velas adoperta cucullo

Skelton almost certainly has this passage in mind when he
attacks Wolsey in *Why Come Ye Nat to Courte*. But what he writes
is:

> Ye may weare a cockes come;
> Your fonde hed in your furred hood,
> Holde ye your tong, ye can no goode:

Juvenal's line embodies penetrating diagnosis of a fact, and an
attitude of angry superiority to it; Skelton replaces this by the
common sense, and the impudence towards the great, of the
plain man.[29] In the *Garlande of Laurell* there is an account of how
the legendary phoenix consumes itself in the fire. Skelton
probably had a passage from Ovid's *Metamorphoses*, Book xv, in
mind. But he adds something of his own about this phoenix:

> her wynges betwene
> *She bet up a fyre* with the sparkis full kene.

---

[29] Juvenal, *Satires*, viii. 144–5; *Why Come Ye Nat to Courte*, ll. 1232–4. It should be
noticed that at l. 1224 Skelton has quoted verbatim part of l. 140 of the Eighth Satire.

Perhaps it is not fanciful to suggest that this comes nearer to an early morning scene in Skelton's own Norfolk parsonage than it does to Ovid. Again, when Skelton in the same poem describes the bard Iopas singing his song in the garden of the Muses, he follows the closing lines of the first book of the *Aeneid*; but there is nothing in Virgil which corresponds to the lively turn of thought, humorous rather than witty, whereby Skelton's Iopas, in his songs about the constellations, includes

> that pole artike which doth remayne
> *Behynde the taile* of Vrsa so clere

and there is nothing in Virgil, beyond a plain 'rainy Hyades', which could produce the vividness in Skelton's homely touch of the Hyades' 'misling eye'.

Thus Skelton's manner of drawing *on* proverbial language, and of drawing *away* from literary models, both show the essential quality of his mind. So, more important perhaps, do his rhythms. Dr Nelson argues that of all the various progenitors which have been suggested for Skelton's short-line verse, the brief, chiming cadences of Latin rhyming prose are the most likely.[30] In this he seems clearly right. It is much more open to question, though, whether he is right in suggesting that the transition from prose to verse was, in Skelton's case, one towards smoothness and regularity. Across Skelton's short lines there seems often to be an irregular longer rhythm; one which is essentially a long *spoken* rhythm, the angry accelerating tirade brought to a halt by an emphatic rallentando and pause.[31] If this is so, it is yet another example of how Skelton adapts what is literary in origin, to vehement speech and to the cast of mind which lies behind that kind of speech.

However this may be, a parallel trend is quite indisputable in the case of Skelton's longer metre. His long lines, it is true, can sometimes be seen almost as two short 'Skeltonic' lines combined into one: but that is by no means the whole of the story. The convention that the poet should disparage his own work may have been why Skelton makes one of the characters in *Magnyfycence* say that his big speech—really a dramatic chorus —will be 'In bastarde ryme, after the dogrell gyse'. But again,

---

[30] Op. cit., pp. 90f.
[31] For example, *Why Come Ye Nat to Courte*, ll. 65–81.

that is not the whole story. Ramsay, in his admirable Introduction to *Magnyfycence*, made it clear that Skelton's long line, even in the rhyme-royal sections of this poem, is not the regular five-stress line of Chaucer at all, but a four-stress line, which never carries the sense on from line to line; which is marked by constant alliteration; which may vary in length from seven to fourteen syllables; and which (in its ampler forms) centres round a very emphatic central pause. The result is a loose and exceedingly flexible verse form, which can vary from almost naïve spareness to great amplitude and copiousness, which has as its metrical unit not the foot at all, but the self-dependent phrase, and which is such as we might expect, in fact, if the *sense* of rhythm which we have in Langland were to find expression through a Chaucerian rhythmic *form*. It is essentially a metre dominated by the speaking voice, as against a metre which dominates the voice. Here is one part of its connexion with proverbial utterance, and the cast of mind which goes with that. Another part is how it resists enjambment—each line makes a separate statement—and how it naturally falls into two parts around its central pause, for this is also common in proverbs ('Many hands, light work': 'If wishes were horses, beggars would ride').

Skelton may be the master of this metre, but he did not invent it. A fifteenth-century poem like 'Lex is layde and lethyrly lukys'[32] falls not only into the metre, but also into the gnomic quality, the macaronics, and the general attitudes, which are common in Skelton:

> Veritas is demytt to hange one the ruyde,
> Verecundia was drownytt at the laste fluyde,
> So that few freyndes may a man fynde,
> ffor rectum iudicium commys so farre be-hynde.
> ffraus is fykyll as a fox, and reuys in this lande
> ffuror is hys freynde, as I vnderstande . . .

Another poem of this general period is especially interesting, because it shows the attitude of mind which tended to force a poet into using the stress metre. Like Skelton's *Ancient Aqueyntaunce*, it begins as a deceptively decorous compliment to a lady, and turns into a ribald and telling palinode against her. As it

[32] Carleton Brown (ed.), *Religious Lyrics of the Fifteenth Century* (1939), no. 176, p. 269.

makes this transition in attitude, its rhythm changes from
smooth, regular rhythm by feet, to an abrupt Skeltonic rhythm
of the half-line and the independent phrase.[33] The poem opens:

> O masy Quince hangying by your stalke
> The whyche no man may pluk away ner take

but by the time it is *speaking out*, as it were, we find:

> My louely lewde masterasse take consideracion
> I am so sorrowfull there as yet be absent
> The flowre of the barkfate the fowlyst of all the nacion
>   [tanner's vat
> To loue you but a lytyll hit myne entent.

Counterfeit Countenaunce's chorus speech, to which I referred
just now, is essentially in this stress-rhythm also; and it is this
which enables it to move, with great freedom and ease, out of
abrupt and lively dialogue into what is almost a rhetoric of
moral denunciation. It opens with light rhythms:

> Fansy hath cachyd in a flye net
> This noble man Magnyfycence

and little by little, in a kind of flux and reflux, it is amplified into
lines like:

> Counterfet preaching and byleue the contrary
> Counterfet conscyence, peuysshe pope holy:
> Counterfet sadnesse, with delynge full madly;
> Counterfet holynes is called ypocrysy;
> Counterfet reason is not worth a flye;
> Counterfet wysdome, and workes of foly;
> Counterfet countenaunce every man doth occupy:

In face, the general recurrent movement of this play is to
modulate from dialogue to this kind of moralistic verse, solemn
yet essentially popular, and traditional in both its style and its
attitudes.

   This same kind of poetry is constantly breaking through the
'literary' tedium of *The Garlande of Laurell*:

> He is not wyse ageyne the streme that stryvith;
>   Dun is in the myre, dame, reche me my spur;

---

[33] Henry A. Person (ed.), *Cambridge Middle English Lyrics* (1953), no. 49, p. 40.

Nedes must he rin that the deuyll dryuith;
   When the stede is stolyn, spar the stable dur;
A ientyll hownde shulde neuer play the kur;
It is sone aspyed where the thorne prikketh;
And wele wotith the cat whose berde she likketh.

But it is in *Speke, Parot* that these qualities of Skelton's work are most important; for that extraordinary poem is surely his masterpiece. Historically, this poem marks not only Skelton's hostility to Wolsey, and those policies of Wolsey which were inescapably bringing the whole traditional order to an end, but also Skelton's general hostility to the growing Erastianism of the time,[34] and his now final abandonment of London and the court, for the great conservative family of the Earl of Surrey. Indeed, everything which shows Skelton's place in the culture of his time seems to converge in this poem. Morality based upon the Bible and the people's proverbial wisdom goes here with an essentially vernacular use of language throughout, with a distinctive development of the polyglot macaronic kind of writing (a popular and goliardic mode rather than a literary one), and with a structure perhaps somewhat like those commonplace books which passed from hand to hand in the country houses of the time, and contained, as Dr Person writes, 'poetry and prose, English, Latin or French, long poems and scraps, religion and science, devotional and satiric works, riddles and proverbs'.[35] Yet out of this gallimaufry, Skelton has made a poem which (though chaotic from a mechanical standpoint) is imaginatively perhaps the most unified of his works. It is unified in the persistent vivid presence and exceedingly distinctive tone—the tone of one who threatens and yet is himself in danger—of the parrot. Above all, it is unified in the gathering power and directness of the attack, as this gradually breaks through the speaker's prudence, and at last converts his glancing blows into the finale: a fierce and solemn denunciation of Wolsey himself.

So braynles caluys hedes, so many shepis taylys;
   So bolde a brggyng bocher, and flesshe sold so dere;
So many plucte partryches, and so fat quaylles;

[34] See J. M. Berdan, 'Speke, Parot', *MLN*, xxx (1915), 140.
[35] Person, op. cit., p. iv.

> So mangye a mastyfe curre, the grete grey houndes pere;
> So bygge a bulke of brow antlers cabagyd that yere;
> So many swannes dode, and so small revell;—
> Syns Dewcalyons flodde, I trow, no man can tell.

We scarcely need to trace Wolsey's father the butcher in these lines; nor the Tudor greyhound, nor the swan of the Buckinghams. The passionate, unflinching, comprehensive grasp of reality, and embodiment of it in an idiom wholly the writer's own, are unmistakable. If we think that we are not in the presence here of poetic greatness, it is because there is a kind of poetic greatness which we have not learnt to know.

To make this claim is not to make every claim. Nothing in Skelton has the poignancy, strangeness, and deep compassion of the scene in Henryson's poem where Cressid the leper begs an alms of Prince Troilus, and his memory of her swims half-way to the light, then goes back into darkness. Skelton has nothing of the imaginative brilliance of the opening words of Sensualitie in Sir David Lindsay's *Ane Satire of the Thrie Estatis*:

> Luifers awalk, behald the fyrie spheir,
> Behauld the naturall dochter of Venus.

This is not going far afield. But what we do see in Skelton is one quite distinctive kind of excellence. A variety of vernacular traditions, a vernacular kind of insight, a metre and a rhythm which had for long had contact with vernacular expression —all these are things that come together in Skelton's verse. Once again George Puttenham, cicerone of the new and more literary poetic which succeeded Skelton and put him out of favour, settles the matter for us (though he settles less than he thinks) when he ridicules

small and popular musickes song . . . upon benches and barrels heads where they have none other audience then boys or countrey fellowes that passe them in the streete, or else by blind harpers or such like taverne minstrels that give a fit of mirth for a groat, and their matters being for the most part stories of old time . . . also they be used in Carols and rounds and such light or lascivious Poemes, which are commonly more commodiously uttered by these buffons or vices in plays then by any other person. Such were the rimes of Skelton . . . in our courtly maker we banish them utterly.[36]

---

[36] Op. cit., ed. Willcock and Walker, pp. 83–4.

To accept this view of Skelton as essentially in contact with the apprehension of life of the ordinary man is not to accept what Puttenham thought it meant: that his work was crude and artless. I hope I have shown how he drew upon, or sometimes transformed, the work of his predecessors or models. His rhythmic spontaneity and flexibility is in fact a high technical achievement, towards which we can see him working from *The Bouge of Court* on to *Speke, Parot*. But when we open our minds to what is most truly distinctive of his verse, what we find is amplitude, immediacy, rhythmic vitality, a suggestion of embodied power for growth. What Henry James called 'felt life' seems to operate in the texture of his language with a quite special freedom and directness; and when that language moves, as it often does, beyond plain speech, it moves in a different direction from that which is conspicuous in Donne, say, and the poets who followed Donne: it moves less towards wit and argumentation through figurative language, than towards the proverbial, gnomic solemnity of the traditional and popular mind. The result is no mere mirror of life, no mere Skeltonic realism, but something of an embodiment of life's permanent contours and essential vitality. Much may be absent from Skelton, but this, with the deep refreshment which it brings, is not absent.

When a literature—like our own—is old, and has been forming and re-forming for centuries, and has been reacting with other literatures for centuries also, there is a strong tendency for your courtly maker or his counterpart to predominate; and for writers generally to seek and expect success through naturally and studiously imitating their master Francis Petrarch, or whoever may be the Francis Petrarch of the hour. We cannot but recall at this point the views of Graves and Berenson (I quoted them earlier) about multiplying tricks and devices, achieving a highly individual style, perpetually changing, displaying genius which is as frequently destructive as constructive. 'What has not been done? What is left to do?' seems more and more insistently to become the cry. Perhaps this cannot but tend to happen, as the centuries go by, and the past tends to weigh more and more upon the present. But in Skelton, although he had the interests of a serious poet, and although his civilization was old rather than young, something else has happened. In his work, the dominance of artistry by reality is peculiarly thoroughgoing, peculiarly intimate and genuine. This may or may not be the balance which we find at the very pinnacle of artistic achievement; but I think it is one which we greatly need to contemplate, and to learn from, today.

2. DONNE: A LONDON POET

BY BARBARA EVERETT

DONNE's most recent biographer calls him 'a Londoner born and bred'.[1] Donne was born a few streets east of St Paul's, and it was in the environs of St Paul's and as its dean that he died sixty years later. It is there too that his funeral effigy still stands, one of the very few to survive the Great Fire. The epitaph on it speaks of Donne looking eastward, towards 'eum cuius nomen est Oriens'. But Donne spent his youth and his prime looking westward—west towards the court and towards those centres of power which had in his own lifetime finally established themselves in the capital. Donne was an ambitious man: he desired to be better than he was; and he did not lose his worldliness when he entered the Church—that Church whose bishops had on the king's orders defended the depraved Countess of Essex the year before they ordained the poet. For Donne's life spans a period during which it was not possible, certainly not wise, to think with much simplicity about 'worldliness'; if it had been so, Shakespeare could not have written *Hamlet*. Or, to put the matter in terms of place rather than time, Donne was—despite the abstract habits of thought which might appear to dissociate him from place—a Londoner by nature as well as by birth and breeding, a man who (as Walton put it) 'could not leave his beloved London, to which place he had a natural inclination'. And he was a Londoner at that crucial phase in the city's history when it took on the character by which we recognize it now. For in Donne's lifetime London became a metropolis.

The emergence of London as a metropolis at the end of the sixteenth century—as one of the world's great cities, with a quarter of a million souls in it—is a fact on which historians of the period have recently much insisted, partly because the

---

[1] R. C. Bald, *John Donne: A Life* (1970), p. 19.

inordinate growth of London created such a crisis of awareness in Londoners themselves. When Donne was a boy of 8, London's Lord Mayor and aldermen were already appealing to the Privy Council for legislation whereby the alarming expansion and overcrowding of 'this great metropolis' might be contained.[2] And the Proclamation that answered this appeal was only the first move in four centuries of struggle to meet the human problem posed by the growth of the city. In the forty or so years since Henry VIII had died, London had become a new Rome (and it was, apparently, actually called 'Romeville' in the thieves' jargon of the time). The sense of size is a relative thing: Donne's City and suburbs were small in extent compared with Greater London today, but his contemporaries had a notion of their city not by any means unlike our own. '*Rome* was a *Metropolis*', wrote Thomas Heywood in 1612, 'a place whither all the nations knowne under the Sunne, resorted: so is *London*.'[3] Or, to quote Professor Jordan, the distinguished historian of London's charities: 'The London of 1600 was . . . a great urban complex. It was a metropolis in every sense of the word, with an immense wealth and a size which comparatively made cities of the next rank seem no more than large provincial towns.'[4] Some sense of what was happening to London may be painlessly acquired if one contemplates for a few minutes three of those map-pictures or long views of the City which have survived from the sixteenth and seventeenth centuries. In the 1540s Wyngaerde came to London and drew with economy and delicacy the outline of an airy Tudor river-town that clustered round the curve of the Thames. In about 1600 Visscher sent his traders' and travellers' Thames in a straight line across seven feet of wall space, and banked up behind it an incredible density of houses and towers and spires and shops. The viewer stands in Southwark and looks through the masts of great trading vessels into the City of 'profit and loss' itself. When in the 1640s Wenceslas Hollar came, he drew from above the grand prospect of a city that one now sees as almost Restoration before the Fire and before Wren, so purely and widely urban is the London he surveyed.

[2] See Norman G. Brett-James, *The Growth of Stuart London* (1935), pp. 67–8.
[3] *An Apologie for Actors* (1612), sig. C2.
[4] W. K. Jordan, *The Charities of London 1480–1660* (1960), p. 16.

It was this astonishingly developing city, the 'national centre for risk capital' as Jordan calls it, that produced John Donne; the son of one of those rich London merchants who were as munificently and independently philanthropic as they were mercenary, and who played so large a part in giving their city its standing and its character. Many of London's inhabitants came, made their fortune (or lost it), and went home again. Donne was born there, lived there, and died there. To appreciate this fact adds, I think, something to our understanding of him as a writer. That there is some obvious and simple sense in which Donne was a London poet may be perceived by opening the *Songs and Sonnets* in the format of its first edition and reflecting on the chaotic and formidable variety of available experience that assails the reader there, as it might a country visitor to the capital. The voices of the poems constitute a crowd; and in this milieu to think, to discriminate, or to *be* at all with any individuality it was necessary (so the poems seem to say) to withdraw to that characteristic Donne place, the enclosed bedroom of lovers overlooking a street from which arises all the perpetual noise of life. The restless vitality of these poems, their arrogant expertise and quick boredom, their amusement and anxiety and fatigue—these are recognizably metropolitan qualities. But I should like to go on from this superficial impression to explore some further senses in which Donne might be called a London poet. Some of my definitions are far removed from any literal or topographical meaning. Yet Donne's own sense of London admits of the metaphorical: for him as for anyone a familiar place was pre-eminently a fact of consciousness. As he himself wrote: 'I do not make account that I am come to *London*, when I get within the wall: that which makes it *London* is the meeting of friends.'[5] Necessarily I am concerned here less with the London of history than with 'that which made it London' to Donne.

I

We can none the less meet in Donne a city evoked with that vitality of social observation that was to characterize Donne's

---

[5] *Letters to Severall Persons of Honour: written by John Donne Sometime Deane of St Pauls London* (1651), p. 285.

coeval Jonson nearly a decade later. For Donne's most vivid
evocation of London comes in the first of his Satires, which
must be the product of his early twenties when he was still a
student at Lincoln's Inn. This brilliant, original poem is mainly
a monologue spoken by a young scholar. He meditates on
London—for he is being tempted to forsake his bookish isolation and 'go on the town'. The tempter is the poem's second
voice, from whom we hear snatches, and of whose person we
catch glimpses, in its second half. He is the antithesis of the
scholar—Zany to his Pedant (if we think in terms of the Zanni
and Dottore of the *commedia dell'arte*):[6] a 'fondling motley
humorist' whose hunger to wander equals the other's loyalty to
a life that is for all its narrowness secure and sanctioned by the
wisdom of those dead philosophers, historians, and poets who
line the shelves of his grave-sized study: 'Let me lye / In prison,
and here be coffin'd, when I dye.' The dazzlingly animated
opening fifty lines disclose a prospect of crowded London
streets from which sharp details stand out: here the 'Captaine
. . . / Bright parcell gilt, with forty dead mens pay', there the
silhouetted gesture of salute by which the errant friend prices
the passers-by: 'and to that rate / So high or low, dost raise thy
formall hat.' What Donne is doing here, however, is very
characteristic of him. This animated scene is not (as we soon
learn) the real thing—it is only the young scholar's half-
appalled and half-enchanted fantasy: for this prospect of the
London streets is only a reverie, entertained in anticipation,
and we have still to descend into the London of actuality. The
point at which we do so (hard to discern otherwise) is signalled
by an abrupt change of style. The addressed friend ceases to be
thou and becomes *he*; the reader ceases to stand in for that friend
and becomes an onlooker. The pair move into visible action
before us: we immerse in activity and are surrounded by
crowd-like voices in an acoustic effect almost stereophonic. And
now the voices of the two friends intertwine to the point at
which their identities are confused, despite the fact that their
roles are in theory so far apart:

> Now leaps he upright, joggs me, 'and cryes, 'Do 'you see
> Yonder well favour'd youth?' 'Which?' 'Oh, 'tis hee

[6] The pair recur a decade later as Morose and Truewit in Jonson's first London
comedy *Epicoene* (1609).

That dances so divinely.' 'Oh', said I,
'Stand still, must you dance here for company?'
Hee droop't, wee went . . .

'But Oh, God strengthen thee, why stoop'st thou so?'
'Why? He hath travail'd.' 'Long?' 'No, but to me'
(Which understand none,) 'he doth seeme to be
Perfect French, and Italian.' I reply'd,
'So is the Poxe.'[7]

And then, the two young voices still casually running on, a third
change of style occurs, this time into rapid narrative, to record
with a negligent detachment the fate of the zany friend:

At last his Love he in a windowe spies,
And like light dew exhal'd, he flings from mee
Violently ravish'd to his lechery.
Many were there, he could command no more;
He quarrell'd, fought, bled; and turn'd out of dore
    Directly came to mee hanging the head,
    And constantly a while must keepe his bed.

So the poem ends.

This First Satire appears to drift aimlessly. Indeed its easy
rambling movement, as of a liberated self-abandonment to
whatever happens, is one of its chief charms. It flaunts a lordly
sprezzatura, as if its author isn't really trying. But in the modern
world a sense of the fortuitous may be a main route to the sense
of the real. Moreover the poem's structural peculiarity of
vagrant progress is reinforced by the topicality of reference: one
can learn things from it about the London of the early and
mid-fifteen-nineties as from a newspaper—the rich heiresses,
the thinking horse, the vogue for black feathers. It seems clear
that Donne has been taught by those Roman satirists to whom
he went to school, that satire must be, if not urbane, at least
urban; that it must focus itself on some central civilized community. He borrows Horace's device of a saunter through a
peopled city in which there is much to entertain and much to
provoke derision; he takes over too the sophisticated compli-
cation of Horace's dialogue formula. From Juvenal Donne

[7] Quotations from Donne's Satires and Verse Letters are from the edition by W.
Milgate (Oxford, 1967); from the Elegies and Songs and Sonnets, that by Dame Helen
Gardner (Oxford, 1967); from the Divine Poems, that by Dame Helen Gardner
(Oxford, 1952); from The Anniversaries, that by Sir Herbert Grierson (Oxford, 1912).

perhaps learned that a personal relation to a great city both loved and detested was worth the expressing. In his third Satire (used again by the Augustan Johnson in *his London*) Juvenal had created one of the most brilliant crowd scenes in literature, and its powerful rendering of the feeling of physical immersion may have lingered in Donne's memory. Both these poets of Rome, Horace and Juvenal, helped Donne towards the half-casual re-creation of London in the image of Rome nearly a century before the English Augustans were to do it again. For it was in the last quarter of the sixteenth century, when London became a metropolis, that English poets were first able to make full imaginative use of the most metropolitan of the Roman poets.

There is a third debt to Roman poetry which must be accounted for. The dialogue between the young men which I have quoted takes its conventions neither from Horace's nor from Juvenal's more straightforward exchanges but from the mannered and knotted burst of conversation that opens the first Satire of Horace's younger imitator, Persius. Later in this satire Persius explains the principles of his dialogue: the second voice is, he says, merely an 'imaginary opponent'. I think it possible that Donne took a hint from Persius here in that his poem is as much an internalized debate as it is a piece of reporting. Of Donne's two young men, who are so closely involved with each other as to be at moments indistinguishable, one is a dominant, detached, and talkative scholar (the 'Pedant'), who loves the stability of theory, even though it may resemble the security of the prison and the grave. The other (the 'Zany') is an impulsive and susceptible clown, who wanders as the appetite for mere experience leads him—and it leads him finally to the 'stability' of the lecher's and brawler's sick-bed. It is not difficult to recognize the younger Donne in the learned and fanciful scholar. And though the 'grinning, smacking, shrugging' friend may seem a less familiar persona, it is relevant to recall that in an early verse letter romantically addressed to a young friend Donne refers to himself as 'Thy debtor, thy echo, thy foil, thy zany'—and there is much of the 'zany' that emerges in his poetry. Both young men, scholar and clown, may be twin aspects of the personality of which Walton was later to say: 'The melancholy and pleasant humour were in him so contempered, that each gave advantage to the other, and made his

company one of the delights of mankind' (*pleasant* here meaning
of course 'humorous' or 'amusing'). The zany friend of the First
Satire, at any rate, is foolish mainly through his desire to be at
the centre of things, a desire close to an impulse recurrent in
Donne's writings and derisively captured in one of his Elegies:

> Although we see celestiall bodies move
> Above the earth, the earth we till and love:
> So we her ayres contemplate, words and hart
> And vertues; But we love the Centrique part.

We can in fact speak of the First Satire as less externalized
commentary than internalized debate, a 'dialogue of one' in
which London—though loved and hated as was Juvenal's
Rome—becomes a setting more figurative than the Roman
capital was to Juvenal. In Donne's scenic poems 'The Storm'
and 'The Calm', he was to portray a world of natural phenomena gone almost out of the mind's control. The London of
the Satire has something of the chaotic violence of the Nature of
these two poems—and the two young men are arguing about its
value. Yet to say so much may have the effect of obscuring the
poem's form, which expresses not debate but event. The two
voices which become confused in the course of the dialogue
suggest that what is happening concerns not two persons but
change in one person. For all its realism therefore the anecdote
is a fable suggestive of that natural and necessary passage,
incessantly repeated in an individual's life, by which the mind's
quietness gives way to the confusions of existence, and is
exhilarated, and learns, and suffers loss. The movement here,
that is to say, is closely related to that 'launching out' which
Donne contemplates with a melancholy and humorous reluct-
ance in *The Progresse of the Soule*:

> O let me not launch out, but let mee save
> Th'expense of braine and spirit; that my grave
>   His right and due, a whole unwasted man may have.

This movement finds also a curious echo in the sentence with
which Walton was reflectively to summarize Donne's situation
some years after the writing of this satire, at the marriage
that might have helped his rising fortunes but in fact ruined
them:

Mr Donne's estate was the greatest part spent in many and chargeable travels, books, and dear-bought experience: he out of all employment that might yield a support for himself and wife, who had been
curiously and plentifully educated; both their natures generous, and
accustomed to confer, and not to receive, courtesies.

The First Satire, one might say finally, is a poem about
'chargeable travels' and 'dear-bought experience', a subject
that goes deep into what moved Donne as a poet throughout his
career. There is an implicit acceptance in Donne's writing that
a man must go on his travels and that one must make for the
centre, the metropolis of experience; it also accepts that the trip
is likely to be dear-bought. The scholar in the First Satire is
without any real hesitation as he descends into the streets,
foretelling precisely what will happen—'Come, let's go.' The
lover of the Elegies never questions his sad departures, but
briskly 'bids farewell'. Among the *Songs and Sonnets*, all Donne's
tenderest poems are valedictions. And the speaker in the
magnificent, and magnificently worldly, late Hymn to Christ
sets out without illusion on a journey that he knows will wreck
him:

> To see God only, I goe out of sight:
> And to scape stormy dayes, I chuse
> An Everlasting night.

II

Donne's Ovidian Elegies seem to have been written more or less
contemporaneously with the Satires, during the early and
middle years of the fifteen-nineties. The heroines of these
love-poems (if one can call them heroines, and if one can call it
love) belong with those 'Daughters of London . . . / As gay as
Flora, and as rich as Inde' whom Donne salutes elsewhere. The
sociological interest of these Elegies, the sense in them of the
historical London, does not extend much further than that.
These poems are uneven, perhaps only intermittently focused,
and not at all easy to be dogmatic about, yet parts of them have
power as well as wit. I would suggest that they are most lively
where we feel the friction of divided tones. For in these Elegies
Donne's creativity seems often to be a matter of discovering
situations and tones which reflect an ambiguous response to

experience—of giving voice once more to the Pedant and the Zany, who find themselves this time in a more simply amorous context. It is in this fashion that Donne is a London poet.

By means of this development of dramatically divided tones, Donne reworks Ovid as radically and as originally as he reworked Horace, Persius, and Juvenal in his figurative narrative. He seems to be learning something both from the early comic Shakespeare and from the brilliant Marlowe of the poems, as he creates here and there an almost purely comical relation between the sober and judicious voice of the narrator and the foolish presence of his own zany desires, or of his mistress's body, or of any of the other ludicrous appurtenances of a love intrigue:

> I taught my silkes, their whistling to forbeare,
> Even my opprest shoes, dumbe and speechlesse were.

So says the hero of the Fourth Elegy, 'The Perfume', who tells how a secret affair was wrecked by his hapless choice of too pungent a scent. The young lovers struggle to achieve the Roman pleasures of an illicit amour while plunged up to the neck in the confusions of English family life: threatening father, tired mother, hordes of younger children making their way in and out of the bedroom all night, and with all this the intimate betrayal by *things*—clothes, shoes, the wrong perfume. The hero is in theory an ambitious, even rather nasty, Ovidian seducer, but he finds himself committed to the whole confounding and chaotic world of practical existence: things, bodies, families, smells, London. And so, between intention and performance, he stumbles, an exasperated, affectionate, and would-be brutish dandy. In the Seventh Elegy, 'Tutelage' ('Nature's lay Ideot, I taught thee to love'), we meet again this exasperated dandy, patiently teaching 'the Alphabet of flowers' to one who is clearly the dumbest of girls. Amusing as the image is, and fabricated though it may be, it helps to offset that more prevalent image of Donne as the lewd seducer that takes support from the more apparently simply sensual of the Elegies. For even 'Love's Progress' and 'Going to Bed' share the cool and amused element that one finds in Shakespeare's comic-erotic Mannerist poem *Venus and Adonis* or in Marlowe's more classical—but still funny—*Hero and Leander*. Donne's two Elegies are surprisingly abstract pieces that play theme and variations on what passes for a concrete procedure. 'Love's Progress' wanders round the 'Centrique part' with a movement as erratic as that of the two young men in the First Satire; and the more the lines speak of the 'right true end' of love, the more the vagrancy tells that the lover is both lunatic and poet, his desire indistinguishable from his fantasy. Similarly few first readers of 'Going to Bed' have not, I imagine, been surprised to realize when the poem ends that the proposed event has yet to begin, and that the speaker has so far managed to undress no one but himself.

So much must be said of the ambiguous tone of the Elegies, the metropolitan wariness and humour with which they embark on erotic adventures. But these poems are far from satires, and it would be misleading to overstress their critical tone. To do so, we would have to ignore their 'zany' side, their capacity for total immersion in an experience, so that the most critical of readers is convinced so long as he reads. Even to call the Elegies anything as clear-cut as comedies would be a mistake, from another point of view. A comparison with the early Shakespeare would bring out how relatively unfocused mood and attitude are in these poems. Shakespeare has from the beginning a far firmer grip on his comic subject, the humour and pathos of man's dual nature in love; he achieves early and with little strain an almost classical generality of comic wisdom. But it is perhaps easier for a man to know what he thinks about love in Arcadia (or Navarre, or Athens) than in the City of London.

If one bears in mind such reservations as these, one may be in a better position to appreciate the degree and nature of Donne's success in the most striking of the Elegies, the sixteenth, 'On his Mistris'. He has in this poem invented a situation which, however odd it may seem, serves his needs perfectly. Much of the poem's power lies in the truthfulness of its mixed feelings. From the famous first line—'By our first strange and fatall interview'—a voice speaks with tenderness, exasperation, pain, urgency, and humour. The curiously angular realism of the situation, by which a man persuades a woman *not* to accompany him in the disguise of a page, has been explained in

terms of pure autobiography, but the poem's human warmth
and poignancy have also prompted comparisons with *Romeo and
Juliet*. Neither of these appeals to fact or fiction seems to me to
get quite close enough to the actual substance of the Elegy. On
the fictional side, Donne's sense of pain is not Shakespeare's; he
lacks Shakespeare's *gravitas*, the tranquillity arising from a deep
sense of the natural. Donne is much nearer in this Elegy to a
work more internationally famous in the period than anything
by Shakespeare: the Spanish prose classic *Celestina*. Rojas's long
narrative presents the tragic fall of two young lovers and their
nurse–bawd in a way that blends a piercing romanticism with a
startlingly modern realism and harsh humour. One of the
peculiarities of Rojas's powerful story is that though it contains
great psychological accuracy in the telling, its tragedy is ultimately unexplained. The lovers take it for granted that they
cannot marry and must meet furtively; but no reason is given
why they cannot. This absence of primary motivation in no way
impairs the work. Indeed its refusal to explain throws all the
greater stress on the 'explanation' the reader makes for himself:
he responds in terms of that profound fatalism of true romance
that believes love to be unlucky and that expects a *Liebestod*. The
strangeness of Donne's story—of a girl who wants to assume
disguise—works, I suggest, in precisely the same way as
Celestina. The element of the random, the chancy, projects us
forward immediately into an excited anxiety whose cause is
purely psychological. So too with the urgent repetitions of the
Elegy's opening lines: they take us back by rhetoric to the
plangent desolation of true romanticism, the authentic and
brooding Petrarchan distress in which nothing lies ahead but
Laura in morte.

If the Sixteenth Elegy relates in any way to real life, to
'fact',—and its anecdotal allusiveness awakes a sense of the
real—then its facts are not biographical but psychological. The
poem has a movement, circuitous but purposive, which is
remarkably like that of the First Satire. Donne even uses the
same device of a violently syncopated rhythm to give his sense
of immersion in the world of the debauched Europeans—

> Men of France, changeable Camelions,
> Spittles of diseases, shops of fashions

—as he used when he described the London crowds. And the
friend's rough fate in a brothel brawl ('quarrell'd, fought, bled')
has its parallel—even a verbal echo ('taken, stabb'd, bleede')
—in the imagined death of the lover. But in the Elegy the act of
violence is given a finer form, in keeping with its more complex
function: it here becomes—odd though the notion may seem
—the climax of a nightmare which the lover warns his mistress
not to give way to. The violence is thus deeply inset in a fiction
within a fiction: fear (faced with sufficient bravado) becomes a
controlled fantasy—is even, with luck, exorcized. The poem
ends with the lover telling his mistress to

> walk in expectation, till from thence
> Our greate King call thee into his presence.
> When I am gone, dreame mee some happinesse,
> Nor let thy lookes our long hid love confesse,
> Nor praise, nor dispraise mee, blesse, nor curse
> Openly loves force; nor in bed fright thy nurse
> With midnights startings, crying out, oh, oh
> Nurse, oh my love is slaine; I saw him goe
> Ore the white Alpes, alone; I saw him, I,
> Assayld, fight, taken, stabb'd, bleede, fall, and dye.
> Augure mee better chance, unless dreade Jove
> Think it enough for mee, to 'have had thy love.

In its psychological insight and its exquisite poise the close of
the Sixteenth Elegy looks beyond anything in the First Satire.

At the end of this Elegy we hear for the first time a note that
gives power to some of the best of the *Songs and Sonnets*. The
poet's response blends longing and fear, attraction and recoil:
from the tension between the two comes the nervous charge so
characteristic of Donne's poetry—that almost electrical quality that energizes the reader and yet makes its harassing
demands upon him. It is by virtue of this power that Donne
earns the right to be called our first (perhaps our only) real
master of the poetry of urban anxiety, the love poet of the
'national centre for risk capital'. In their ability to convert
anxiety into an empowering force—to live on their nerves
—any of Donne's lovers might ask

> what other way have wee,
> But to marke when, and where the dark eclipses bee?

One might take as representative of this conversion of apprehension into boldness and balance the archetypal hero and heroine of the 'Lecture upon the Shadow', pacing under the glare of the noonday sun and reflecting upon their condition:

> These three hours that we have spent,
>   Walking here, two shadowes went
> Along with us, which we our selves produc'd;
> But, now the Sunne is just above our head,
>   We doe those shadowes tread;
> And to brave cleareness all things are reduc'd.

These instructive lovers, moving with the upright steadiness the level rhythm suggests, take with them a shadow ahead and a shadow behind, one in space and one in time, one the suspicion of others and the other the doubt of themselves. Their very uprightness derives from the tension of being between shadow and shadow, and knowing it. And their dignity derives also from the dangerousness of the situation, in which love is defined only as some completely central noonday moment of feeling at which all is always crisis: 'And his first minute, after noone, is night.' The poem's sharp-edged brilliance consists in this exclusiveness. Indeed one of the most impressive things about it (as with so many of Donne's poems, but here to an extreme degree) is the amount of the natural which the poem finds expendable. It contains nothing but sun, shadow, lovers, nerves, and rhetoric. The tension that results is quite alien to that natural or pastoral wisdom which might teach its person how to 'abide the change of time', as do the couples of Shakespearian romance. Donne's lovers belong to the great city, and they are powered by an anxiety as acute as it could be without sacrificing their lucidity. Their balance, and the 'brave cleareness' of this whole abrupt and nervous poem, is a poise of alternatives reckoned with, an art of balancing upright on shadows.

III

Comparatively little has been said about Donne as a conscious stylist; not surprisingly, because a marked naturalism is so much a feature of his style. I now want to argue that he is in fact a London artist in another sense: a man who writes out of an extreme consciousness of himself as an artist and an equal consciousness of the 'understanders', that sophisticated audience for whom he writes, men and women likely to miss nothing. The naturalism of the style, that is to say, is in itself—like the apparently random structure of the First Satire and the Sixteenth Elegy—an effect of art. In the Verse Letters we meet, in place of the flawless cantabile of some of the *Songs and Sonnets*, a poet making himself master of that essentially English mode, the off-hand style. For Donne writes here as angularly to his friends as to those great ladies he was obliged to flatter. He likes to seem to be involved in a stumbling, stammering battle with language from which a cadence or a tenderness will suddenly float free, as though friendship or civility or writing at all were a matter of working against the grain of things until the miraculous happens:

> For 'twere in us ambition to write
> Soe, that because wee two, you two unite,
> Our letter should as you, bee infinite.

And at times he does this also, though more sweetly, in the lyrics of the *Songs and Sonnets*:

> These burning fits but meteors bee,
> Whose matter in thee is soone spent.
> Thy beauty, 'and all parts, which are thee,
> Are unchangeable firmament.

Donne distrusts the conventionally aesthetic, and often devotes his large verbal mastery to writing like an amateur: sometimes, as in the echoic and parodic Fourth Satire, with an effect of virtuoso clowning. There is possibly a clue here to two of his most famous stylisms, his rhythmic syncopation and his use of conceits. He will with deliberation destroy the harmony of a blank verse line; or withdraw from an emotional effect, by interposing a conceit that forces upon us the coolest intellectuality. He is a master of certain kinds of aesthetic or emotional spell, but like many artists of his time will repeatedly break that spell in order to assert the claims of life and reason.

The later sixteenth century was of course a great age of applied rhetoric; all the major arts of the time were public arts, arts for an audience. It is no accident that Donne, who was trained in the law, was in youth 'a great frequenter of plays', and later became a famous preacher. It throws some light on the peculiar artistry of the *Songs and Sonnets*, to recall that place in the letters where Donne speaks of the blessings and delights of good company, of family and friends, and then adds that he tends to be 'not the lesse alone, for being in the midst of them'.[8] Similarly, in his poems there is often a perfect equilibrium between their exact truth to mood and feeling and their acute awareness of an audience. Like an actor, he can give to any attitude, however complex and difficult, a splendidly full consciousness; he brings it, one might say, into full daylight. The reader of such poems finds a pleasure of concentration, of commitment, wittily involved with the pleasure of freedom: one thinks this because one chooses, not because one is compelled; and having thought it one may go on to think something else. This is the side of Donne that he himself described as a 'vertiginous giddiness', a ceaseless awareness of the mind's and will's alternatives. And in the libertine poems especially he shows himself to be (to quote him once again, this time from *Pseudo-Martyr*) a man who needed 'freedome and libertie, as in all other indifferent things, so in my studies also, not to betroth or enthral my self, to any one science, which should possesse or denominate me'.[9] So he writes

> Thus I reclaim'd my buzard love, to flye
> At what, and when, and how, and where I chuse;
>   Now negligent of sport I lye,
>   And now as other Fawkners use,
> I spring a mistresse, sweare, write, sigh and weepe;
> And the game kill'd, or lost, goe talke, and sleepe.

Many of the slighter of the *Songs and Sonnets*—and libertine poems like 'Loves Diet', which I have just quoted, are among them—have this special virtue of their own: their splendid surface lucidity gives pleasure in itself, but it also rides, or controls, considerable inward complexity, tonal or psychological or referential. If we look back at 'Loves Diet' we see that the man who speaks with such careless savagery of the 'game' does so in a tone whose chief effect is one of controlled purity. And it is clear from the rest of 'Loves Diet' that the speaker's libertinism has a good deal to do with failed or reluctant

---

[8] *Letters*, p. 45.   [9] *Pseudo-Martyr*, Preface, sig. B2 (London, 1610).

devotion, is an idealism *manqué*. Some of these libertine poems
are complex in a different way. The title of 'The Indifferent', the
phrase 'things indifferent' in 'Communitie', and possibly 'indifferent things' in the sentence I have just quoted from *Pseudo-
Martyr* all (I would suggest) make glancing allusion to the
important Reformation doctrine (associated mainly with
rationalism and with the radical or Lutheran left wing) of
adiaphorism, or indifferentism—some things only are necessary to salvation, the rest are indifferent to it.[10] To meet such
allusions is to be alerted to the breadth of range in which
Donne's libertine poetry operates. It is focused on erotic experience but it resonates in a wider area that is moral, intellectual,
and theological.[11] This is very much poetry of the Elizabethan
university graduate, setting to work his large but otherwise
underemployed talents. We should not at any rate underesti-
mate the degree of tonal complexity in even the lightest of these
poems. 'Marke but this flea' opens a seduction poem with the
prosy gravity of a sermonizing parson, a tone supported by
theological allusion throughout; and the comparison throws an
odd light on both preacher and seducer. The limpid directness
of the moralist of 'Communitie'—

> Good wee must love, and must hate ill,
> For ill is ill, and good good still

—leads, as it happens, straight into sexual anarchy. And
the man who discovers, in 'The Indifferent', an uproarious
promiscuity—

> I can love both faire and browne,
> Her whom abundance melts, and her whom want betraies

—is given by the liturgical rhythms of the piece all the modest
pride of some well-brought-up lad just awarded the prize for
universal charity. The presence of these bright tones is always a
danger signal in Donne. Later in life, and hoping to make his
way in the world, he preferred these worldly but provocative
poems not to pass around too freely. They are not 'safe' poems:

---

[10] See, for example, the brief discussions of adiaphorism in A. G. Dickens, *The
English Reformation* (1964), pp. 78–9, 180.
[11] William Empson discusses the theological bearing of some of Donne's love poems
in 'Donne the Space Man', *Kenyon Review* (1957).

they have all the dangerousness of 'brave cleareness', the capacity to hold on to the logic of an idea until it emerges into an alarming daylight. Their 'free speech' has sometimes even a self-destructiveness in it, the power to undermine its own apparent premises. The preposterous comminator in 'The Curse' gets so involved in the artistry of his hatred as finally to lose interest in hating; the deserted lover in 'The Apparition' hates so hard that he finds out that he must be in love after all. This sharp paradoxicality occurs even in such things as the beautiful, pellucid opening of 'A Feaver':

> Oh doe not die, for I shall hate
> All women so, when thou art gone,
> That thee I shall not celebrate,
> When I remember, thou wast one

—when Donne comes very close to suggesting that for this beneficent lady to give up the ghost just then would be a foolish, or even a fatal, mistake as far as he is concerned. In all these poems conventional surfaces are both brilliantly displayed and yet dangerously undermined. This elusive 'dangerousness' makes one want to demur somewhat over that epithet most often applied to Donne: 'passionate'. The word is not unjust, since it takes account of what is most there to be noticed, the strange strength of the author's personality as it issues in a voice almost unnervingly close to the ear, and the candour and generosity with which that voice speaks. But in ordinary human and social terms, what one meets as often is not so much 'passion' as that amiable rancour, that wary civility, that distinguishes the tone of English social communication, but most particularly in the social centre, London itself. The real motto of the City that was already in Donne's day a great trade centre ought to be *Caveat Emptor*; and one of the most candid and generous sayings of the 'passionate' Donne is 'Take heed of loving me'.

It is not only in his slighter, merely libertine or complimentary poems that Donne works this kind of effect. One of the most haunting and tender of the *Songs and Sonnets*, the 'Valediction: forbidding Mourning', moves and convinces by the way it sets up an attitude or tone which is strongly threatened but which does not finally give way. In terms of subject the poem is a kind of perfect abstraction of that original experience so vividly present at the close of Elegy 16, but here refined almost out of sight. The situation of the 'Valediction', the parting of lovers, is introduced with an abruptness that gives it the raw immediacy of a street accident. Yet Donne handles it throughout with an extraordinarily sophisticated obliquity, almost with evasiveness, with secrecy. The poem opens with the removed conceit of the death of good men:

> As virtuous men passe mildly 'away,
>> And whisper to their soules, to goe,
> Whilst some of their sad friends doe say,
>> The breath goes now, and some say, no:
> So let us melt . . .

And it closes with the famous, even more abstract, three-stanza conceit of parting and rejoining compasses. Both images are at a remarkable distance from the world of 'yonge fressche folkes, he or she', and in that distance resides both the austerity and the reassurance of the poem. The tone of the 'Valediction' is less that of mere kindness than of a bracingly high style shared: we are involved in something halfway between the lightness of a courtier's *Coraggio!* and such cheerfully distracting games as might be played with a child in the face of a danger both great and imminent.

> Moving of th'earth brings harmes and feares,
>> Men reckon what it did and meant,
> But trepidation of the spheares,
>> Though greater farre, is innocent.

In the ambiguities of the word *innocent* here lies much of the power of the poem. The 'Valediction' has a note of experience, of the adult need to play games, deep enough to discount much belief in innocence; and yet the games themselves are innocent. Given all the freedom therefore of being necessarily half-ironical, or only half-believed, the whole poem carries a quality of light numinousness that comes to rest in its last conceit, that of the compasses, a suspended and spiralling image that never finally proves quite what it seems to.

In the 'Valediction', courage is a tone of voice, tenderness a high style. This tacit artistry, and a suggestion of the milieu it arises from, reappears at the climax of Ford's tragedy *The Broken Heart*, when the princess Calantha hears the news of the death of all those closest to her but continues impassively her formal dance, allowing herself to prepare to die of grief only when the music has ceased and the dance is over. Donne, who longed to break into the court circle but never succeeded, despite himself retained the independent humanity and undermining intelligence that could authenticate such marvellous gestures. Without these qualities we are left, as we are perhaps in Ford's case, with an art of surface, that second-generation art by which the radical revolution of Marlowe, Donne, and Jonson—their invention of an intellectual élitist culture—has quietly changed its terms and become a social élitism: the gentleman's art that governs seventeenth-century letters.[12]

IV

The obliquity of the 'Valediction: forbidding Mourning' is a part of its own special wit. Not many of the *Songs and Sonnets* work in this way, by an explicit art of indirection. They have that 'brave cleareness' which gives the 'Lecture upon the Shadow' its strength and which is an essential characteristic of Donne's mind. Yet almost invariably the movement of feeling in these poems is subject to an opposing current: there are few statements which do not find the implied pressure of opposing counter-statements. To take one brief example of this: the poem in which most would agree that Donne's affirmation of the sense of security in love is at its height, 'The Anniversarie', magnificently celebrates a timeless love in lines whose movement is like that of a ship riding in deep water:

> Only our love hath no decay;
> This, no tomorrow hath, nor yesterday,
> Running it never runs from us away,
> But truly keepes his first, last, everlasting day.

But the whole of the rest of the poem is about 'yesterday' and 'tomorrow'; the deep water is, so to speak, fresh and flowing, a current that animates the poem. To make association between love and what must be (judging by the imagery that fills the last

---

[12] Cf. Grierson: 'There are no poets . . . whose style in so entirely that of an English gentleman of the best type' (*Metaphysical Lyrics and Poems* (1921), p. xxxi).

stanza of the poem) the Accession Day ceremonies of either an ageing queen or an unageless king is to understand why those 'true and false feares' enter the poem. The monumental quality of 'The Anniversarie' lies in its affirmativeness; but its power to move derives from that truthful detachment that places Donne always outside the event, able to see a thing in its frailty as well as in its strength. The end of the poem converts a Catullan assertion into something far more touchingly English: an honest anticlimax, that in its precision takes the scale of the endeavour:

> Let us love nobly, 'and live, and adde againe
> Yeares and yeares unto yeares, till we attaine
> To write threescore: this is the second of our raigne.

It does not seem to me helpful to see this mixture of commitment and withdrawal as a symptom of some personal neurosis. The terms of 'The Anniversarie' (with its 'honors, beauties, wits') allow us to say that Donne is placing his love fairly and squarely in a capital city. And this placing of love makes his language of feeling perpetually vulnerable, arousing always, directly or by association, echoes of the primary love-language of his time, that of courtly Petrarchism—a language that had become open to corruption and hence made the man who used it subject to considerable stresses. The nature and uses of the Petrarchan love-language in the sixteenth century is a large subject which, even if I had the competence, I do not have time to explore. It can summarily be said, however, that the formality of the courtly love-speech of the period gave it always some qualities of a game. But it was a game that could be played with intense seriousness and in various contexts, some of them well outside the area of private feeling. A literary scholar has recently reminded us of the 'Machiavellian' uses made of the Petrarchan love-code by Queen Elizabeth, particularly in the last decade of her reign when the waning of her personal power made even greater political demands on the myth.[13] Similarly a political historian has written of the fall of Essex in terms that perhaps throw light on Donne's ambiguous relation to this love-code—for whether or not he was in fact of the Essex party

[13] Leonard Forster, *The Icy Fire* (1962). See chapter 4, 'The political petrarchism of the Virgin Queen'.

Donne seems to have felt some degree of involvement with
Essex's fate when he spoke of himself as having died in that grey
year when the courtier fell and he himself married.[14] Professor
Hurstfield says of Elizabeth's court in the last years of her reign:

> Everything was in fact conducted on two levels: in the adorned
> language of amorous devotion, and beneath it in the sharp cut-and-
> thrust for office and power, in which the queen held the unbreached
> authority to decide . . . Essex made the fatal mistake of treating the
> façade as though it were the reality . . . He hoped that in gaining a
> peculiar place in the queen's affections, he would win a dominant
> voice in the queen's government. He broke the rules of the game.[15]

Any man who was of the world, or who hoped to be, played this
game. We can observe Donne playing it by looking at the first
letter in the volume which his son published after Donne's
death. Unlike the reticent though often warmly friendly letters
to men that fill so much of the volume, this one, with all its
exquisite hyperboles, is glacially cold:

> Madame, I could make some guesse whether souls that go to heaven,
> retain any memory of us that stay behinde, if I knew whether you ever
> thought of us, since you enjoyed your heaven, which is your self, at
> home. Your going away hath made *London* a dead carkasse. A Tearm,
> and a Court do a little spice and embalme it, and keep it from
> putrefaction, but the soul went away in you: and I think the onely
> reason why the plague is somewhat slackened, is, because the place is
> dead already, and nobody left worth the killing. Wheresoever you are,
> there is *London* enough.[16]

It scarcely needs arguing that this courtly medium has its place
in the *Songs and Sonnets*, whether directly or in the commoner
anti-Petrarchan forms. But it would be a mistake to go on from
there and assume that Donne is too simply conditioned by this
social and Petrarchan medium, that his poems are mere 'social
gestures'.[17] True, Donne was a master of the urbane love-game,

---

[14] 'If at last, I must confess, that I dyed ten yeares ago, yet as the Primitive Church
admitted some of the *Jews* Ceremonies, not for perpetuall use, but because they would
bury the Synagogue honourably, though I dyed at a blow then when my courses were
diverted, yet it wil please me a little to have had a long funerall, and to have kept myself
so long above ground without putrefaction.' *Letters*, p. 122.

[15] Joel Hurstfield, *Elizabeth I and the Unity of England* (1963), p. 187.   [16] *Letters*, p. 1.

[17] Cf. 'His lyrics . . . do not define private sensations. Instead, they make public
gestures, and produce social effects . . . Donne's Petrarchism shows his poems to be
gestures made from social situations.' See Donald L. Guss, *John Donne, Petrarchist*
(Detroit, 1966), pp. 108–11.

as of many games. But he was also a man—as all his writings
surely make plain—for whom the notions of truth and sincerity
were important.

It is relevant here that there are some lyrics in the *Songs and
Sonnets* which leave us uncertain whether they were addressed
to a beloved mistress (or wife) or to a patroness who was
expected to pay the poet for the tributes he addressed to her.
The great age of English love poetry was also, significantly
enough, the time of the literary patroness—and Donne pursued the Countess of Bedford manfully. It was in fact in the
relationship of poet to patroness that the problem of sincerity,
of purity of motive in love and in art, confronted him in one of its
most searching and explicit forms. Donne has been compared
unfavourably with Samuel Daniel, on the ground that as a
patronized poet he was over-subject to anxiety.[18] Yet there was
clearly good cause for anxiety in this situation, as there was for
the many hopeless suitors who peopled Elizabeth's court.
Moreover, the patronized poet—if honest and intelligent
enough—might find in his situation anxieties other than the
simply material: namely the more abstract doubts and complexities of any thoroughly worldly love. A man can tell a truth
when he writes of love for a person by whom he hopes to profit,
and he can tell a truth too when he considers how fruitless his
love has been; and to discover and express these truths without
cynicism or self-pity demands a peculiar steadiness and clarity
in the poet. This situation and these qualities unite two men
otherwise so different, Donne and Ralegh. In Ralegh's splendid
line, 'Twelve years intire I wasted in this warr', the courtly poet
is love's fool but no other man's and certainly not his own; and
this is the note—as of mere digested experience—that is heard
in Donne's writing. Where Ralegh is tragic and retrospective,
the more lucid (although more fantastic) Donne will present
the game of worldly love as a wild farce in a strict form:

> Till then, Love, let my body raigne, and let
> Mee travell, sojourne, snatch, plot, have, forget,
> Resume my last yeares relict: thinke that yet
>   We 'had never met.

18 In 'The Literature of Patronage 1580–1630' by Patricia Thomson, *Essays in
Criticism*, ii (1952).

The same lucidity shows itself as Donne reflects in his Letters on his relation to his patroness. One kind of honesty appears in that letter in which he states his flat disappointment at the small sum at last paid to him by the countess and regrets writing the elegy which had moved her compassionate interest (and so aroused his hopes).[19] Another kind of honesty, more anxious but not therefore inferior, appears in the letter in which he actually speaks of the problem of sincerity and truth, and of past and present experience, as it affects the relation with a patroness; and the language he used carries a regretful and complicated echo of the Petrarchan sentiment itself:

> I should be loath that in any thing of mine, composed of her, she should not appear much better then some of those of whom I have written. And yet I cannot hope for better expressings then I have given of them. So you see how much I should wrong her, by making her but equall to others. I would I could be beleeved, when I say that all that is written of them, is but prophecy of her.[20]

A confusion of categories, or a heroic or merely brutish will to unify them, broke the courtier Essex. Donne too 'broke' his fortunes in the year of his disastrous and devoted marriage. But in his poems the effort to unify, the note of 'I would I could be beleeved', continues. This need to master and shape the disparities of experience, and to write truthfully of a London love, takes one of its simpler (even cruder) forms in 'The Blossome', a gay courtly poem presumably addressed to a patroness but seeming to commune with the poet's own 'naked thinking heart'. The 'heart' is behaving somewhat over-romantically, and so, as a tart corrective, Donne allows it a short spell longer with the *donna* before returning to its proper place:

> Meet mee at London, then . . .
> > I would give you
> There, to another friend, whom wee shall finde
> As glad to have my body, as my minde.

The London of 'other friends', other times, other experiences, always forms a ground of actuality even to the most high-flying of Donne's poems, so that assertion is always a

---

[19] *Letters*, p. 219.
[20] *Letters*, p. 260.

personal, sometimes paradoxical, sometimes heroic, will to
believe. It is only safe to treat 'The Good-morrow', for instance,
as confident assertion if one notes that it opens with 'I wonder'
and closes with an 'If'—that the 'good morrow to our waking
soules' takes place in a moment of present time enclosed in a
questionable past and a conditional future, a London always
outside the window. No poem is more firmly located in the
courtly London world than that exquisite and remarkably cold
romance 'Aire and Angels', which should perhaps make
its readers wonder more than they appear to whether its
nominal addressee was a mistress or a patroness—and wonder
too about the exact mode of the 'passionate' poet about
whom this can be said. It opens with the headiest of angelic
compliments—

> Twice or thrice had I lov'd thee,
> Before I knew thy face or name;
> So in a voice, so in a shapeless flame,
> *Angells* affect us oft, and worship'd bee . . .

—and it closes with a flatly depressed statement of the incompatibility of men and women. But the distance between beginning and end is not as great as it may at first seem; in one of his
sermons Donne surprisingly refers to 'Angels and Arch Angels'
in the same breath and with the same scepticism as he does to
the 'Giants, Witches, Spirits, Wild Beasts' in the maps of the
'Old Cosmographers'.[21] Angels are hypothetical creations.
Love for an angelic mistress (or patroness) is an 'I would I
could be beleeved' that suffers a certain attrition—or at least
change of state—from the passage of time, and we are made to
feel that passage in the poem's uncharacteristically loose,
flaccid, paratactic narrative structure. As we read through the
poem, from line to line, we seem to pass through a stylized
accelerated version of real time, an effect reinforced by the odd
but purposeful variations of tense. And much of the beautiful
and slightly melancholy character of 'Aire and Angels' resides
in the disjunction between this precise actuality and the soaring
abstraction which is also its mode.

---

[21] 'A Sermon of the Commemoration of the Lady Danvers'; in *The Sermons of John
Donne*, ed. Evelyn M. Simpson and George R. Potter, viii. 81–2.

This whole aspect of Donne's mind is crystallized in 'The Canonization'. It is a poem that manages to define a heroic solitariness of love in terms of the city it excludes; and that takes much of its power and life from the life of that excluded city. It is important, I think, that the first two stanzas of this poem are based on Ovid's Defence of Poetry.[22] For 'The Canonization' is a formal Defence of Love in five stanzas, but its strategy is so paradoxical that its formal nature may not be recognized at once.[23] In stanzas one and two Donne rebuts the opposing claims of the busy world on the underminingly modest ground that his love is at least harmless; but his wit does little to diminish the real energy of the world he rebuts. In stanza three he races through the conventional claims *for* love with a reductive airiness that displays taper and phoenix, eagle and dove as what they are in terms of real experience: emblems, no more. The point of rest for the poem, the fulcrum on which 'love's whole world doth wheel' in poetic terms, is the tired, terse line that opens the fourth stanza and that seems to proceed as by a peculiar inward logic from the incompatibilities of the first three:

> We can dye by it, if not live by love.

The claim that follows in the fourth stanza is technically a paradox of self-reference: 'it will be fit for verse', said in verse. Thus Donne's last soaring stanza, the fifth, is something allied to a legal fiction; it has the lightness of pure levity, for nothing rational keeps it up, beyond the sheer self-referent wish that has driven the poem itself into being. The poem is a paradox, a worldly *Contra mundum*, that defends love and poetry by 'ringing the bell backward'. It is entirely characteristic of 'The Canonization' that Donne's lovers in the 'hermitage' of the last stanza should speak with the tongues of 'Countries, towns', and 'courts'; and that the most lucid and moving definition of love Donne ever made, 'You to whom love was peace that now is

---

[22] i.e. the fifteenth and last Elegy of the First Book of *Amores*—apparently a favourite poem with Elizabethan poets, translated by both Marlowe and Jonson, and the poem from which Shakespeare took his epigraph for *Venus and Adonis*.

[23] Though the device of opening and closing every stanza with the rhyme-word *love* neatly expresses Donne's firm but finite involvement with his subject: 'Love, love, nothing but love'.

rage', is here a notion about the past locked up in a mind imagined in the future by a poet existing in an all too para-doxical present.

V

I have been arguing that these poems, like so many in the *Songs and Sonnets*, are London poems in a double sense: first, because of their hold on the dense medium of actual experience, which qualifies all romantic abstracts; second, because of their author's self-consciousness as an artist, his extreme awareness of himself in relation to a surrounding audience. I want to close by suggesting that this understanding of Donne as a metropolitan writer may be used to throw light on one of his more difficult and least apparently metropolitan poems, 'The Exstasie'. The difficulty of 'The Exstasie' does not, I think, lie in the abstruseness of its subject; it lies, rather, in the elusiveness of its treatment. The eloquence and power of the poem are undeniable, but its intention and even its tone are so disputable as to cause the sharpest disagreement as to its final meaning.

One way to approach 'The Exstasie' is to recall that there is a great deal of late Renaissance European art, in both its Mannerist and Baroque phases, in which the relation of the spectator to the artwork becomes a large part of the artist's subject. Many of such works demand a sceptical approach to their subject if one is not to ascend a staircase that ends in mid-air. Donne's relationship with this kind of work is sug-gested in 'The Exstasie' by a detachment which is, even for him (and considering the nature of the overt subject) unusually marked. Three features make this plain. The first is that, from the very beginning of the poem, the experience of the lovers is uncompromisingly set back in the past:

> Where, like a pillow on a bed,
> A Pregnant banke swel'd up, to rest
> The violets reclining head,
> Sat we two, one anothers best.

A man who can write (as Donne did in his *Devotions*) 'This minute I was well, and am ill, this minute', does not use a past tense unguardedly. And the problematical valuation of past experience is, as I have hoped to show, a subject to which Donne recurs. Indeed, one of the period's most constant themes is

> Poore cousened cousenor, *that* she, and *that* thou,
> Which did begin to love, are neither now;
> You are both fluid, chang'd since yesterday.

From the first stanza until the point—wherever it occurs—at which we are so possessed by the lovers' experience that it becomes our 'now', 'The Exstasie' is set in 'yesterday'.

Secondly, this peculiarity of time is reinforced by a peculiarity of place, which is manifested in terms of style. The opening is very oddly written, with a turgid, knotted abstractness that one would guess was meant to sound old-fashioned but which is hard to explain with any certainty: the twisted eye-beams and cemented hands, the reclining violet and sepulchral statues are presumably there by design and for a purpose. The lovers appear to be not merely in the past but in a semi-symbolic past: one might guess, in a state of nature. Wherever they are, they are clearly (at least at the opening) not where *we* are.

Hence Donne's third device of detachment: the invention of at least one intermediary (there may be more) in the middle distance between us and them:

> If any, so by love refin'd,
>   That he soules language understood,
> And by good love were grown all minde,
>   Within convenient distance stood . . .

If it were not that the lovers are so very emblematic, a state of being in a state of nature, it is true that one might be worried by these intermediaries or lookers-on at a love-scene; and there are readers of the poem who resent, and are even repelled by, their presence. But few of those who visit the church of Santa Maria della Vittoria in Rome to see the most famous of Baroque sculptural groups can fail to be startled by the fact that the on-stage ecstasy of Bernini's St Teresa is being watched by modest stone cardinals in side-boxes. They are there because the thing has, so to speak, to be seen to be believed; they are sceptical reason embodied and sanctified, 'by good love grown all minde'.

These devices of detachment establish themselves strongly at the start of the poem; they dominate it much as Donne's authorial voice does in other poems. When we arrive at the ecstatic lovers, therefore, we meet them with a certain preserved equilibrium. It is not irony, of which there are only faint traces in the poem, and even less is it a satirical impulse. What works on us in the opening of the poem is something inherent in the mere movement of the verse and the tone of voice we seem to hear through it. It is a sophisticated mind which sees a grassy bank as 'pregnant' and two young lovers as 'two equal armies', and it is an intelligent and knowledgeable mind which places us so securely in possession of the past. In the scepticism of this tone there is the essentially metropolitan awareness that other experiences are always also true.[24] As a result of this, when the lovers begin to talk—and by definition they are persons for whom no other experience is as true as this—they sound like elevated infants. For Donne invents for them a reedy limpidity of diction such as the 'dead birds' of Shakespeare's 'Phoenix and Turtle' might have used:

> This Exstasie doth unperplex
> (We said) and tell us what we love,
> Wee see by this, it was not sexe,
> Wee see, we saw not what did move.

Ben Jonson's Young Shepherd was to use just such a diction some years later:

> Though I am young and cannot tell
> Either what death or love is, well . . .

and Marvell's Nymph Complaining, after him:

> The wanton troupers riding by
> Have shot my faun and it will die . . .

Donne is the earliest of these three sophisticated poets to register innocence by means of a child-like syntax and rhythm and a monosyllabic simplicity of diction. The impulse, however, is an impulse to register, not to deride. We may feel from

---

[24] Cf.: 'The effect of London is apparent; the author has become a critic of men, surveying them from a consistent and developed point of view; he is more formidable and disconcerting; in short, much more mature.' T. S. Eliot on Pound in (the anonymous) *Ezra Pound* (New York, 1917), pp. 16–17.

outside the poem that the lovers' sentiments are, if scrutinized, turgid and even a little silly. But no poem is read from the outside: its truth must be read to be believed, for the reading is in itself a species of 'ecstasy'. It is important that Donne himself is quite as much interested in this kind of ecstasy as in any other. An ecstasy is to him a passion of human communication, outgoing the self, and the literary may well be more authentic than the amatory. So he will write to a friend, 'this writing of letters . . . is a kind of extasie',[25] and again, 'Sir, more then kisses, letters mingle Soules'. It is this 'ecstasy' of literary sympathy on the part of both poet and reader that makes our poem, where it succeeds, as elated as it is aloof. For when the lovers speak, all Donne's poetic energy gets inside these leaden quatrains and by sheer force of sympathy lifts them up until they float. The detached man falls silent, and the inset lovers give voice to a sense of glory.

But Donne cannot simply maintain these divided voices; for he is not a dramatist who can leave his persons unreconciled, but a poet thinking, and to some conclusion. The substance of the poem tempts us always to suppose that his 'thought' is a matter of the arguments produced. But the young people's intellectual contortions, like all the arguments in Donne's poems, remain that—mere arguments: a gesture towards, rather than the real substance of, that tough and thorough intellectuality which characterized the poet. His lovers here are troubled by the relation of soul and sense. But Donne has already introduced into the poem a person (that one 'grown all mind' who is his own and the reader's surrogate) who from his 'convenient distance' sees the lovers as souls talking sense; and 'mind' has the right to assume therefore that the essential mark of the love-ecstasy is the happy inability of soul and sense to be distinct. So much for the lovers' arguments. The poet's thinking (as apart from the lovers') goes into the shaping that obtains this effect; and, more, into the penumbra of intonations and associations that surrounds all that the lovers say. They talk about a timeless love for twelve steady stanzas, which comes to

---

[25] *Letters*, p. 11. 'I make account that this writing of letters, when it is with any seriousness, is a kind of extasie, and a departure and secession and suspension of the soul, wch doth then communicate it self to two bodies.'

seem a remarkably long time; and while they talk, things begin to happen to them; or if not to them, then at least to that more time-bound mind which listens to them. For while he overhears with sympathy and even some awe their single-minded discourse, he has time to regain what he perhaps never lost, that scepticism with which he met them first. As a result, the arguments of innocence take on more and more of the complex and touching intonations of an imputed experience; and we begin to hear the familiar sound of 'I would I could be beleeved':

> But O alas, so long, so farre
> Our bodies why do wee forbeare?

'So long, so farre' is not the cadence of a child; and the listener hearing it may well echo with the beginnings of irony, 'O alas . . . our bodies'. And this note in the poem, as of a life lived, deepens with the categorical imperative of the stanza with which 'The Exstasie' begins to close:

> So must pure lovers soules descend
> T'affections, and to faculties,
> Which sense may reach and apprehend,
> Else a great Prince in prison lies.[26]

The resonances here move right outside the soul–sense debate, and it does not matter that the lovers' sentiments are at this point somewhat confused—indeed, it may be a necessary part of the effect that they are so. What we hear is the word *must*, and talk of a *descent* and of a *prison*; and the reader who—like the poet—has not the freedom to argue that fictive lovers enjoy but inhabits a prison of 'musts' thinks of the other descents which await the rapt speakers: from innocence into experience, from thought into action, from the past into the present and out of the poem. These last stanzas are involved in a curious, always perceptible melancholy, but also in a quickening of rhythm into a brisk decisiveness. Both moods meet in the magnificent image of the prince in prison, who seems so much greater than his immediate context needs him to be, and who brings into a knotted and self-analytical love-poem all the clarity and

---

[26] I do not adopt here Professor Gardner's controversial new reading of 'That' for 'Which'.

strength that Renaissance humanism could sometimes achieve. There are princes in prison in Sidney, Shakespeare, and Calderón, but the one most important to Donne here can be met in his own *Biathanatos*, where he writes of 'the search and discovery of truth, who else being the greatest Prince in the world, should have no progresse, but be straightned in a wretched corner'.[27]

It may be said that 'The Exstasie' is in itself a 'progresse of truth'. What gives the poem its weight, in fact, is less the conclusion that the arguing lovers come to, than the conclusion they bring poet and readers to. And that conclusion is an ending, not a thing that can be stated as any theory of soul and sense in love. For the poet, and for the reader after him, poetic love in this otherwise curiously loveless though luminous poem is a raising up of a highly personal truth out of some 'wretched corner' of the mind into the daylight of a nobly common reason, where human confusions and contradictions exist in a clearer, more truthful equilibrium. And this is the daylight that poet and reader share, and where they may be said to meet in a rational ecstasy peculiarly their own. So Donne mingles the amatory and the literary in the last stanza of this highly self-conscious poem:

> And if some lover, such as wee,
>   Have heard this dialogue of one,
> Let him still marke us, he shall see
>   Small change, when we're to bodies gone.

Using the *we* and *us* of lovers, Donne writes from within the now receding fictive love-situation.[28] But his authorial plural is directed at the poet's non-amatory partner, the reader—that person who is in the end his only audience. Donne is, I think, taking a hint here from Ovid's elegy in defence of poetry (which I earlier proposed as a 'source' for 'The Canonization'). Ovid ended his elegy by saying that he could endure contumely and unsuccess in this world in the thought of his posthumous fame:

---

[27] *Biathanatos* (1609), p. 84.
[28] The Renaissance device of breaking a convention before the close in order to establish another more apparently realistic takes various forms: e.g. the endings of Shakespeare's *Love's Labour's Lost* and *The Tempest*, Donne's own 'The Indifferent', and Milton's *Lycidas*.

'I will', he says, 'always be read by the careworn lover', 'I shall live, and the great part of me survive'.[29] Donne's last stanza, which has often been found difficult, holds perhaps an oblique echo of Ovid's resonant close. Like the Roman poet, the English poet and his lovers will surely survive their bodies. But these lines also contain a phrase—'this dialogue of one'—that is wholly Donne's, and it serves to epitomize all the poem's different kinds of communication: those between lover and lover, between lover and poet, between poet and reader. For even here, in a poem as apparently private and self-communing as 'The Exstasie', Donne appeals to some human metropolis of letters, a London which is 'the meeting of friends'.

[29] 'atque ita sollicito multus amante legar . . . vivam, parsque mei multa superstes erit.' Ovid, *Amores* i. 15, ll. 38–42.

3. JOHN WILMOT, EARL OF ROCHESTER

BY ANNE BARTON

In the second act of Jonson's *Volpone*, the Fox disguised as a mountebank harangues a crowd of Venetians beneath Celia's window. His aim is quite straightforward. By pretending to be Scoto of Mantua, the possessor of a marvellous elixir, he hopes to obtain a glimpse of Corvino's young and jealously guarded wife. Volpone's long speech of self-advertisement, cluttered though it is with medieval jargon and false learning, is basically simple. He recognizes that other mountebanks, the charlatans of the profession, may parade accomplishments superficially like his own.

Indeed, very many have assay'd, like apes, in imitation of that, which is really and essentially in me, to make of this oil; bestow'd great cost in furnaces, stills, alembics, continual fires, and preparation of the ingredients (as indeed there goes to it six hundred several simples, besides some quantity of human fat, for the conglutination, which we buy of the anatomists), but when these practitioners come to the last decoction, blow, blow, puff, puff and all flies in fumo: ha, ha, ha! Poor wretches! I rather pity their folly and indiscretion, than their loss of time and money; for those may be recovered by industry: but to be a fool born is a disease incurable.

Here, and throughout his oration, the Fox insists strenuously that he represents truth as opposed to the specious claims of his rivals. Meanwhile, every word he utters reveals him clearly as an impostor. The rational and intelligent members of his stage audience are not deceived for an instant; only the credulous and the foolish—the Sir Politic Would-Be's of the world—could possibly mistake this arrant counterfeit for the true man he pretends to be.

At some point during the winter of 1675–6 John Wilmot, Earl of Rochester, acting not on a stage but in the middle of that Restoration London in which he normally lived, chose to

submerge his own extraordinary identity in that of a fictitious
Italian mountebank of his devising. Rochester was consti-
tutionally restless and also insatiably curious; he had recently
been banished from the court for irreverence; he had a passion
for disguise. These are the generalities of the situation. More
precise reasons underlying his impersonation of Alexander
Bendo, if indeed they existed, remain obscure. Like Volpone
in Jonson's play, Rochester in real life addressed a formal
peroration to his potential customers.

However Gentlemen in a world like this, where Virtue is so frequently
exactly Counterfeited, and hypocrisie so generally taken notice of,
that every one armed with Suspicion stands upon his Guard against
it, 'twill be very hard, for a Stranger especially, to escape a Censure:
All I shall say for myself on this Score is this, if I appear to anyone like
a Counterfeit, even for the sake of that chiefly, ought I to be constru'd
a true Man, who is the Counterfeit's example, his Original, and that
which he imploys his Industry, and Pains to Imitate, & Copy. Is it,
therefore my fault, if ye Cheat, by his Witts and Endeavours, makes
himself so like me, that consequently I cannot avoid resembling him?[1]

On Volpone's lips, truth and falsehood had remained fixed
counters: traditional opposites. He hoped to persuade his
listeners to mistake the one for the other, certainly, but he did
not doubt the validity of the distinction. In fact, his mock-
righteousness played upon it. The movement of mind described
by Rochester's prose, by comparison with Jonson's, is posi-
tively dizzying. Not even Shakespeare had gone this far when
he allowed Imogen, in the third act of *Cymbeline*, to reflect upon
the power of hypocrisy to breed a distrust of the honesty it
mimics.

> True honest men, being heard like false Aeneas,
> Were in his time thought false: and Sinon's weeping
> Did scandal many a holy tear, took pity
> From most true wretchedness: so thou, Posthumus,
> Wilt lay the leaven on all proper men;
> Goodly and gallant shall be false and perjur'd
> From thy great fail.

---

[1] Thomas Alcock and John Wilmot, Earl of Rochester, *The Famous Pathologist or The Noble Mountebank*, ed. Vivian de Sola Pinto, Nottingham University Miscellany No. 1 (Nottingham, 1961), p. 33.

The reasoning here may seem convoluted; none the less, behind Imogen's speech the values of truth and falsehood stand distanced but inviolate. Honesty may for a time be slandered by its opposite, reality mistaken for appearance, in reversal of the more usual Elizabethan error. Fundamentally, however, these qualities are not interchangeable. Like Jonson, Shakespeare maintained a basic conviction of antithesis, a conviction which Rochester as Bendo overthrows.

It is, Dr Bendo points out, the principal aim of the counterfeit to be taken for a true man, the thing he imitates. He fulfils his nature only in so far as he can promulgate this confusion. The man who appears false, therefore, is by definition unlikely to be engaged in any duplicity. The one who seems true and honest is the candidate for suspicion. What stance, under these circumstances, can the man who is genuinely honest adopt? How can he distinguish himself from his double, the counterfeit? A pose of deliberate dishonesty would seem to be all that is open to him. To embark upon it, however, would be to contradict his very nature as an honest man. At this point, language breaks down. We are in the country of Epimenides's paradox: the statement that 'All Cretans are liars' made by a man who is himself a Cretan. Truth and falsehood, reason itself, begin to run round in circles. Antipodes touch; extremes and contradictions, bewilderingly, coalesce. This tendency to confound antithesis in identity is not, of course, peculiar to Rochester, though I should wish to claim that both as a person and as a poet he was perhaps its most brilliant seventeenth-century exemplar. The Restoration as a period seems to have been drawn to this activity; its comedy in particular regularly annihilates traditional polarities. 'I know no effectual Difference between continued Affectation and Reality', says Mr Scandal in Congreve's *Love For Love*. The remark is recognizably part of the world of Dr Bendo.

To compare Rochester with Byron has become a biographical and critical cliché. The common ground is obvious: aristocracy, exceptional physical beauty, sexual licence, scepticism, immense personal charm, an early death. Both of them minimized and underplayed their own poetry; neither could live without it. Between Rochester's despairing remark in a letter to his wife about the 'disproportion 'twixt our desires

and what is ordained to content them'[2] and Byron's description
of Cain as a man exasperated by 'the inadequacy of his state to
his conceptions'[3] the line runs straight and true. Confirmed
empiricists, taking nothing on trust, both Rochester and Byron
were committed to a world of fact and sense experience. These
were the boundaries of knowledge in which they believed.
Unfortunately, because they were the people they were, they
persistently asked of sense experience things which were not
only in excess of what it could give, but inappropriate to it.
They lived intensely; they pushed individual experience as far
as it could go, only to find that even in the rarefied air of the
extreme it was disappointing. Dedication to a reality which
they could not help recognizing as limited, imperfect, and in the
proof maddeningly below expectation, left them hankering
after intangible absolutes, values fixed beyond sense in a world
from which they were debarred by their own rationalism. In the
last weeks of his life, Rochester surrendered; he took the leap in
the dark into religious faith. Byron, despite his sessions with
that earnest Methodist Dr Kennedy at Missolonghi, did not.
On the way to these very different final positions, both men
used poetry as a means of coming to terms with a personal
quandary that was essentially the same. Neither really believed
in poetry in the sense of a man like Keats, yet with both the
relationship of life to the art which it generated became
so immediate and complex as to call the whole time-worn
antithesis into question.

From *Childe Harold* to *Don Juan* Byron systematically
mythologized his life in his verse. He came, reluctantly, to
depend upon poetry as a means of heightening and transforming a world of objective fact which claimed his allegiance, but
which he felt to be basically inadequate. Interestingly enough,
Byron was a man who had absolutely no capacity for disguise,
either in his life or his verse. No matter where he travelled, no
matter how exotic or incongruous his adventures, whether he
was sitting at the feet of Ali Pasha in Albania or attempting to
seduce the wife of a Venetian baker, he remained Milord

[2] *The Collected Works of John Wilmot, Earl of Rochester*, ed. John Hayward (London,
1926), p. 288 (Letter LXX).
[3] *The Works of Lord Byron . . . Letters and Journals*, edited by R. E. Prothero, v. 470 (to
Murray, 3 Nov. 1821).

Byron. His poetry too is always spoken in his own voice. On those infrequent occasions when he did try to conceal his own identity behind that of a fictitious spokesman—as he did briefly in the first canto of *Don Juan*—the pretence invariably failed and had to be discontinued. All of Byron's heroes, Childe Harold, Lara, the Corsair, the narrators of the satires, are over-life-size versions of himself. It was Byron's characteristic way of overcoming the limitations of things as they are.

The mythologizing of Rochester's life and personality, on the other hand, was for the most part accomplished by people other than himself. Dryden's dedication to *Marriage à la Mode*, in which he claims that 'the best comic writers of our age, will join with me to acknowledge, that they have copied the gallantries of courts, the delicacies of expression, and the decencies of behaviour, from your Lordship' may sound impossibly sycophantic. The fact remains that the drama of the Restoration is filled with Rochester-figures, with (more or less garbled) memories of his conversation, refractions of his wit, attempts to mirror his style. According to John Dennis, all of the town that mattered went away from the first performance of Etherege's *The Man of Mode* in 1676 agreeing that the rake-hero Dorimant was an avatar of Rochester. And Dorimant is the archetype and model for a whole series of later libertines. Nat Lee, baffled by the complexity and contradiction of his former patron's character, introduced him into his strange and brilliant comedy *The Princess of Cleve* (1680) as two separate people: the dead Count Rosidore, whose memory haunts the courtiers who have survived him, and the living Nemours. In the pages of Anthony Hamilton, in a flood of contemporary and posthumous anecdotes, allusions, and lampoons, Rochester achieved semi-legendary stature. His spectacular deathbed conversion added a new dimension to the myth. Even Charlotte Brontë, of all people, seems to have had him in mind when she bestowed his name and a number of his personal characteristics, including the penchant for disguise, upon the hero of *Jane Eyre*.

Only once, however, as far as one knows, did Rochester himself make a literary contribution to his own myth. 'The Earl of Rochester's Conference with a Post Boy' is not a polite poem, but neither is it negligible.

Son of A whore, God damn you can you tell
A Peerless Peer the Readyest way to Hell?
Ive out swilld Baccus sworn of my own make
Oaths wod fright furies, & make Pluto quake
Ive swived more whores more ways y^n Sodoms walls
Ere knew or the College of Romes Cardinalls
Witness Heroick scars, Look here neer go
sere Cloaths & ulcers from ye top to toe
frighted at my own mischiefes I have fled
and bravely left my lifes defender dead
Broke houses to break chastity & died
that floor with murder which my lust denyed
Pox on it why do I speak of these poor things
I have blasphemed my god & libelld Kings
the readyest way to Hell come quick!
BOY.   Nere stirr
The readyest way my Lords by Rochester

As Mr David Vieth has pointed out, in his book *Attribution in Restoration Poetry*, this is a better lampoon than any Rochester's enemies were able to compose.[4] As a self-portrait, it is unsparing, worlds away from the kind of romantic self-magnification which Byron practised in his *Oriental Tales*. Rochester's characteristic oaths, the scars and running sores left by the venereal disease which, a few years later, was to kill him, the suggestion not merely of sexual excess but of perversion, the allusion to that gesture of drunken cowardice in the Epsom affair of 1676 which cost the life of his friend Downes, the unlovely propensity to slander: all of these details were based on fact. None are pretty. The efforts of the wretched post boy to escape from the company of this unsavoury and drunken interlocutor are both comic and entirely understandable. Yet, oddly enough, the final effect of the poem is not that of a lampoon, in the sense that it annihilates or even breeds contempt for its subject. The amoral energy, almost daemonism, of the speaker in his deliberate rush to hell is simply too attractive, and so of course is the intelligence of his self-mockery. The verse employs a hyperbolic style which is persuasive and, at the same time, ironically

[4] David M. Vieth, *Attribution in Restoration Poetry* (New Haven and London, 1963), p. 199. I have used the version of 'The Post Boy' printed by Vieth. Otherwise, all quotations from Rochester's poetry come from the edition of Vivian de Sola Pinto (London, 1953).

conscious of its own exaggeration. It manages simultaneously to magnify and deflate *both* its subject and the orthodox values by which that subject is being judged, to invite belief and to undercut it.

In 'The Post Boy' as a whole, reality and pretence, the counterfeit and the true, take up positions like those they occupy in the vertiginous world of Dr Bendo. Formally, although not ultimately, the lines belong to the genre of the lampoon. To write a lampoon on oneself is not exactly unique; it is, however, fundamentally paradoxical. The complexity of this situation is only increased by the pretence that the poem represents an actual incident. Professor Pinto prints it in his edition among the other 'Impromptus', alongside the three lines of rueful compliment paid to the Duchess of Cleveland after she had just knocked Rochester down in the street for presuming to steal a kiss. As an immediate response to a real situation, the discomfited epigram addressed to Samuel Pepys's beloved duchess is conceivable: no man, however witty, produces extempore verse like that of 'The Post Boy'. If a genuine encounter lies behind the poem, it lies a long way behind. The important consideration here is not biographical truth, but the contribution which the anecdotal pose of the dialogue makes to a confusion worked out on a variety of other levels.

Rochester's sins as recorded in 'The Post Boy' have a particularized reality which must have been even more striking to his contemporaries than to us. They are described, however, in terms which force the reader to question the possibility that a monster like this could exist. He becomes a caricature of vice. Lines 11 and 12 in particular ('Broke houses to break chastity & died / that floor with murder which my lust denyed') suggest an allegorical figure of Lechery invented by some canting and overwrought divine. Here, as in the scurrilous reference to Rome's cardinals and their sexual predilections, satire glances off to targets other than himself. Those orthodox values by which the wicked Earl of Rochester stands self-condemned are themselves mocked. In the act of invoking traditional verities of good and evil, virtue and sin, 'The Post Boy' blurs their identity. It is not at all clear in the end how we are meant to feel about this mythologized Earl of Rochester who asks, so

peremptorily, for directions to another world. He repels, but he
also attracts. The poem is amusing; it is also horrifying. Even
more perplexing: what is the point at which one should separate
this dramatic character, the subject of the lampoon, from the
witty poet of the same name who stage-managed the incident in
the first place and who controls in so complex a fashion the tone
and language of his self-presentation?

I suggested earlier that 'The Post Boy' was the only surviving
poem of Rochester's in which, like Byron, although with very
different results, he mythologized his own life and personality
directly. His more characteristic mode was the one which
Byron shunned: disguise. Rochester's life is filled with extraordinary impersonations, of which the mountebank Bendo is
only one. Hamilton's account of how Rochester exchanged
identities with Killigrew in order to deceive two of the queen's
maids of honour reads like a scene from Restoration comedy.
He seems also to have transformed himself into a solid mer-
chant, in which role he vanished for a time among the citizens of
London, earning their approbation by the vigour with which he
railed against the profligacies of the court—particularly those
of the wicked Earl of Rochester. (Etherege was perhaps thinking of this particular caper when he had Dorimant charm
Harriet's mother Lady Woodvil in *The Man of Mode* by pretending to be the sober and censorious Mr Courtage.) Even more
daringly, Rochester is said to have lost himself among the
beggars and the common whores of London in the guise of a
porter. The town of Burford retains the tradition of his sudden
appearance there as a tinker, in which unglamorous form he
collected pots and pans to mend, and then systematically
destroyed them. He was released from the stocks upon the
arrival of his own coach and four. The kitchen-ware, magnani-
mously, was replaced.

In much of this, obviously, there is a quality of Haroun-al-
Raschid, the caliph of *The Arabian Nights* who liked to walk the
streets of Baghdad incognito, in search of the marvellous and
the strange. Other members of the court of Charles II, including the king himself, also resorted occasionally to disguise, as
Bishop Burnet testifies in his *History of his Own Time*. No one,
however, took it as far as Rochester, used it as inventively, or
out of as deep a need. By his own admission, he was drunk for

five years on end, without an interval of sobriety: excess, as he himself recognized, was another kind of role-playing, permitting him to assume manners and a persona heightened and more extravagant than normal. The famous contradiction between his gallantry in the naval action of 1666 and his supposed cowardice in the duel with Mulgrave a few years later probably explains itself in similar terms. 'He thought it necessary', he told Burnet, 'to begin his life with those Demonstrations of his Courage in an Element and way of fighting, which is acknowledged to be the greatest trial of clear and undoubted Valour'.[5] Having done so to his own satisfaction, he discarded the role. In the Mulgrave affair, he was playing another and more wryly exploratory part, as he was presumably when he tried the odd experiment of having his own wife converted to Catholicism by means of an intermediary hired, secretly, by himself. Over and over again in his short life, Rochester seems to have been impelled to alter his perspective on reality, to seek yet another vantage point, by adopting some form of disguise. If (and there seems no reason to doubt the story) he was in fact the architect of Mrs Barry's genius—rehearsing her over and over again in the parts she had to play until, from being the worst and most incompetent actress on the Restoration stage, she became its acknowledged queen—his success is in no way surprising. This was a man who understood the actor's art.

Not unexpectedly, therefore, Rochester's own poetry involves a whole series of impersonations, is spoken in a variety of different voices. He invented the cynical old rake counselling his successors in 'The Maim'd Debauchee', the overblown braggart who addresses his mistress in so insufferable a style in the 'Heroical Epistle in Answer to Ephelia', and the arrogant but misguided author who pens the 'Epistolary Essay from M.G. to O.B. Upon their Mutual Poems'. The extremely indecent but impressive 'Ramble in St James' Park' represents the point of view of a jaded stallion consumed by sexual hate, a man who speaks out of the ruins of wit and sense. Rochester's 'Dialogue

[5] Gilbert Burnet, *Some Passages of the Life and Death of the Right Hon. John Earl of Rochester* (London, 1680), p. 11.

Between Strephon and Daphne' is much better than the usual Restoration pastoral and one of the reasons is the dramatic credibility of this nymph and shepherd: the individuality of their voices. He was an adept at women's parts as well as men's (there is at least the tradition of a transvestite episode in his own life), as witness that somewhat dismaying young lady who showers dubious endearments upon the ancient person of her heart in the poem 'To Her Ancient Lover'.

As a study in feminine character alone, the marvellous 'Letter from Artemesia in the Town to Cloe in the Country' repays attention. Artemesia herself, the woman composing the letter, is a kind of seventeenth-century Elizabeth Bennett. Witty and self-aware, both amused and exasperated, delighted and saddened by the follies she describes, she is the sister of Jane Austen's heroines. What is astonishing about the poem is the fact that that anonymous knight's lady whose affectations and conversation Artemesia reports at such length is not, as she so easily might have been, a mere caricature. She too is a fully realized character of some integrity, and her discourse is filled with telling points as well as with absurdity. Artemesia, the detached observer, watches more in sorrow than in anger while the lady cuddles a pet monkey in the house they are both visiting:

> The dirty, chatt'ring Monster she embrac'd;
> And made it this fine Tender Speech at last.
>   Kiss me, thou curious Miniature of Man;
> How odd thou art, how pretty, how japan:
> Oh! I could live and dye with thee; then on
> For half an Hour, in Complements she ran.
> I took this Time to think what Nature meant,
> When this mixt thing into the world she sent,
> So very wise, yet so impertinent.
> One that knows ev'rything, that God thought fit
> Shou'd be an Ass through Choice, not want of wit.
> Whose Foppery, without the help of sense,
> Cou'd ne'er have rose to such an excellence . . .
> An eminent Fool must be a Fool of parts.
> And such a one was she; who had turn'd o're
> As many Books as Men; lov'd much, read more:
> Had discerning Wit; to her was known
> Ev'ry one's Fault, or Merit, but her own.

> All the good qualities that ever blest
> A Woman so distinguished from the rest,
> Except Discretion only, she possest.

The attitudes which the knight's lady strikes are ridiculous; her mind and endowments are not. A generosity which is both Artemesia's and, ultimately, Rochester's allows her, in what is in effect the play within the play of the letter, to relate with real understanding the scarifying story of Corinna, the girl undone by a Wit, who now

> unheard of, as a Flie,
> In some dark hole must all the Winter lye;
> And want, and dirt, endure a whole half year,
> That, for one month, she Tawdry may appear.

Disguise, as an aspect of Rochester's verse, governs more than the various personae of his poems. There is also the question of literary imitation. In an article published in 1949, 'The Imitation in English Poetry', Dr Harold Brooks has argued that what was to become with Pope and Johnson the approved method of transmuting a classical or French original appears for the first time in Rochester's satire 'An Allusion to Horace'.[6] The poet presents, consecutively, his own equivalent of a pre-existing text. If the reader is fully to appreciate the new creation, he must constantly measure it against the original from which it departs. Ideally, he himself will know this original so well that reference back and forth with every line becomes virtually automatic. The imitation is a poem in its own right; it can stand alone, if necessary, but it fulfils itself only in terms of its relationship—a relationship involving both resemblance and contrast—to the work of art it shadows. According to Dr Brooks, 'An Allusion to Horace' is the only one of Rochester's poems which exacts this kind of point-by-point comparison with its original. It stands in the true Augustan line, as the more independent arabesques performed against the basic groundwork of Boileau in the 'Satyr Against Reason and Mankind' do not.

I do not mean to question Dr Brooks's general argument.

[6] H. F. Brooks, 'The Imitation in English Poetry', *Review of English Studies*, xxv (1949), 124–40.

However, I do think that there is one other poem of Rochester's, not a satire and emphatically not in the Augustan line, which asks to be read in the manner of 'An Allusion to Horace'. On the whole, Rochester's editors have regarded the poem 'To His Mistress' beginning 'Why do'st thou shade thy lovely face?' with a certain amount of nervousness and suspicion.

> Why do'st thou shade thy lovely face? O why
> Does that Eclipsing hand of thine deny
> The Sun-Shine of the Suns enlivening Eye:
>
> Without thy light, what light remains in me
> Thou art my Life, my way my Light's in Thee,
> I live, I move and by thy beams I see.
>
> Thou art my Life, if thou but turn away
> My Life's a thousand Deaths, thou art my way
> Without thee (Love) I travel not but Stray.

There is not a line here, or in the rest of the poem, which does not derive immediately from Francis Quarles, from either the seventh or the twelfth poem in the second book of his *Emblems*. Whole stanzas are, in some cases, identical.

To accuse Rochester of plagiarism, as some critics have done, is obviously to miss the point. What in Quarles had been a passionate expression of the sinner's abasement before God becomes, in Rochester, the despairing cry of a lover to his mistress. The whole object of the exercise is to change as little as possible of the original while wresting it in a different direction, transforming it into its opposite. The closeness of the Christian language of spiritual adoration to that describing the raptures of physical love is, of course, a well-known psychological phenomenon. This is a place where antinomies cross: body and soul, finite and infinite, sexuality and a world of the spirit. It is a paradox worked out on one level in the occasionally embarrassing language of the great fourteenth-century mystics, agonizing after what comes to seem a physical union with God. On another, it means that the libertine pursuing sense experience to its extremes is precisely the man most susceptible to a dramatic religious conversion. A great deal of the poetry of the seventeenth century—one thinks immediately of Donne and Herbert—deliberately avails itself of the language of transcendence in order to celebrate earthly love, and of a fairly straightforward eroticism in speaking of God. The sacred parody, religious poetry strongly influenced by or even based upon a profane model was by no means an uncommon English form.[7] No one, however, as far as I know, conducted an experiment quite like Rochester's in 'To His Mistress'. The poem is an analytic enquiry, an attempt to define the exact point at which opposites merge.

Sensuality is inherent in the very rhythms of Quarles's two poems, in the passionate monotony of his reiterated appeals, and Rochester allows it to speak for itself. He is forced to make certain obvious changes: the word 'Lord' becomes 'Love'; 'Great Shepherd' metamorphoses into 'Dear Lover'. On the whole, however, he alters Quarles only where he must, and these alterations, many of them extremely subtle, become a guide to the fragile but genuine distinctions which can be drawn between earthly and heavenly love. Stanza 11 of Quarles's 'Emblem VII' reads as follows:

> If that be all, shine forth and draw thee nigher;
> Let me behold, and die, for my desire
> Is phoenix-like, to perish in that fire.

In Rochester, this becomes:

> If that be all Shine forth and draw thou nigher
> Let me be bold and Dye for my Desire.
> A *Phenix* likes to perish in the Fire.

There are only two verbal substitutions here of any consequence: the witty and almost imperceptible metamorphosis of 'behold' into 'be bold', and the more striking introduction of the word 'likes' in Rochester's version of the third line. Otherwise, the transformation has been effected by means which are not properly linguistic: by end-stopping the second line where Quarles had permitted an enjambment and by a change in punctuation and accentual stress which suddenly throws the erotic connotations of the word 'die' (submerged and unconscious in the original poem) into relief. The lines are the same and not the same; another voice is speaking Quarles's words, from another point of view.

---

[7] Louis L. Martz, *The Poetry of Meditation* (New Haven, 1954), pp. 179–93.

Obviously, 'To His Mistress' is a far more extreme and idiosyncratic poem than 'An Allusion to Horace'. If Rochester ever subjected another text to this kind of treatment, no record of the experiment survives. Imitation generally, however, was as essential a principle in his verse as in his life. Seneca, Anacreon, Horace, Ovid, Lucretius, Passerat, and Boileau were only a few of the writers upon whose work he built. In his hands, Fletcher's tragedy *Valentinian* became a different and much more interesting play. Nothing, of course, is unique about this method of composition in itself. The idea that an individual style was best achieved through the study and reproduction of (preferably) classical models is a standard part of seventeenth-century aesthetic. As literary archaeologists, Rochester's contemporaries were as assiduous as he. They also tended to imitate one another. Even without considering the whole vexed issue of whether there really was a clear-cut school of Jonson as opposed to the school of Donne, the minor poetry of the Caroline and Restoration periods displays an extremely high and in a certain sense unhealthy mutual awareness. The writers represented in the three volumes of Saintsbury's *Caroline Poets* seem at times to be involved in a kind of never-ending *New Statesman* competition. Fruition (for and against), honour, chastity, the pastoral life: topics like these became an artificial sports ground on which poets consciously vied with one another. Not surprisingly, the exercise tended to become academic, a mere game of rackets played between one poem and its successor.

Elizabethan handling of conventional subject-matter had been different. When Philip Sidney buried time-worn Petrarchan conceits in the structure of his sonnets, he did so because he needed to work by way of their anonymity towards a particularized and felt emotional statement. A poem like Suckling's 'Out upon it, I have lov'd / Three whole days together', on the other hand, invites only one response. And Sir Tobie Matthews provided it: 'Say, but did you love so long? / In troth I needs must blame you.' An already unconvincing because logically imposed stance has been pushed a degree further in a way that is literary in the worst sense of that term. Where can the conversation possibly go beyond Matthews? For most Restoration poets, there was no answer except graceful restatement of what had been said before. With Rochester, something else happens:

> All my past Life is mine no more,
>   The flying hours are gone:
> Like transitory dreams giv'n o'er,
> Whose Images are kept in store,
>   By Memory alone.
>
> The Time that is to come is not,
>   How can it then be mine?
> The present Moment's all my Lot,
> And that, as fast as it is got,
>   *Phillis*, is only thine.
>
> Then talk not of Inconstancy,
>   False hearts, and broken Vows;
> If I, by Miracle, can be
> This live-long Minute true to thee,
>   'Tis all that Heav'n allows.

The technique here is not unlike Sidney's: a convention is revealed in the last lines, but it has been arrived at in such a way that it stands transformed. Melodious and elegant, the poem is ultimately terrifying in its denial of the continuum of life, and the consequences of that denial for human relationships. Neither past nor future exists; man is reduced to the needlepoint of the immediate present, and even this reality is in motion. Essentially, this is a Heraclitean poem: it also points forward to Kierkegaard's analysis of Mozart's seducer Don Juan in *Either/Or*: 'he does not have existence at all, but he hurries in a perpetual vanishing, precisely like music, about which it is true that it is over as soon as it has ceased to sound, and only comes into being again, when it again sounds'.[8] The defence of inconstancy, that weariest of Restoration clichés, is revitalized in Rochester's lyric. No one but Donne perhaps could have formulated and placed the phrase 'this live-long Minute' with such sureness. The compression is typical of Rochester; so is the essential seriousness of the wit.

It is, I believe, fair to say that at the time Rochester was writing, English verse was facing a double crisis: of language and of

---

[8] Søren Kierkegaard, *Either/Or*, trans. David F. Swenson and Lillian M. Swenson (London, 1944), Part i ('The Immediate Stages of the Erotic'), p. 83.

subject-matter. The problem was most acute in what had been the glory of the preceding age: the poetry of love. Both Cleveland and Cowley seem to me better poets than they are currently given credit for being, but it would be hard to deny that their work reflects a sense that all the words of love have already been used, and its possible attitudes exhausted. The obvious temptation was to reach out for the extravagant and bizarre, both linguistically and in terms of subject-matter. What has come to be known as 'Clevelandism' is an intelligent dead end as far as language is concerned, but it is a dead end all the same. As for subject-matter: not by accident are there so many Caroline and Restoration poems about the love affairs of dwarfs, hermaphrodites, or very young girls married to very old men. It was a way, although a fairly desperate one, of ensuring a certain novelty. The blatant obscenity of much Restoration love poetry can also be explained, in part if not entirely, as a response to this situation. A good deal of Rochester, even after the canon has been purified of the improprieties fathered upon it by other writers, remains extremely obscene. Nor was he above the exploitation of abnormal situations, as witness the 'Young Lady to her Ancient Lover', or the song beginning 'Fair Cloris in a Pig-Stye Lay'. Nevertheless, although the solution he found to the problem was too personal to be of use to other poets, Rochester's love poetry at its best seems to me to cut through the dilemma.

Dr Johnson thought that Rochester's lyrics had no particular character. 'They tell, like other songs, in smooth and easy language of scorn and kindness, dismission and desertion, absence and inconstancy, with the common places of artificial courtship. They are commonly smooth and easy; but have little nature, and little sentiment.' With all respect to Dr Johnson, this is one of his 'Lycidas' judgements. Admittedly, there are Rochester lyrics—'My dear Mistress has a heart / Soft as those kind looks she gave me', or ''Twas a dispute 'twixt Heav'n and Earth'—over which one is not tempted to linger, although even here the formal perfection and beauty of sound make one feel churlish in requiring any more of them. At its best, however, Rochester's love poetry achieves individuality and passion by way of an illusory simplicity and coolness of tone.

It is true that the language of these poems is for the most part clear, almost transparent. The vocabulary employed is not wide. Compressed and economical, they make only a sparing use of images and conceits. It has become a commonplace to talk about the gradual shift during the Restoration from the rich, ambiguous, essentially connotative language of Shakespeare and Donne to a kind of Royal Society plain style in which words and images limit themselves to precise and denotative meanings. At first sight, Rochester may appear to belong to the new school in most of his poems. Yet behind the deceptively limpid surface lies a complexity of attitude, an air of strain and doubt, that links him with the metaphysicals. It is worked out, however, by means alien to the school of Donne.

Much of the excitement generated by Rochester's best lyrics springs from their character as tentative and immediate explorations of a particular situation or state of mind. They tend to conclude surprisingly, to arrive at a position in the last lines which seems in some way to be a product of the actual writing of the poem, not a preconceived attitude clothed in verse. If it is often difficult to determine how the poet arrived at this conclusion, it is also obligatory. Yet analysis is made difficult by the fact that so much of what happens in Rochester is a matter of tone. The progression is essentially non-linguistic, one of attitude, and you cannot come to grips with it through the relatively available medium of metaphor and conceit as you can with metaphysical poetry. In the end, of course, this method has a complicating effect of its own upon language. Nothing is more characteristic of Rochester than the way a single word, particularly in the final stanza of a poem, will suddenly move into focus and reveal its possession of a variety of warring meanings. This happens with the word 'severe' in the penultimate line of 'The Fall', as it does with the word 'innocent', upon which such a terrible illumination is suddenly cast, in the obscene final stanza of 'Fair Cloris'.

Fundamentally, however, a discussion of the lyrics must involve itself with somewhat intangible considerations. They are characterized in the first place by the fact that in them the sense tends to flow both forwards and back. A single line, a whole stanza, which had one apparent meaning when first encountered will alter in retrospect: from the vantage point of the end of the poem, or even of the next stanza. This technique

can be observed at its most straightforward in Rochester's
pastoral 'Dialogue Between Strephon and Daphne', at the end
of which the forsaken nymph declares abruptly to her incon-
stant lover that every word she has uttered up to this point was
a lie. The volte-face of this particular ending is reminiscent of
the plays of Fletcher, and indeed it can be defended in terms
very like those employed by Professor Philip Edwards in his
article, 'The Danger Not the Death: The Art of John Fletcher.'[9]
The poem is not summed up and exhausted once the trick
conclusion is known, because there is another kind of pleasure
to be derived from noticing its effect upon what has gone before, from understanding now the real, below the assumed,
meaning of the character's words. With 'Strephon and
Daphne', a further complexity—characteristic of the creator of
Dr Bendo—is introduced by a certain doubt as to whether
Daphne's final assertion that she has been lying is not in itself a
face-saving and despairing lie.

'Strephon and Daphne' is anything but a simple poem, but it
is more conventional than most of Rochester's lyrics. The
brilliant and horrifying 'Fair Cloris', for instance, turns not
upon a shock ending in itself, but upon the opportunity for
misreading or at least misintonation in the second stanza. It is a
mistake which it is almost impossible not to make every time,
no matter how well you know the poem, so cleverly has
Rochester constructed the trap.

> Fair *Cloris* in a Pig-Stye lay,
>   Her tender Herd lay by her:
> She slept, in murmuring gruntlings they,
> Complaining of the scorching Day,
>   Her slumbers thus inspire.
>
> She dreamt, while she with careful pains
>   Her Snowy Arms employ'd,
> In Ivory Pails, to fill out Grains,
> One of her Love-convicted Swains,
>   Thus hasting to her cry'd.

Verse rhythm, position in the line and sense all persuade the
reader to take 'she dreamt' as part of a construction syntactically

[9] Philip Edwards, 'The Danger Not the Death: The Art of John Fletcher', *Jacobean Theatre*, Stratford-upon-Avon Studies I, ed. John Russell Brown and Bernard Harris (London, 1960), pp. 159–77.

parallel with that introduced by 'She slept' in the preceding stanza. But the suggestion of symmetry is indeed the trick. Because of it, everything that follows in the poem: the treachery of the swain, the brutal rape of poor Cloris whose honour 'not one God took care to save' looks like a real incident in a waking world clearly distinguished from her interrupted dream of ivory pails. This impression is carefully furthered by the tone of Rochester's description of the rape: deprecating, brutal, matter of fact. Not until the final stanza (unfortunately suppressed in most editions) does the true meaning of the poem become clear: 'Frighted she wakes.' The whole episode was a dream and indeed one inspired appropriately by pigs. Cloris has been the victim, not of an unfeeling rustic, but of her own lustful imagination, and she proceeds to seek sexual gratification in the only way available to her.

Scepticism about the pastoral pretence was not, of course, original with Rochester. Ralegh and Donne before him had cast a mocking eye upon the innocent pleasures of sheep-folds and bowers. 'Fair Cloris' is in fact part of the whole dialogue initiated by Marlowe's 'Come Live with Me and be my Love' and Ralegh's reply. The poem is not, however, either a simple parody or a hyperbolic extension of a given attitude in the manner of Sir Tobie Matthews's answer to Suckling. Imitation is essential to it; like most Restoration exercises in the pastoral, it presupposes all the pros and cons of earlier poets, speaks largely through a mask. What is remarkable is its ability (admittedly with the assistance of the psychological realism of Hobbes) genuinely to re-create a traditional mode. The ending of 'Fair Cloris' is not pleasant, but neither is it trivial, pornographic, nor ultimately derivative.

Most important of all, perhaps, the basic technique of this poem could be and was applied by Rochester to subjects of a different nature. Syntactical ambiguity marks many of his lyrics, and it is used for a variety of purposes. In general, he seems to have been fond of words or clauses in apposition:

> Let the Porter and the Groom,
>   Things design'd for dirty Slaves;
> Drudge in fair Aurelia's Womb,
>   To get Supplies for Age and Graves.

Here, the dependence of the second line upon the first is relatively straightforward—although in the context of the third ('Drudge in fair Aurelia's Womb') the seemingly innocent phrase 'design'd for' shifts meaning and direction, attacking Aurelia herself and not simply her ignominious lovers. Far more complex is the situation in the final stanza of 'The Fall':

> Then, *Cloris*, while I Duty pay,
>   The Nobler Tribute of my Heart,
> Be not You so severe to say,
>   You love me for a frailer Part.

In this instance, the appositive second line transforms the first from which it apparently derives, underscoring the whole body/soul paradox of the poem. Over and over again in Rochester, constructions of this kind jolt the reader into attention. They force a decision as to the real equivalence of the two halves of a parallel. Does the second part consolidate the meaning of the first, or does it subtly annihilate it?

Syntactical ambiguity of another kind ensures, in the second stanza of that beautiful poem 'An Age in her Embraces Past', that the conventional dependence of the lover's soul upon the eyes of his mistress should be a grammatical fact, built in to the structure of the lyric, and not simply an imposed conceit:

> But, oh! how slowly Minutes rowl,
>   When absent from her Eyes;
> That feed my Love, which is my Soul,
>   It languishes and dyes.

What seems at first to be the subject of this poem—the relativity of love's time—is a seventeenth-century commonplace. Cowley, one of the English poets Rochester most admired, has two poems on the subject in his collection *The Mistress*, neither of them negligible, both dependent upon metaphysical imagery and style: 'Love and Life' and 'The Long Life'. Rochester begins, apparently, in their manner:

> An Age, in her Embraces past,
>   Would seem a Winters Day;
> Where Life and Light, with envious hast,
>   Are torn and snatch'd away.

This great celebratory opening, a statement in the grand manner, is oddly disturbing, although only the reader already well acquainted with the poem will be able to articulate, at this point, precisely why. In fact, the positive image at the centre is being contradicted by the tone and balance of the stanza as a whole. A sense of deprivation, of violence and negation, threatens to overbear the fragile felicity it is ostensibly there to magnify. The meaning of the words is clear and straightforward: an eternity spent in the lady's arms would seem too short. Cowley had thought so too. The emotional stress of Rochester's stanza, on the other hand, running counter to its intellectual content, falls upon the winter's day and its tragic abridgement. Why it should do so it is the business of the rest of the poem, with its exploration of what Professor George Williamson has rightly called Rochester's 'ethic of pain',[10] to make clear:

> Fantastick Fancies fondly move;
>   And in frail Joys believe;
> Taking false Pleasure for true Love;
>   But Pain can ne're deceive.
>
> Kind Jealous Doubts, tormenting Fears,
>   And Anxious Cares, when past,
> Prove our Hearts Treasure fixt and dear,
>   And make us blest at last.

The great poem 'Upon Nothing' also both invokes and passes beyond the metaphysical style. The basic joke, the paradoxical idea of writing Something in praise of Nothing had been explored by at least two Continental poets before Rochester, as he must have known. His own poem is an inversion of the first chapter of the Book of Genesis and also, in a more limited sense, of Cowley's 'Hymn to Light'. Most immediately of all, it wanders in the country of the pre-Socratic philosopher Parmenides, playing with concepts of Being and non-Being in a way designed to call the structure of language itself into question. After all, how is it possible to articulate an adoration of primal Chaos without sacrilege: without repeating poetically precisely what Rochester castigates as the primal rape of Nothingness by Creation? The poet is a maker, and the act of writing bestows shape and order perforce upon what had

---

[10] George Williamson, *The Proper Wit of Poetry* (London, 1961), pp. 125–6.

previously been formless. Simply by being at all, Rochester's poem perpetuates that contamination of the abstract by the concrete, of Nothing by Something, which it is out to deplore. 'Upon Nothing' is an even more dizzying poetic equivalent of Dr Bendo's bill. This is, with a vengeance, the place where fundamental opposites meet and relinquish their identities, and they do not do so simply in terms of witty images like 'thy fruitful emptiness's hand'. Man's efforts to conceptualize, language itself, is under attack in this poem and verbal analysis can go only so far. Oddly enough, Henry Vaughan can help.

> I saw Eternity the other night
> Like a great *Ring* of pure and endless light,
>   All calm, as it was bright,
> And round beneath it, Time in hours, days, years,
>   Driv'n by the spheres
> Like a vast shadow mov'd, In which the world
>   And all her train were hurl'd;
> The doting Lover in his queintest strain
>   Did their Complain.

After a staggering opening, Vaughan's poem collapses into triviality. The doting lover and his quaint strain are simply not compatible with the ring of endless light, as innumerable critics have pointed out. But this incompatibility is, of course, the whole point. The abrupt downward movement is deliberate, a demonstration of the gap between Heaven and Earth, between great abstractions and a finite world of small fact. Rochester's 'Upon Nothing' does something similar, in pursuit of another end. Within fifty-one lines, the poem moves from the noble abstractions of Nothingness, through Creation, to the debased minutiae of a contemporary reality: 'King's Promises, Whores Vows . . . Dutch Prowess, British Policy'. The very form of the poem is a demonstration of its basic premiss, that Nothing is best. Increasingly satirical as it becomes more detailed and concrete, its construction is a silent witness to the ignominy of Being.

Let me end with what seems to me the best of Rochester's lyrics.

> Absent from thee I languish still,
>   Then ask me not, when I return?
> The straying Fool t'will plainly kill,
>   To wish all Day, all Night to Mourn.

Dear; from thine arms then let me flie,
  That my Fantastick Mind may prove
The Torments it deserves to try,
  That tears my fixt Heart from my Love.

When wearied with a world of Woe
  To thy safe Bosom I retire,
Where Love, and Peace, and Truth does flow,
  May I contented there expire.

Lest once more wand'ring from that Heav'n,
  I fall on some base heart unblest;
Faithless to thee, False, unforgiv'n,
  And lose my Everlasting rest.

Here once again is an opening contradicted by what follows. The first line, 'Absent from thee I languish still', seems to introduce a conventional lament in absence. The impression is immediately corrected. This lover has not yet left his lady's arms, nor is he compelled to do so by either the world or time. It is his own fantastic mind which is about to impose a separation which his heart regrets. In the moment of leave-taking, he foresees clearly the pain and loathsomeness of his self-imposed exile; he also foresees his return 'wearied with a world of woe' to a place he should never have left. A man asks leave to be faithless, knowing it will disgust him, predicting his renunci-ation of what he already recognizes as folly. This would seem a sufficient burden of meaning for any sixteen-line lyric to carry, but Rochester goes further. His narrator can see, beyond this initial separation and return, still another betrayal, a wanton repetition of the whole process. This clear-sightedness is terrify-ing in itself. Even worse is his recognition that this next absence but one may end in a commitment to 'some base heart unblest', a permanent exile from the true heaven which claims his devotion, but which he can neither live with nor without. Appalled at the possibilities of the future, he asks for death in his lady's arms—not, significantly, now, but at the stage of his first return.

Rochester's conversations with Bishop Burnet provide the real gloss on this poem. It both is and it is not a secular love song. I have not touched in this lecture upon Rochester's 'Satyr Against Reason and Mankind'. This is his best-known poem, and it has always been able, unlike the lyrics, to speak for

itself. I would, however, remind you of its poise between a firm
conviction of the empirical limits of man's mind and an underlying agony that he should in fact be bounded by sense experience. The theme of limitation is everywhere in Rochester and
never, not even in poems where it seems most straightforwardly
a physical matter ('The Fall' or that wry grafting of Donne's
'Extasie' on to Ovid, 'The Imperfect Enjoyment'), is it without
its transcendental shadow. Jeremy Collier once pointed out
irately that the association of one's mistress with heaven had
become a blasphemous Restoration commonplace. In 'Absent
from Thee', it is far more than this. The poem embodies the
state of mind in which Burnet found Rochester before his final
illness and mystical experience: desirous but at the same time
despairing of commitment, haunted by the idea of a position of
rest and stasis involving more than mere sexual fidelity, but
unable to encompass it.

   Rochester's deathbed conversion caused rejoicing among the
godly, but also a good deal of perplexity to his old friends. The
temptation then, as indeed now, was to regard it as yet another
of his roles, the last part assumed. There are certain indications
that Rochester himself feared for its permanence. He wished to
die before there could be any risk of his mind's alteration. Nat
Lee, in *The Princess of Cleve*, could not resist a sneer at the man
his play otherwise mourns so movingly. Nemours points out
acidly in the last lines that

> He well Repents that will not Sin, yet can,
> But Death-bed Sorrow rarely shews the Man.

Rochester's old companion and fellow-reveller Fanshaw fled
from the obsessive pieties of the deathbed at Woodstock convinced that his friend had gone mad. He hadn't, but he had
effectively ceased to be Rochester. The very anonymity of the
last letters, and of the recantation and apology for his past life
which he dictated and signed on 19 June 1680 is startling. They
could have been written by anyone. A whole personality has
collapsed simultaneously with the doubts and contradictions at
its centre. Rochester told Robert Parsons, his mother's chap-
lain, that he intended to turn to the composition of religious
poetry if he lived. What it might have been like is an interesting
speculation, considering that by his conversion the whole

former basis of his art—doubt, rationalism, the confusion of good and evil, sensuality, the assumption of false faces—had been swept away. In a sense, the final scene of his life was inevitable from the beginning. Looking at the poetry, at the letters, the biography, and at that strange portrait in Warwick Castle in which he is depicted crowning an ape with the laurels of poetry, it is hard not to think of Rochester as the archetypal Man of Herbert's 'The Pulley'. Endowed by God with beauty, strength, wisdom, honour, and pleasure, he had everything but peace of mind. And that, in the end, was the point of this sinister compact.

> Yet let him keep the rest,
> But keep them with repining restlessness;
> Let him be rich and wearie, that at least,
> If goodnesse leade him not, yet wearinesse
>   May tosse him to my breast.

4. CARVING TRIFLES: WILLIAM KING'S IMITATION OF HORACE

BY JOHN FULLER

I

EATING, like making love, is an intimate sensual act, fundamental to the perpetuation of life, but whereas we do not have to look far to find love-poetry, eating has produced no comparably serious poetry concerned with human emotion. On the other hand, it has produced poetry with a distinctly moral purpose, and in this it is, of course, similar to other apparently prosaic subjects popular with poets in the eighteenth century, such as money or horticulture. Often treated in a detailed and technical way in themselves, these subjects nearly always involve the larger issue of what kind of moral stance is desirable in life, a concern which may redeem whatever may in the first instance have seemed commonplace. Thus Augustan poets may make jokes about banknotes or tell you which kinds of apple make the best cider, but are never far from seeing such concerns as part of a way of life really possible for their contemporaries and worth helping to bring about.

Eating immediately suggests a range of moral attitudes. Unlike making love, it appears not to involve others, but in fact its occurrence is usually more frequent and certainly less private and is the occasion of the exercise of many virtues such as friendship or hospitality. Its effects are both less momentous and less avoidable: the celibate of the dinner-table will not live long. Eating has become more complicated than making love, even though it is more involuntary, and therefore it is able in a sly sort of way to rival the sublimer passion. Seeing it as a passion does, usually, enable the poet to draw comparable lessons: in the eighteenth century the moral consequences of excess in both activities were felt to be similar. The lecher and the glutton offended against a common ideal of temperate living, and themselves acted as paradigms of social corruption.

The poet's point of view varied, of course. Food in Pope is frequently a kind of Horatian test of character; Gay (a fat poet) aestheticizes food; Rochester cannot help viewing it in terms of what to him was the primary appetite, as when, for instance, in *Timon*, a meal is described in terms of the sexual organs. But what is most interesting about Augustan food poems is that they can so happily find themselves concerned primarily with a detailed rationale of the finer points of eating. In many of them the chosen mode is etiological or preceptive, deriving, no doubt, from Virgil's *Georgics*. In the case of William King's *The Art of Cookery* (1708)[1] the instructional element is provided by the mock form of the poem (it is an imitation of Horace's *Ars poetica*), but one may detect characteristics of the Georgic, such as the readiness to make patriotic gestures or to invoke the Golden Age. Moreover, the connection between husbandry and cooking (both concerned with the preparation of food) is plain. Gastronomic information, like erotic information, cannot fail to interest us in itself.

King, a slightly older contemporary of Swift and Arbuthnot, was something of a pioneer of the kind of Tory satire that we associate with these two.[2] Indeed, for this reason, *A Tale of a Tub* was ascribed to King on its first anonymous appearance. A lawyer who never cared much for the law, King was, however, a compulsive reader, an able translator, and a ready polemicist. He fell in with Atterbury's circle at Christ Church and joined with them in publishing in 1698 the work known as *Boyle on Bentley*. Bentley, it will be remembered, had a few years earlier demonstrated with some brilliance that for dialectal reasons the supposed *Epistles* of Phalaris could not be genuine. King's contribution to *Boyle on Bentley* made use of Bentley's method to prove that he could not have written his own dissertation.[3] In

---

[1] My references to the first edition will consist of page numbers for the prose and line numbers for the verse. All other references to King's works are to the three-volume edition of the *Original Works* (1776), edited by John Nichols.

[2] William King (1663–1712) was a Doctor of Civil Law and a Student of Christ Church. He is still occasionally confused with his namesakes and contemporaries, the Archbishop of Dublin and the Principal of St Mary Hall, Oxford. For an account of King see Johnson's *Lives of the Poets*, Nichols's memoir in his edition of the *Works*, or G. A. Aitkin in *DNB*.

[3] According to Atterbury, via Pope and Warburton. See Colin J. Horne, 'The Phalaris Controversy: King *versus* Bentley', *RES* 22 (1946), 289–303.

the same year, King published *A Journey to London*, an attack on
Martin Lister's topographical and antiquarian enquiries in
his *A Journey to Paris*, and two years later he made fun of
Hans Sloane in the absurd dialogues of *The Transactioneer*,
Sloane having revived the publication of the Royal Society's
Philosophical Transactions in 1693.

These works are less the casual *jeux d'esprit* of a busy man of
letters than the first sketches of a lifelong satirical obsession. In
Bentley, Lister, and Sloane, King had acquired a scholar, a
zoologist, and a botanist wholly representative of contemporary scientific enquiry, a triumvirate of Moderns. King disliked
what he felt was inaccuracy and lack of elegance in the prose
style of these writers, and his satire often depends, sometimes
tediously, on exposing their stylistic roughness and incon-
sequence. He also found their scientific attention to detail a
great joke, and here his sense of absurdity is more creative. The
misplaced energy of the virtuosi is transformed in King's work
into a joyous celebration of the bizarre.

Shadwell's Sir Nicholas had appeared to propound their first
article of faith in declaring: "'Tis below a *Virtuoso*, to trouble
himself with Men and Manners. I study Insects.'[4] Such anti-
humanism, as King saw it, yielded a jumble of trivial commonplaces, superstitions, microscopic irrelevances, and downright
untruths solemnly dressed up as a serious investigation of the
real world. With the aim of holding up such material to the
mockery of common sense, King continued his attack on
Bentley, Lister, and Sloane in his best-remembered works,
Dialogues of the Dead (1699), *The Art of Cookery* (1708), and *Useful
Transactions in Philosophy* (1709), showing, as did the members of
the later Scriblerus Club, an understandable and genuine
comic fascination with the material of his satire, such things as
'Cows that sh–t Fire, Verses on an Eel and a Pike, A Lamb
suckled by a Wether, Martial Discipline of Grasshoppers, A
stout Butcher's Dog that run under a bed, Mr Hone O Hone's
traveling Irish Bog, Mr Greatrax's Excellence in Stroaking'
and so on.[5] The effect of such satire is ambivalent, though

    [4] Thomas Shadwell, *The Virtuoso*, Act III (*The Complete Works*, ed. Montague
Summers (1927), iii. 142).
    [5] Some consecutive items from the 'Contents of the Transactioneer', *Works*, ii. 56.

encouraged to find them contemptible, we feel that these things
are strange enough to be really significant. Indeed, his own
private memoranda show King himself to have been infected by
the wide-ranging curiosity of this period, as when he has the
idea of translating English poets into Latin for foreign readers,
makes note of a Tudor religious manual discovered in the belly
of a cod, or wonders whether rice would grow on boggy ground,
vowing to 'try to sow all sorts of things upon Bogs'.[6] This
reminds us that King was in Ireland between 1701 and 1707 as
vicar-general of Armagh and Keeper of the Records at Dublin
Castle, and that his best poems, such as *Mully of Mountown* and
The Art of Cookery, were written there. These and many other
poems are about food, and reveal a not dissimilar ambivalence
of attitude to which I shall return later.

Food was an habitual subject with King. The keynote is
struck by his imaginary Parisian goggling at the size of British
joints of meat in *A Journey to London*, and his attacks on the
virtuosi return again and again to the theme. Sloane is shown to
be interested in making bread out of turnips, the food of
philosophers.[7] Bentley is presented as a monstrous cook, offering Greek dishes with such impossibly long names that they
make you forget the essential ingredients.[8] King's contributions to the *Tatler* also make use of the subject,[9] and it is not
surprising that he translated the opening chapters of Hall's
Mundus,[10] taking evident delight in its Rabelaisian version of
Cockaigne and possibly some inspiration from its explicit
connection between drinking and poetry (in 1. 2. iii Hall's note
quotes Horace's 'Aut insanit homo, aut versus facit'). King

[6] From 'Adversaria', *Works*, i. 237, 232, and 261.
[7] In *The Transactioneer*, *Works*, ii. 37. D'Urfey's philosopher Gonzales eats turnips and
other root vegetables in *Wonders in the Sun*, Act I, scene i.
[8] See Dialogue VI of *Dialogues of the Dead*, *Works*, i. 160.
[9] According to Nichols, 'when the *fifth* volume of Tatlers was begun by Mr Harrison,
Dr King was a regular associate in that work'. Nichols only prints no. 22, 8–10 Mar.
1711, 'The Analogy between Physicians, Cooks, and Playwrights' (*Works*, ii. 304). I
would guess no. 32, on the appropriateness of certain kinds of poetry to different times
of the year, also to be by King. He had contributed to the *Examiner* in the previous year.
The Bodleian copy (Hope fol. 17) ascribes nos. 5 and 11 to King, while nos. 8 and 9 on
political terminology are also in King's manner.
[10] 'Crapulia; or, the Region of the Cropsicks: A Fragment, in the Manner of
Rabelais', *Works*, iii. 278. The title was no doubt bestowed by the editor of the *Remains of
the late learned and ingenious Dr William King* (1732), Joseph Browne, who did not
recognize it as a translation of Hall.

himself was a notoriously bibulous writer, his publisher Lintott
remembering that 'Dr King would write verses in a tavern three
hours after he couldn't speak'.[11]

The subjects of many of these verses characteristically concern the stomach: the mock-heroic defence of a furmety shop by
the porters and drivers who frequent it; tributes to a variety of
puddings, some in the form of recipes; compliments to the
steward of an estate on his skill in the most important of his
duties, brewing; a tale about the efforts of a parish schoolmaster
to get asked out to dinner every night of the week; a passionate
invocation of the gastronomic resources of the idyllic country
house of a hospitable Dublin friend; and so on.[12] A few lines
from the beginning of this last poem will show something of
King's ability to use words with exactness and knowing tact in
order to convey a delicate ambiguity between tender feelings
and hearty appetite:

> Mountown! thou sweet retreat from Dublin cares,
> Be famous for thy apples and thy pears,
> For turnips, carrots, lettuce, beans and pease,
> For Peggy's butter, and for Peggy's cheese.
> May clouds of pigeons round about thee fly,
> But condescend sometimes to make a pie!
> May fat geese gaggle with melodious voice,
> And ne'er want gooseberries or apple-sauce!
>
> (Part i, 1–8.)

King appears to suggest, reasonably, that the geese will have no
desire to find themselves served up with gooseberries or apple-
sauce, but we know he is really saying that he hopes there will
never be a *lack* of these traditional accompaniments. Similarly,
if the pictorially grand and elevated 'clouds of pigeons' con-

[11] Reported by Pope to Burlington in 1716 (*The Correspondence of Alexander Pope*, ed.
Sherburn, i. 373).

[12] 'The Furmetary'; 'The Art of Making Puddings'; 'To Mr. Carter'; 'The Vestry';
'Mully of Mountown' (*Works*, iii. 195, 262, 265, 254, 203). The poem 'Apple-pye', really
by Leonard Welsted, is printed in *Works*, iii. 259, and was once thought to be King's
(see C. J. Horne, 'Welsted's Apple-pye', *N & Q* 17 Nov. 1945). It is worth noting not
only the similarity of this poem to 'The Art of Making Puddings', *The Art of Cookery*
(47 ff.) or Part ii of 'Mully of Mountown', but also its reference to King Cole (cf. King,
Works, ii. 87) and the parody of *Absalom and Achitophel* at l. 59. King liked to parody
Dryden (e.g. 'Orpheus and Eurydice', ll. 269 ff. and *The Art of Cookery*, 134). A
possibility not so far canvassed is that the young Welsted sent the poem to King, who
tinkered with it, in particular adding the last four lines which Welsted did not reprint.

descend like goddesses to make a pie, it would appear that they really wish to do so, acquiescing voluntarily and with dignity, as though the secret of making pies were something they are willing to impart to the eager household. In fact they will have to *con-descend*, that is to say, be brought down *en masse* with quantities of lead shot in order to fill the capacious Mountown pie-dishes, a very different sort of incarnation. The whole description is a fine exercise in gourmet restraint.

II

The Art of Cookery, which is King's most sustained poetic achievement in the field of gastronomy, relies for much of its initial impact upon the pleasant humour of the parallels with the *Ars poetica*. This is not the place to discuss the vexed question of the structure of Horace's poem. It is enough to say that King's imitation is of necessity even more gnomic, more miscellaneous. Its subject is the concern of cooks ('Buy it and then give it to your Servants', says King) but much of it is the concern of hosts, too, just as Pope's *An Essay on Criticism*, suggesting that criticism is too important to be left to professionals, becomes an essay on how to read. Other preceptive poems of the period, such as Gay's *Trivia, or the Art of Walking the Streets of London* or Breval's *The Art of Dress*, are more obviously the province of the knowledgeable amateur.

The parallels are cool and ingenious. Horace's advice that murders and metamorphoses are better narrated than presented on stage (*Ars*, 179–88) is turned into the necessary distinction between parlour and kitchen when it comes to the unpleasantness of preparing some kinds of food, slimy eels, for instance (244–9); the point about having only three speaking characters on stage at one time (*Ars*, 192) becomes an injunction to limit the number of guests at table (259); the nine-year rule (*Ars*, 388) is represented by the information that a roasting pig is done when its eyes pop out (484) and the *deus ex machina* (*Ars*, 191) by a surprise in a pie. Horace forbids a god to intervene in a play 'nisi dignus vindice nodus / inciderit' ('unless a tangle should arise worthy of such a deliverer'). For the Tory King an occasion of this importance would be a City banquet, where the feasted dignitaries (Whig businessmen one and all, no doubt) are merely children beneath their robes:

Let never fresh Machines your Pastry try,
Unless Grandees or Magistrates are by,
Then you may put a Dwarf into a Pye.
Or if you'd fright an Alderman and Mayor,
Within a Pasty lodge a living Hare;
Then midst their gravest Furs shall Mirth arise,
And all the Guild pursue with joyful Cries.

(252-8.)

King is always alert to passages which contrast style and
substance. Just as a play with ideas in it, however crude, is more
popular than fine-sounding vacuities (*Ars*, 319-22), so you can
better win round the 'huzzaing Mob' with beef and beer than
with ragouts of peacocks' brains (396-9). Typically, King
seems here to flatter the taste of the dreaded *mobile* more than he
intends to. The spirit of the observation may be close to
Bounderby's scorn of a hypothetical proletarian taste for turtle
soup eaten with a golden spoon, but it is in fact conditioned
both by Horace's tribute to the unerring though unprofessional
judgement of Roman audiences and by the powerful symbolism
of beef, about which I shall have more to say later. 'Non satis est
pulchra esse poemata; dulcia sunto', says Horace (*Ars*, 99: 'It
isn't enough for poems to be beautiful; they must have charm').
This line introduces an important paragraph in the *Ars poetica*
about the emotional power of poetry, but the word *dulcia*,
translated by Fairclough in the Loeb edition as 'charm',
happens also to be the word used by Apicius for a sweet, or
pudding. This is a useful hint to King, who imitates the line as:
'Unless some Sweetness at the Botton lye, / Who cares for all
the crinkling of the Pye?' (137-8). The appropriateness of
diction to the various kinds of (and occasions for) emotion in
poetry then prompts King into some remarks on the social
decorum of eating habits, but he rounds off the paragraph by
returning to Horace's statement that it makes a great difference
to the poet's style whether the character speaking is a god or a
hero, an old man or a young one, a woman of rank or a bustling
nurse and so on (*Ars*, 114ff.) with a deft parallel to such
distinctions, moving from the general to the typical and introducing a final tribute to the purely topographical element in
these gastronomic distinctions:

Old Age is frugal, gay Youth will abound
With Heat, and see the flowing Cup go round.
A Widow has cold Pye, Nurse gives you Cake,
From gen'rous Merchants Ham or Sturgeon take.
The Farmer has brown Bread as fresh as Day,
And Butter fragrant as the Dew of *May*.
Cornwal Squab-Pye, and *Devon* White-Pot brings,
And *Lei'ster* Beans and Bacon, Food of Kings!

(159–66.)

I have said enough of *The Art of Cookery* as a formal imitation. The element of parody is unignorable despite King's claim that Horace is simply 'an Author to be imitated in the Delivery of *Precepts*, for any Art or Science' (p. 18). The illumination of similarity and contrast goes far beyond borrowed method into burlesque, although, as I now hope to show, Horace was chosen for another and more important reason. Clues to this further relevance of Horace may be found on almost every page of *The Art of Cookery*. For instance, the culminating dish in my last quotation, the '*Lei'ster* Beans and Bacon', is typical of Horace's own unpretentious preferences in food, and we may suspect that if the phrase 'Food of Kings' has nothing to do with royalty, then King is equating himself with Horace here. Compare the Latin poet's longing for his farm in the sixth satire of the second book: 'O quando faba Pythagorae cognata simulque / uncta satis pingui ponentur holusula lardo!' (ll. 63–4: 'O when shall beans, brethren of Pythagoras, be served me, and with them greens well larded with fat bacon!').[13] Such plain diet is, in the context, a necessary adjunct to a serious discussion with friends of the fundamental questions of ethical philosophy. Elsewhere in Horace we find a dish of leeks, peas, and fritters as the preliminary to sound sleep untroubled by the ambitious man's insomnia (*Serm.* 1. vi. 115 ff.); an unpretentious *vin ordinaire* that nonetheless has had its owner's care bestowed upon it, and is associated in date with the recovery from illness of his friend and patron (*Carm.* 1. xx); and a prayer at a new shrine to Apollo not for great riches but for olives, endives, and mallows as aids to a good digestion (*Carm.* 1. xxi. 15 ff.: olives,

---

[13] This was to be translated by Pope as 'Beans and Bacon' (*An Imitation of the Sixth Satire of the Second Book of Horace*, l. 137).

sorrel, and mallows turn up in *Epod.* ii. 56 ff.). In this way, simple tastes are associated with virtue, and with just that interest in human nature and moral philosophy which the virtuosi appeared to neglect.

We are reminded that the full title of King's poem is *The Art of Cookery, in imitation of Horace's Art of Poetry. With some Letters to Dr Lister, and others: occasion'd principally by the Title of a Book publish'd by the Doctor, being the Works of Apicius Coelius, concerning the Soups and Sauces of the Ancients.* The whole work, consisting of the poem itself and its nine accompanying prose letters (one of which contains another Horatian imitation, of the fifth epistle of the first book) is a good-natured assault upon Lister's latest and rather uncharacteristic venture, his edition of Apicius.[14] It is important to stress the essential unity of the whole. Like Mandeville's *The Fable of the Bees* or Pope's *Dunciad*, *The Art of Cookery* is a Menippean satire, mixing verse and prose, and containing a great deal of miscellaneous illustrative material. Taken in this way, the satirical focus shifts from the *Ars poetica* to Martin Lister's curious resurrection of the forgotten Apicius, who is seen to be suspect on several grounds which the letters teasingly unravel. When modern scholarship pays attention to an ancient cookery book, much of which seems at least quaint if not downright sybaritic to the ordinary reader, satire such as King's, relying heavily on a mistrust of learning and extolling traditional virtues of common sense and temperate living, is in its element. Apicius annotated by Lister looms large in the work, therefore, in a way not apparent from the poem taken on its own. We find, too, a shift of emphasis in King's use of Horace, from the *Ars poetica* to the attitudes revealed in such satires as the second, fourth, sixth, and eighth of the second book, where the simple life is praised and fun made of extravagant or pretentious dining.

Typical of Horace's delicate treatment of this common classical theme is the way in which in the Fourth Satire of the

---

[14] *Apicii Coelii de opsoniis et condimentis, sive arte coquinaria, libri decem, cum annotationibus Martini Lister* (1705). My references (to 'Lister') will be to the second edition (Amsterdam, 1709). There is a modern edition with an English translation by Barbara Flower and Elizabeth Rosenbaum, *The Roman Cookery Book* (1958). 'Apicius Coelius' is M. Gavius Apicius, who lived in the first century AD, although about two-fifths of the work consists of middle-class additions by a fourth-or early fifth-century editor.

second book he gently encourages Catius to recount what he can remember of a gastronomic lecture he has attended. Catius is just dashing off when we meet him, in order to jot down the precepts he has heard, precepts which he describes as 'qualia vincent / Pythagoran Anytique reum doctumque Platona' (ll. 2–3: 'such as will surpass Pythagoras, and the sage [Socrates] whom Anytus accused, and the learned Plato'). Horace's remarks in the dialogue convey a secret smile to the reader as he elicits the precious and recondite information that makes up the bulk of the Satire: this is raillery at its finest. King cannot match it, but his stance is remarkably similar.

As Catius reports the unknown gastronomic lecturer to Horace, so Lister, through his edition, brings Apicius to the notice of King, whose fascinated incredulity is paraded throughout the prose letters in *The Art of Cookery*. His ruse (like Horace's) is to counterfeit a desire to partake of such learning, and also to boast of his own achievements in that line. In the fifth letter he actually quotes Catius' first precept, prefacing it with a remark which signals the assumed allegiance with beautiful guile:

He [Horace] is indeed severe upon our sort of Learning in some of his *Satyrs*; but even there he instructs, as in the fourth Satyr of the second Book;

> *Longa quibus facies ovis erit, illa memento,*
> *Ut succi melioris, & ut magis alba rotundis,*
> *Ponere; namque Marem cohibent callosa vitellum.*
> 'Choose Eggs oblong, remember they'll be found
> 'Of sweeter tast, and whither than the Round;
> 'The Firmness of that Shell includes the Male.

I am much of his Opinion, and could only wish that the World was thoroughly inform'd of two other Truths concerning *Eggs*: One is, how incomparably better *Roasted Eggs* are than boil'd; the other, never to eat any Butter with *Eggs* in the *Shell*: You cannot imagine how much more you will have of their Flavour, and how much easier they will sit upon your Stomach. The worthy Person who recommended it to me made many Proselytes; and I have the Vanity to think that I have not been altogether unsuccessful.   (pp. 18–19)[15]

---

[15] For other classical views on the subject see Aristotle, *Hist. anim.* 6. 2. 2 and Pliny, *Hist. nat.* 10. 145. King's own advice here contrasts notably with Apicius (see Lister, p. 214: '*Ova elixa*: Liquamine, oleo, mero', etc.).

It is true, I suppose, that the best learning in this field is traditional household wisdom, but King's Listerian language turns it almost into a matter of sectarian belief. It is the language of Big-endians and Little-endians.

King's desire to learn is principally conveyed by the device of suspense. *The Art of Cookery* proclaimed itself 'Occasion'd principally by the Title of a Book publish'd by the Doctor'. In the first letter King professes himself tantalized to hear of such a work, and begs his friend to send it with all speed. By the third letter he is so suffused with the spirit of antiquarian research that he is writing to Lister a long rambling account of toothpicks, cutlery, and chopsticks. In the fourth letter he tells his friend that he is writing his poem on the art of cookery. In the fifth he says that he encloses it, and he gives instructions as to how it shall be read. In ensuing letters he talks about the importance of food in poetry, elaborately showing how a play written by Lord Grimstone when he was 13 conforms to rules laid down in the poem: the level of excitement is high, and yet by the eighth letter he has still not read Lister's Apicius. He mentions a 'surprising Happiness', which is simply to have met someone who *has* seen it, and who has 'a Promise of Leave to read it'. The tension is unbearable. At this point, King's poem itself is printed, and we have to wait for the long ninth and final letter before we have his description of the book and his comments upon it, based on this friend's report. The first edition of Lister's Apicius was indeed a rarity, but there is no reason to suppose that King did not actually have a copy. His device gives a dramatic shape to his work, and conforms to the spirit of restless enquiry of much contemporary scientific correspondence. Later editions of *The Art of Cookery* that print the letters together and the poem at the end are missing King's point, which is to allow the native English good sense of the poem to steal the thunder of the indulgences of classical cuisine as pondered by Lister, Humelberg, and other scholarly authorities on Apicius.

III

Lister had been guilty of treating French food and drink with respect in his *A Journey to Paris*.[16] King cannot resist elaborating

[16] *A Journey to Paris in the Year 1698* (1699), pp. 146–70.

upon Horace's tribute to Homer in the *Ars poetica* (140 ff.) in
order to reintroduce this topic:

> *Homer* more modest, if we search his Books,
> Will shew us that his Heroes all were Cooks:
> How lov'd *Patroclus* with *Achilles* joins,
> To quarter out the Ox, and spit the Loins.
> Oh cou'd that Poet Live! cou'd he rehearse
> The Journey *L——* in immortal Verse!
>
> *Muse sing the Man that did to* Paris *go,*
> *That he might taste their Soups and Mushrooms know.*
>
> Oh how would *Homer* praise their Dancing Dogs,
> Their stinking Cheese, and Fricasy of Frogs!
>
> (200–9.)[17]

This contrast between beef, the food of heroes, and the particularly nasty forms of food attributed to the taste of England's
enemy is central to an understanding of what King is up to. The
growing ascendancy of the French in cooking was something to
feel sensitive about, no doubt, and nervous laughter about
frogs, snails, and high meat is an attitude we can still recognize.
King was quick to perceive that Lister as a zoologist had a
scientific interest in snails and maggots. In the ninth of the
Dialogues of the Dead, for example, the virtuosi's obsession with
maggots is contrasted with the fact that the Ancients ate their
meat as soon as they had killed it.[18] The Homeric attitude to
food was entirely without fastidiousness or foppishness, as King
ironically observes in *The Art of Cookery*:

Homer makes his Heroes feed so grossly, that they seem to have
had more occasion for *Scewers* than *Goosequills*. He is very tedious
in describing a Smith's Forge, and an Anvil; whereas he might
have been more polite in setting out the *Tooth-pick-case* or painted
Snuff-Box of *Achilles*, if that Age had not been so barbarous as to want
them. (p. 9.)

The sheer bulk of beef, therefore, and the essential simplicity of
its preparation, becomes a triumphant national symbol to

[17] Patroclus and Achilles are later associated with Guy of Warwick in the same
context in King's Dedication of his *Miscellanies* (1709), *Works*, iii. 291.
[18] *Works*, i. 169. Lister's delineation of the sexual organs of snails in his *De buccinis
fluviatilibus & marinis exercitatio* is mentioned with delight at the end of the eighth letter of
The Art of Cookery, and his studies of cockles, beetles, snails, and spiders at the beginning
of the ninth.

oppose to the poverty, triviality, and unnecessary complexity of
French cuisine. In war, for instance, soldiers at one time
expected only simple food, stewing their beef in their helmets
(of course they had to have beef) and putting anything else they
could find into the common pot (281 ff.). Paralleling Horace's
ironical account of supposed cultural progress in the gradually
elaborated role of the flute in leading the chorus of post-
classical tragedy (*Ars*, 202 ff.), King suggests that the military
style of great leaders like Marlborough is now, in contrast,
effete and Frenchified:

> But when our Conquests were extensive grown,
> And thro' the World our *British* Worth was known,
> Wealth on Commanders then flow'd in apace,
> Their Champaign sparkl'd equal with their Lace:
> Quails, Beccofico's, Ortelans were sent
> To grace the Levee of a General's Tent.
> In their gilt Plate all Delicates were seen,
> And what was Earth before became a rich Terrene.

> (290–7.)

Champagne, ortolans, gilt plate? Could infant imperialism
suffer such ostentation? 'Sic priscae motumque et luxuriem
addidit arti / tibicen traxitque vagus per pulpita vestem' (*Ars*,
214–15: 'Thus to the basic art the flute-player added movement
and display, and strutting across the stage trailed his robe').
King's simple 'Earth' is at once the common camp cooking-pot
and the world that remains to be conquered by the British. A
'Terrene' is a novelty, and King feels obliged to explain it in the
fifth letter as 'a Silver Vessel fill'd with the most costly Dainties'
(p. 22). The pun in effect hands over our conquests to the
enemy. What is the point of fighting the French if we become
French ourselves?

Though the French were actually supreme in the art of
making sauces, King casts aspersions on such superfluous and
luxurious inventions of the Ancients: '. . . the *Goths* and *Vandals*
over ran the *Western* Empire, and . . . they by Use, Exercise, and
Necessity of Abstinence, introduc'd the eating of Cheese and
Venison without those additional Sauces, which the Physitians
of old found out to restore the deprav'd Appetites of such great
Men as had lost their Stomachs by an Excess of Luxury'
(pp. 140–1). Indeed, King declares: 'As for my self I take him

to abstain, / Who has good Meat, with Decency, tho' plain' (373–4). Beef unadorned, therefore, becomes a moral, even a patriotic, virtue. The French are thought not only to like bad meat, but actually to have very little meat at all, as King's French traveller to London observes:

. . . whereas we have a great deal of cabbage and but a little bit of meat, they will have monstrous pieces of beef (I think they call them *rumps* and *buttocks*) with a few carrots, that stand at a distance, as if they were frightened; nay, I have seen a thing they call a *sir-loin*, without any herbs at all, so immense, that a French footman could scarce set it upon the table. (*Works*, i. 204–5.)

Joints of this kind, that need an Achilles to carve them, prove the heroic superiority of the British. Fifty years later, such a joint was to put in a central appearance in Hogarth's popular engraving *The Gate of Calais*, sometimes known as *O the Roast-Beef of Old England*, where it is presented as an object of amazement to the soup-eating and priest-ridden French.[19] Hogarth himself assisted in the founding of the Sublime Society of Beef-steaks, in which beef-eating was intended to encourage and celebrate strength, independence, and the love of freedom. But a similar society, Richard Estcourt's Beef-steak Club, was in existence in King's day, and *The Art of Cookery* is dedicated to it:

> He that of Honour, Wit and Mirth partakes,
> May be a fit Companion o'er Beef steaks,
> His Name may be to future Times enroll'd
> In *Estcourt*'s Book, whose Gridir'ns fram'd of Gold.
> (515–18.)

Ned Ward dwells on the presumption that the eating of beef increases sexual appetite,[20] but although King recognizes that certain foods influence our passions, he does not claim that beef is an aphrodisiac; indeed, by a specific juxtaposition, he refutes it:

[19] Plate 192 in Ronald Paulson's *Hogharth's Graphic Works* (1965). The alternative title derives from Air xlv in Fielding's *Welsh* (or *Grub-Street*) *Opera* (1731). See also Derek Jarrett, *England in the Age of Hogarth* (1974), chap. 1. When King reprinted *A Journey to London* in his *Miscellanies* (1709), he particularly represented it as 'a vindication of [his] own country' against France.
[20] *The Secret History of Clubs* (1709), pp. 378 ff.

The things we eat by various Juice controul,
The Narrowness or Largeness of our Soul.
Onions will make ev'n Heirs or Widows weep,
The tender Lettuce brings on softer Sleep,
Eat Beef or Pye-crust if you'd serious be:
Your Shell-fish raises *Venus* from the Sea.   (141–6.)

One may be serious about love, no doubt, but true seriousness
belongs to honour and virtue, the moral qualities of the hero.
King's allegiance to Estcourt's Tory Beef-steak Club may thus
be explained on grounds of virtue and patriotism. The members of Jacob Tonson's Whig Kit-Cat Club only ate mutton pies
and custard, after all. King does pay a tribute to Christopher
Catt's mutton pies in the poem (424), but elsewhere he shares
the delight which Tory writers had in poking fun at Tonson's
profitable relations with the Kit-Cat Club.[21] I would guess that
King originated the reversed name 'Nosnotbocai' (later to be
taken up by Ward and Shippen) in his poem *Orpheus and
Eurydice* (1704), where the ugly publisher is associated with a
Papist purgatory and with a fairyland where Orpheus is fed, in
Herrick's manner, with a very insubstantial dinner:

'Sir, a roasted ant, that's nicely done
By one small atom of the sun.
These are flies' eggs in moonshine poach'd;
This a flea's thigh in collops Scotch'd;
'Twas hunted yesterday i' th' Park,
And like t'have 'scap'd us in the dark.
This is a dish entirely new,
Butterflies' brains dissolv'd in dew;
These, lovers' vows, these courtiers' hopes,
Things to be eat by microscopes;
These, sucking mites, a glow-worm's heart,
This is a delicious rainbow tart!'

(*Works*, iii. 212.)

This kind of food is very far from serious beef, and links the
microscopic concerns of the virtuoso with the empty world of

---

[21] See Kathleen M. Lynch, *Jacob Tonson, Kit-Cat Publisher* (Knoxville, 1971), chap. 3.
Ward contrasts beef and pies in *The Secret History of Clubs*, p. 391: '*Who then can blame such
Worthies, who despise / For noble* Beef, *that Childish Diet* Pies.'

political ambition and frivolous amours—a collocation to be exploited by Pope.[22]

What King objects to in the various kinds of food he contrasts with beef is that they give one nothing to carve. French food is mostly soups and ragouts, and Chinese food 'is all boil'd to Rags'. You certainly could not carve a Turkey-cock or a Chine of Beef with chopsticks, as King explicitly remarks (p. 11). In discussing Roman food, he surprisingly links comfortable chairs and bibliographical studies as modern phenomena likely to reintroduce idleness and luxury:

There is a curious Observation concerning the diversity of *Roman* and *British* Dishes, the first delighting in Hodge-podge, Gallimaufreys, Forc'd Meats, Jussels, and Salmagundies; the latter in Spear-ribs, Surloins, Chines and Barons; and thence our Terms of Art, both as to Dressing and Carving become very different; for they lying upon a sort of Couch cou'd not have carv'd those Dishes which our Ancestors, when they set upon Formes us'd to do. But since the Use of Cushions and Elbow Chairs, and the Editions of good Books and Authors, it may be hop'd in time we may come up to them.   (p. 148.)

Carving was a serious business, and King shows that he has read Wynkyn de Worde.[23] If a joint is stuffed with too many other ingredients it turns into something else impossible to get one's knife into:

> Meat forc'd too much, untouch'd at Table lies,
> Few care for carving Trifles in Disguise,
> Or that fantastick Dish, some call *Surprise*.
>
> (418–20.)

These lines are King's version of Horace's advice that stories should be 'proxima veris' (that is, close to reality) in order to

[22] For example, at the conclusion of *The Rape of the Lock*, when the lock is thought by some to have mounted 'to the Lunar Sphere':

> There broken Vows, and Death-bed Alms are found,
> And Lovers' Hearts with Ends of Riband bound;
> The Courtier's Promises, and Sick Man's Pray'rs,
> The Smiles of Harlots, and the Tears of Heirs,
> Cages for Gnats, and Chains to Yoak a Flea;
> Dry'd Butterflies, and Tomes of Casuistry.
>
> (v. 117–22.)

[23] The 'termes of a Kerver', from Worde's *Book of Kerving* (1508), are mentioned in the sixth letter, pp. 33–4.

please, and that 'neu pransae Lamiae vivum puerum extrahat alvo' (*Ars*, 340: 'one shouldn't pull the boy out alive from the lamia's stomach after her meal'), a literary denouement familiar to us from fairy-tales like *Little Red Riding Hood*. If meat is so stuffed that it is like a trifle, however, it is getting perilously close to being simply stuffing without meat at all, even if it takes the shape of meat. Apicius has several recipes of this kind, such as 'Patina de *Apua sine Apua*' (Patina of anchovy without anchovy) of which he remarks 'Nemo agnoscet, quid manducet' ('No one will know what he is eating'). In a later recipe, ground liver is moulded into the shape of a fish.[24] As Lister points out in his notes to the first of these, this is the kind of thing meant by *coena dubia* alluded to by Horace in the second satire of the second book and embodied in the pretentious feast of Nasidienus in the eighth of the second book. It is puzzling, even dishonest, food, trifle in disguise, ancestor of the nut cutlet and soya steak. Together with the Roman habit of eating comic and unheroic animals such as dormice, it casts doubt upon the valour and virtue of the later Roman Empire, the text of Apicius dating, as Lister claimed, from the time of the Emperor Heliogabalus.[25] In his final letter, King is particularly taken with the dormice and by the fact that Lister in his notes mentions his patient observation of their habits.[26] Much fun is made of the reader's likely weariness at this stage of the long précis. Such a 'soporiferous Dainty' as dormouse served with poppies and honey, as recommended by Petronius ('as good as Owl Pye to such as want a Nap after Dinner') is seen as particularly appropriate (pp. 152–5).

Foreign meat, absurd meat, fairy meat, insect meat, pretend meat: there remains one further and possibly more serious threat to beef running through King's work, and that is vegetarianism. Horace's offer in the fifth epistle of the first book of a

[24] Lister, pp. 110–11 and 260.   [25] Lister, sig. *7ᵛ.

[26] Lister, p. 244. King resumes his fun at the expense of dormice in *A Voyage to the Island of Cajamai*: 'Were the Northern Nations as exquisite in their tastes at the Romans, they would in their country seats have their separate Parks for their Snails, and another for their Rats; for so I interpret the Latin word *glires*, though I know the generality of persons take them for Dormice. . . . But I think a Friend of mine has surpassed them all, by a Park which he made for his Spiders; the largest of which was a very sensible creature, knew his master's Voice, and answered to the name of Robin.' (*Works*, ii. 176–7.)

dinner of vegetables only, eaten out of an unpretentious dish
(l. 2: 'nec modica cenare times holus omne patella') is translated by King as 'few dishes': it obviously didn't seem like anything very much to him. In general, vegetarianism is associated
with poverty, miserliness, and nonconformism, and King has
predictable jokes about turnips or about tailors and cucumbers
(p. 24, and ll. 127–8). However, vegetarianism was not to be
lightly dismissed. There were dietary reasons for stressing
'*white, young, tender animal* Food, *Bread, Milk* and *Vegetables*' as
opposed to 'high *animal* Food and *rich Wine*',[27] which we would
recognize today and which were not unknown to the ancients,
as for instance when Juvenal in his simple dinner for Persicus
offers a kid because it is desirably fuller of milk than blood.[28]
Milk itself can be a direct alternative to beef, as King's poem
Mully of Mountown pathetically demonstrates:

> Mully, a cow sprung from a beauteous race,
> With spreading front did Mountown's pastures grace:
> Gentle she was, and, with a gentle stream,
> Each morn and night, gave milk that equall'd cream.
>
> (Part iii, 18–21.)

This is not enough for the churlish cowherd Robin, who is an
eater of beef:

> ''Tis a brave cow! O, Sirs! when Christmas comes,
> These shins shall make the porridge grac'd with plums;
> Then, midst our cups, whilst we profusely *dine*,
> This blade shall enter deep in Mully's chine.
> What ribs, what rumps, what bak'd, boil'd, stew'd, and roast!
> There sha'n't one single tripe of her be lost!'
>
> (36–41.)

Peggy speaks up for the innocent creature, and various other
servants join in the debate. King's own ambivalent view is, I
think, expressed by Terence, whose deliberate equivocation is
emphasized by the rather good triplet:

[27] George Cheyne, *The Natural Method of Cureing the Diseases of the Body* (1742), pp. 56
and 69.
[28] 'Qui plus lactis habet quam sanguinis', *Sat.* xi. 68.

> Then Terence spoke, oraculous and sly;
> He'd neither grant the question, nor deny;
> Pleading for milk, his thoughts were on mince pie.
>
> (52–4.)

King breaks off the poem in an elaborate profession of grief, but the mock-Virgilian terms of the whole poem should not distract us from its basic point, which is that behind a country idyll lie the hard facts of farming, killing for food.

IV

More truly Horatian are the many places in *The Art of Cookery* where King celebrates the content which simple tastes are bound to bring:

> Happy the Man that has each Fortune try'd,
> To whom she much has giv'n, and much deny'd:
> With Abstinence all Delicates he sees,
> And can regale himself with Toast and Cheese.
>
> (149–52)

The *beatus ille* formula comes, of course, not from the *Ars Poetica* but from the second epode, where a man may feel blessed on his small plot of inherited land, his *rura paterna* which even the great may envy. The theme is also King's:

> A Prince who in a forest rides astray,
> And weary to some Cottage finds the way,
> Talks of no Pyramids of Fowl or Bisks of Fish,
> But hungry sups his Cream serv'd up in Earthen Dish:
> Quenches his Thirst with Ale in nut-brown Bowls,
> And takes the hasty Rasher from the Coals:
> Pleas'd as King *Henry* with the Miller free,
> Who thought himself as good a Man as He.
>
> (129–36.)

Such hospitality is real because it lacks ostentation. Pyramids of fowl are not appropriate here, and nor would they be so among friends:

> When among Friends good Humour takes its Birth,
> 'Tis not a tedious Feast prolongs the Mirth.
>
> (118–19.)

This is exactly the sentiment of Horace (*Serm.* II. vi. 65 ff.).

The hospitality of cottager to prince, or of friend to friend, is paralleled by that of the lord to his tenants. Hospitality is always accused of being moribund, and English satire from Hall (*Virgidemiarum*, v. ii. 55 ff.) to Pope (*Epistle to Bathurst*, 179 ff.) laments the overgrown courtyards and smokeless chimneys of great houses that should be welcoming visitors. King's tribute to Judge Upton's hospitality at Mountown has already been glanced at. The following passage from *The Art of Cookery* links hospitality with the strong sense of tradition that runs through the poem:

> At Christmas time be careful of your Fame,
> See the old Tenant's Table be the same;
> Then if you wou'd send up the Brawner's Head,
> Sweet Rosemary and Bays around it spread:
> His foaming Tusks let some large Pippin grace,
> Or midst those thund'ring Spears an Orange place,
> Sauce like himself, offensive to its Foes,
> The Roguish Mustard, dang'rous to the Nose.
> Sack and the well-spic'd *Hippocras* the Wine,
> Wassail the Bowl with ancient Ribbands fine,
> Porridge with Plumbs, and Turkey with the Chine.
>
> (167–77.)

Ceremony of this kind may exist largely in the imagination, certainly in that part of the mind furnished with good intentions or nostalgia. The comfortable tone is established at the very outset of the work, by the words of the publisher to the reader. The author shows, it is said,

his Aversion to the Introduction of Luxury, which may tend to the Corruption of Manners, and declare[s] his Love to the old British *Hospitality, Charity and Valour, when the Arms of the Family, the old Pikes, Muskets and Halberds hung up in the Hall over the long Table, and the Marrow Bones lay on the Floor, and* Chivey Chase *and the* Old Courtier of the Queen's *were plac'd over the Carv'd Mantle Piece, and the Beef and Brown Bread were carried every Day to the Poor.*

Satirists who praise the simple life, its happiness and its responsibilities, will inevitably attack depravity and excess. In the poem, King is more concerned to stress styles of eating

appropriate to the occasion (as in imitation of the *Ars poetica* he
was perhaps bound to do), though the letters make plain the
role played by Apicius himself in introducing luxury and
corrupting manners. King claims that Seneca and the Stoics
abhorred his work, and finds it wholly understandable that
the treatise was transcribed in the reign of an emperor like
Heliogabalus rather than, say, Antoninus, 'who had gain'd his
Reputation by a temperate, austere, and solid Virtue' (p. 139).
One of King's earliest works, incidentally, was a translation of
a Life of Antoninus. He twice refers to Athanaeus' anecdote
about Apicius' impulsive and disappointed journey to Africa in
search of enormous lobsters (pp. 155–6, and *Crapulia*, ch. 5). In
Crapulia, the dead gourmet had become something of a national
hero. Their schools, for instance, were in fact public-houses
where fragments of Apicius were studied (*Works*, iii. 286). Since
Apicius, via Lister and Horace, is the ultimate *raison d'être* of *The
Art of Cookery*, it should be remembered that King's homely
precepts are continually designed to counter the whimsicality
of Apicius' salacaccabies or dormouse sausages. The work
really is, then, as it claims to be, a native art of cookery, and we
can read it in the spirit in which we read Mrs Glasse, whose own
Art of Cookery was published thirty-nine years later:

> Buy it and then give it to your Servants: For I hope to live to see the
> Day when every Mistress of a Family, and every Steward shall call up
> their Children and Servants with, Come Miss *Betty*, how much have
> you got of your Art of Cookery? Where did you leave off, Miss *Isbel*?
> Miss *Katty*, are you no farther than *King Henry and the Miller*? . . . What
> a glorious sight it will be, and how becoming a great Family, to see the
> Butler out-learning the Steward, and the painful Skullery Maid
> exerting her Memory far beyond the mumping House-keeper.

> (pp. 39–40.)

There is, however, a twist to the story. Despite these sound
Horatian attitudes, which constitute, as I have suggested, the
concealed layer of imitation in *The Art of Cookery*, there is
an obvious weakness in King's position. Whereas Horace's
professional success as a civil servant was in some sense
necessary before he could have 'the little farm which made him
himself again' (*Epist.* I. xiv. 1), King was not a competent
administrator, for example leaving the Irish Record Office in

no better condition than he found it.²⁹ He was a 'poor starving wit', according to Swift.³⁰ He squandered what wealth he had, and could not hold down a job. The 'hoc erat in votis' mood of *Mully of Mountown* applies to someone else's farm, and once settled again in London, he became memorable only for drinking and practical jokes. Naturally a writer's personal habits will often defeat the professions of virtue which may be found in his work. Pope, for instance, despite a much higher moral tone than King, can in fact be accused of gormandizing,³¹ and Horace himself, of course, is found to be in two minds about country and city, humble life and rich life. His servant Davus' accusations in the seventh satire of the second book locate the ambivalence succinctly: 'Romae rus optas; absentem rusticus urbem / tollis ad astra levis' (ll. 28–9: 'In Rome you long for the country; in the country, changeable as you are, you elevate the absent town to the stars'). There seems to be one rule for the servant and another for the master: 'Obsequium ventris mihi perniciosius est cur?' asks Davus (l. 104: 'Why is it worse for me to follow my stomach?'). The answer lies in the force of circumstance. At the end of his epistle to the wealthy Vala asking for information about seaside resorts, Horace confesses that although he is likely to praise the simple life, given the chance he would naturally seize the opportunity to indulge himself (*Epist.* i. xv. 42 ff.), and in the epistle to Scaeva he reproduces the repartee between Diogenes the Cynic and Aristippus: 'Si pranderet holus patienter, regibus uti / nollet Aristippus.' 'Si sciret regibus uti, / fastidiret holus qui me notat' (*Epist.* i. xvii. 13–15: 'If Aristippus could be content to dine on greens, he would not want to live with princes.' 'If he who censures me knew how to live with princes, he would sniff at

---

²⁹ In 1709, Addison found the Irish public records disordered and in poor condition, and proposed a thoroughgoing transcription and cataloguing. See Peter Smithers, *The Life of Joseph Addison* (1968), pp. 168 ff.

³⁰ *Journal to Stella*, 19 Dec. 1711.

³¹ Bathurst to the Countess of Suffolk in 1734: 'You do well to reprove [Pope] about his intemperance; for he makes himself sick every meal at your most moderate and plain table in England. Yesterday I had a little piece of salmon just caught out of the Severn, and a fresh pike that was brought me from the other side of your house out of the Thames. He ate as much as he could of both, and insisted on his moderation, because he made his dinner upon one dish.' (*Letters to and from Henrietta, Countess of Suffolk* (1824), ii. 81.) Perhaps one should point out that 1734 was the year in which Pope imitated Horace's *Serm.* ii. ii in *To Bethel* (cf. ll. 137 ff.).

greens'). Horace, therefore, can be seen as an Epicurean if one wishes, though his philosophy was notoriously eclectic.

King would have well understood this, approving the licence to mock a Catius or a Nasidienus, while reserving the right to believe 'bene qui cenat bene vivit' (*Epist.* i. vi. 56: 'he who dines well lives well'). There is an amusing instance of this in King's *Useful Miscellanies* (1712), where he gives 'Some Account of Horace's Behaviour during his Stay at Trinity College in Cambridge.'[32] Bentley, Master of Trinity College since 1700, had been in trouble with his governing body. The newly decorated Master's Lodge, for instance, had cost five times the expected sum, and he was accused of unfairly obtaining provisions at the College's expense.[33] In 1711, Bentley published his edition of Horace, in which in the dedication to Harley he metaphorically referred to Horace as a guest who 'after having been kindly entertain'd by me for many Years, at last seem'd willing to get Abroad'.[34] It was a typical pleasantry of King's to take up this metaphor and prove that Bentley's high-handedness and financial deviousness as Master was the result of entertaining for so long such a demanding guest. It was not hard for him to construct a comic argument proving that the Epicurean Roman poet could really be responsible for the vast bills run up by the Master. Bentley, King's first and last literary victim, was even hounded from the grave, since it seems clear that the vulgarizing translation of Bentley's notes, and the 'Notes upon Notes', in Oldisworth's edition of Horace of 1712/13 were also by King, though mostly appearing after his death.[35] This final twist, then, is analogous to finding a wine-snob attacked by a connoisseur who preaches abstinence. King's work in fact shows an uncommon interest in the niceties of eating. There is no harm in caring about food, but how then

---

[32] *Works*, iii. 24.

[33] See J. H. Monk, *The Life of Richard Bentley, D.D.*, 2nd edn. revised (Cambridge, 1833), chaps. 7 and 8.

[34] *Q. Horatius Flaccus, ex recensione et cum notis atque emendationibus Richardi Bentleii* (Cambridge, 1711), sig. A1[r]. The translation is from Oldisworth's *Horace (The Odes, Epodes and Carmen Seculare, with a translation of Dr. Bentley's notes; to which are added Notes upon Notes done in the Bentleian stile* (24 parts, 1712/13; 2 vols, 1714).

[35] See Horne, *RES* 22 (1946), 301. Monk, op. cit., p. 319, writes: 'A copy of the book [Oldisworth's edition], in an old binding, shown to me by Mr Evans the eminent bookseller of Pall-Mall, is lettered *King's Horace*.'

do you show where someone else oversteps the mark? In *The Art of Cookery*, King treads a fine wire, and is perhaps being truly Horatian in having it both ways.

William King devoted his literary talent to the defence of tradition, common sense, and civilized moderation. It is a minor achievement, uneven and, for an undoubted *bon viveur*, perhaps a morally precarious one. Some of his poetry is without interest (the Prior-like tales and bawdy anecdotes in particular) but much is delightfully fresh: his *Art of Love*, in imitation of Ovid, was deservedly popular, and I am sorry to have had no opportunity to deal with it. Johnson's Life of King represents, I am inclined to think, rather too dampening a view of the poet, while nowadays in literary histories and bibliographies he is apt to be mentioned largely as a 'miscellaneous writer' and his poetic achievement to be almost lost from sight. King is an interesting man for his time, and much of this interest could, it is agreed, only be described as miscellaneous, but among much forgotten political and religious controversy a distinct literary independence may be noted: the invention of the satirical index,[36] the pioneering of the genre of dialogues of the dead,[37] translation of Persian tales,[38] the writing of a sonnet in a largely sonnetless age and of a poem composed in a dream,[39] the first quotation in print of such nursery rhymes as 'The Lion and the Unicorn', 'Good King Cole', and 'Boys and Girls come out to Play',[40] and the lucrative publication of a classical dictionary for schools.[41] One could continue such a list, and of course it could be taken to reinforce the dilettantism of which Johnson tacitly disapproved.

But King does claim our attention as a poet of modest but

[36] According to D'Israeli. See Horne, *RES* 22 (1946), 294.

[37] Horne, *RES* 22 (1946), 295, writes that King goes back directly to Lucian. Contemporary examples of the form may be found in the works of Brown and Prior.

[38] *The Persian and Turkish tales, compleat, translated into French by M. Pétis de la Croix and now into English by Dr King* (1714).

[39] 'To Laura, in imitation of Petrarch' and 'I waked speaking these out of a dream in the morning' in *Works*, iii. 240 and 269.

[40] In *Useful Transactions in Philosophy, Works*, ii. 90, 87, and 84. King pretends that the rhymes derive from Arabic, Old English, and Greek versions which he prints and discusses.

[41] *An Historical Account of the Heathen Gods and Heroes Necessary for an Understanding of the Ancient Poets* [1711]. The volume was dedicated to one of King's old schoolmasters, Dr Knipe of Westminster.

memorable achievement in his imitations, particularly in *The Art of Cookery*. This in turn derives its imaginative energy as much from his pre-Scriblerian scorn of contemporary science and scholarship as from his need to celebrate one particular aspect of the Horatian good life. From this point of view, the most celebrated judgement upon King strikes at the heart of the satirical attitudes of the time. He was, Johnson said, 'one of those who tried what wit could perform in opposition to learning, on a question which learning only could decide'. And as a corollary to this, Johnson concluded: 'His purpose is to be merry; but perhaps, to enjoy his mirth, it may be sometimes necessary to think well of his opinions.' Now there is a class of satirist of whom this is not really true: Swift on Wotton, Arbuthnot on Woodward, Gay on Dennis, Pope on Bentley. With one's hand on one's heart one could not honestly agree with their opinions: the reader is too fully aware of the part played by prejudice, misunderstanding, or personal animosity in such satirical victimization. One might perhaps reverse Johnson's conclusion, and say that to enjoy their opinions it may be sometimes necessary to think well of their mirth. In satire of this kind, it is the humour that is of prime importance, not the *parti pris*. If the joke works, we do not care whether the satirist is right or wrong. Much of the time the Tory wits clearly *were* wrong, even though we cannot now quite ignore their comic and damaging qualifications of the overall intellectual achievements of their age. In his efforts to make dunces of men like Bentley, Sloane, and Lister, I would admit King to this class of satirist. In missing the point, he sets up an illuminating cultural discrepancy. Their kind of learning, parent of our own specialized research programmes and scholarly footnotes upon footnotes, seemed to him in some disturbing sense uncivilized. Their blinkered attention to minutiae was absurd, and the acute intelligence, approaching to dissect, too frequently encountered only a trifle.

5. POPE AND DULNESS
BY EMRYS JONES

I

THE strangeness of Pope's *Dunciad* is a quality that often gets lost from sight. During the last few decades criticism has worked so devotedly to assimilate the poem and make it more generally accessible, that, inevitably perhaps, we may now have reached the point of distorting it out of its original oddity. The *Dunciad* is both a work of art and something else: it is, or was, a historical event, a part of literary and social history, an episode in the life of Pope as well as in those of his enemies. And its textual complications—the different versions it went through—present unwieldy problems to editor and critic alike, which add to the difficulty of seeing clearly what it is. When the *Dunciad* is mentioned do we think of one, or more than one, poem? And do we include the elaborate editorial apparatus supplied by Pope, or do we suppress it, as being inessential? Is it in fact necessary to understand·Pope's references to his now often totally obscure contemporaries? The *Dunciad* is so deeply immersed in history—the final version contains references or allusions to about two hundred actual persons—that its status as poetry is problematical, and has perhaps always seemed so.

In so far as the poem has been read at all, and it has surely never been widely read, the real critical effort has been to find in it some coherent meaning independent of its dead personalities. In the nineteenth century one tendency was to see the poem so much in terms of Pope's private character, to see it so confinedly within the context of his war with Grub-street, that it was impossible to take seriously any of its supra-personal, cultural pretensions. In this period the *Dunciad* was, so to speak, under-generalized. In recent years, on the contrary, a prevalent temptation—or so it seems to me—has been to over-generalize it, or to generalize it in a dubiously valuable way. I am thinking of the current tendency to praise the poem for taking a stand

against barbarism on behalf of civilization, and to argue that,
since such cultural issues are always with us, Pope has given
expression to a permanent dilemma. The *Dunciad* may then be
compared—indeed has been—with Arnold's *Culture and Anarchy*. The implication is that we read Pope as we might read a
cultural or educational treatise, with a view to finding some
guidance for practical activity. There is of course something to
be said for this approach, for there is a genuine Arnoldian side
to the *Dunciad* which comes out especially in the fourth Book,
and no doubt general issues such as these may legitimately arise
from a discussion of the poem. But it may be doubted whether
they are the reasons why we read the poem in the first place, or,
more important, why those of us who enjoy the poem return to
it.

To say so much is certainly not to be ungrateful for such a
scrupulous and thorough work of scholarship as Aubrey
Williams's *Pope's Dunciad: A Study of its Meaning* (1955), despite
some reservations one might feel about the limited sense in
which 'meaning' is being used here. In their study of Pope's
'meaning' Aubrey Williams and those who share his approach
confine their attention to Pope's deliberate artistry, his conscious intentions so far as these can be ascertained; and for their
purpose they are quite right to do so. They emphasize the
intellectual qualities of the *Dunciad* and those parts of it which
comprise statement or allegory or approximate to either. And in
such a treatment the great fourth Book rightly gets pre-eminent
attention. And yet it is possible to read the *Dunciad* again and to
feel that there is something else to say, that such accounts of the
poem's 'meaning' do not wholly tell us what it feels like to read,
and that the first three books especially have a good deal in
them which seems to elude such treatment.

The *Dunciad* on the page is a formidable *object*, dense, opaque,
intransigently and uncompromisingly itself. Its apparatus of
prefatory material, voluminous annotation, and after-pieces
helps to create something like a spatial sense of the area
occupied by the central object, the poetic text. One can indeed
contemplate it as something with real physical dimensions. Just
as the Lilliputians one day found the sleeping man–giant
Gulliver within their kingdom, so Pope's contemporaries can
be imagined as discovering this strange offensive object, lying

in a public place like an enemy weapon or a ponderous missile: essentially not a set of abstract verbal statements but a thing, to be walked around and examined, interpreted, and possibly dealt with. Certainly the *Dunciad* when printed simply as a poetic text, without its surrounding paraphernalia, is not quite itself; it has lost something of its solid three-dimensional presence. This impression that the *Dunciad* makes of being a thing, an object, is important to our sense of a quality with which I shall be particularly concerned here: its energy. When we read the poem we can, I think, sometimes feel that there is great energy and vitality in it, that Pope transmits formidable waves of power which affect us emotionally and psychologically, and that this aspect of the poem's impact—its emotional and psychological effect—is not really accounted for in those descriptions of the *Dunciad* which seem to have now become widely accepted. Works of satire can often seem more emotionally straightforward, the sources of their power less mysterious, than they really are. And when, as in the *Dunciad*, the verse is crammed with the names of actual persons and with references to real events, the poetic end-product may all seem a triumph of the controlled will—and of nothing else.

If Pope were in complete control of his material, it would be easier than it is to speak of the unity of the *Dunciad*. For critics still debate whether it is one poem in four books, or two in three and one. Ian Jack concludes that Pope shows 'a fundamental uncertainty about the subject of the poem, a fatal indefiniteness of purpose'.[1] He has been challenged by H. H. Erskine-Hill,[2] who finds a satisfying unity of purpose in the final four-book version; but although his argument is a highly interesting one he does not, to my mind, altogether dispose of Ian Jack's original objections. But whatever one thinks about this question, there can be no doubt that the poem did go through several stages after its first appearance in print, that Pope did change his intentions to some extent, and that this happened with no other of his major poems with the exception of that other mock-heroic *The Rape of the Lock*. Uncertainty of

[1] *Augustan Satire* (1952), p. 134.
[2] 'The "New World" of Pope's *Dunciad*', *Renaissance and Modern Studies* vi (1962); reprinted in *Essential Articles for the Study of Alexander Pope*, ed. Maynard Mack (1964).

purpose—if that is what it is—is not the same thing as mysteriousness, but these external considerations might be borne in mind when one tries to account for the *Dunciad*'s strange power. Pope himself may not have been clear what it was he wanted to do.

Like some other great works of its age, like *A Tale of a Tub* and *Clarissa*, the *Dunciad* seems to engage us on more than one level. The first level one might describe as a level of deliberate artistry: the poet works in terms of play of wit, purposeful allegory, triumphantly pointed writing, in all of which we are made aware of the pressure of a highly critical and aggressive mind. But on another level the poetry works more mysteriously and obscurely: one seems to see *past* the personal names and topical allusions to a large fantasy-world, an imaginative realm which is infused with a powerful sense of gratification and indulgence. The first level is primarily stimulating to the mind, while the second works affectively in altogether more obscure ways. It is indeed relevant here to recall Johnson's remarks about the 'unnatural delight' which the poet of the *Dunciad* took in 'ideas physically impure'—a notion to which I shall return.

It seems altogether too simple to think of Pope as a defender of cultural standards confronting an army of midget barbarians. It might be nearer the truth to regard the *Dunciad* as having something of the quality of a *psychomachia*, to see Pope as dramatizing, or trying to reduce to order, his own feelings, which were possibly more divided and mixed than he was willing or able to acknowledge. In what follows I shall be using several approaches to justify the feeling that the poem is often more deeply ambiguous than Pope's overt purposes suggest; and I use several routes because there are different ways of explaining and describing this state of affairs.

II

I shall begin by observing that the Scriblerus Club has a markedly retrospective, even somewhat archaic, character for the reign of Queen Anne. In an age much given to club activity this one stands out for certain qualities which recall nothing so much as the circle of More and Erasmus: not only literary cultivation and critical stringency but an almost conspiratorial intimacy and high spirits. The admiration in which Swift held

More and the reverence which Pope more than once expressed
for Erasmus are too well known to need insisting on: *Gulliver's
Travels* is, of course, an example of Utopian fiction, while in one
or two respects (which I shall return to) Pope's Praise of
Dulness, the *Dunciad*, recalls *The Praise of Folly* (and was dedicated to Swift just as *The Praise of Folly* was to More). But more
generally the later seventeenth and early eighteenth centuries
seem to have been much engaged in taking stock of the early
and middle sixteenth century, the age of the New Learning and
the Reformation. Bishop Burnet wrote a great *History of the
Reformation* and translated the *Utopia*; during Pope's lifetime *The
Praise of Folly* was available in two new versions, Samuel
Knight's *Life of Erasmus* appeared in 1726, and Nathan Bailey's
standard translation of the *Colloquies* in 1733, while a few years
earlier (1703–6) the *editio princeps* of Erasmus's collected works
had been published at Leyden. Montaigne was newly translated by Cotton in 1685, and the great Urquhart–Motteux
translation of Rabelais—an important event for Augustan
literature—was finally completed in 1708. The *Epistolae obscurorum virorum* were not translated, but were reprinted in 1710,
dedicated to Steele. And Pope himself edited a selection of
Latin poetry of the Italian Renaissance. Indeed when Pope
wrote the first *Dunciad* in the 1720s, he was not (as readers fresh
to the poem often suppose) simply scoring off his enemies by
adapting a few of the incidents in Virgil, Milton, and others to
the degraded setting of contemporary Grub-street—although
he did of course do this. But he was also fusing together certain
other traditional kinds of writing, some of which had previously
been associated with prose. Pope's concern to preserve the
names of men who would, most of them, otherwise have been
forgotten is comparable with the intention of the authors of the
prose *Epistolae obscurorum virorum* (1515, 1517). And their satirical interest in obscure men in turn gains definition from such a
work as Petrarch's *De viris illustribus*, with its characteristic
Renaissance concern with true fame. Petrarch, who stands on
the threshold of the Renaissance, seems to have invented the
concept of the Dark Ages: at the end of his epic poem *Africa*
—the first Renaissance neo-classical epic—he affirmed the
hope that the dark age in which he was fated to live would not
last for ever: posterity would emerge again into a radiance like

that of antiquity.[3] Pope, at the end of the Renaissance, closes the cycle: his poem ushers in an age of darkness more profound than any envisaged by Petrarch:

And Universal Darkness buries All.

The connections of the Augustan satirists, including Pope, with the early and high Renaissance probably deserve more attention than they have yet received.[4]

More precisely, it is becoming increasingly clear[5] that the *Dunciad* owes something to a literary tradition whose chief classical exponent was Lucian. In the sixteenth century Lucian was particularly associated with More and Erasmus, who both translated some of his satires and whose *Utopia* and *Praise of Folly* were in part Lucianic in inspiration; and the same is true of the *Epistolae obscurorum virorum* and Rabelais's *Gargantua* (except that in them Erasmus's own influence is also important). These Christian humanist works have all caught something of the Lucianic flavour: an elusive scepticism, a vein of cool, ironical fantasy, and an irreverent critical spirit, which has often been attacked as merely reductive and irresponsible.[6] (Especially useful to More and Rabelais was Lucian's way of describing the manners of fabulous peoples, so as to produce an unsettling sense of relativity.) The Lucianic mode might be epitomized as a serio-comic style, in which the extent to which the writer is in jest or earnest is often left deliberately unclear.

There is one direct connection between this serio-comic tradition and the *Dunciad*. During the Renaissance a classical genre was revived which was not especially Lucianic, although Lucian did contribute to it. This genre has been given the name *adoxography*: the rhetorical praise or defence of things of doubtful value. The writing of such perverse or paradoxical encomia had been a recognized rhetorical exercise in antiquity, and was enthusiastically taken up again in the Renaissance. A bulky

[3] See Theodor E. Mommsen, 'Petrarch's Conception of the Dark Ages', *Speculum* xvii (1942), 226–42; quoted by Erwin Panofsky, *Renaissance and Renascences in Western Art* (Stockholm, 1960), p. 10.

[4] For example, the third of Oldham's *Satires upon the Jesuits* was modelled on George Buchanan's Latin satire against the Franciscans, *Franciscanus*. See *Poems on Affairs of State*, ii (1678–81), p. 44, ed. Elias F. Mengel, jun. (Yale, 1965).

[5] See Aubrey Williams and H. H. Erskine-Hill, op. cit.

[6] The use made of Lucian by Erasmus and More is fully discussed in H. A. Mason's *Humanism and Poetry in the Early Tudor Period* (1959).

collection of such writings, in Latin, appeared in Hanover in
1619, and was followed by other editions; it was edited by
Caspar Dornavius and called *Amphitheatrum sapientiae socraticae
joco-seriae.*[7] It includes elaborate rhetorical praises of such
things as hair (and baldness), gout, deafness, poverty, fleas,
lice, and so on; Erasmus's *Praise of Folly* is included, since that
work belongs to this genre; so is Lucian's *Encomium of the Fly.*[8]
There are, interestingly, several poems in praise of Nothing
—interesting because they form precursors of Rochester's
famous poem *Upon Nothing*, which is itself probably an important formative influence on the *Dunciad.*[9] (Pope's imitation of it,
Upon Silence, comes into the same *genre*; and, as is well known,
Pope helped to improve Wycherley's 'adoxographical' poem
A Panegyric of Dulness.) Also included in this collection are
several works of a rather different nature, which treat indecent
or 'scatological' subjects.[10] Considerable verbal ingenuity is
lavished on these scurrilous *nugae*, and one is strongly reminded
of some of the effects of mock-heroic: the treatment is ludicrously verbalistic, the tone earnest, the style solemnly elevated and
necessarily much given to circumlocution. What further anticipates Swift and Pope—and among Pope's poems the *Dunciad* in
particular—is the combination of scholastic method with gross
and indecent subjects. The result is a manner or tone which
might be called a learned puerility.

I remarked that the *Dunciad* can be seen as Pope's Praise of
Dulness, a work which, at however great a remove, owes
something to *The Praise of Folly.* Mr Erskine-Hill has convinc-
ingly described Pope's ambiguity of response towards the
'world' of Dulness created in the *Dunciad*, and has related
Pope's Goddess Dulness to Erasmus's Folly. Structurally, too,

[7] See A. S. Pease, 'Things without Honor', *Classical Philology* xxi (1926), 27–42;
quoted by Charles Osborne McDonald, *The Rhetoric of Tragedy* (Massachusetts, 1966),
pp. 89 ff.
[8] Pope's insect-winged Sylphs perhaps owe something to Lucian's Fly. Lucian's
Podagra (Gout) formed the basis of a poem, *The Triumphs of the Gout*, by Pope's
contemporary Gilbert West.
[9] V. de Sola Pinto suggested a connection between the two poems in 'John Wilmot,
Earl of Rochester and the Right Veine of Satire', *Essays and Studies* (1953). Dornavius's
collection includes Passerat's *Nihil*, which was quoted in full (apparently from
memory) by Johnson in his *Life of Rochester*.
[10] Such things as *Podicis encomium, Latrinae querela*, and *Stercoris encomium*, and several
pages each under the titles *Problemata de crepitu ventris* and *De peditu eiusque speciebus*.

The Praise of Folly may have helped Pope to organize his poem. Erasmus's Folly is presented as a kind of universal principle: everyone is in some sense a fool, and Erasmus's ironical understanding of the multiple applications of *folly* as he uses it allows him to embark on a survey of mankind from which no walk of life is exempt. Between Erasmus and Pope came Rochester, whose poem *Upon Nothing*, for all its brevity, is similarly all-inclusive or potentially so, since everyone and everything contains the principle of 'nothingness'. Like Erasmus's Folly and Rochester's Nothing, Pope's Dulness is a fundamental principle of being, and the phrase 'great Negative' which Rochester applied to Nothing could equally be applied to Dulness. The concept of Dulness becomes for Pope a structural device which makes possible a certain kind of poem: its inclusiveness allows him to treat a wide variety of subjects so that in the *Dunciad* he managed to write a poem which impinges on much more than its subject would seem to promise. F. R. Leavis's phrase, 'a packed heterogeneity', which occurs in his essay on the *Dunciad*, very aptly characterizes it.[11] In one of Pope's prefatory pieces to the *Dunciad* he says: 'And the third book, if well consider'd, seemeth to embrace the whole world.' *The Praise of Folly* also embraces the whole world, and like the *Dunciad* it could be indefinitely extended: the structure is a capacious hold-all. The author does put an end to it, but it is possible to imagine it given repeated additional material, as Pope found with his poem. In this respect—its tendency to accumulate additional material—the *Dunciad* foreshadows two other works which share a relation to the Lucianic Rabelaisian tradition: Sterne's *Tristram Shandy* and Byron's *Don Juan*. Neither is finished, and in theory both could be (and in a sense were) extended for as long as the author lived. In the case of *A Tale of a Tub* and the *Dunciad*, part of their power seems to derive from the appeal, inherent in the subject-matter, of formlessness: both authors are overtly hostile to the chaotic threat embodied in their subject, but both betray a strong interest, indeed fascination, in it. In this they are interestingly different from Sterne and Byron, who are frankly delighted by the rule of accident, the unpredictable flow of things, which is perceived as the principle of Nature, the inexhaustible source of organic

---

[11] 'The *Dunciad*', in *The Common Pursuit* (1952), p. 95.

form. The attitudes of Swift and Pope are more divided: hostile
on the face of it, but in their overall treatment of the subject
more equivocal.

The point I want to stress is this. The traditions and genres of
writing which I have just been referring to were of a kind to
exert a two-sided influence. They could be liberating, but they
could also be unstabilizing; they could help a writer to realize
his creative impulse, but they might do so at the expense
of his rational equilibrium. His powers of judgement might
be compromised by a spirit of reckless, possibly generous,
irresponsibility.

III

A comparable influence, liberating but in some ways unsettling, might be ascribed to the mock-heroic kind itself, to
which of course the *Dunciad* belongs—if it belongs to anything.

It is in the first place remarkable that some of the best
imaginative writing from the Restoration to about 1730 is
mock-heroic or burlesque or in some way parodic in form. The
mock-heroic has been very fully discussed in terms of its literary
conventions, its comic use of epical situations, characters,
diction, and so on, but the secret of its fascination remains not
wholly accounted for. These mocking parodic forms had been
available to English writers since the sixteenth century, but
they have usually taken a very subsidiary place in the literary
scene. But in the later seventeenth and early eighteenth centuries they seem to move to the centre of things: they attract
writers of power. The result is such works as *Mac Flecknoe*, *A
Tale of a Tub*, *The Battle of the Books*, *Gulliver's Travels*, and *The
Beggar's Opera*, as well as, on a lower level, Cotton's *Virgil
Travestie* and his versifications of Lucian, and such burlesque
plays as Buckingham's *Rehearsal*, Gay's *What D'you Call It*, and
some of Fielding's farces. Certainly no other period in English
history shows such a predilection for these forms. Why were
so many of the best writers of the time drawn to mock-heroic
and burlesque? No doubt it is useless to look for a single
comprehensive answer, but a partial explanation may be
sought by considering the time, the age, itself.

The period from the Restoration to Pope's death was one
whose prevailing ethos was avowedly hostile to some of the

traditional uses of the poetic imagination. It disapproved of the romantic and fabulous, and saw little reason for the existence of fiction. 'The rejection and contempt of fiction is rational and manly': the author is Dr Johnson, writing in 1780,[12] but the attitude was common, even prevalent, during Pope's lifetime. The literary world into which the young Pope grew up was, it seems fair to say, relatively poor in imaginative opportunities. The poets writing immediately before Pope were without fables and without myths, except those taken in an etiolated form from classical antiquity; they seemed content with verses that made little demand on the imaginative life of their readers. It is suggestive that in his final collection of poems, *Fables Ancient and Modern* (1700), Dryden drew away from contemporary manners and affairs with versions of Ovid, Boccaccio, and Chaucer: the fabulous and romantic are readmitted through translation and imitation. Otherwise the literary scene as Pope must have viewed it as a young man was, at its best, lucidly and modestly sensible; but in feeling and imagination it was undeniably somewhat impoverished. What characterizes the literature of the Restoration is a brightly lit, somewhat dry clarity, a dogmatic simplicity; it is above everything the expression of an aggressively alert rational consciousness.

Something of this imaginative depletion can be observed in the structure of single poems. If we leave Milton aside, the poetry of the Restoration with most life in it suffers from a certain formal laxity: there is brilliance of detail but often a shambling structure. Parts are added to parts in a merely additive way, with often little concern for the whole: poems go on and on and then they stop. The poets often seem too close to actual social life, as if the poetic imagination had surrendered so much of its autonomous realm that they were reduced to a merely journalistic role; their longer poems seem to lack 'inside'. At one time Milton thought of Dryden as 'a good rimist, but no poet'. And T. S. Eliot's words still seem true of much of Dryden's verse: 'Dryden's words . . . are precise, they state immensely, but their suggestiveness is often nothing.'

In such a period the mock-heroic and burlesque forms seem to minister to a need for complexity. The mock-heroic, for

---

[12] *The Life of Addison.*

example, gave the poet the possibility of making an 'extended metaphor', a powerful instrument for poetic thought—as opposed to thought of more rationally discursive kinds. It allowed him entry into an imaginative space in which his mythopœic faculties could be freed to get to work. And yet, while offering him a means of escape from a poetry of statement, from a superficially truthful treatment of the world around him, it at the same time seemed to guarantee his status as a sensible adult person—as a 'wit'—since what arouses laughter in the mock-heroic is precisely a perception of the ludicrous incongruities between the heroic fabulous world of epic and the unheroic, non-fabulous world of contemporary society. Presumably few people nowadays think that the essence of mock-heroic is really mockery of the heroic, but neither is simply the reverse true: mockery, by means of the heroic, of the unheroic contemporary world. It would be truer to say that the mock-heroic poet—at his best, at any rate—discovers a relationship of tension between the two realms, certainly including mockery of the unheroic present, but not by any means confined to that. It might be nearer the full truth to think of him as setting out to exploit the relationship between the two realms, but ending up by calling a new realm, a new world, into being.[13] And this new realm does not correspond either to the coherent imagined world of classical epic or to the actual world in which the poet and his readers live and which it is ostensibly the poet's intention to satirize. It is to some extent self-subsistent, intrinsically delightful, like the worlds of pastoral and romance. In various ways it gratifies an appetite, perhaps all the more satisfyingly for doing so without the readers' conscious awareness. And in any case, mock-heroic, with its multiple layers of integument, its inherent obliquity, was temperamentally suited to a man like Pope, who 'hardly drank tea without a stratagem'.

Before coming to the *Dunciad* I should like to glance at Pope's first great success in mock-heroic, *The Rape of the Lock*. It takes 'fine ladies' as its main satirical subject, and the terms in which the satire works are explained in Ariel's long speech in the first canto. Since the sylphs are the airy essences of 'fine ladies', Ariel's object is to impress such young ladies as Belinda with a

---

[13] This is the argument of H. H. Erskine-Hill.

sense of their own importance and to confirm them in their
dishevelled scale of values:

> Some secret Truths from Learned Pride conceal'd,
> To Maids alone and Children are reveal'd:
> What tho' no Credit doubting Wits may give?
> The Fair and Innocent shall still believe.

Pope characteristically blurs his moral terms, so that his own
position as a man of good sense is represented by the ironical
phrases 'Learned Pride' and 'doubting Wits', whereas the
empty-headed young girls have access to 'secret Truths': they
are 'Fair and Innocent', they shall have faith. Such faith abhors
any tincture of good sense, for fine ladies are characterized by
an absence of good sense. They are preoccupied with their own
appearance, with the outward forms of society, and—it is
suggested—with amours. 'Melting Maids' are not held in
check by anything corresponding to sound moral principles;
they are checked only by something as insubstantial, or as
unreal, as their 'Sylph'. Mere female caprice or whim prevents
a young girl from surrendering her honour to the importunity of
rakes. Pope is working on a double standard: as readers of the
poem we enjoy the fiction of the sylphs, but the satire can only
work if we are also men and women of good sense who do not
confuse fiction with fact—so that we do not 'believe in' the
sylphs any more than we 'believe in' fairies. Judged from this
sensible point of view, the sylphs are nothing, thin air. So in
answer to Ariel's question, 'What guards the purity of melting
Maids?' our sensible answer is 'Nothing': if a young lady rejects
a man's improper proposal it is simply because—she doesn't
want to accept it: she is restrained by her 'Sylph'. For the
principles of female conduct are not rational: they are, as Ariel
says, 'mystic mazes', and sometimes mere giddy inconstancy
will happen to keep a young lady chaste.

> When *Florio* speaks, what Virgin could withstand,
> If gentle *Damon* did not squeeze her Hand?
> With varying Vanities, from ev'ry Part,
> They shift the moving Toyshop of their Heart . . .

and so to the conclusive irony:

> This erring Mortals Levity may call,
> Oh blind to Truth! the *Sylphs* contrive it all.

What is the nature of Pope's poetic interest in 'fine ladies' in *The Rape of the Lock*? From the standpoint of men of good sense—the 'doubting Wits' of Ariel's speech—such women are silly, vain, and ignorant. They are of course badly educated: they may be able to read and write a little, but their letters, ludicrously phrased and spelt, will only move a gentleman to condescending amusement. (As Gulliver found with the Lilliputians: 'Their manner of writing is very peculiar, being neither from the left to the right, like the Europeans; nor from the right to the left, like the Arabians; nor from up to down, like the Chinese; but aslant, from one corner of the paper to the other, like ladies in England.') This at least is how women, or many of them, often appeared in the *Tatler* and the *Spectator* —and how they appeared to Pope to the extent that he was a satirist. However, simply because women were less rational than men, they were also, from another point of view, more imaginative because more fanciful than their male superiors. They were more credulous, more superstitious, more given to absurd notions. For if gentlemen, or 'wits', were creatures of modern enlightenment, women could be regarded as belonging to the fabulous dark ages. Accordingly what women, or women of this kind, provided for a poet like Pope, a poet working in a *milieu* of somewhat narrow and dogmatic rationalism, was a means of entry to a delightful world of folly and bad sense. For although Pope as a satirist pokes fun at them, he is yet as a poet clearly fascinated by them. Women are closer than men to the fantastic and fabulous world of older poetry, such as that of *A Midsummer Night's Dream*, and it is precisely the 'fantastic' nature of women that allows Pope to create his fantastic, fairy-like beings, the sylphs. *The Rape of the Lock* is full of the small objects and appurtenances of the feminine world which arouse Pope's aesthetic interest: such things as 'white curtains', combs, puffs, fans, and so on. This world of the feminine sensibility is one which offers a challenge to the larger world of the masculine reason. The man of good sense might laugh at it, but he could not destroy it; and to some extent he had to recognize an alternative system of values.

The subject I have been keeping in mind is the more general one of the imaginative appeal of mock-heroic, and what I have just said about the poetic attraction of the feminine world applies also, with certain modifications, to the attraction of the *low*. The age in which Pope lived seems to have been markedly aware of the high and the low in life as in literature. The high level of polite letters, indeed the contemporary cult of politeness, and the genteel social tone of the Augustan heroic couplet seem to have coexisted with a strong awareness of what they left out below. That is to say, in this period of somewhat exaggerated politeness, correctness, rationalism, there existed a correspondingly strong interest in the low, the little, the trivial, the mean, the squalid, and the indecent—to the extent of giving all these things expression in imaginative writing. The structure of mock-heroic and burlesque forms provided a means of getting at this kind of material and thus gratifying a desire which might otherwise have been hard to reconcile with the poet's and his readers' dignity as sensible and adult men and women. For all Pope's and Swift's different intentions, one can discern something distinctly similar in Pope's sylph-attended young ladies and Swift's Lilliputians: Pope's young ladies have something of the aesthetic fascination of children's dolls, while the Lilliputians—as when the army parades on Gulliver's handkerchief—call to mind in a rather similar way the nursery world of toy soldiers; they are both enchantingly *below* our own level. *The Rape of the Lock* and Gulliver's Voyage to Lilliput are undoubtedly remarkable creative efforts: in Pope's case his poem for a good many of his readers (and not necessarily the undiscerning many) has represented the climax of his fictive powers: it has an achieved roundness, a plenitude, and an affectionate warmth, for the absence of which nothing in his later poems compensates. And yet in both works—this is a matter I shall take up later—the creative impulse seems close to something childish or childlike in the minds of their authors.

IV

It is easy enough to see how Pope came to value the *little* in the form it took in his earlier mock-heroic poem: the feminine and the absurd. More problematical is the use he makes of the *low*, especially in the form it takes in the *Dunciad*: the gross and the obscene. I want to consider mainly the first three books, which are mock-heroic in a way in which the fourth is not. Each of these books treats a different aspect of Dulness as Pope

imagined it, and does so through an appropriate action or setting.
The result is to create in each book one or two large composite
images which—such is the interest with which Pope invests
them—are exciting, or disturbing, or even exhilarating, to
contemplate. However, as I suggested earlier, we can be said to
contemplate these images only obliquely, since what engages
the foreground of our attention is the luxuriantly profuse detail
of the poem's verbal activity. Our minds are stimulated and
energized by a ceaseless flow of wit, word-play, allusion, and so
on, which exercise a control over us almost hypnotic—and
particularly important is the arresting use of proper names.
Obliquely, however, we are made aware of these larger images,
and it is these that I want very tentatively to investigate.

Book One presents the Grub-street poet in his setting:
Grub-street, a nighttown of poverty, hunger, mercenary
writers, and urban squalor. As usual Pope is at his happiest as a
poet when dealing with a body of material which had been
frequently used before: he can then treat it allusively, confident
that his readers will be familiar with the *kind* of material he is
alluding to. Pope came at the end of forty or fifty years of an
Augustan tradition which had taken the topic of bad mercenary
poets as itself a poetic subject; the result was some poetry of a
startling intensity. Pope could of course take for granted the
most famous of Grub-street poems, Dryden's *Mac Flecknoe*; he
would certainly have known, even if some of his readers might
not, Oldham's *Satyr Concerning Poetry* and Swift's *Progress of
Poetry*; while Juvenal's Third Satire, which Oldham had imitated, and which Pope quoted in one of his notes to the *Dunciad*,
supplied the authoritative classical version of the 'Cave of
Poverty and Poetry'. Oldham's imitation of part of the Juvenal
includes the following:

> The moveables of *P——ge* were a Bed   } [Pordage]
> For him and 's Wife, a Piss-pot by its side,   }
> A looking-glass upon the Cupboards Head,   }
> A Comb-case, Candlestick and Pewter-spoon,
> For want of Plate, with Desk to write upon:
> A Box without a Lid serv'd to contain
> Few Authors, which made up his *Vatican*:
> And there his own immortal Works were laid,
> On which the barbarous Mice for hunger prey'd. . . .

Some lines from Oldham's *Satyr upon a Printer* contain more
Grub-street imagery, and end with a horrifying simile:

> May'st thou ne'er rise to History, but what ⎫
> Poor Grubstreet Penny Chronicles relate,   ⎬
> Memoirs of *Tyburn* and the mournful State ⎭
> Of Cut-purses in *Holborn*'s Cavalcade,
> Till thou thy self be the same Subject made.
> Compell'd by Want, may'st thou print Popery, ⎫
> For which, be the Carts Arse and Pillory,   ⎬
> Turnips, and rotten Eggs thy Destiny.   ⎭
> Maul'd worse than *Reading*, *Christian*, or *Cellier*,
> Till thou, daub'd o'er with loathsome filth, appear
> Like Brat of some vile Drab in Privy found,
> Which there has lain three Months in Ordure drown'd.

Images such as those of the hack writer's garret, the bookseller's stall or post—

> The meanest Felons who thro' *Holborn* go,
> More eyes and looks than twenty Poets draw:
> If this be all, go have thy posted Name
> Fix'd up with Bills of Quack, and publick Sham;
> To be the stop of gaping Prentices,
> And read by reeling Drunkards, when they piss . . .[14]

—the whole underworld of prostitute, thief, and gamester
merge in Pope's mind with such images as the following (from
an ironical dispraise of learning):

> Let *Bodley* now in its own ruins lie,
> By th'common Hangman burnt for Heresie.
> Avoid the nasty *learned* dust, 'twill breed
> More Plagues than ever Jakes or Dunghill did.
> The want of Dulness will the World undo,
> This learning makes us mad and Rebels too.[15]

The *Dunciad*'s original connection with Theobald, the restorer
of Shakespeare, entailed admitting into the poem the dulness
of learning—the world of silent libraries, unread tomes, the

---

[14]From Oldham's *Satyr Concerning Poetry*. Quotations from Oldham are from the 1710
edition.
[15] From an elegy on Oldham by T. Wood, dated 1684, in *Remains of Oldham* (1710).
Pope uses the phrase 'learned dust' in *Dunciad*, iii. 186, a parallel not noted by
Sutherland.

brains of scholars laden with unusable data—and mixing it with the socially different milieu of Grub-street. Indeed in the person of Theobald, as far as Pope was concerned, the two worlds were actually united: he was a learned emendator, treading in Bentley's footsteps, but he also wrote pantomime libretti to keep himself alive.

This is the world which Pope so allusively and economically re-creates in the first book of the *Dunciad*. The question arises: why does this Grub-street imagery arouse such an intense response? The Grub-street mythology, which fuses together the concerns of 'high', polite literature with material poverty and every sort of personal deprivation, produced—one may conjecture—a peculiar thrill in Pope and his contemporaries, one which may still be felt, to some extent, by a reader of his poetry. (A single line in the *Epistle to Arbuthnot*—'Lull'd by soft Zephyrs thro' the broken Pane'—brilliantly evokes the whole of this mythology.) No doubt merely to glimpse such misery, degradation, and squalor produced a fascinated shudder in some readers. But in Pope's handling there is more to it than that. The condition of Grub-street's inhabitants was, above all, one of deprivation: a state of physical need combined with a state of mental vacuity. We may consider the two constituents separately.

Pope exposed himself to a good deal of adverse criticism, on moral and humanitarian grounds, for taking poverty as a subject for satire. He defended himself in various ways: by citing the authority of Juvenal, or, more often, by claiming that what he was attacking was the *pride* of dull writers who had only their own lack of self-knowledge or their dishonesty to blame for landing themselves in a condition which might otherwise be pitiable. But these high-minded professions of Pope do not wholly carry conviction: one may at least feel that there must have been more to it than that. The literary treatment of poverty in Pope and his predecessors seems to have something in common with the harsh comic treatment of hunger or even starvation which is a common feature of Spanish literature of the sixteenth and seventeenth centuries—the constant stress on pangs of hunger, bellies emptily rumbling, and so on, which we find in Spanish drama and picaresque fiction. Oldham, Pope, and the others find the subject funny, but also—it seems—in some way interesting and stimulating.

One of the aspects of the Grub-street setting which they give marked attention to is that of ludicrous physical discomfort: the material conditions of life press with a harsh and unwelcome force on the hack writer's consciousness; the unlovely objects which furnish his garret loom large in his vision of the world —and the fact that they do so is given mirthful emphasis for us because the Grub-street hack is, after all, attempting to write *poetry* in this setting: he is 'Lull'd by soft Zephyrs thro' the broken Pane', or as Oldham put it:

> And there his own immortal Works were laid,
> On which the barbarous Mice for hunger prey'd.

What the Grub-street setting does is to force into violent antithesis the notions of body and mind by showing the ethereally spirited poet of tradition yoked to a clumsy machine of a body which constantly craves to be fed, clothed, warmed, and cleaned. Such a poet drags out a doleful existence—which we are invited to find funny—in a world of unsympathetic *objects*, an environment totally hostile to and unsuggestive of mental and literary activity. The traditional garret setting seems to make the writing of poetry—any poetry—absurd; it derides it. And it derides it, it calls in question the necessity of its existence, by insisting on the primacy of matter, mere things, mere bodies. The Grub-street myth is primarily a Restoration creation: it has some classical prototypes, but it makes its full appearance in English poetry in the satires of Marvell, Rochester, Oldham, and others, and it may be that its strong appeal is to be related to the rise of the new philosophy with its strong bias against the poetic and the imaginative. Such poets as Oldham may have seen in the reduced condition of the Grub-street poet as they imagined him, a grotesque reflection of the impoverishment of themselves. And so the peculiarly radical nature of the challenge put to the poet by the Grub-street myth was one to arouse powerful and mixed feelings: an intense curiosity (possibly unconscious of its own motive), intense mirth, and perhaps a vague feeling of alarm. There seems at times something almost hysterical in the violent response of such a poet as Oldham.

But there is another side to the subject. Poverty reduced the hack poet to a man struggling for survival amidst unfriendly

objects; and one way in which Pope and his predecessors
exploit the Grub-street theme is to insist on the gross materiality of *poems*, to focus attention on the poem not as a mental
artefact but as so many pages of solid paper, something that can
be eaten by mice, burnt for fuel, used for 'wrapping Drugs and
Wares' (Oldham), lining trunks (Pope), or, as Oldham put it,
addressing the hack poet:

> Then who'll not laugh to see th' immortal Name
> To vile *Mundungus* made a Martyr flame?
> And all thy deathless Monuments of Wit,
> Wipe Porters Tails, or mount in Paper-kite?[16]

Both Oldham and Rochester degrade poetry further even than
this by zestfully comparing it to excrement—a peculiarly
Restoration conceit. Of course the satirical target in such
passages is ostensibly *bad* poetry, but the satirical strategy is
such as to involve good poetry—poetry of whatever quality
—along with it. In the *Dunciad* Pope too uses this theme, but
with less intensity than the Restoration satirists. The action
of Book One takes place, we may say, in the archetypal
Grub-street night, with Cibber writing in his garret surrounded
by the fragments of his literary efforts:

> Round him much Embryo, much Abortion lay,
> Much future Ode, and abdicated Play;
> Nonsense precipitate, like running Lead,
> That slipp'd thro' Cracks and Zigzags of the Head . . .

and later, in despair, he addresses some of his literary works
(his 'better and more christian progeny') before consigning
them to the flames:

> Ye shall not beg, like gratis-given Bland,
> Sent with a Pass, and vagrant thro' the land;
> Not sail, with Ward, to Ape-and-monkey climes,
> Where vile Mundungus trucks for viler rhymes;
> Not sulphur-tipt, emblaze an Ale-house fire;
> Not wrap up Oranges, to pelt your Sire!

---

[16] There was a strong element of realism in this topic. Cf. an observation by T. J. B.
Spencer: 'The demand for waste paper, for a variety of domestic and other uses, has,
until comparatively recent times, been heavy and continuous and urgent and far in
excess of the supply. The consequences for English literature have been serious.'
('Shakespeare *v.* The Rest: The Old Controversy', *Shakespeare Survey* xiv (1961), 81.)

—the last line one of Pope's brilliant effects of agile concentration. Poems ('papers of verses') had frequently been made to wrap foodstuffs in satires before Pope, but to make them wrap oranges for theatre audiences to use as missiles is a new refinement. Pope uses the theme of the materiality of literary works with much less emotional involvement than his Restoration forebears, but the topic still has enough life in it to arouse him to considerable artistic excitement. His treatment of Cibber here is less ferocious than Oldham would have made it, but more elaborate and ingenious. And Pope's verse is of course rhetorically orchestrated, shaped, and climaxed in a fashion beyond Oldham's reach.

This aspect of the Grub-street setting has to do with the hack poet's physical need, his uncomfortable awareness of his physical environment. The other aspect I mentioned concerned the poet's own *mental* poverty. To some extent what I have said of the materiality of poetry has already touched on this. For the bad poet's mental vacuity, his mental dulness, is imagined in terms of solid inert matter, heaviness, retarding friction, torpor, and so on, in a manner learnt from Dryden's example in *Mac Flecknoe*. The whole topic has been admirably treated by D. W. Jefferson.[17] Like Dryden, Pope is keenly stimulated by images of solidity and inertness—he has a remarkably sensitive insight into insensitivity.

I am suggesting that images such as these of the sordid and the grossly material are as exciting to Pope as they are repulsive. The deprived social underworld of Grub-street presented a challenge and stimulus to a poet who was placed in a position of social comfort and even superiority; as did the spectacle of insensitivity to a mind acutely sensitive. In both, the poet of consciousness and wit can be said to be contemplating a form of the mindless. A further related aspect of Pope's treatment of Dulness might be called the challenge of the unconscious to a mind keenly conscious, perhaps even over-confidently so. This is an area of my subject about which I want to remain tentative, and which I will approach somewhat obliquely.

There is in the further dim recesses of the *Dunciad* a region of Dulness, created for us by hints and allusions, which is an

---

[17] 'Aspects of Dryden's Imagery', *Essays in Criticism* iv (1954), 20–41.

important element in the imaginative impact of the poem. It is
there in Cibber's address to his literary offspring:

> O! pass more innocent, in infant state,
> To the mild limbo of our Father Tate:
> Or peaceably forgot, at once be blest,
> In Shadwell's bosom with eternal rest!

as well as in single lines like that describing the poets of
Grub-street:

> Sleepless themselves, to give their readers sleep

or the dunce's 'Gothic Library', where

> high above, more solid learning shone,
> The Classics of an Age that heard of none.

This is an elusive region, but recognizable to anyone familiar
with the poem: a vast dim hinterland of book-writing, book-
reading, and book-learning, not so much a dream of learning
as a nightmare of dead knowledge. This striking fantasy
seems essentially a late-Renaissance phenomenon, something
peculiar to a period not too far removed from the first age of
print to have altogether lost its sense of the power and objec-
tivity of printed books, but so late in the era of humanism that
its sense of the closing of a cycle was very strong.[18] Milton had
said that 'books are not absolutely dead things', and that a good
book was 'the precious life blood of a master spirit, embalmed
and treasured up on purpose to a life beyond life'. Pope, in
effect, shows that bad books too do not die, but if they do not
achieve the empyrean of fame they are at least consigned to an
eternity in limbo, a place of soft, gently decaying verbal matter
—'the mild limbo of our Father Tate'. Pope is sounding the
great Augustan theme—it is of course a lasting pre-occupation
of humanism—of the use of knowledge: how to make knowledge live by making it useful to the real business of living.
Cibber, about to burn his own literary productions, says they
are

---

[18] Marshall McLuhan ends *The Gutenberg Galaxy* (1962) with a discussion of the
Dunciad. He declares that 'the first age of print introduced the first age of the
unconscious', p. 245.

>   Soon to that mass of Nonsense to return,
>   Where things destroy'd are swept to things unborn

—and an obscure region is evoked where things not dead, but dormant or only potentially alive, maintain their phantom-like existence. They lurk in a kind of lumber-room of the mind, useless and irrelevant, in a manner comparable to the physical fate of the dead in Rochester's powerful line: 'Dead, we become the Lumber of the World'.[19] (The word *lumber*—'old furniture' —like *frippery*—'old clothes'—is a favourite with Augustan writers, and is often given imaginative definition by the opposite concept of *use*. Pope finds a place for both words in the *Dunciad*.[20])

There is, I think, a strange intensity in these glimpses into a limbo of the mind, not altogether explained by the Augustan commonplace concerning useless knowledge. Pope seems to be communicating here, however obscurely and momentarily, a sense of non-conscious life—a form of vitality which is alien to the conscious mind and felt to be a threat to it. It is of interest that the word *unconscious* first makes its appearance in English a few years before the *Dunciad*;[21] and indeed Pope's own image in Book Two of an 'unconscious' pool is a suggestive one:

>   No noise, no stir, no motion canst thou make,
>   Th' unconscious stream sleeps o'er thee like a lake.

In this connection—Pope's poetic interest in mindlessness, which is one form of Dulness—Lancelot Law Whyte's book *The Unconscious before Freud* (1962) is illuminating: its theme is 'the

[19] From *The latter End of the Chorus of the second act of Seneca's Troas, translated* (*Poems*, ed. Pinto, 49). The couplet quoted above is, as Sutherland points out, adapted by Pope from the same poem:

>   And to that Mass of Matter shall be swept,
>   Where things destroy'd, with things unborn are kept . . .

[20] For a late example (1791) of *lumber* in a context concerning the use of learning, cf. Boswell's summing up of Johnson's character at the end of his *Life*: 'But his superiority over other learned men consisted chiefly in what may be called the art of thinking, the art of using his mind; a certain continual power of seizing the useful substance of all that he knew, and exhibiting it in a clear and forcible manner; so that knowledge, which we often see to be no better than lumber in men of dull understanding, was, in him, true, evident, and actual wisdom.'

[21] According to the *OED unconscious* is first recorded in 1712: Sir Richard Blackmore uses it several times in his poem *The Creation*, of which the seventh book is concerned with the operations of the human mind.

development of European man from overemphasis of self-consciousness to recognition of the unconscious'.[22] Especially valuable in Whyte's book is his anthology of sayings from writers of the two and a half centuries before Freud. Pascal is quoted: '. . . never does reason override the imagination, whereas the imagination often unseats reason', and the remark has its value in this context. Another, which would certainly have been known to Pope, is from Dryden: '. . . long before it was a play; when it was only a confused mass of thoughts, tumbling over one another in the dark; when the fancy was yet in its first work, moving the sleeping images of things towards the light . . . .'[23] The *Dunciad* seems to have a peculiarly rich commerce with this twilight zone where intuitions have not yet been polished and clarified into an acceptable good sense. For what Pope as a deliberate satirist rejects as dully lifeless his imagination communicates as obscurely energetic—states of being densely, but often unconsciously, animated. Pope himself was undoubtedly committed to defending conscious mental alertness, vigilance, keen critical activity. Yet the poem as a whole makes us aware of the possibility of another tenable attitude, the value of what the Cambridge Platonist Ralph Cudworth called, in speaking of the mind's powers, 'a drowsy unawakened cogitation'.[24] In *The Castle of Indolence* (to take a slighter poem than the *Dunciad* and a far simpler case, but one not far removed in time) Thomson eventually works round to a useful moral recommending 'Industry', but what is agreed to be the best part of the poem celebrates the allure of 'Indolence'. Nearly a hundred years after the first *Dunciad* Keats was to take the theme much further so as to make plain the association of Indolence, or Dulness in one of its senses, with artistic creativity.

V

I take my last ambiguous image of Dulness from a part of the poem which has hardly been the most popular or appreciated:

---

[22] Whyte's book is quoted by McLuhan, op. cit., p. 245.
[23] From an epistle To Roger, Earl of Orrery, prefixed to *The Rival Ladies* (1664) (*Of Dramatic Poesy and Other Critical Essays*, ed. George Watson (1962), i. 2).
[24] Quoted by Whyte, op. cit., p. 96.

the second Book. This Book, which describes the heroic games of the duces, is the most notorious part of the poem, perhaps the most notorious part of all Pope's works. Here the satire against the booksellers, critics, patrons, and Grub-street writers takes the form of making them go through ludicrous actions of a humiliating and even disgustingly sordid nature. At least, this is one way of looking at it—although a way which takes a rather external view of the actual working of the poetry. For this is not, I think, what it feels like to read. What the book communicates is a curious warmth, a gusto, even a geniality —which, notably, G. Wilson Knight has testified to and described.[25] Certainly Pope lavished a good deal of work on this Book, and most of it is admirably written. He might have been expected to have shied away from it himself when he revised the *Dunciad*. But far from that, he carefully improved it, and added to it, making it the second longest of the four Books.

First of all, what is the dominant effect of Book Two—apart from its indecency? Some of the power of its imaginative conception comes from the fact that the action now moves out of the Grub-street garret into the more publicly exposed setting of the City of London, but a city fantastically simplified, seen as in dream. This is London seen as Lud's-town—or Dul-town, as Pope brings out in a couplet in the 1728 version (its leaden thud was sacrificed in the recasting):

> Slow moves the Goddess from the sable flood,
> (Her Priest preceding) thro' the gates of Lud.

'Dul-town' is inhabited not by starving poets but by vividly felt, if faceless, presences who are sometimes infantile and sometimes maniac. (The notion of an *infant* can be related to the *Dunciad*'s verbal and literary concerns through its literal meaning: 'a person unable to speak or use words'.)

Wilson Knight has remarked on the absence of cruelty in this

[25] Wilson Knight notes that 'there is a strange and happy absence of the sadistic. The comedy is not precisely cruel: the duces are all happy, are not shown as realizing their absurdity, and are allowed to maintain a certain physical, though ludicrous, dignity.' He further comments on Pope's 'delicate emotional and sensuous touch, felt in the softness, the nature-tone, of the whole atmosphere'. See *Laureate of Peace* (1954), pp. 61, 62. In his essay on the *Dunciad*, in a discussion of a passage in Book Four, F. R. Leavis remarks on 'the predominant feeling, which, in fact, might fairly be called genial'.

narrative of the games. On the contrary, every one is having a wonderful time, for within the imaginative world of the poem no one is conscious of humiliation. These dunces are, in fact, like unabashed small children—but children viewed with the distance and distaste of the Augustan adult. The world they inhabit is, like that of early infancy, wholly given to feeling and sensation, and so all the activities are of a simple physical nature: they run races, have urinating, tickling, shouting, and diving competitions, and finally vie with each other in keeping awake until 'the soft gifts of Sleep conclude the day'. The poetic atmosphere is soft and delicate, the feelings expressed by the dunces playful, occasionally petulant, but essentially affectionate. As a satirist Pope is of course degrading his enemies: all the characters are given the names of actual persons. Yet, as usual, the poetry is doing something more interesting than a narrowly satirical account would suggest. What it is doing, in part, is creating a world free of adult and social restraints. 'Here strip, my children!' cries their mother Dulness at one point, and they strut about naked, play games, quarrel, and shout, as free of inhibition and shame as any small infant. Pope evokes the unrestrained glee of childhood, its unthinking sensuality (as in the tickling match) and the deafening noise made by children at play:

> Now thousand tongues are heard in one loud din;
> The monkey-mimics rush discordant in;
> 'Twas chatt'ring, grinning, mouthing, jabb'ring all,
> And Noise and Norton, Brangling and Breval . . .

The world of Book Two seems in many ways a version of pre-literate infancy, and to enter it is to experience a primitive sense of liberation. Not only is it innocent; it is completely without self-consciousness: again Pope's poetic concern is with a form of unconscious vitality. The comparison of the dunces with small children, however, is only implicit; it does not exhaust the whole of the poetic image. The dunces are, after all, not in fact children, and in so far as they are adult they call to mind the inhabitants of Bedlam, madmen resembling small children in being without restraint and without manners. Bedlam is one of the places which Pope is careful to include on his simplified map of London: in the first book it is said to be close to the 'Cave of Poverty and Poetry' which is Cibber's Grub-street residence. In this second book the implicit Bedlamite metaphor becomes more insistent. (One of the prints in the early editions of *A Tale of a Tub* gives an intensely dismal picture of Bedlam hospital: naked madmen lie chained on filthy mattresses in a large cell, while being peered at through grilles by members of the public.)

Let me give an example of a dunce who combines qualities of infantility with the manic energy of a madman. This is Blackmore in the shouting competition:

> But far o'er all, sonorous Blackmore's strain;
> Walls, steeples, skies, bray back to him again.
> In Tot'nham fields, the brethren, with amaze,
> Prick all their ears up, and forget to graze;
> Long Chanc'ry-lane retentive rolls the sound,
> And courts to courts return it round and round;
> Thames wafts it thence to Rufus' roaring hall,
> And Hungerford re-echoes bawl for bawl.

It is as if this dunce has grown to a figure of Brobdingnagian size, or as if the City has shrunk to the dimensions of a toy-town with a child standing astride over it. Aubrey Williams's account of this passage is a good example of his method. He shows that the place-names mentioned here are chosen to mark Westminster's boundaries, so that the voice of Blackmore the 'City Bard' resounding all over Westminster represents the invasion of the West End by dulness.[26] His commentary is helpful and entirely convincing, but such an account may have the effect of shielding us from the full impact of the image as Pope has conceived it. For the image of deafening, gigantesque noise—as of a giant *shouting* over London—is, though comic, a disturbingly powerful one; and although it has an allegorical meaning which we should know, the image itself in all its rude force ought, it seems to me, to come first. This after all is what one remembers after reading the book: the games themselves, not what they 'stand for'; the poetic fiction is primary.

No doubt most readers of Pope will never do other than shrink from this second book. But if one is willing to explore it, one beneficial result might be a clearer perception of Pope's

---

[26] Op. cit., pp. 36–8.

extraordinarily rich, but undoubtedly very strange, sensibility. It seems possible that the impression of an unusual degree of creative release given by such parts of the *Dunciad* as these is due to Pope's being able to indulge intense feelings of an infantile nature by taking advantage of the permissive decorum of mock-heroic. There is a quality of complicity in the writing— 'Heav'n rings with laughter' (ii. 121), and the mirth seems to include both poet and reader—that makes it hard to bear in mind that, from the 'satirical' point of view, such writing is supposed to show Pope making a fierce retaliatory attack on his enemies. But so often this other point of view, which occasionally finds expression in Pope's own notes, seems to belong to a quite different mood and spirit. One of Pope's notes to the second book opens in a tone of high moral indignation: 'In this game is expos'd in the most contemptuous manner, the profligate licentiousness of those shameless scriblers . . .' But the corresponding part of the poem reads:

> See in the circle next, Eliza plac'd,
> Two babes of love close clinging to her waist . . .

The poetry, as Wilson Knight says, has a 'nature-tone', and it seems not altogether absurd to find here a certain real tenderness—of course set against the incongruously risible circumstances, but none the less a modifying element in the full poetic effect. In a similar way the account of the mud-diving and the encounter with the mud-nymphs is, as several critics have remarked, strangely attractive, and has the effect of robbing the huge open sewer of Fleet-ditch, the actual scene of the action, of its horrible offensiveness. The effect is quite un-Swiftian, not nasty in the reading. In a related way such a passage as the following achieves an inimitably Popian beauty:

> Thro' Lud's fam'd gates, along the well-known Fleet
> Rolls the black troop, and overshades the street,
> 'Till show'rs of Sermons, Characters, Essays,
> In circling fleeces whiten all the ways:
> So clouds replenish'd from some bog below,
> Mount in dark volumes, and descend in snow.

This draws its vitality from its absorption of 'base' matter into forms pleasurable to contemplate and from an attitude to experience which refuses to find anything repulsive or offensive: the 'disagreeables' are evaporated.

But the element of the obtrusively childish and dirty in this part of the *Dunciad* remains an issue to be faced. Pope often seems to have been attracted to indecent or equivocal subjects, as if he derived a stimulus from affronting conventional good taste: indeed, of all the considerable English poets he remains perhaps the one with the greatest power to shock—no doubt partly because the social restraints which make the sense of shock possible are themselves powerfully represented in his verse. However we may respond to this side of Pope, it does not seem helpful to call it 'immature', since it may well have been an indispensable part of his creative temperament. Indeed Pope might have been a less comprehensive poet, even a less balanced one, without it. It has been suggested that during this period 'various forms of play and irresponsibility may have been a chief outlet for the poetic impulse',[27] and certainly without their disconcertingly childish side not only Pope but also his fellow Scriblerians Swift and Gay would be considerably less forceful and original writers. Ambrose Philips's undistinguished, if innocuous, little poems addressed to children (such as those written for the Pulteney girls: one is dated 1724, another 1727, the years immediately preceding the first *Dunciad*) were mercilessly attacked and parodied (for example by Henry Carey as well as by Pope[28]), presumably because they contravened the current assumption that childish feelings might be indulged obliquely in comic and parodic forms but not expressed directly in all their unwitty vulnerability. For the Augustans, Pope included, mock-heroic provided the perfect protective form for the expression of childish feelings, since (as I suggested earlier) its built-in critical apparatus served to absolve the poet from a possible charge of too outrageous an irresponsibility. Similarly such versicles as Henry Carey's and Pope's Lilliputian Odes (written, for the most part, in lines of

[27] William K. Wimsatt, jun. and Cleanth Brooks, *Literary Criticism: A Short History* (New York, 1957), p. 217 n. 2.
[28] Pope refers to Philips's 'Infantine stile' in his note to 1728 *Dunciad*, iii. 322. Chapter 11 of *The Art of Sinking in Poetry* (1727) had dealt with 'The Infantine', 'where a Poet grows so very simple, as to think and talk like a child'. Cf. also Pope's reference to Philips in a letter to Swift, 14 Dec. 1725 (*Correspondence*, ii. 250, ed. George Sherburn).

two and three syllables respectively) take advantage of the
Lilliputian fiction for writing of an undiluted frivolity.

VI

In what I have been saying I have been deliberately stressing
one side of Pope's genius: the peculiar *energy* of his poetry and its
power to excite. I want finally to add a few remarks on this
subject from a rather different point of view.

The *Dunciad* is so often discussed simply in terms of its topics,
its ideas, attitudes, literary conventions, and so on, or its
individual effects of wit—its grotesque metaphors, its low
puns, its studiedly indecorous diction—that it might seem that
the poem as a whole was fully accounted for. Yet something
more fundamental seems to escape such discussions: everything that can be included under the idea of *form*—the overall
shape of the poetic experience, the contributions made by
Pope's use of the couplet, the paragraph, the episode and each
Book of the poem. When Pope is writing well, the verse moves
with a strong purposefully directed energy, the couplets are
pointed, the paragraphs draw to a climax, and the individual
Books each have a true conclusion—they do not merely stop.
The couplets, for example, are never allowed to succeed each
other in a merely additive way; instead they are held firmly in
place in the verse paragraph, and the paragraph itself often
follows a large rhythmic curve which makes possible a dynamic
verse movement. When read with a sympathetic mimetic
co-operation, such verse has an exceptional capacity to arouse
nervous excitement. However, this energy sometimes has
an ambiguous effect, which may be such that an account of
the poem which stays too close to its satirical paraphrasable
meaning may distort the real effect of the poetry.

In his liking for exuberant or agitated movement, for vehement emphasis, and for intense surface vivacity, Pope reveals
himself as baroque in sensibility; as he does in his nervous sense
of tempo, especially at those moments when he gathers speed
for an overwhelming climax.[29] Among English poets in this one
respect his true predecessor is Crashaw, whom Pope had read

[29] One of the most impressive of such climactic movements, the conclusion to the
Epilogue to the Satires, Dialogue 1—the 'triumph of Vice'—was compared by Joseph
Warton to a painting by Rubens.

carefully and used, although it is not necessary to suppose that he needed Crashaw to discover these qualities in himself: there were numerous other influences. But nowhere in seventeenth-century English poetry except in the *Hymn to Saint Teresa* and the magnificent, and in some ways curiously Popian,[30] *Music's Duel*, can one find a comparable verve and ardour, such an acute response to sensory experience, or such a flamboyantly dynamic sense of movement.

These qualities are to be found in all Pope's greater poems, not least in the work he was engaged on immediately before the first *Dunciad*: the translation of Homer. This, in its energy, its sustained 'elasticity' (Pope's term[31]), and in the way in which its personages are so often posed in brilliant theatrically lit tableaux, can certainly be seen as an outstanding example of the late baroque sensibility in poetry. In a comparable way the fantastic action of the *Dunciad* also allowed Pope to devise forms amenable to baroque taste. Some baroque art seems designed to express movement or animation almost for its own sake; and Dulness, as imagined by Pope—anarchic, 'busy, bold, and blind'—encouraged the invention of such effects as those in the passage I have already quoted:

> 'Till show'rs of Sermons, Characters, Essays,
> In circling fleeces whiten all the ways:
> So clouds replenish'd from some bog below,
> Mount in dark volumes, and descend in snow

—with its repeated swirling movement, an effect which receives a number of variations:

> Not with more glee, by hands Pontific crown'd,
> With scarlet hats wide-waving circled round . . .

and

> As man's Mæanders to the vital spring
> Roll all their tides, then back their circles bring . . .

[30] The account of the tickling contest in Book Two of the *Dunciad* possibly owes something to *Music's Duel*. Pope perhaps remembered Crashaw's reference to tickling: 'that tickled with rare art / The tatling strings' (47–8). Pope's line 212, 'And quick sensations skip from vein to vein' may recall Crashaw's 'then quicke returning skipps / And snatches this againe' (32–3), while his phrase 'the pleasing pain' (211) is reminiscent of some of Crashaw's peculiar interests.

[31] Cf. *Dunciad*, i. 186.

POPE AND DULNESS 135

The sensibility which took pleasure in these and similar effects informs the entire poem, and, despite all the personal and topical allusions and all the brilliant local explosions of wit, sets going (in the first three books at least) a powerful current of feeling; at times the larger movements take on a demonic momentum. This may be felt particularly in the concluding phases of the Books, which are given an emphasis as if each Book were a self-contained poem.[32] Throughout his career the endings of Pope's poems are conspicuously strong and deeply felt: indeed some of his poems sound at their conclusions an almost apocalyptic note—a desire to relate the poetic subject to ultimate ends. In the 'Elegy to the Memory of an Unfortunate Lady' the poet finally anticipates his own death, the end of time for himself, while in '*Eloisa to Abelard*' the heroine looks forward to as far in the future as her story will be read—which may again be interpreted as the end of time. And *The Rape of the Lock* has an ending whose startling power has to do with its looking forward to the death of Belinda, and again to an eternity made possible by poetry. In the *Dunciad* the first and third books both end on sustained climactic movements; both record, in a high incantatory strain, a visionary moment when the order of things as they are, appears to be dissolving to give place to a totally different order. In the first version Book Three (originally, of course, the final book) ends with the uplifted strains of Settle's prophecy—in the last line of which Pope's own name is introduced—before entering upon the great Conclusion to the whole poem. And this Conclusion is an ending in the grandest possible sense: the end of Nature itself.

The Conclusion to the *Dunciad* is uninterruptedly solemn and sublime: indeed its sublimity may be felt to be somewhat disconcertingly absolute. It seems entirely in keeping with the mode of the poem that we do not, perhaps, quite know how to take it; and indeed in the first version a note by Pope introduces a sense of wavering or qualification into the reader's mind.[33] In the same version the poem ends with a couplet which 'contains' the vision of 'Universal Darkness' and consigns it to the realm of false dreams:

[32] Book Two is an exception: it cannot end with a powerful climax, since it shows the dunces falling asleep—although the falling asleep is in itself an elaborate set-piece.
[33] 1728 *Dunciad*, iii. 337.

> 'Enough! enough!' the raptur'd Monarch cries;
> And thro' the Ivory Gate the Vision flies.

But in the final version of 1743 the Conclusion is no longer framed by this couplet, but ends uncompromisingly with

> Thy hand, great Anarch! lets the curtain fall;
> And Universal Darkness buries All.

And there is no note here to suggest that the poet is not fully committed to what his poem is saying. The Conclusion has become a final, grandiose, annihilating gesture, sublime but also grotesque—for it is surely hugely disproportionate, not really prepared for in terms of the poem's own fiction. Moreover it has the effect, not uncommon in baroque paintings, of overflowing the bounds of the frame so as to engulf the spectator. Pope is of course cornering the reader, forcing upon him an acknowledgement of his responsibility, pulling him into the world of the poem—by making the poem reach out to him. But even here, it seems to me, where Pope is at his greatest as a poet of prophecy and lament, our feelings are not simple, nor simply tragic, and in one part of our minds we move through the Conclusion with a powerful sense of pleasure: the emotional drive of the poem, its baroque afflatus, seem to require a consummation as absolute as this. Pope's imaginative desire for completeness, for making an end, is here fused with his poetic delight in images of cataclysmic destruction. It is an important part of his greatness as a poet that he could not only recognize, judge, and repudiate the anarchic but feel within himself its vitality and excitement, and communicate what he felt. So it is here in the Conclusion. The poet at once succumbs to and defies the power of Dulness; and what destroys the world completes the poem.

APPENDIX

The Conclusion to the Dunciad

It has apparently not been noticed that as a poetic unit the Conclusion to the *Dunciad* was probably, though in a very general way, modelled on Ovid's account of the coming of the Iron Age (*Metamorphoses*, i. 125–50).

In Book One Pope had written of Dulness:

Here pleas'd behold her mighty wings outspread
To hatch a new Saturnian age of Lead.   (27–8.)

To which he appended a note: 'The ancient Golden Age is by Poets
stiled *Saturnian*: but in the Chymical language *Saturn* is Lead. She is
said here only to be spreading her wings to hatch this age; which is not
produced completely till the fourth book.' Pope here probably has in
mind Ovid's account of the four ages (Gold, Silver, Brass, Iron),
so that the Golden Age of Dulness—Pope's 'new Saturnian age of
Lead'—corresponds to Ovid's last, and worst, Iron Age.

   The best-known version of the *Metamorphoses* in English was that in
heroic couplets (1626) by George Sandys, whom Dryden had called
'the best versifier of the former age' (*Preface to the Fables*). Pope had
read Sandys's translation as a child and had 'liked [it] extremely'
('Spence's *Anecdotes*', ed. James Osborn (1966), i. 14). Sandys trans-
lates the coming of the Iron Age as follows (it is not, as it happens, a
particularly good specimen of his style):

> Next unto this succeeds the *Brazen Age*;
> Worse natur'd, prompt to horrid warre, and rage:
> But yet not wicked. Stubborn *Yr'n* the last.
> Then, blushlesse crimes, which all degrees surpast,
> The World surround. Shame, Truth, and Faith depart:
> Fraud enters, ignorant in no bad Art;
> Force, Treason, and the wicked love of gain.
> Their sails, those winds, which yet they knew not, strain:
> And ships, which long on loftie Mountains stood,
> Then plow'd th'unpractis'd bosome of the Flood.
> The Ground, as common earst as Light, or Aire,
> By limit-giving Geometry they share.
> Nor with rich Earth's just nourishments content,
> For treasure they her secret entrailes rent;
> The powerful Evill, which all power invades,
> By her well hid, and wrapt in Stygian shades.
> Curst Steele, more cursed Gold she now forth brought:
> And bloody-handed Warre, who with both fought:
> All live by spoyle. The Host his Guest betrayes;
> Sons, Fathers-in-law: 'twixt Brethren love decayes.
> Wives husbands, Husbands wives attempt to kill.
> And cruell Step-mothers pale poysons fill.
> The Sonne his Fathers hastie death desires:
> Foild Pietie, trod underfoot, expires.
> *Astraea*, last of all the heavenly birth,
> Affrighted, leaves the blood-defiled Earth.

(I have quoted from the edition of 1640, p. 2). There is no doubt that
Pope used Book One of the *Metamorphoses* elsewhere in the Conclusion,
since his note to lines 637–8—

> As Argus' eyes by Hermes' wand opprest,
> Clos'd one by one to everlasting rest;

—refers to the source in *Metam.* i. 686–7, 713–14.

Ovid's description and Pope's Conclusion share a concern with a rapid decline or degeneration in human life. In structure too they have a good deal in common: like so many of the great set-pieces in the *Metamorphoses*, this one proceeds by enumerating circumstances line by line, working by accumulation to a climax—a procedure adapted here by Pope. But only the first twenty-six lines of Pope's Conclusion (627–52) are modelled on Ovid: his final four lines, in which Dulness is apostrophized, are his own invention:

> Lo! thy dread Empire, CHAOS! is restor'd;
> Light dies before thy uncreating word:
> Thy hand, great Anarch! lets the curtain fall;
> And Universal Darkness buries All.

The fact that Sandys's verse paragraph also fills twenty-six lines suggests that Pope used Sandys, rather than the original Latin, as a structural model. Moreover Pope's lines 649–52 are close in substance and tone to the last four of Sandys, and in the case of one line (650)—which was, in fact, added only in the final version—has one identical word, also in the final position:

> *Religion* blushing veils her sacred fires,
> And unawares *Morality* expires.
> Nor *public* Flame, nor *private*, dares to shine;
> Nor *human* Spark is left, nor Glimpse *divine!*

Of course the effects made by Ovid's description and Pope's Conclusion are very different. Pope transforms Ovid's description by substituting his own more abstractly metaphysical circumstances and building up to a far grander climax. But quite as important is the placing of each passage within the poem as a whole. In Pope's hands the Ovidian set-piece is removed from its place within the seemingly endless sequence of the *Metamorphoses* to a position right at the end of a long poem, unsoftened (in the final version) by any narrative framework, and left to make its full impact in all its massive abruptness.

Pope's Conclusion (unlike Johnson's in *Rasselas*) is a conclusion in which *everything* is concluded. And just as the whole poem works up to the great Conclusion, so the Conclusion itself works up to the immensely resonant last line:

> And Universal Darkness buries All.

The line had an earlier form, in which Pope tried out 'Dulness' and 'cover' in place of 'Darkness' and 'buries'. Sutherland also notes three lines in Pope's *Iliad* which anticipate it (iv. 199, vi. 73—he wrongly cites 199—and xii. 80); and Constance Smith in a note, 'An Echo of Dryden in Pope' (*Notes and Queries* NS xii (1965), 451), suggests as a closer parallel line 117 in Dryden's 'Last Parting of Hector and Andromache from *Iliad*, vi:

> And Universal Ruine cover all

—only this parallel having the words *Universal* and *cover* (which Pope had used in the 1728 *Dunciad*). Two other parallels that I would add are from Crashaw's *Music's Duel*, 156:

> A full-mouth *Diapason* swallowes all

and from Creech's translation of Manilius's *Astronomicon* (1697, p. 52):

> *Earth* would not keep its place, the *Skies* would fall,
> And universal Stiffness deaden All.

There are no doubt other examples of this form of verse-sentence, with a similarly placed verb and a final *All*. These lines are all concerned with striving to accomplish something absolute and final—to swallow, cover, deaden, bury, *all*; their quasi-erotic energy is very characteristic of baroque sensibility. Among the poets who use this form of line, however, Pope achieves unquestionably the greatest effect. In his final version of the *Dunciad*, by virtue of its perfect phrasing and by being placed last in a long poem, the line reaches what seems an ultimate degree of intensity.

6. THE POETRY OF THOMAS GRAY: VERSIONS OF THE SELF

BY ROGER LONSDALE

THERE is no more familiar comment on Gray's poetry than Johnson's praise of the Elegy Written in a Country Churchyard as a poem which 'abounds with images which find a mirrour in every mind, and with sentiments to which every bosom returns an echo'.[1] In one form or another Johnson's tribute to Gray's eloquent generalities about rich and poor, life and death, has been reiterated down to the present day. There are signs, however, that the 'Elegy' produces fewer or more complicated echoes in the bosoms of modern readers than in those of earlier generations. We are less confident about the basic truths of common human experience, or less grateful to the poet for attending to them. In his recent book *Sincerity and Authenticity*, Professor Lionel Trilling shows how the 'commonplace' has become for some contemporary writers precisely the treacherous illusion which frustrates the search for 'the authenticity of particular being', attainable only through 'intransigent subjectivity'.[2] Gray's own commonplaces have seemed sinister in another respect. In the opening pages of *Some Versions of Pastoral* Professor William Empson takes for granted the irritation many modern readers feel with 'the complacence in the massive calm' of the 'Elegy', and goes on to analyse with characteristic subtlety one of its most familiar stanzas to lay bare the latent political implications. Gray is meditating on the potential talents of the dead villagers which had never enjoyed any opportunity of fulfilment:

> Full many a gem of purest ray serene
> The dark unfathomed caves of ocean bear;
> Full many a flower is born to blush unseen
> And waste its sweetness on the desert air.

[1] Lives of the Poets, ed. G. B. Hill, 3 vols (Oxford, 1905), iii. 441.
[2] *Sincerity and Authenticity* (1972), pp. 104–5.

By means of these images, Professor Empson argues, such a waste of talents 'is stated as pathetic, but the reader is put into a mood in which one would not try to alter it'. Their effect is to make an unfair social arrangement seem both natural and dignified, to trick the reader into feeling that the deprived villager 'is better off without opportunities'. In general, the 'universality and impersonality' of Gray's truisms in the 'Elegy' claim that 'we ought to accept the injustice of society as we do the inevitability of death'.[3]

Even if he does not agree with these conclusions about them, the careful reader of the 'Elegy' will still do well to ponder the function of these images. What is surely most obvious about the hidden gem and unseen flower is that they have each fulfilled all their natural potential. The sense of 'pathetic' waste springs entirely from the isolation and therefore neglect of such perfected beauty and sweetness, and this seems oddly inappropriate to what has been said of the plight of the villagers, whose talents had been repressed and frozen by 'Chill Penury'. Their potential had been stunted and therefore unfulfilled; what the 'mute inglorious Milton' might have achieved was accessible only to the sympathetic imagination of the poet. (In his unfinished didactic poem *Education and Government*, Gray had used appropriate images of 'sickly plants' and blossoms nipped in the bud to describe how natural potential could be stunted by lack of education and a tyrannical government.)

Some explanation of the role of the gem and the flower can be found in the earliest surviving draft of the 'Elegy', preserved in the Eton MS, which contains the first eighteen stanzas as we know them and four concluding stanzas which were later to be dropped. This original conclusion to the poem has particular interest since it returns us, as the final text does not, to the poet himself meditating in the darkness of the churchyard as at the beginning of the poem. In this version, the poet's reflections on the contrast between the humble lives and graves of the dead villagers and the splendid futility of the memorials to the arrogant great, his balancing of the wasted talents of the poor against the possibility that opportunity might only have corrupted that potential virtue and genius, have all been

---

[3] *Some Versions of Pastoral* (2nd imp., 1950), pp. 4–5.

considerations in an essentially personal debate. Having weighed the deprivations of a life of obscurity against the opportunities and evils of the great world, the poet has reached the conclusion that his own preference should lie with the 'innocence' and 'safety' represented by the village:

> The thoughtless World to Majesty may bow
> Exalt the brave, & idolise Success
> But more to Innocence their Safety owe
> Than Power & Genius e'er conspired to bless
>
> And thou, who mindful of the unhonour'd Dead
> Dost in these Notes their artless Tale relate
> By Night & lonely Contemplation led
> To linger in the gloomy Walks of Fate
>
> Hark how the sacred Calm, that broods around
> Bids ev'ry fierce tumultuous Passion cease
> In still small Accents whisp'ring from the Ground
> A grateful Earnest of eternal Peace
>
> No more with Reason & thyself at strife;
> Give anxious Cares & endless Wishes room
> But thro' the cool sequester'd Vale of Life
> Pursue the silent Tenour of thy Doom.

This renunciation draws on both the classical tradition of praise of retirement from the corrupt city and the Christian consolation of eternal peace hereafter. Yet the attempted calm of this conclusion to the poem seems precarious. What threatens it is the very acknowledgement of the 'fierce tumultuous' passions, the 'strife' with reason and the self, the 'anxious Cares & endless Wishes', which have apparently been the occasion of the poet's meditations. The belated admission of such inner turmoil has the effect of leaving us with it rather than of purging it.

We can now see in retrospect how unusually emphatic for its period is the fourth line of the familiar opening stanza of the poem in which the ploughman 'leaves the world to darkness and to me'. The heavy final rhyme on 'me' seems to invite us to concentrate on the poet himself: as for Adam and Eve at the end of *Paradise Lost*, the world, even if shrouded in darkness, is all before the poet where to choose. The particularity of time and place, the poet's isolation (enhanced by the gradual withdrawal

THE POETRY OF THOMAS GRAY 143

of human and animal life from the landscape), the sense that we are overhearing a direct utterance in the present, the sense of an individual consciousness delicately perceiving the fading away of sound and light, all seem to be preparing us in these opening stanzas to focus on the poet as a unique self. Yet the choice the poet is going to make can not after all be expounded in subjective terms. It has instead to be objectified into the contrasts of the rich and poor, and so convincing is the 'massive calm' of those familiar balanced quatrains, so assured and harmonious the rendering of truths which generations of earlier poets seem only to have been fumbling towards, that the personal predicament is virtually eliminated. It is as if there are two selves in the poem: a judicious, normative self, resting confidently on traditional wisdom and values, and a deeper unofficial self of confused and subversive passions which can only be acknowledged as the debate is closed in the concluding lines.

Yet the elimination of the self is not total even in the impersonal body of the poem: the potent images of the gem and the flower, irrelevant to the plight of the deprived villagers, define exactly in their fulfilled but neglected perfection the poet's sense of his own isolation, to which he teaches himself to be resigned. There is no question in this version of the poem of the poet trying to trick the reader into feeling that the humble villager is 'better off without opportunities', as Professor Empson suggests: he is trying to persuade himself that he prefers to remain in obscurity. The poet's imaginative re-creation of the lives of the dead villagers combines a sympathy for their lot, unusual for its age, with a degree of envy of their vitality and usefulness, but his feelings about them are essentially subservient to his concern about the meaning of his own life.

The fact that Gray provided the 'Elegy' with a quite different conclusion in 1750 suggests that he may himself have been aware of a split in the poem between an aspiration to express timeless truths about human experience and an impulse to render a particular subjective predicament existing and uttered in a troubled present. The original conclusion, the poet's apparent identification with the humble and innocent lives of the villagers, may also have come to seem facile and self-deceiving. Two hundred years later another, and equally self-conscious, Etonian faced that problem literally in declaring that 'it is no use clapping a proletarian on the back and telling him that he is as good a man as I am: if I want real contact with him . . . I have got to alter myself so completely that at the end I should hardly be recognizable as the same person'.[4] The solution attempted in the revised conclusion to the poem takes the opposite direction to George Orwell's: not to alter the self beyond recognition, even poetically, but to find a way of expressing and claiming some value for a self which rejected the corruption of the great world only to find itself cut off by education and self-consciousness—by the very ability to contemplate a choice—from the innocence, vitality, and purposeful energy of the lives it attributes to the humble villagers.

The new ending which Gray supplied for the 'Elegy' has disappointed and puzzled most readers and critics. The clear and balanced structure contrasting the rich and poor survives in the first part of the poem but no longer to provide the poet with the grounds for making a personal choice. Apparently impersonal reflections now pursue the contrast between the grandiose monuments to the great and the 'frail memorials' to the poor in the churchyard, and then dwell on the general human desire for sympathy at the hour of death and for remembrance after death. If there is uncertainty in both the syntax and the broader movement of thought in this section of the poem it perhaps betrays the poet's uneasiness as he tries to bridge the gap between the impersonal assurance of the earlier stanzas and what he is now intent on describing: the memorial and the sympathy he can imagine himself receiving after his own death. As in the concluding stanzas of the first version, one of which he at first planned to transfer to this transition, the poet eventually addresses himself (as 'Thee'—the use of the second person perhaps betraying the split between the judicious and problematic selves), and then imagines what may happen in his own special case: some sympathetic 'kindred spirit' coming to the churchyard to enquire about his fate. The enquirer will receive from a 'hoary-headed swain' an account of the poet which will indicate just how far he had been from

<hr />

[4] *The Road to Wigan Pier*, ch. 10.

comfortable identification with the lives of the villagers, and
how far, on the other hand, from the Augustan ideal of urbane,
rural retirement dedicated to moderation and wisdom.

A solitary, distant, puzzling figure, the poet had wandered
aimlessly round the village, hastening to meet the dawn,
listlessly poring on the stream under the trees at noon and then,
even more ominously,

> Hard by yon wood, now smiling as in scorn,
> Muttering his wayward fancies he would rove,
> Now drooping, woeful wan, like one forlorn,
> Or crazed with care, or crossed in hopeless love.

The mysterious young man had suddenly disappeared and two
days later had been buried in the churchyard. It is not simply
the later fate of Thomas Chatterton, the poet in whose memory
this annual lecture is given, which leads one to ponder the
circumstances of the death that the meditating poet envisages
for himself. Although modern critics have ignored the matter,
at least one eighteenth-century reader suspected that the poet
had committed suicide.[5] It would seem that such a deduction is
at least left open to us, by his youth, his misery, the abruptness
of his death, and the warning in the 'Epitaph' not to enquire too
closely into his frailties.

The very possibility of a 'dramatic' interpretation of the
'Elegy'—that, for example, the meditating poet in the churchyard is contemplating suicide—serves at least to remind us of
what is logically the case, that this curious, melancholy figure
described by the swain is the poet himself: his evening meditations in the darkness which we are overhearing, when sensible
villagers are indoors, are part of the same eccentric pattern of
behaviour observed by the swain. And yet the poet's whole
strategy is now to reduce our memory of the particularity of the
opening of the poem, of the whole poetic utterance as existing in
the present. (It was perhaps for this reason that Gray finally
omitted a stanza in the Eton MS at this point in which the swain
describes the poet watching the setting sun 'With whistful
Eyes', and which has the effect of identifying the poet's present
utterance with the behaviour of the doomed youth.) The

---

[5] John Young, *A Criticism on the Elegy* (1783), p. 78.

psychological turmoil, kept at bay in the first version by
classical and Christian resources, remains, but its existence in
the present consciousness of the poet is doubly screened: by
externalization into a version of the poet himself as observed by
the innocent and uncomprehending villager, and by the deliberate escape from the present into an imaginary swain's
narrative in an imaginary future, which will speak of an
imaginary past. The suffering present is ingeniously vacated.
The embarrassment of direct personal utterance is avoided.

The result is the swain's depiction of the lonely, distraught,
and doomed, perhaps self-doomed, poet. Its poetic weakness,
the self-consciousness of the swain's pastoral diction, culled
from Spenser, Shakespeare, and Milton, is revealing, for it is a
significant version of the self which emerges here: an anticipation of the sorrows and alienation which a generation later
would drive Young Werther in similar circumstances to
suicide, and a prefigurement, however tentative, of the isolation, mysterious suffering, and special sensibility, which were
later to become familiar attributes of the image of the artist in
an unsympathetic or hostile society. Gray's portrait of the artist
remains, of course, a far from defiant one: seen through the
swain's eyes the poet's behaviour is more baffling than anything else and even, in the context of village life, faintly
ludicrous. Yet the swain will also guide the enquiring 'kindred
spirit' to the 'Epitaph' on the poet's gravestone. In a poem
unified if at all in its final form by a concern with monuments
and memorials, the 'Epitaph' must be intended to offer a
definitive version of the self. Wordsworth later said that the
essence of an epitaph was 'Truth hallowed by Love',[6] and this is
precisely what the poet provides himself with here. The 'voice
of nature', which had earlier been described as crying even
from the tomb for sympathetic remembrance, cries from the
'Epitaph'. Of course, the poet is only imagining himself to be
dead, but the strangeness and vulnerability of his present needs
are once more doubly disguised: by the attribution of the
'Epitaph' to the truth and love of an unknown sympathizer, and
by the relative permanence of its inscription on stone, which

---

[6] *Literary Criticism of William Wordsworth*, ed. P. M. Zall (Lincoln, Nebr., 1966),
p. 102.

seems to take the fantasy not merely out of the present or the imaginary future but into apparent timelessness:

> Here rests his head upon the lap of earth
> A youth to fortune and to fame unknown.
> Fair Science frowned not on his humble birth,
> And Melancholy marked him for her own.

Critics have rarely approved of the 'Epitaph'; and from the eighteenth century onwards they have wanted that 'And' to be a 'But' in the last line of the stanza. Why should the 'Epitaph' imply that the blessings of Science or Knowledge—of which the villagers were explicitly deprived—might *naturally* lead to melancholy? The answer seems to be that the sensitive poet was educated but deprived of opportunity: knowledge merely replaced innocence with a burden of painful self-consciousness. He was neglected like the gem and the flower but, unlike them, knew that he was neglected. And yet the 'Epitaph' goes on to claim tentatively for the poet a value lacked by both the arrogant great and, as the fact that the swain cannot read these lines suggests, the humble villagers. Melancholy leads to sensibility and true sensibility to pity and compassion for others: away finally from the self towards sympathy with, for example, the lot of the humble villagers, as the poem itself has shown:

> Large was his bounty and his soul sincere . . .
> He gave to Misery all he had, a tear . . .

The self-consuming passions are at last refined into the benevolent sensibility which renders the poet superior to the inhabitants of the 'thoughtless World', yet also grants him a compensatory value in the natural rustic world. To put it another way, the poet has found an acceptable escape route from the self in the growing contemporary doctrine of the ethical centrality of sympathy.

Such emphasis on the self-absorption of the 'Elegy' has both advantages and disadvantages. It may be felt that to lay emphasis on the poem's conclusion merely draws attention away from the poem's undoubted strengths, the assured and eloquent utterance of timeless truths about man, society, and history, to its most diffident and uncertain areas. And yet it is too easy to read as static and marmoreal what is in one aspect a sustained struggle to find decorous ways of talking about the self and about the meaning of one's own life. The poet's circuitous technique of self-dramatization has misled some modern critics into arguing that the poet must be visualizing not his own death but that of someone else: Gray's friend, the young poet Richard West, who had died in 1742, for example; or, more desperately, the 'stonecutter', a village poet who must have been responsible for the stark inscriptions on the 'frail memorials', and who accordingly joins the dramatis personae of the 'Elegy' in some modern interpretations. I have no doubt that the poet is talking about himself at the end of the 'Elegy', yet the problem that interests me is not in the first instance a biographical one. I have tried so far to keep Gray the man out of my discussion and to deal rather with the 'self' created by the poem. The complexity of the relationship between the man and the poetic 'self' may be suggested by a letter Gray wrote in April 1749 (about a year before the final version of the 'Elegy'), in which he also anticipates his death, but in a somewhat different tone. The letter describes the laziness, the ennui, and the trivial pleasures of his life in Cambridge, and contemplates with wry amusement the numerous errors which will appear in his eventual obituary notice:

Brandy will finish what Port begun; & a Month after the Time you will see in some Corner of a London Even:ng Post, Yesterday, died the Revnd Mr John Grey, Senior-Fellow of Clare-Hall, a facetious Companion, & well-respected by all that knew him. his death is supposed to have been occasion'd by a Fit of an Apoplexy, being found fall'n out of Bed with his Head in the Chamber-Pot.[7]

That is only one more, and in its own way complex, version of the self. My particular concern so far has been with the way in which a mid-eighteenth-century poet felt that he could approach and express private experience, the unique self, that point 'Where all stand single', as Wordsworth later phrased it,[8] even if we accept that self as a poetic creation only. Why did Gray have to be so devious in the 'Elegy'? A simple explanation would be that there was little or no respectable precedent for

[7] Correspondence of Thomas Gray, ed. P. Toynbee and L. Whibley, 3 vols (Oxford, 1935), i. 318.
[8] The Prelude, iii. 187.

genuinely introspective poetry and that Gray was himself a
conventional enough poet to obey contemporary injunctions
that the business of the poet was to utter basic truths about
shared human experience rather than to describe private spiritual turmoil. The cautious progress of autobiography in the
eighteenth century in itself indicates the suspicion of introspec-
tion as morbid or egocentric. (Introspective or confessional
autobiography in England before 1740 was almost entirely
religious in character, a purposeful scrutiny of private experience for spiritual ends.) English poetry, as Gray knew it,
portrayed the self only in conventional religious or amatory
postures and predicaments. The dominant recent influence,
Alexander Pope, had dramatized himself in his poetry often
enough, but as an idealized, public self, usually fortified and
biographically confused by a skilful merger with Horace. In
1738 Henry Pemberton had quoted as definitive a dictum of
Fénelon: 'To make a work truely excellent it is necessary, that
the author should so forget himself, that the reader may forget
him likewise, and have his attention engaged only on the
subject.'[9]

   The time had not yet come for the profound exploration of
the self which would seem more or less compulsory to the
Romantics. Even so, there were signs of growing interest in
personal experience in literature and Gray himself was perhaps
caught at a crucial transitional moment. In accounts of this
development importance is usually granted to John Locke,
whose philosophy made the problem of consciousness central
and established a new concern with what we would now call
psychology. The most ambitious of Gray's many early Latin
poems, the unfinished 'De principiis cogitandi' (1740–2), is in
fact a versification of parts of Locke's *Essay on Human Understanding*. After dealing at length with the various senses, Gray comes
to the crucial moment when the maturing human mind can
recognize and contemplate its own activities. He chooses to
describe it in a long simile, which attempts to render Locke's
concept of 'reflection' as literally as possible. A hamadryad who
has wandered alone through a deserted landscape lies down on
the bank of a stream, silent, chilly, and darkly shadowed,

[9] *Observations on Poetry* (1738), p. 102.

discovers her own reflection in the water, and eventually recognizes herself.[10] Gray has not merely given a decidedly melancholy atmosphere to this moment of self-discovery. He has also admitted ominous literary overtones, for the passage as a whole irresistibly recalls not merely Narcissus falling in love with himself in Ovid's *Metamorphoses*, but Milton's newly created Eve admiring herself in the lake in Eden, an act foreboding the eventual Fall.[11] Self-knowledge apparently involves for Gray the danger of self-absorption and the loss of innocence.

The English poetry which Gray began to write in a uniquely creative period in 1742 so repeatedly finds itself at such a moment of self-discovery as to explain the emphasis I have placed on this element in the 'Elegy', written several years later. From a purely biographical point of view such a preoccupation with the self as an isolated, unique identity need not be surprising. In the previous year Gray, aged 24, had returned to England alone after quarrelling in Italy with the companion who had taken him abroad, Horace Walpole, probably the closest of the few friends he had made at Eton and Cambridge. However affectionate it had once been, the friendship had always seemed likely to lead to tension once it moved into the real world. Walpole was the son of a powerful Prime Minister, Gray of relatively humble origins. To the effects of the serious breach with his friend was added uncertainty about his future: his father had died recently, he was uprooted, and, since he had quarrelled with the one man whose influence could have helped him to rapid preferment, without any obvious role in society.

Gray spent those early months of 1742 reading, corresponding about literature with another Etonian friend, Richard West, and, for the first time with any seriousness, writing English poetry. In May 1742 he sent West his 'Ode on the Spring'. His capacity for distilling the essence of a whole tradition of earlier poetry on the subject into his own condensed, suggestive, lyrical creation is already astonishingly clear, but the basic situation of the poem, and its development to the end of the penultimate stanza, are all too familiar. Surrounded by the beauty and fertility of the spring, the

[10] A translation of the passage can be found in my edition of *The Poems of Gray, Collins and Goldsmith* (1969), p. 331.
[11] *Paradise Lost*, iv. 456–69.

poet—a mere representative self—meditates complacently on the absurd ardour of the crowd, the folly and meanness of the proud and great. The sportive insects of the spring become emblematic of the futile activities of busy, frivolous, and ephemeral humanity. But in the final stanza the façade of this comfortable traditional moralist suddenly collapses to reveal the lonely and frustrated private self which lies behind:

> Methinks I hear in accent low
> The sportive kind reply:
> Poor moralist! and what art thou?
> A solitary fly!
> Thy joys no glittering female meets,
> No hive hast thou of hoarded sweets,
> No painted plumage to display:
> On hasty wings thy youth is flown;
> Thy sun is set, thy spring is gone—
> We frolic, while 'tis May.

Relying on the humorous sympathy of Richard West, the poet can present ironically this discovery of the sterility of the self, measured against the fertility and 'untaught harmony' of the spring, and even against the activities of other men. In retrospect the moral commonplaces offered earlier in the poem turn out to have been equally sterile compensatory rationalizing.

The letter containing this poem was returned unopened, for Richard West, the only audience of Gray's poetry, was already dead at the age of 25. In this state of isolation Gray wrote three other poems at Stoke Poges in August 1742. He was never himself to publish his sonnet in memory of West, perhaps because, for all its restraint, it is so totally self-enclosed in a grief for which no resolution can be discovered. The poet is trapped syntactically by the self: 'My lonely anguish melts no heart but mine.' The poem begins and ends with the words 'In vain'. Grieving for the loss of the only one who would have sympathized with such grief, the poet, as in the 'Ode on the Spring', is again surrounded by the instinctive activities of nature, fertile, amorous, harmonious, indifferent to his deprivation. As Philip Larkin has said in his own poem on Spring, 'those she has least use for know her best'.

In the same month Gray wrote his 'Ode on a Distant Prospect of Eton College', which explores the same situation: or rather, it may be felt, fails to explore it. The details of the observed landscape and the historical associations of Eton, appropriate to a topographical poem, are followed by a stanza of apparently spontaneous and particularized personal statement. The distant prospect of Eton is not merely spatial but temporal: the poet is contemplating his own past and the observing self threatens momentarily to become as important a subject as what it observes:

> Ah, happy hills, ah, pleasing shade,
> Ah, fields beloved in vain,
> Where once my careless childhood strayed,
> A stranger yet to pain!
> I feel the gales, that from ye blow,
> A momentary bliss bestow,
> As waving fresh their gladsome wing,
> My weary soul they seem to soothe,
> And, redolent of joy and youth,
> To breathe a second spring.

The freshening winds blowing across the valley travel also across the years from his own childhood. But this is not the 'correspondent breeze', the reanimating, liberating, creative power, fusing the imagination with nature, which blows through the pages of Romantic poetry; nor is this that characteristic kind of Romantic poem in which, through the interplay of memory, imagination, and nature, the individual contemplating a significant landscape can work through a private predicament towards self-discovery and reaffirmation. The poet of the 'Eton' ode has come as close as he can to confronting his own weariness and pain: there is a gulf between past and present selves which cannot be explored or given meaning. The soothing winds bring no 'second spring' after all, but leave the poet only a more painful sense of an unresolved and unspecific deprivation. There is a rhetorical appeal to Father Thames to describe the present generation of schoolboys, an evocation of what has been lost, not of what might be regained: hope, joy, resilience, the possibility of breaking through restraints:

> Some bold adventurers disdain
> The limits of their little reign
> And unknown regions dare descry:

> Still as they run they look behind,
> They hear a voice in every wind,
> And snatch a fearful joy.

The description of the boys repeatedly echoes earlier descriptions of prelapsarian man by Milton and James Thomson: what has been lost above all is innocence. The poet himself has gained only the superior but useless knowledge of what awaits the inhabitants of paradise: the onset of destructive human passions, misfortunes, disease, and death. Through the formal tableaux of menacing personifications private anguish is desperately generalized into the experience of all men. Yet at the end, as in the 'Ode on the Spring' and the sonnet on West, the poem has to admit its own futility, or to cancel whatever assertions it has made:

> Thought would destroy their paradise.
> No more; where ignorance is bliss,
> 'Tis folly to be wise.

The poet has gained from experience only a destructive capacity to warn the happy and innocent. For Wordsworth the poet was to be one 'who rejoices more than other men in the spirit of life that is in him', a heart which is not 'scared at its own liberty', which can itself project life and passion into nature.[12] In these three poems of Gray, the poet's self-consciousness, cut off from the innocence and vitality of nature or childhood, illuminates only his own isolation and sterility.

The remaining poem Gray wrote in the summer of 1742 was the 'Ode to Adversity', a disciplined effort to move outward from this self-enclosed predicament. Although the poem accepts with the 'Eton' ode that all men are born to suffer, it also asserts that human suffering is not meaningless, for it can lead to wisdom and the melancholy sensibility which brings in its train compassion for the sufferings of others. The fact that Gray himself sometimes entitled the poem a 'Hymn to Adversity' suggests that he has fallen back here on a more ritualized and therefore less directly subjective form for fervent personal utterance. Only at the end of the poem does the poet plead in his own person for the benign 'philosophic' fruits of his suffering.

---

[12] *Literary Criticism*, ed. Zall, p. 48; *Prelude*, i. 16.

> To soften, not to wound, my heart.
> The generous spark extinct revive,
> Teach me to love and to forgive,
> Exact my own defects to scan,
> What others are to feel, and know myself a man.

The capacity for sympathy, love, and self-knowledge desired here was to be claimed for the poet in the 'Epitaph' of the 'Elegy'. In other ways also the two versions of the later poem represent renewed efforts to order and resolve the preoccupations of 1742. One recurrent theme had in fact appeared in the very first of Gray's surviving English poems, the lines he had sent to Walpole at the age of 18 in 1734, in which he speaks as a ghost rising at Walpole's command to describe how 'That little, naked, melancholy thing, My soul' had travelled after death to a twilit underworld of sexual frustration and humorous social chaos. The 1742 poems had all described or implied a kind of living death in the poet: his 'sun is set' in the 'Ode on the Spring'; his exclusion from the processes of nature in the sonnet on West left him essentially as dead as his friend; the useless wisdom of the 'Eton' ode was offered as if by one who had already experienced the entire cycle of life and was acquainted with 'The painful family of Death'. In the second version of the 'Elegy' the poet is excluded from the innocent lives of the villagers, as earlier from nature or childhood. Yet he contrives, as we have seen, finally to escape the living death of the present by an imaginative enactment of his own death into a timeless state of unfulfilled but uncorrupted potential, which he can share with the dead villagers. And the self commemorated thus is no longer simply sterile nor its wisdom merely futile: the whole poem has been an act of that sympathetic sensibility which claims at the end a special value of its own and its own right to comparable sympathy.

On the purely biographical level, which it becomes increasingly hard to ignore, we might speculate that these claims at the end of the 'Elegy' were directed unconsciously at Horace Walpole, with whom a cautious reconciliation had taken place in 1745, who probably remained for Gray a permanent focus for all his complicated feelings about his own relationship with the great world, and who had eventually replaced Richard West as the audience of his poetry. It was to Walpole that the 'Elegy' was first sent in 1750, through Walpole that it was circulated in manuscript and eventually published. Ironically, the instantaneous success of the poem in itself provided Gray with a new identity which at once enters his poetry. 'A Long Story' was a reply in verse to an invitation from a fashionable lady who had admired the 'Elegy' in manuscript. The humorous self-representation in 'A Long Story' makes clear Gray's uneasy fascination with this new role: the poet (and he is now specifically identified as such), pursued by emphatically militant women, appears as an awkward, nervous figure to whom dubious and possibly malign powers are attributed by the local community, but who is eventually and to his own surprise absorbed into respectable society by an aristocratic invitation to dinner.

Gray later tried to suppress this occasional poem, in which humour and self-consciousness mingle uneasily. Indeed, he was to continue writing serious poetry for only a few more years, as if the 'Elegy' and its success had helped to render his problematic dealings with the poetic self unnecessary. In the stanzas he addressed to Richard Bentley, the illustrator of an elaborate edition of his poems which Walpole insisted on supervising in 1753, Gray modestly expressed only the hope that his poetry, whatever its other limitations, might inspire a 'secret sympathy' in some other 'feeling breast'. The trouble was that there were suddenly too many 'feeling breasts' and 'kindred spirits', all eager to respond to the 'Elegy'. He had exposed as much of himself or *a* self as he wished, perhaps too much, and had no desire to become, in Keats's phrase, 'A pet-lamb in a sentimental farce'. He never attempted another poem in the manner of the 'Elegy', although countless imitators for the rest of the century were only too delighted to do so for him.

Yet how was he to follow the 'Elegy', which had gained him that new identity as a poet? Perhaps inevitably, the subject of Gray's two remaining serious poems was poetry itself. In the two Pindaric odes which he published in 1757, he set out quite consciously to baffle the popular audience he had so recently acquired. 'The Progress of Poesy' now claims for poetry all the energy, fertility, passion, harmony, and life-enhancing powers which had formerly always contrasted with the poet's own sterility; and its visionary power, richness of texture, and technical virtuosity are an attempt to embody everything that Gray could claim for his art. Poetry itself, the 'heavenly Muse', is now explicitly a providential compensation for the real and imaginary ills of life.

The last great embodiment of the popular Augustan 'progress' formula, 'The Progress of Poesy' follows the movement of poetry westward from Ancient Greece to Britain, expounding the close connection of poetry and liberty and so asserting the importance of the poet to society. An Augustan 'progress' poem naturally ends in the glorious British present. The trouble with a 'progress of poesy' is that it naturally ends with the poet himself. Gray can celebrate the great poets of the English tradition, Shakespeare, Milton, Dryden, with whom he always allied himself, but this native tradition turns out to be itself a burden on his shoulders. Even along this route the poet finally comes face to face with himself, although the closing lines of the poem are obscure enough to have prevented many readers from grasping that he is here talking about his own inadequacy and rashness in daring to imitate Pindar and to follow the achievements of the earlier English masters.

Gray was, of course, expressing here not merely a sense of personal inadequacy, but a more general uncertainty about the capacity of his own over-civilized society to maintain the tradition. The final attempt at a solution appeared in the second Pindaric, 'The Bard', in which the embarrassing self and the ever-burdensome present are at last eluded through an escape into history. Yet the escape from the self is achieved only by total self-projection into the poem's protagonist, the figure of the medieval Welsh bard. When a friend asked Gray how he felt when writing the poem, he replied, 'Why I felt myself the bard'.[13] This is the final version of Gray's isolated poet, surrounded by poetic ghosts in a veritable graveyard of the bards. Gray has not merely provided his poet with flowing locks and bardic robes, but has invested him with everything he and his contemporaries could identify as a lost source of poetic power, as if hoping to channel into his poem the authentic springs of all the great poetry of the past: the Pindaric sublime, biblical

---

[13] *Correspondence*, iii. 1290.

prophecy, the unselfconscious poetic passion of primitive societies, the medieval and the Celtic. Thus formidably equipped, the Bard, the sole survivor of the Welsh bards supposedly slaughtered by Edward I, can thunder denunciation and defiance at the tyrant and at all the forces hostile to poetry; the ghosts of the dead bards can foretell in prophetic vision the future revival and high destiny of poetry in a better society.

Yet at the end the Bard—and this time there is no ambiguity —has to commit suicide, and that spectacular plunge to death also marks the end of Gray's serious career as a poet at the age of 40. During the 1760s he was to write occasional epitaphs by request, two or three humorous poems, a few translations for their historical interest of fragments of Norse and Welsh poetry, whose primitive violence only points up the sobriety of the life he himself had been leading rather resentfully in Cambridge since 1742, devoted largely to antiquarian and, later, botanical pursuits. An affectionate and highly amusing friend to a small circle, as his superb letters show, Gray could otherwise seem an aloof, fastidious, and proud figure. His final poetic effort, the 'Ode for Music' he dutifully provided in 1769 for the Installation of the Chancellor of the University, was not a production in which he took any pride. 'The musick is as good as the words: the former might be taken for mine, & the latter for Dr Randal's', he confided to a friend.[14] Most striking is the fact that the once neglected gem and flower of the 'Elegy' now make a disconcerting reappearance, as if to confirm that the problematic self had now been exorcized:

> Thy liberal heart, thy judging eye,
> The flower unheeded shall descry,
> And bid it round heaven's altars shed
> The fragrance of its blushing head:
> Shall raise from earth the latent gem
> To glitter on the diadem.

And yet as late as 1768 Gray had produced one of the most impressive, if still neglected, of his poems, his contemptuous verses on the fashionable ruins with which Lord Holland had adorned his bleak estate on the Kent coast. Gray makes these

[14] Ibid., iii. 1065.

ruins symbolic of the devastation this corrupt and unscrupu-
lous politician would have visited on the nation as a whole if his
colleagues had not abandoned him:

> Far other scenes than these had blessed our view
>   And realised the ruins that we feign.
> Purged by the sword and beautified by fire,
>   Then had we seen proud London's hated walls:
> Owls might have hooted in St Peter's choir,
>   And foxes stunk and littered in St Paul's.

The sudden satiric intensity of this late poem seems to appear
from nowhere. Or could it be that it sprang from some deep
response in the poet to the sterile, destructive vision he attributes to Holland, as if some part of him were avenging a still
latent barrenness and emptiness of his own, for which poetry
itself had come to be no compensation?

Here, it may be as well to admit that an enquiry into the ways
in which a private poetic self could be expressed or dramatized
can go no further without resort to evidence of a purely
biographical nature, a resort which may not be misleading if we
are not confused about the limitations of what we are doing.
The perpetual but inhibited preoccupation with the self in
Gray's poetry may be explicable simply in terms of the theor-
etical pressure on a poet of his generation to avoid morbid
self-centredness and to express the truths of common human
experience. The other possibility can be presented only in
biographical terms. No one who has read through Gray's
admirable correspondence will have failed to be struck, and
moved, by the tone of the letters he wrote early in 1770 to a
young Swiss friend, Charles de Bonstetten, who had studied in
Cambridge for a few months under the poet's supervision. The
bewilderment of painful self-discovery is clear in the letters he
wrote to the young man after his departure:

Never did I feel, my dear Bonstetten, to what a tedious length the few
short moments of our life may be extended by impatience and
expectation, till you had left me: nor ever knew before with so strong a
conviction how much this frail body sympathizes with the inquietude
of the mind. I am grown old in the compass of less than three
weeks. . . . I did not conceive till now (I own) what it was to lose you,
nor felt the solitude and insipidity of my own condition, before I
possess'd the happiness of your friendship.

And a week later:

My life now is but a perpetual conversation with your shadow.—The known sound of your voice still rings in my ears.—There, on the corner of the fender, you are standing, or tinkling on the Pianoforte, or stretch'd at length on the sofa.—Do you reflect, my dearest Friend, that it is a week or eight days, before I can receive a letter from you and as much more before you can have my answer, that all that time (with more than Herculean toil) I am employ'd in pushing the tedious hours along, and wishing to annihilate them; the more I strive, the heavier they move and the longer they grow.

The last letter was written in May 1770:

I know and have too often felt the disadvantages I lay myself under, how much I hurt the little interest I have in you, by this air of sadness so contrary to your nature and present enjoyments: but sure you will forgive, tho' you can not sympathize with me. It is impossible with me to dissemble with you. Such as I am, I expose my heart to your view, nor wish to conceal a single thought from your penetrating eyes.[15]

Gray died in the following year. Bonstetten survived until 1832, to publish these letters and to express the opinion that the trouble with Gray was that he had never loved anyone.

This one, sad, unignorable exposure of the heart does not provide us with a key which unlocks the secret of Gray's poetry. Yet it may suggest why his poetic career as a whole had become a process of escape from a dimly understood sense of a private predicament, which was in itself the real spring of his creativity. If such a conclusion might help to explain why his output was so small and fragmentary, it does nothing to account for the undoubted distinction of much of his poetry. Although he was content at last to see himself as merely 'a shrimp of an author', Gray's handful of lyrical or resonant poems were to affect the sensibility of a whole generation and the best of them have not been forgotten. I have myself been concerned only to suggest that poetry which might seem 'complacent' in its 'massive calm' was in reality neither complacent nor calm; or, at least, that such calm as it ever achieved was the result of a personal and poetic struggle which can not but be moving, if viewed with the sympathetic imagination which was its own unifying theme.

[15] *Correspondence*, iii. 1117–18, 1127, 1132.

7. THE POETRY OF THE EARLY WAVERLEY NOVELS

BY CLAIRE LAMONT

MY subject this evening is the lyrics, songs, and ballad snatches in the early novels of Sir Walter Scott. I shall say a little about the songs in his longer poems, but talk primarily about the poetry of the novels, up to *The Bride of Lammermoor* of 1819. It has often been pointed out that Scott's novels contain some of his finest poetry. John Buchan, for instance, claimed that it is there that Scott attained 'his real poetic stature', and added 'in his greater lyrics Scott penetrated to the final mystery of the poet.'[1] The short poems in the novels are quite different from Scott's narrative verse, 'that poetry of careless glance, and reckless rhyme'.[2] In the poetry of the novels there is seldom any carelessness, seldom any failure of eye or ear. The songs and ballad snatches in the novels are usually impersonal, and are in one way or another overheard. We are not now dealing with the minstrel tradition which welcomes the listener into the tale. The short songs are simply sung, and there is not usually a listener although there may be a hearer. Scott knew himself to be a story-teller; and in many places in his work he shows himself preoccupied with the task of the minstrel or bard; did he in a more private part of his mind know that he had that more elusive gift, as a lyric poet?

In talking about the poetry of the novels I have used various terms, songs, lyrics, ballad snatches. As regards the ballad, I shall be dealing with only one ballad which occurs in anything like its narrative completeness, Elspeth's ballad of the Red

I am grateful to the Trustees of the National Library of Scotland, the Curator of Autograph Manuscripts in the Pierpoint Morgan Library, and the Curators of the Signet Library for permission to quote from manuscripts in their possession. My visit to the Pierpont Morgan Library was made possible by a grant from the Newcastle University Research Fund, to which I am much indebted.

[1] John Buchan, *Sir Walter Scott* (1932), p. 115.
[2] John Ruskin, *Modern Painters*, Part iv (1856), iii. 265.

Harlaw in *The Antiquary*. The rest are ballad snatches which, in the way that Scott quotes and alters them, are half-way to existing as separate songs. There is also the question of ownership. Am I going to give Scott credit for composing what he merely quoted? I shall distinguish as carefully as I can, but it is notoriously difficult and sometimes even Scott himself would not have known with certainty.[3] The fact that the songs in the novels are sung by fictitious singers renders the problem of 'authorship' more intricate. A fictitious character may be supposed either to compose or quote; and if he quotes he may do so from another fictitious character, or from a fictitious tradition. In practice, however, the origin of a song in Scott's novels is usually less important than the fact that the singer knew it and sang it at the right moment.

The verse romances, most of which were published before he produced his first novel, show Scott creating various settings for his interspersed songs. In *The Lay of the Last Minstrel* (1805) there are none until the last canto when a group of songs is sung at the feast to celebrate the marriage of the heroine. Scott confessed in a letter that he had been short of material for the last canto, 'so I was fain to eke it out with the songs of the minstrels'.[4] It was a happy accident if it enabled him to discover his talent for writing songs in a context. In *Marmion* (1808) there are two songs. The first, Constance's song 'Where shall the lover rest',[5] with its statement about the fates of the lover and the traitor, is clearly related to the poem as a whole. Perhaps more interesting is the relation of the other, the very different song in Canto V, the story of young Lochinvar. It is sung by Lady Heron, the wily Englishwoman who was King James's favourite, while the court is assembling in preparation for battle. James is about to embark on the rash venture that led to the field of Flodden. The song tells of the victory of the bold man who rode off with his bride on the eve of her marriage to another.

> So daring in love, and so dauntless in war,
> Have ye e'er heard of gallant like young Lochinvar?

[3] See, for instance, *Letters 1821–1823*, p. 179. (All references to Scott's letters are to volumes of *The Letters of Sir Walter Scott*, ed. H. J. C. Grierson (1932 ff.).)

[4] To Anna Seward, 1805. *Letters 1787–1807*, p. 243.

[5] Canto II, x–xi.

The song, with its irrepressible metre, suggests inexorable success for the man who boldly takes, and is not calculated to bring moderation to the counsels of the king.

There are many more songs in *The Lady of the Lake* (1810). One of the most beautiful is the song sung by the madwoman, Blanche, to warn the King of treachery ahead.

> The toils are pitched, and the stakes are set,
>   Ever sing merrily, merrily;
> The bows they bend, and the knives they whet,
>   Hunters live so cheerily.
>
> It was a stag, a stag of ten,
>   Bearing his branches sturdily;
> He came stately down the glen,
>   Ever sing hardily, hardily.
>
>   .   .   .   .   .
>
> He had an eye, and he could heed,
>   Ever sing warily, warily;
> He had a foot, and he could speed—
>   Hunters watch so narrowly.
>
>   (Canto IV, xxv.)

The hearer is given information by one to whom he would not normally turn for counsel. The madwoman sees through disguise (she recognizes the 'stag of ten'), and presents herself to give her vital warning. The inspiration for Blanche came from a poor woman whom Scott had seen in the Pass of Glencoe many years earlier,[6] and in the rather hasty filling in of her life story we can see the germ of a character like Madge Wildfire.

Equally interesting from the point of view of the songs in the novels are those sung by Edmund in *Rokeby* (1813). Here for the first time Scott has created a character to sing his songs who has a sustained part in the action of the poem. Edmund is a peasant boy who has joined a robber gang, and he sings hauntingly of the way of life of the outlaw community:

> 'And when I'm with my comrades met,
>   Beneath the greenwood bough,
> What once we were we all forget,
>   Nor think what we are now.

---

[6] *Letters 1808–1811*, p. 411.

CHORUS.

Yet Brignal banks are fresh and fair,
   And Greta woods are green,
And you may gather garlands there
   Would grace a summer queen.'—

(Canto III, xviii.)

That song, Scott said, was one of his favourites.[7] There are no such inset songs in *The Lord of the Isles*, though one wonders if Edith would not have sung in her disguise as a page, had he not been 'from earliest childhood mute'.[8] But *The Lord of the Isles* appeared in 1815, six months after the first of the novels, *Waverley*.

As the songs I am talking about were sung, it should be asked whether Scott had in mind any particular music. Sometimes he had; for instance Constance's song in *Marmion* was inspired by the singing of Highland reapers in the Lowlands, and was written to fit a specific tune.[9] Scott was not particularly musical, but could write to a tune if it were hummed over to him often enough.[10] For the songs in the novels he did not usually have specific tunes in mind, but he often indicates what the reader should be hearing by a phrase or two of verbal description. One of Madge Wildfire's dying songs, for instance, 'rather resembled the music of the Methodist hymns'.[11]

Before turning to the novels I should say a word about the manuscripts, as most of Scott's novel manuscripts survive. It is surprising to anyone looking at a Scott novel manuscript for the first time how smoothly the songs appear inset in their places. A closer look reveals that some of the songs we know from the printed texts are not present in the manuscript, for instance Glossin's rather uncharacteristic drinking-song in *Guy*

[7] *Letters 1811–1814*, pp. 194 and 201.

[8] Canto III, xxiii.

[9] See *Letters 1787–1807*, pp. 363, 393, and 403; *Letters 1801–1811*, pp. 67 and 162; and *Letters 1831–1832*, p. 300.

[10] See *Letters 1815–1817*, p. 179. This is one of an interesting series of letters about the songs in the verse romances addressed to Dr John Clarke Whitfeld, the Cambridge musician who set many of them to music. Because the novels were published anonymously the correspondence unfortunately does not extend to the songs in the novels.

[11] *Tales of My Landlord*, 2nd series (*The Heart of Midlothian*), iv. 68; ch. 40. (The first reference is to the first edition, from which the quotation is taken; the second is to the chapter number in any one-volume edition.)

Mannering.[12] In some cases the song is clearly needed in the first draft of the manuscript, and was presumably sent on a separate sheet. In others there was apparently no expectation of a song, and its addition, presumably in proof, required some slight alteration of the text to accommodate it. But still the majority of the songs occur in the manuscript, with very little correction. Did Scott compose the songs as he wrote; or had he worked them out in his capacious memory earlier? Many years later in his *Journal* he recalled the speed at which passages in the novels were written: 'the pen passed over the whole as fast as it could move and the eye never again saw them excepting in proof'. He added immediately afterwards, 'Verse I write twice and some-times three times over'.[13]

By 1814 the songs and ballad snatches in Scott's work were so well known that they threatened the anonymity of the new novel, *Waverley*.[14] There is a wide range of poetry in *Waverley*. Besides the narrator's snatches of quotation, all the main characters sing or write verses. I want to concentrate on the most famous singer in the novel, Davie Gellatley. Davie Gellatley is the Baron of Bradwardine's *innocent*, which Scott glosses as 'a natural fool'.[15] He is the first person whom Edward Waverley met on his arrival at Tully Veolan, and on coming up to Waverley he sang 'a fragment of an old Scotch ditty', starting 'False love, and hast thou play'd me this . . .'[16] The reader hardly notices that the heir to an English Jacobite family, newly signed on in the Hanoverian army, is being addressed as a faithless lover. When there was a pause in Davie's singing and dancing Waverley asked if Mr Bradwardine were at home. The reply came:

> The Knight's to the mountain
> His bugle to wind;
> The Lady's to greenwood
> Her garland to bind.

[12] ii. 248; ch. 34. The manuscript is in the Pierpont Morgan Library, New York, press-mark VIIB, MA 436–8. The passage referred to here is ii. 78.

[13] *The Journal of Sir Walter Scott*, ed. W. E. K. Anderson (1972), p. 86.

[14] See, for instance, the review in the *British Critic* (August 1814), reprinted in *Scott: The Critical Heritage*, ed. John O. Hayden (1970), p. 73.   [15] i. 124; ch. 9.

[16] i. 118; ch. 9. The song is slightly altered from one in David Herd's *Ancient and Modern Scottish Songs* (1776), ii. 6. See also F. J. Child, *The English and Scottish Popular Ballads* (1882–98), no. 218.

> The bower of Burd Ellen
> Has moss on the floor,
> That the step of Lord William
> Be silent and sure.

'This conveyed no information . . .', and Edward had to repeat his enquiry. And he finished up following Davie Gellatley down the garden. '"A strange guide this," thought Edward, "and not much unlike one of Shakespeare's roynish clowns . . ."' 'The Knight's to the mountain' Scott wrote himself.[17] While alluding to the absence of the baron, it alludes also to the fact that the daughter's lover is entering the house. But the situation is rendered general and impersonal by the references to the knight and the greenwood, and to Lord William and Burd Ellen, archetypal lover and beloved of the ballad tradition. It is not surprising that to the young Englishman, who had in any case so much to learn about Scotland, 'This conveyed no information.'

Before his next meeting with Davie Gellatley Waverley learns something of his history from Rose Bradwardine, including that he had 'a prodigious memory, stored with miscellaneous snatches and fragments of all tunes and songs, which he sometimes applied, with considerable address, as the vehicles of remonstrance, explanation, or satire'.[18] The source of Davie's songs was his elder brother, now dead, who had been folk-singer and composer—it was he who wrote

> Hie away, hie away,
> Over bank and over brae,
> Where the copsewood is the greenest,
> Where the fountains glisten sheenest, . . .[19]

a song of escape from the world that had dashed his hopes. So that behind the character of Davie Gellatley Scott has created a folk-singer and poet. In Davie's songs we feel the inherent pathos of the oral tradition: the reason that we have songs to

[17] That is according to Scott's note on some typeset pages containing the poems from vol. i. of *Waverley*, which were sent to him by Constable as a specimen for his volume *The Poetry contained in the Novels . . . of the Author of Waverley* (1822). Scott annotated the pages indicating which poems were original. They are in the National Library of Scotland, MS 743, fos. 27–36, and I am grateful to Dr David Hewitt for drawing them to my attention.

[18] i. 169–70; ch. 12.   [19] i. 171; ch. 12.

sing is that the elders who used to sing them have passed away.

The next meeting between Waverley and Davie Gellatley
took place early in the morning; Waverley rose early and going
out of doors found Davie with his dog.

One quick glance of his [Davie's] eye recognised Waverley, when,
instantly turning his back, as if he had not observed him, he began to
sing part of an old ballad:

> Young men will love thee more fair and more fast;
>> *Heard ye so merry the little bird sing?*
> Old men's love the longest will last,
>> *And the throstle-cock's head is under his wing.*
>
> The young man's wrath is like light straw on fire;
>> *Heard ye so merry the little bird sing?*
> But like red-hot steel is the old man's ire,
>> *And the throstle-cock's head is under his wing.*
>
> The young man will brawl at the evening board;
>> *Heard ye so merry the little bird sing?*
> But the old man will draw at the dawning the sword,
>> *And the throstle-cock's head is under his wing.*[20]

Although this is introduced as 'part of an old ballad', Scott later
admitted to having written it himself.[21] Waverley has by now
learned that Davie's songs indicate something he should know,
and he tries by direct enquiry to get Davie to tell him outright.
But Davie will not. He had after all turned his back on
Waverley before singing it, pretending not to see him. The song
refers apparently to the quarrel with the young Laird of
Balmawhapple two days earlier; but that quarrel was of political origin, and the song's deeper allusion is to the Jacobites, at
the time—the summer of 1745—coming together to rise
against the government that Waverley serves. It is one of the
hints that the rising is shortly to come to a head. But it is a dark
one, couched in terms of the contrast between the young man
and the old, the young man hasty, impetuous, and quickly
dashed, the old man true, owning old loyalties, undeflected.
The pace at which the contrast emerges is slowed down by the
refrain, with its reference to the rhythms of the natural world.
The imminent situation is sketched in terms of the psychologi-

---

[20] i. 195–6; ch. 14.
[21] See National Library of Scotland, MS 743, fo. 33ᵛ.

cal traits of its participants—Balmawhapple and the Baron of Bradwardine, but not only them.

The allusiveness of Davie's song contrasts with the explicitness of the Bard's song about the impending rising which Waverley hears at the feast at Glennaquoich, and which is subsequently translated from Gaelic for him by Flora Mac-Ivor.[22] The Bard's song is historical, exhortatory, and sung in a communal setting. Yet for all the mass response to the performance of Mac-Murrough the Bard, in which Waverley shares, we feel that the poetry is with Davie.

For all the central part of the novel Davie Gellatley is out of our ken while we watch Waverley join the Jacobite army, march with it into England, and during the retreat from Derby become separated from it in a nocturnal skirmish. It is months later, after the battle of Culloden, that Waverley, alone, makes his way to the deserted and devastated Tully Veolan.

While . . . he was looking around for some one who might explain the fate of the inhabitants, he heard a voice from the interior of the building, singing, in well-remembered accents, an old Scottish song:

> 'They came upon us in the night,
> And brake my bower and slew my knight;
> My servants a' for life did flee,
> And left us in extremitie.
>
> They slew my knight, to me sae dear;
> They slew my knight, and drave his gear;
> The moon may set, the sun may rise,
> But a deadly sleep has closed his eyes.'[23]

Scott later added a note on this song: 'The first three couplets are from an old ballad, called the Border Widow's Lament'.[24] This ballad, which derives from James Hogg, had been included in Scott's collection, *The Minstrelsy of the Scottish Border*:[25] it is about the murder of a Border chieftain by the King of Scotland. In turning two stanzas of it into a song for Davie Gellatley Scott has made the king into an unspecified enemy,

[22] i, chs. 20–2.   [23] iii. 226–7; ch. 63.   [24] 1829 edition, ii. 328.

[25] 2nd edition (1803), ii. 80. The stanzas in question had a history of being portable before Scott used them. Similar ones occur in a broadside ballad, 'The Lady turned Serving-Man', printed by Percy in *The Reliques of Ancient English Poetry* (1765) iii. 87. See also Child, no. 106.

and has added two lines at the end which give a feeling of finality, rather than lamentation. It is a statement of emotion rather than of fact, which Waverley, fortunately, seems partly to realize. By this late stage in the novel he is much matured, and he understands Davie Gellatley much better than before. As Davie made to flee the intruder, 'Waverley, remembering his habits, began to whistle a tune . . . which Davie had expressed great pleasure in listening to, . . . Davie again stole from his lurking place . . .' Davie Gellatley's poetry is both a commentary on the action of the novel, and a measure of the growing maturity of its hero. And it is, I think, an indication of the relative optimism of *Waverley*, despite Culloden in the background, that the poor foolish singer plays a valuable part in saving the family that protects him, and that the dashing young hero learns to listen and communicate with him.

In *Waverley* Scott created for himself an opportunity to be a folk poet; in *The Antiquary* he provided himself with a similar opportunity to become a ballad singer. Although versions of a ballad on the battle of Harlaw are known, old Elspeth's ballad of the Red Harlaw is unlike them, and is thought to be Scott's own work.[26] It is interesting to see how it is introduced. The Antiquary, Mr Oldbuck, wishes to get from the crazed old Elspeth a statement 'in a formal manner'[27] of the events long in the past which she has just revealed to Lord Glenallan. Oldbuck, his nephew Hector, and the old wandering beggar Edie Ochiltree, approach Elspeth's hut for that purpose.

As the Antiquary lifted the latch of the hut, he was surprised to hear the shrill tremulous voice of Elspeth chaunting forth an old ballad in a wild and doleful recitative:—

> 'The herring loves the merry moon-light,
>   The mackerel loves the wind,
> But the oyster loves the dredging sang,
>   For they come of a gentle kind.'[28]

A diligent collector of these legendary scraps of ancient poetry, his foot refused to cross the threshold when his ear was thus arrested, and

---

[26] See the note in *Sir Walter Scott: Selected Poems*, ed. Thomas Crawford (1972), pp. 277–8.
[27] iii. 150; ch. 36.

his hand instinctively took pencil and memorandum-book. From time to time the old woman spoke as if to the children—'O aye, hinnies, whisht, whisht! and I'll begin a bonnier ane than that—

> 'Now haud your tongue, baith wife and carle,
>   And listen, great and sma',
> And I will sing of Glenallan's Earl
>   That fought on the red Harlaw.'[29]

And she continues with a ballad about the battle of Harlaw, fought in 1411, the battle which, in Scott's words, determined 'whether the Gaelic or the Saxon race should be predominant in Scotland'. As she sings she is held up by failure of memory and wandering thoughts, and then, when she gets to a passage of particular interest, by the need to explain it to her supposed auditors, for she imagines her grandchildren to be present.[30]

> '"To turn the rein were sin and shame,
>   To fight were wond'rous peril,
> What would ye do now, Rowland Cheyne,
>   Were ye Glenallan's Earl?"'

'Ye maun ken, hinnies, that this Roland Cheyne, for as poor and auld as I sit in the chimney-neuk, was my forbear, and an awfu' man he was that day in the fight, but specially after the Earl had fa'en; for he blamed himsel for the counsel he gave . . .'

One can imagine that historical ballads were frequently glossed in that manner when they were fulfilling one of their basic functions, that of preserving a family's history.

But what about her actual auditors? Hector is impatient, Oldbuck is overcome with the lust of the ballad collector, only

---

[28] This stanza does not occur in the manuscript, which is in the Pierpont Morgan Library, press-mark VIIB, MA 1073–5. See iii. 61. It is apparently Scott's composition, perhaps influenced by two lines in 'The Dreg Song' in David Herd's *Ancient and Modern Scottish Songs* (1776), ii. 163:

> The oysters are a gentle kin,
> They winna tak unless you sing.

See 'The Poetry contained in the Novels . . . of the Author of Waverley', in *The Retrospective Review*, 2nd series, i (1827) 21.

[29] iii. 220 ff.; ch. 40.

Edie Ochiltree has any sympathy for her elderly and bereaved condition. Their voices disturb her, she stops singing and bids them enter; and they start the enquiries which they hope will lead to a confession of her complicity in the Glenallan tragedy. But old Elspeth refuses to make any admission, and in a last disjointed assertion of loyalty to her former mistress she falls dead. So the formal statement was not obtained, and in the end any proofs required are got from elsewhere. But has not Oldbuck in his antiquarian zeal missed something? He came for a statement, and got a ballad—a ballad about an earlier Glenallan whose downfall was brought about by the advice of Elspeth's ancestor.

> ' "Were I Glenallan's Earl this tide,
>   And ye were Roland Cheyne,
> The spur[31] should be in my horse's side,
>   And the bridle upon his mane.
>
> ' "If they hae twenty thousand blades,
>   And we twice ten times ten,
> Yet they hae but their tartan plaids,
>   And we are mail-clad men." ' '

The countess and Elspeth had been just as ruthless, and it was Elspeth who had given her mistress the fatal advice which destroyed her son's happiness.[32] And like her ancestor Roland Cheyne, after the miscarriage of her advice she fought the more loyally. In view of the mental world in which Elspeth is still living is there any hope that she will submit to a magistrate's enquiry? And likewise is there any hope that Oldbuck will attempt to discover the significance of his much-prized historical ballad?

Probably the most famous of Scott's fictitious singers is Madge Wildfire in *The Heart of Midlothian*. Scott says that the initial inspiration for Madge Wildfire came from 'Feckless Fanny', a girl who had lost her senses on the death of her lover.[33] Some details, for instance Madge's ducking near Carlisle, clearly come from the gipsy lore which had called forth

[30] The manuscript shows that Scott at first envisaged the children as present, but made a small alteration to indicate that Elspeth only thought them so. See MS iii. 61.

[31] MS 'spur'; the first edition, wrongly, reads 'spear'.

[32] ii. 75; ch. 33.

[33] See his note to the 1830 edition, iii. 36–9.

the character of Meg Merrilies in *Guy Mannering*.[34] Other influences on this story of the girl rendered mad by sorrow and singing in her madness are Wordsworth's mysterious mad-women, and the mad singers of German literature. And in the background, of course, there is Ophelia. The suggestion is made only to be qualified: 'Of all the mad-women who have sung and said, since the days of Hamlet the Dane, if Ophelia be the most affecting, Madge Wildfire was the most provoking'.[35] Madge Wildfire, like Davie Gellatley, sings snatches of song to warn, predict, and explain, could the hearer only interpret her message. Madge seldom offers information—though some-times she has vital information; she is usually led into betraying it by just that playing on her feelings and weaknesses which the Baron of Bradwardine forbids to be practised on Davie Gellat-ley. For Davie is a protected member of the household at Tully Veolan, whereas Madge is an outcast.

Miss Lascelles has drawn our attention to Scott's interest in a character from an 'alternative society', for instance the gipsy society of Meg Merrilies, a clearly defined way of life drawing on different traditions which may impinge on the rest of society for good or ill, but only according to its own laws.[36] *The Heart of Midlothian* shows his preoccupation with a character slightly different, the person who has left the ordinary society of which he was once a member, either voluntarily, as George Staunton, or because he was driven out of it, like Madge Wildfire and her mother. Edmund in *Rokeby* is one who voluntarily adopts the life of an outlaw, and can sing of it most attractively:

> Allen-a-Dale has no faggot for burning,
> Allen-a-Dale has no furrow for turning,
> Allen-a-Dale has no fleece for the spinning,
> Yet Allen-a-Dale has red gold for the winning.
> Come, read me my riddle! come, hearken my tale!
> And tell me the craft of bold Allen-a-Dale.[37]

(Canto III, xxx.)

[34] See the *Quarterly Review* xvi (1817), 439–41; and 'Notices concerning the Scottish Gypsies' in *Blackwood's Magazine* i (1817), 43–58, 154–61, and 615–20.

[35] ii. 99; ch. 16.

[36] See Mary Lascelles, 'Jane Austen and Walter Scott: a Minor Point of Compari-son', in *Notions and Facts* (1972), pp. 230–46.

[37] The name presumably comes from the ballad of 'Robin Hood and Allen a Dale', see Child, no. 138.

We must enjoy its bravado, but the desperate fate of Bertram in
the same poem shows that its freedom is illusory, or at most
only a young man's freedom. The flamboyant outlaw becomes
mere robber at last. And what about the girl invited to join such
a society?

> 'If, Maiden, thou wouldst wend with me,
>   To leave both tower and town,
> Thou first must guess what life lead we,
>   That dwell by dale and down.
> And if thou canst that riddle read,
>   As read full well you may,
> Then to the green wood shalt thou speed,
>   As blithe as Queen of May.'—
>
> CHORUS.
>
> Yet sung she, 'Brignal banks are fair,
>   And Greta woods are green;
> I'd rather range with Edmund there,
>   Then reign our English queen.'
>
> (Canto III, xvi.)

The next song shows the next stage:

> 'A weary lot is thine, fair maid,
>   A weary lot is thine!
> To pull the thorn thy brow to braid,
>   And press the rue for wine!
> A lightsome eye, a soldier's mien,
>   A feather of the blue,
> A doublet of the Lincoln green,—
>   No more of me you knew,
>   My love!
>   No more of me you knew.'
>
> (Canto III, xxviii.)

The two songs represent 'innocence' and 'experience', and the
emotional pull of each is equally balanced.

George Staunton, alias Robertson, with all the explanations
proper to a novel, has left ordinary society, and has seduced a
vain, giddy girl, Madge Murdockson, in a way that ensures that
she will have to leave it too. He wrote for her the song which in
the novel becomes, as it were, Madge's 'signature tune', crop-

ping up here and there like wildfire.[38] George made it for her at
Lockington wake, a festival in Leicestershire:

> 'I'm Madge of the country, I'm Madge of the town,
> And I'm Madge of the lad I am blithest to own—
> The Lady of Beever[39] in diamonds may shine,
> But has not a heart half so lightsome as mine.
>
> I am Queen of the Wake, and I'm Lady of May,
> And I lead the blithe ring round the May-pole to-day:
> The wild-fire that flashes so fair and so free
> Was never so bright, or so bonnie as me.'[40]

The rest of the novel shows us the pathos of this 'Queen of the
May'.

It is surprising to realize that the first snatch of song to be
sung in *The Heart of Midlothian* is not sung by Madge Wildfire.

> 'The elfin knight sate on the brae,
>   The broom grows bonnie, the broom grows fair;
> And by there came lilting a lady so gay,
>   And we daurna gang down to the broom nae mair.'[41]

It is sung by Effie Deans, to cover her confusion at meeting her
sister shortly after parting from Staunton. This little snatch,
which betrays her apprehensiveness, is sung by the daughter of
the strict Presbyterian who had no time for 'fule sangs'; Effie
Deans, who like Madge Wildfire was to be ruined by bearing a
child to George Staunton. In her description of the dancing
where she met Staunton Effie comes close to the world of
Madge Wildfire, with its singing, dancing, laughter, and vanity. Yet it is the other sister, Jeanie, who has more to do with
Madge in the novel. In her efforts to save Effie, Jeanie meets the
dark side of Madge's world. And there, in the midst of her
alarm, Jeanie finds that Madge's vanity is mingled with something deeper, though she scarcely understands it. As the two of
them leave the barn where Jeanie had been unwillingly
detained on her journey to London, Madge likens them to
characters from *The Pilgrim's Progress* and sings one of Bunyan's

[38] In the senses described by *OED*, 2, c. 'will-o'-the-wisp, *ignis fatuus*' and
d. 'lightning; *esp*. sheet lightning without audible thunder'.
[39] Belvoir, seat of the Duke of Rutland.   [40] iii. 145; ch. 31.
[41] i. 246; ch. 10. The refrain is found in the traditional ballad, see for instance Child,
no. 16, 'Sheath and Knife'. The broom is often a setting for seduction in the ballad
world.

songs. Davie Deans's sectarian zeal had prevented his children
from reading Bunyan, and Jeanie has to make what little she
can of Madge's fancy. Jeanie's compassion ensures that she will
always do what she can to help Madge, but her religion, to
which she is so faithful, makes it difficult for her to recognize a
groping in the same direction when it does not take the same
path.

Madge's position gives her freedom from the restrictions of
the ordinary world, whether confining or shaping and reassuring. It gives her the freedom to say some things which need
saying in the novel. Jeanie, having stumbled unwittingly on the
fact that Madge had had and lost a child, says ' "I am very sorry
for your misfortune—" ' Only to be interrupted by Madge,
' "Sorry? what wad ye be sorry for? The bairn was a blessing
—" '[42] There is a blessing in the bairn that the rigours of law
and theology in the novel fail to recognize, and the spokesman is
Madge Wildfire.

We see no more of Madge after she and Jeanie part until, on
her return journey from London, Jeanie visits Madge on her
deathbed in the workhouse in Carlisle. Madge is singing as she
enters, and does not recognize her visitor. Jeanie calls her by
name; Madge replies by summoning the nurse, ' "Nurse—
nurse, turn my face to the wa', that I may never answer to that
name ony mair, and never see mair of a wicked world." '[43]
There follow three songs. The first is religious:

> 'When the fight of grace is fought,—
> When the marriage vest is wrought,—
> When Faith hath chased cold Doubt away,
> And Hope but sickens at delay,—
> When Charity, imprisoned here,
> Longs for a more expanded sphere,
> Doff thy robes of sin and clay;
> Christian, rise, and come away.'

The first two lines are reminiscent of Meg Merrilies's 'Dirge';[44]
the rest remind one of the last lines of Johnson's *The Vanity of
Human Wishes*, a poem which Scott particularly admired.[45] As
Madge becomes weaker the style of her song changes:

[42] iii. 136; ch. 30.   [43] iv. 67–8; ch. 40.   [44] *Guy Mannering*, ii. 87; ch. 27.
[45] See J. G. Lockhart, *Memoirs of the Life of Sir Walter Scott, Bart.* (1837–8), ii. 307.

'Cauld is my bed, Lord Archibald,
  And sad my sleep of sorrow;
But thine sall be as sad and cauld,
  My fause true-love! to-morrow.'

—a ballad snatch, with as usual a prophetic and monitory element. Then comes her final song:

Again she changed the tune to one wilder, less monotonous, and less regular. But of the words only a fragment or two could be collected by those who listened to this singular scene.

'Proud Maisie is in the wood,
  Walking so early;
Sweet Robin sits on the bush,
  Singing so rarely.

' "Tell me, thou bonny bird,
  When shall I marry me?"—
"When six braw gentlemen
  Kirkward shall carry ye."

*   *   *

' "Who makes the bridal bed,
  Birdie, say truly?"
"The gray-headed sexton
  That delves the grave duly."

*   *   *

'The glow-worm o'er grave and stone
  Shall light thee steady;
The owl from the steeple sing,
  "Welcome, proud lady." ' '

Asterisks between the second and third, and third and fourth stanzas in the manuscript and early printed editions[46] indicate that other stanzas are supposedly missing. It is after all 'only a fragment or two'. One is left to imagine a longer question-and-answer ballad, but the fragment which the listeners could hear is just enough, and enough to give it full emotional intensity. The manuscript shows also that Scott first attempted the song in the past tense:

[46] They are not always reproduced when the song is printed separately.

> Proud Maisie was in the wood
> Walking so early
> Sweet Robin sat on the bush
> Singing so rarely[47]

but he changed the verbs to the present, probably as he wrote. If we feel entitled to apply this most impersonal song to its singer we see that it expresses her situation and character.

> The lightning that flashes so bright and so free,
> Is scarcely so blithe or so bonny as me.

The giddy singer of that song is here labelled with laconic finality, 'Proud Maisie', and as for the wildfire:

> 'The glow-worm o'er grave and stone
> Shall light thee steady.'

The last novel that I want to mention is *The Bride of Lammermoor*. Lucy Ashton's song, in the third chapter, has often been claimed one of Scott's finest lyrics. Critics concur in the view that the song expresses the character of the singer, and that more than any other song in Scott's novels it is indicative of the theme and mood of the whole work. But a curious feature of this criticism is that so many agree in finding Lucy a weak and passive character. Perhaps John Buchan may be allowed to speak for those who have expressed that view: 'Lucy Ashton is a passive creature, a green-sick girl unfit to strive with destiny . . .'[48] But is Lucy purely passive? No one would claim that she is strong, but is it not only in the company and under the power of her mother that she is weak?

Perhaps I may look at Lucy Ashton's song in more detail in its context. We have not met Lucy, though we have been told that she is 17, when her father, leaving his library where he had been meditating further vengeance on the Ravenswood family whom he has superseded, overhears his daughter sing the following song to her own accompaniment on the lute:

> Look not thou on Beautys charming
> Sit thou still when Kings are arming
> Taste not when the wine-cup glistens
> Speak not when the people listens

[47] National Library of Scotland, MS 1548, fo. 254.
[48] John Buchan, op. cit., p. 195.

> Stop thine ear against the singer
> From the red gold keep thy finger
> Vacant heart & hand & eye
> Easy live and quiet die.[49]

As Mr Maxwell has pointed out, the song has elements of both the ballad and the cavalier lyric,[50] and apparently it advocates a rejection of active life. Sir William Ashton's first remark to his daughter indicates the same interpretation: '"So Lucy, . . . does your musical philosopher teach you to contemn the world before you know it? . . ."'

> Look not thou on Beautys charming
> Sit thou still when Kings are arming . . .

A series of commands, each rendered in one way or another negative. And then the final couplet, the consequence of the withdrawal advocated,

> Vacant heart & hand & eye
> Easy live and quiet die.

The song is in one sense worldly wisdom couched in terms of advice and command. But if that is the surface meaning there is a strong undertow in the opposite direction. In another sense the whole poem can be cast in the conditional; *if* you withdraw from full participation in living, *then* all you will have is an easy life and a quiet death. You may buy peace, but at what cost.

Well, how does this relate to the character of the singer? The novelist comments, shortly after the conclusion of the song, 'The words she had chosen seemed particularly adapted to her character; for Lucy Ashton's exquisitely beautiful, yet girlish features, were formed to express peace of mind, serenity, and indifference to the tinsel of worldly pleasure.' And the passage goes on to describe the gentleness of Lucy's character, and the affection in which she was held by all except her mother, who, believing her to be 'unfit for courts, or crowded halls', can only plan her daughter's withdrawal from life by marriage to 'some country laird'.

---

[49] i. 68; ch. 3. Here transcribed from the manuscript, in the Signet Library, Edinburgh, fo. 15.

[50] J. C. Maxwell, 'Lucy Ashton's Song', *Notes and Queries* cxcv (1950), 210.

But, like many a parent of hot and impatient character, she was mistaken in estimating the feelings of her daughter, who, under a semblance of extreme indifference, nourished the germ of those passions which sometimes spring up in one night, like the gourd of the prophet, and astonish the observer by their unexpected ardour and intensity. In fact, Lucy's sentiments seemed chill, because nothing had occurred to interest or awaken them.

This passage, which occurs between the end of Lucy's song and her father's first remark, indicates that Scott did not want Lucy to appear solely passive. We are introduced to someone of an apparently passive temperament, but with strong hints that she could prove otherwise. With her character as with her song, there is a current pulling against the most obvious interpretation.

'So Lucy,' said her father, entering as her song was ended, 'does your musical philosopher teach you to contemn the world before you know it?—that is surely something premature.—Or did you but speak according to the fashion of fair maidens, who are always to hold the pleasures of life in contempt till they are pressed upon them by the address of some gentle knight?'

Lucy blushed, disclaimed any inference respecting her own choice being inferred from her selection of a song, and readily laid aside her instrument at her father's request that she would attend him in his walk.

Father and daughter take their walk in the park—this is all in the same chapter, chapter three. There they meet a forester, and there follows a conversation in which the forester complains that there has been no sport in the park since the Ashtons took over the estate. Skill in outdoor sports lay with the Ravenswoods; and the forester extols in particular the prowess of Edgar, Master of Ravenswood, who is, of course, to become Lucy's lover. There are only two songs sung in *The Bride of Lammermoor* and they are both in this chapter. As the forester goes off he sings a song:

> The monk must arise when the matins ring,
>   The abbot may sleep to their chime;
> But the yeoman must start when the bugles sing,
>   'Tis time, my hearts, 'tis time.

> There's bucks and raes on Bilhope braes,
>   There's a herd in Shortwood Shaw;
> But a lily white doe in the garden goes,[51]
>   She's fairly worth them a'.

Hunting is often in Scott an analogue of the active life, of the life that must be lived although it is not without danger and cruelty.[52] The second stanza alludes also to the tradition, particularly strong in medieval literature, of the Chase of Love, where the progress of love is described in terms of a stag-hunt.[53]

> But a lily white doe in the garden goes,
>   She's fairly worth them a'.

The 'lily white doe' is of course Lucy Ashton. Although she can be brought to follow a hunt, Lucy is in the end not the pursuer but the pursued. After her long persecution by her mother and Dame Gourlay, the hurt to Lucy is described thus: 'the arrow was shot, and was rankling barb-deep in the side of the wounded deer'.[54] But long before the 'lily white doe' of the song becomes the 'wounded deer' of the end of the novel, there is the hunting scene in chapter nine, Lord Bittlebrain's hunting party. In the course of it the stag turns at bay: 'the hunted animal had now in his turn become an object of intimidation to his pursuers'.[55] Bucklaw is the hero of the occasion, and after rather awkwardly paying his compliments to Lucy goes on to explain to her the particular danger from a stag at bay, '. . . for a hurt with a buck's horn is a perilous and somewhat venomous matter,[56]—a lesson he will learn to his cost on his wedding night.

I think the songs in *The Bride of Lammermoor* are misread if we see Lucy Ashton as innately passive, that is before the strange passivity that comes over her just before her marriage to Bucklaw. We must remember the Lucy Ashton who engaged herself to her father's enemy in a moment of passion. Her tragedy is the result of her attempt to participate in life. As her

---

[51] Transcribed from the first edition, i. 81; ch. 3. The manuscript reads 'gaes' which preserves the rhyme, but loses an internal assonance. fo. 18.

[52] The analogy is present in the first song which Scott inset in a novel, 'Waken lords and ladies gay', which appears in his continuation of Joseph Strutt's *Queen-Hoo Hall* (1808), p. 47.

[53] See Marcelle Thiébaux, *The Stag of Love: The Chase in Medieval Literature* (1974).

[54] iii. 51–2; ch. 31.   [55] i. 230; ch. 9.   [56] i. 233; ch. 9.

father had suggested, she was awakened to life by the addresses
of a gentle knight. Immediately the engagement causes trouble,
because Lucy knows that her mother will oppose it. The reader
is shown in what fear Lucy stands of her mother, and with what
justification. The strength of the mother should not be miti-
gated by declaring the daughter impossibly weak. The mother
in the source story, a story of the Stair family in the seventeenth
century, was supposed to have had supernatural power,[57] and
Lady Ashton is said to have used 'diabolical' means to coerce
Lucy to renounce Ravenswood. Lady Ashton is one of Scott's
formidably strong women, successor to the Lady in *The Lay of
the Last Minstrel*, and the Countess of Glenallan in *The Antiquary*.
Bucklaw curiously enough recognizes Lady Ashton's strength:
'"I'll be bound Lady Ashton understands every machine for
breaking in the human mind, and there are as many as there are
cannon-bits, martingals, and cavessons for young colts."'[58]
Ravenswood never seems to appreciate it, and sees in Lucy's
fears a softness of mind which, however attractive, amounts
'almost to feebleness'. Does he ever understand her last falter-
ing words of him, '"It was my mother"'?[59] I think it is a
mistake for the reader to fail there too.

Perhaps I have given enough examples to be allowed to draw
one or two conclusions. The lyric voice in Scott is curiously
impersonal; it is not the impassioned 'I' that we associate with
the lyric in the post-renaissance tradition. That is one reason
why it is possible for the lyric and ballad impulses in Scott to be
so inextricably linked. Miss Woolf in the introduction to her
study of *The English Religious Lyric in the Middle Ages* has pointed
out two kinds of anonymity in literature: the accidental anonymity whereby history has lost for us the name of an author
whose cast of mind we recognize to be individual; and what she
calls natural or genuine anonymity, where the unknown poet
obtruded no individual peculiarities of style or thought, where
personality is not known because it is not relevant.[60] For a
popular author in the early nineteenth century there was not
much likelihood of either. Scott played with the idea of the first,

[57] See Scott's Introduction to the edition of 1830.
[58] iii. 8; ch. 28.
[59] iii. 78; ch. 33.
[60] Rosemary Woolf, *The English Religious Lyric in the Middle Ages* (1968), p. 5.

but, paradoxically, seems on occasions to be searching for the second. Sometimes in his poetry Scott seems to have wanted to step out of his own personality and into a self-effacing tradition. This is when he creates and steps into the world of his fictitious singers. Even in very slight snatches of poetry Scott often hints just enough to deflect the reader from too closely associating it with himself: the short mottoes which he wrote to head chapters in the novels, from *The Antiquary* onwards, frequently have this disclaimer, 'Old Ballad' or 'Old Play'. What is being said is better vouched for by impersonal utterance than by personal affidavit.

A fair number of Scott's fictitious singers are mad, or crazed with age or grief, apparently not in ordinary command of speech or action. This annoyed Jeffrey, reviewing *The Lady of the Lake*:

The Maniacs of poetry have indeed had a prescriptive right to be musical, since the days of Ophelia downwards; but it is rather a rash extension of this privilege to make them sing good sense, and to make sensible people be guided by them.[61]

Can anything be said to counter Jeffrey's criticism? Is the mad singer of a sane song a mere literary convention, apt to become tiresome with over-use? Or is it, like any good convention, an indication of something more? Can the mad singer and his hearer tell us anything about the nature of poetry and its place in the rest of life? The mad singer raises the problem of consciousness in the writing of poetry: the poetic gift enables one to express something that one may not be consciously aware of; the linking of words and sound, the convention seems to indicate, may be beyond the conscious decision of the writer. In the individual this gift suggests a many-layered consciousness: one part of the singer's mind can produce a penetrating insight about life, while another is unable to cope with life's most mundane demands. It is an impulse 'rather part of us than ours'.[62] I think this may indicate why Scott always jibbed at the idea of being a professional poet. In his longer poems he often adopts the figure of the conscious mover of men; in the short

---

[61] *The Edinburgh Review* xvi (1810), 279.
[62] Introduction to the third canto of *Marmion*, l. 122.

lyrics and songs he displays another gift, less amenable to times and seasons. The figure of the mad singer is there to defeat our enquiry about the source of the lyric impulse, deliberately to baffle rational enquiry.

The mad singers in the novels have hearers, and this is where the figure of the mad singer illustrates aspects of poetry in its relation to the rest of life. Throughout the novels I have been discussing the hearers are offered information by those to whom they would not normally go for it. Matured by tribulation they learn to listen; wrapped in their own certainties and mental categories they hear but fail to understand; like old Elspeth's grandchildren they creep out of the room to play. The mature character in these novels has to learn that society is many-layered, that one layer can see what another cannot, and that if he can recognize what separates and what links them he may discover that, almost in another language, there is some sort of common utterance. The relation of the hearers to the singers in Scott's novels is an elaboration of the ironic injunction, 'Stop thine ear against the singer'. One may have to hear and act on information whose accuracy is only certain after one has done so—requiring a leap of faith again not readily amenable to the rational mind.

If the mad singer and his hearer is one image of poetry in society, the fact of verse printed in a novel is another. The rest of the novel, in all its variety, is the 'life' in which the poetry occurs. The songs usurp the role of dialogue (often in Scott another sort of poetry)—you are told something and you cannot answer; you cannot even be sure that you have heard properly.

Cumulatively these songs suggest that truth is reached by sudden insights. What you are offered is this statement beside which you must put that. You relish the bravado of the outlaw's song, and then you must put beside it the sad little refrain of the next song, 'Adieu for evermore'. And there are the contrasting songs on the death of Madge Wildfire: the religious lyric seeing death as a new life, and the laconic ballad of Proud Maisie stating the finality of our death in nature. The tragic emotion is allowed to exist in Scott without relief. There may be hope, but somehow that is another song. We are given two emotions, and one is not allowed to contain the other; only the order in which we hear the songs may indicate the dominance of one note over another. They express the apparently conflicting emotions which exist concurrently and with equal strength in the mind.

It follows that one is defeated in any attempt to build a system from these songs. Nevertheless there is what I may call a bias in favour of action and living life to the full whatever the cost. Scott's ideal is the man of action; he himself would have wished to be a soldier had he not been prevented by lameness.[63] As it is he is expert in the psychology of the active life, fighting, hunting, loving, and their almost inevitable consequences, death, loss, jealousy, remorse. It is interesting that when he writes of death in a way other than tragic it is in terms of action,

> Doff thy robes of sin and clay,
> Christian, rise, and come away.

Scott's poems and novels offer a wide range of effects. The lyric voice is only one of them, but it is one in which his fitful genius is particularly sustained. Perhaps I may end by quoting a passage from the Introduction to the third canto of *Marmion*, a favourite analogy between Scott's poetry and the Border landscape of his youth:

> It was a barren scene, and wild,
> Where naked cliffs were rudely piled;
> But ever and anon between
> Lay velvet tufts of loveliest green.

[63] See *Letters 1808–1811*, p. 478.

8. KEATS AND REALITY

BY JOHN BAYLEY

I

I SUPPOSE that most people who enjoy poetry see little point in calling it real or unreal. And they are surely right. It is difficult enough for philosophers to make meaningful use of such terms, let alone literary critics. Critical antitheses—Nature and Art, Art and life, moral and aesthetic—have always vanished into abstraction if their power to contrast and divide is too much insisted on. But Keats does press such an insistence upon us. 'Reality' must be admitted to have a special importance in any discussion of his poetry, because it means so much to Keats himself. It meant to him what it means to us; for like him we have come to be aware that we spend as much of our time in literature as in life, and it is for this reason that the idea of reality assumes a meaning and an emphasis for us. We need it because we feel the possibility of being outside it.

The feeling that reality may be elsewhere—this is surely a characteristically modern kind of uneasiness, and one which we find neither in the eighteenth century nor in Keats's predecessors in the Romantic movement. Bagehot calls Keats 'the most essentially modern of recent poets',[1] and the remark is quite in keeping with Arnold's judgement that he 'did not apply modern ideas to life'.[2] Both suggest the direction in which to look. Compare Keats's anxiety and self-distrust with the serenity of Blake, the confidence of Wordsworth and Coleridge —'explaining metaphysics to the nation'—in the sheer worldliness of their powers; their conviction of being in the centre of things and of taking part in changes of political belief and practice as well as changes of heart and style. It is a confidence that appears in the garrulous ease with which Coleridge seeks a

[1] *Literary Studies*, vol. i, Essay on Shelley.
[2] *Essays in Criticism*, vol. i, Heinrich Heine.

subject for a poem 'that should give equal room for description, incident, and impassioned reflections on men, nature, and society, yet supply in itself a natural connexion to the parts and unity to the whole'.[3] True, of course, that for all its easy projection of things, the spacious reference to commerce and politics as well as to mountains and the moral life, this poem 'The Brook' never actually got itself written, but then neither does The Ancient Mariner exhibit any anxiety on the score of its distance from real life. The 'willing suspension of disbelief' it asks for is emphatically not a suspension of our ordinary sense of reality. And Shelley is as confident as Cowper or as Coleridge; perhaps, as Keats hints, because the 'magnanimity' of his uncurbed fantasies leads them straight into the muddle of human passion and event.

No, among the English Romantics it is Keats and—oddly enough—Byron who reveal the kind of anxiety and guilt about the relation of art to reality which is still so much with us today. Frequently enough to show that it is a sensitive point in his armour of worldly confidence, Byron's letters emphasize that his poetry is unusually real, that 'it may be profligate but is it not *life*, is it not *the thing*? Could any man have written it who has not lived in the world?'[4] We might set this beside Keats's claim: 'The imagination may be compared to Adam's dream—he awoke and found it truth' (the exact converse, be it noted in passing, of the Knight-at-arms' experience on 'the cold hill side'); and we might also recall Dickens's strident claim that however apparently implausible and extravagant what he wrote was TRUE![5] The three assertions are a long way from the confidence of the earlier Romantics that what they felt and wrote could not well be otherwise. And the guilt they reveal is not of course that exuberant guilt—if one may so describe it—for the moods of dejection, paralysis, and loss of faith and zest in nature, which haunted Coleridge and bothered Words-worth, but the kind of uneasiness which compels its victims today (if they happen to be literary spokesmen) to dwell on a poet's 'essential relevance to living', or a novel's 'central human theme'; which impelled Tennyson to write The Palace of Art and

---

[3] *Biographia literaria*, ch. 10.
[4] Letter to Douglas Kinnaird, 26 Oct. 1819.
[5] Preface to *Oliver Twist*.

Arnold to emphasize that poetry is 'a criticism of life'; Yeats, to
grow the shell of legend under which all his poetic life was lived;
and W. H. Auden, to insist on the poet's legitimate irresponsibility in the looking-glass world of his art, and his necessary
responsibility in the real world 'in which you have to live
whether you like it or not'. To be so much aware of the division
between life and literature is to see life, involuntarily, as a
literary concept: 'life for life's sake' is no more and no less
meaningful than 'art for art's sake', because it expresses the
same attitude to both.

All this begins to be true for Keats. In 'the hateful siege of
contraries' which oppressed his working mind, poetry was both
the whole of life and a dream that must be rejected in favour of
life. His ambitions never sound so unreal—to beg our question
for a moment—as when he is striving for a new image of reality
and rejecting as fantasy some former mode of poetic being.
From dreamer to poet, from a fancy to a truth, from luxuriant
ignorance to deeper understanding, from feathers to iron—
these are the kinds of contrast by which he sees himself as
coming to knowledge of things as they really are.

> Ye tranced visions—ye flights ideal—
> Nothing are ye to life so dainty real!

Keats suppressed this exclamation of Endymion in the published poem, but it never left his own mind. And the same
passion for the real strives to make words themselves give the
feel of a physical experience to an imaginary longing.

> —one human kiss!
> One sigh of real breath—one gentle squeeze,
> Warm as a dove's nest among summer trees,
> And warm with dew at ooze from living blood.

The words are most real—embarrassingly real perhaps—
when fantasy is most apparent. 'La Belle Dame sans Merci' has
often been called a perfect example of the romantic temper, but
in Keats these contrasts between reality and dream are more
than that: they are extremely personal, and his own awareness
of them continually reveals, in the Letters, his special kind of
vulnerable endearing intelligence. It is not in the nature of the
Letters to reveal a poetic pilgrimage: that has to be done by

Keats's critics. And it is all but impossible for the critic, imposing order on their rapid asides and intelligent confusions, not to direct the flow into a ready-made channel. There is so much—too much—material to draw upon, and Keats's tendency to abstraction, so hesitant and spontaneous in his living utterance, acquires an almost Teutonic shape and purpose in our appraisal of it.

While he was writing Endymion he had realised that the poet must bear 'the burthen of the mystery', and he knew he could not shut out 'the still sad music of humanity'. In *Isabella* and *The Eve of St Agnes* he luxuriated in the world of romance, but his imagination had been enriched and disciplined by his experiences, and he was fully aware that these poems, describing events of far away and long ago, were only a temporary escape from the pressure of reality.[6]

Already, in this quotation from one of Keats's most sympathetic critics, do we not begin to experience a sense of removal from the actual poems, as if Keats, like the Victorian Shakespeare, were being gravely escorted by posterity from the Forest of Arden, into the depths, and perhaps onward to the serene heights?

It may be objected that Keats himself saw his poetic life as a pilgrimage, so it is surely the job of the critic to complete and clarify the stages of it. I cannot feel this. There are many indications that Keats was not a good judge of his own poetry, and that he imposed upon it and upon himself patterns of romantic aspiration that do not fit. Even the famous 'negative capability', which I must refer to again in a moment, seems to me to be one of these. To discuss his poetry as if the patterns did fit leads us ever further into abstraction, into the regions where Keats himself was only too anxious to go, but where his poetry obstinately refused to follow. For instance, the whole question of *identity*, of what the poet's identity was and should be, exercised his speculation, and has in consequence been exhaustively examined by the critics, but it is an impasse that leads not to what is of excellence in his poetry but to a number of contradictory ideas about Keats. His sense of himself, and our sense of him, begins in what Verlaine called *littérature*, in 'a lovely tale of human life'—

[6] *John Keats: A Reassessment*, ed. Kenneth Muir, Introd.

> the silver flow
> Of Hero's tears, the swoon of Imogen,
> Fair Pastorella in the bandit's den
> Are things to brood on . . .

So they were for the Elizabethans, for Spenser and Chapman, for William Browne and Shakespeare himself, but the Elizabethans did not feel as they brooded that they were renouncing life to do so, or letting it go by. Keats did, and prepared himself for the Romantic's progress.

> Then will I pass the countries that I see
> In long perspective, and continually
> Taste their pure fountains. First the realm I'll pass
> Of Flora and Old Pan . . .

'An ocean dim, sprinkled with many an isle', stretches before him, and though it is here that 'the agonies, the strife of human hearts' await him, and the thought fills him with excitement and awe, the geography of his imagination is still literary and magical. If it ceases to be, he loses himself, loses the power to *be* himself in the poem.

> A sense of real things comes doubly strong,
> And, like a muddy stream, would bear along
> My soul to nothingness.

It looks as though 'real things' are not only Keats's enemy here but ours, for the success of the poem depends on our vivid sympathy with him in it, and that sympathy is felt for a person, a particular young man who is expressing here the fear that he may lose that particularity which he has in the nurturing 'lap of legends old'. Like Saturn in *Hyperion* he fears that

> I am gone
> Away from my own bosom, I have left
> My strong identity, my real self—

but lose it he must if, like Apollo, he is to undergo the fierce but abstract anguish of 'dying into life'. The trouble is that there is a world of difference between our informal and engrossing communion with a young man and his ambitions and ideas, in 'Sleep and Poetry' and the 'Epistle to Reynolds', and the spectacle of the same young man renouncing his nature in

terms of grave heroic allegory. Paradoxically it is the renunci-
ation of self that strikes us as self-absorbed, even solipsistic,
while 'Sleep and Poetry' and the 'Epistle' do not.

The business of identity distracts Keats. He must renounce it
as a poet, and yet find his true identity as a man. 'The world is a
vale of soul-making', he writes to his brother and sister-in-law,
'and souls are not souls till they acquire identities, till each one
is personally itself.' The unidentified poet must end as an
identified soul? It is a sterile quibble for the critic, but it was no
contradiction to Keats. As well as being a genius he was the best
of men. His humility was seraphic; his loving-kindness inexhaustible. He can speak of a vale of soul-making in a way that
both moves and shames us, for he had the right to speak. His
humour, even on this vexed question of striving to know
himself, is delightful. 'Perhaps I eat to persuade myself I am
somebody', he interjects to Wodehouse, just before copying out
the 'Ode to Autumn'. He çould never say like Yeats:

> Now shall I make my soul,
> Compelling it to study
> In a learned school . . .

And he could never 'remake himself' by remaking a poem.
Although he had to 'o'erwhelm' himself in it, he had too true a
sense of the unimportance of poetry. 'I have no faith whatever
in poetry, sometimes I wonder that people read so much of it.'
The sanity in that is a part of his goodness, the goodness which,
for all his insistence on the poet's delight in an Iago as well as an
Imogen, is so transparently revealed in his poetry.

And yet his obsession with poethood does run like a flaw
through the sound intelligence of his insights, surfacing most
conspicuously in his attitude to Shakespeare. 'Shakespeare led
a life of allegory; his works are the comments on it.' It is not only
untrue, it shows why Keats's relationship to Shakespeare is in
fact so profoundly deceived. 'Lord Byron', he goes on, 'cuts a
figure, but his works are not figurative', a comment he may be
said to gloss in a later letter by saying of Byron: 'He describes
what he sees, I describe what I imagine.' The briskness is the
tone of Keats at his best, but it is disconcerting that the prime
activity of the imagination, lacking to Byron as a mere observer
of the outward show, should be assumed to be a kind of

allegorizing of the inner life. Keats cannot help seeing the Bard's progress as 'full of symbols for the spiritual eye', a progress from the maiden thought of comedy to the tragic deeps and up to the serene heights—an allegory of supreme poetic mystery. 'His plan of tasks to come were not of this world—how tremendous must have been his conception of ultimates.' It is the Victorian image of Shakespeare (and it has now become for many critics the image of Keats), but more important it is the image in which Keats confided his hope of writing 'a few fine plays'.

A drama like Shakespeare's is the opposite of allegory, for the characters cannot be identified as embodying some experience or preoccupation of the author. They do not represent him: they do not even represent the 'uncertainties, mysteries, doubts' in which Keats feels that the 'writer of achievement' has the 'negative capability' to live. The notion of 'negative capability', like that of 'a life of allegory', ignores the reality of the drama by concentrating on the personality of the dramatist. Keats is not really rejecting the usual Romantic emphasis on the poet's ego, but offering a different version of it. Shakespeare, the diffident and neutral-minded genius, is no more credible or necessary a hypothesis than Shakespeare the authoritative sage, for in both versions the dramatic point is missed. Even when he is stressing its 'camelion' nature, Keats cannot help but emphasize the poetic personality, perhaps because his own is so important to his poetry. His uncertainties are as characteristic and in their way as obtrusive in his poetry as are Wordsworth's certainties in his. The thrush of the 'Epistle to Reynolds', the Grecian Urn, the narrator of *The Fall of Hyperion*, are no less earnest about the truth of what they tell us than the Pedlar and the Narrator of 'Peter Bell'.

Certainly Keats has no trademark of identity as a critic. He was no phrase-maker: he never referred to 'negative capability' again, and he did not retain it in his critical quiver for further use. When he deputized for Reynolds on *The Champion* he subdued his pen wholly to the outlook of his friend and the enthusiasms of their set. He proposed to ask Hazlitt 'in about a year time, the best metaphysical road that I can take', but it does not seem necessary to defend him against the imputation of excessive reliance on Hazlitt, as Professor Muir has done, by

maintaining that 'Hazlitt is a good critic: Keats is a great one'.[7]
In setting up as a critic Hazlitt made himself the embodiment of
an attitude which it became his business to define and defend.
Keats needed to do neither. His passion for 'truths' is for
himself, not to convince others, and if Hazlitt could help him so
much the better. He 'cared not to be in the right', and he was
always ready to admit that 'I and myself cannot agree about
this at all'. He has no wish to testify publicly: 'everyone', he
said, 'has his speculations, just as everyone has his troubles'.
And his speculations were troubles to Keats, not possessions.

And yet as a poet his identity is unmistakable. We must
continue to say 'poet' with some emphasis, for it is true that his
life and letters have been dredged to provide an ideal poet
figure, who can either be transferred into the poetry and
worshipped there, or else can be severely ignored by readers
who prefer the *vates absconditus* of negative capability, the poet
whose rather unfortunate early manner vanishes into a grave
maturity, which gives promise of still more mature and impersonal things to come. Because we know so much about Keats's
life we are unable, or unwilling, to accept as it is the distinct life
of his poetry—distinct and different because Keats's own
personality was in the most impressive sense *provisional*, while
that of his poetry is not. He is not like Byron or D. H. Lawrence:
his self and his work are not an inseparable and completed
whole. Few readers seem prepared to accept the personality of
his poetry in the way that we accept Chaucer's, about whose life
we know little. But the reality of his poetry is to be found in its
personality, if we are not in search of what we think the poetry
should be, or what it might have become. What then is this
personality, which seems to me so vital and in a way so
neglected?

II

Its most decisive ingredient is vulgarity. What is real in his
poetry is also what is vulgar: indeed, 'Keats and Vulgarity'
would perhaps be the proper title for this lecture. He is, happily,
the most vulgar of poets; he is vulgar not as a man but as a
poet—vulgarity is his poetry's 'material sublime'. It goes down

[7] *John Keats: A Reassessment*, ed. Kenneth Muir.

into the root and sinew of his poetic language; it is not just a
surface genteelism, as in words like 'dainty', or in cockney
spellings ('exhalt', 'ear' for 'hear', and so on), but vulgarity in
the heroic sense in which Antony and Cleopatra are vulgar, in
which the dung we palate is 'the beggar's nurse and Caesar's'.
It is the true commonness which in German is called *das
Gemeine*, a word which weightily subsumes and generalizes the
more local and trivial sense of English. It is the soil which, in
German Romanticism, drags down Pegasus and stifles the fire
of poetic thought.[8] It implies above all a kind of helpless being
oneself—'habitual self'—as Keats says; the vulgar man is sunk
in his own selfhood, and yet is unaware of it.

Keats's poetic personality is magnificently *gemein*. In it the
earth reveals the rift of ore; it turns what might appear mean
and embarrassing into what is rich and *disconcerting*: for at his
most characteristic Keats always disconcerts. Now a mark of
the man of poise and breeding is to object beyond all things to
being disconcerted, and it was no doubt for this reason that
Byron hated Keats. 'Burns is often coarse but never vulgar',[9] he
observed, implying that the cockney school is too vulgar even to
aspire to coarseness. (There is the further implication that
Burns knew he was coarse and did not care—indeed took a
pride in it—but one cannot take a pride in vulgarity.) And
Keats came to detest Byron. Their personalities reacted
violently against each other, and this gives the clue to a point of
some interest to which we must return—the point that Keats
and Byron are in fact more closely related to one another than
to any other Romantic poet. Both transform poetry by their
personality, though one exploits the process and the other seeks
to evade it. Byron was ready enough to extend a tribute to the
safe, depersonalized Keats of *Hyperion*.

Byron is the most easily self-conscious of poets; by contrast,
Keats is vulgar when he does not know what he is doing, uneasy
when he does. Vulgarity cuts both ways: an author may be
vulgar when he is unaware, like Keats or Dickens, of the
disagreeable impression he is creating; or when, like Hugo, he is
making sure that we notice an effect which yet does not impress

---

[8] Cf. especially Goethe, *Epilog zu Schiller's Glocke*, and the dedication of *Letters to Schiller*.

[9] *Journal*, Nov. 1813.

us as he seems to think it should: in Goethe's phrase, one sees the intention and one is embarrassed. Keats's brand of vulgarity is as far as possible removed from such an appearance of deliberation, of 'the artist's humour'. His language continually strikes us as fulfilling Yeats's requirement of 'the right word that is also the surprising word', but never in a way that suggests contrivance: the word would not be right for anyone except Keats, and is often right for him only in the most impossible way. Even less does he practise the 'studious meanness'[10] of language cultivated by James Joyce; and still less again—to push our necessary point to an *ad absurdum*—does he revel in the ritual of linguistic vulgarity for its own sake, like an original and personal poet of our own day, John Betjeman. No, like Chaucer's Squire, Keats deploys style 'with ful devout corage'; like that innocent rhetorician he puts his heart and soul into it. Keats is most fully his poetic self, most wholly involved in what he is writing, when he is, in the usual and technical sense, 'bad', or on the edge of 'badness'. One might say that the full reality of his poetry is revealed in the presence of this badness; the poetry needs it. Its greatness, its heavy truth, is profoundly involved with badness and cannot seem to exist without it.

My use of the word 'bad' here begs as many questions as my borrowing of *gemein*, and both are more easily demonstrated in Keats than defined. The clue is, I repeat, that Keats's language is right only for him, and even in him will only seem right after we have accepted his poetic nature whole; it is no good 'by naming the faults to distinguish the beauties'. Keats's badness reveals his kinship with Shakespeare more clearly than his agreed excellence. In both we can find the same apparent lack of close scrutiny and sure taste. Who but Shakespeare could have brought off the repetition in Macbeth's speech?

> And with some sweet oblivious antidote
> Cleanse the stufft bosom of that perillous stuffe
> Which weighes upon the heart?

Early editors did all they could to remove or emend it; to us it seems the only possible word. Keats often echoes this primal Elizabethan certainty, though the *gemein* in him is also his own. He describes Isabella after Lorenzo's disappearance as

[10] Letter to Joyce from his brother, quoted in *The Critical Writings of James Joyce*, ed. Mason and Ellmann, p. 86.

> Spreading her perfect arms upon the air
> And on her couch low murmuring 'Where? O where?'

In most poets such an epithet at such a moment would
be merely vacuous—in Dryden a routine insensibility, in
Hunt a routine archness (it is applied, in *The Story of Rimini*, to
Francesca's waist)—but is it not, in Keats, intensely moving?
Keats assumes with such 'corage' that a cliché is the burning
word for him that it becomes so: everything works together for
good, even when Isabella turned up Lorenzo's 'soiled glove'

> And put it in her bosom where it dries,
> And freezes utterly unto the bone
> Those dainties made to still an infant's cries.

The congruity between the genteelism and the situation is
uncannily touching, as far removed from banality as the
apparition of Lorenzo out of the 'kernel of the grave', which,

> past his loamed ears
> Had made a miry channel for his tears

is removed from any suggestion of the ridiculous. *The Story of
Rimini*, of course, subsides continually into both, but Hunt's
'trusting animal spirits'[11] are not entirely unselfconscious—he
gives us a sidelong glance as he plays the eager enthusiast.
Keats's temperament transforms his attitude without altering
its idiom.

This 'badness' in Keats, then, might be summed up as a
devout, 'unmisgiving' (Hunt's admirable word) acceptance of
the first eager brainwave, and a subsequent unawareness that it
might be modified or corrected. Keats of course alters much,
but he does not polish. His alterations do not, as it were, take
the bloom off his characteristic efforts, but show them in a
sharper relief. The 'deceitful elf' of the 'Ode To A Nightingale'
is changed to 'deceiving', but the disconcertingly Keatsian
entity remains (all his 'self' rhymes are unsuspiciously clumsy)
weighing down with its queer passionate awkwardness the last
stanza of the Ode, an awkwardness marvellously in contrast
with the nightingale's invisible departure

---

[11] Leigh Hunt, Preface to *Poetical Works*.

> Past the near meadows, over the still stream,
> Up the hill-side . . .

I do not want to suggest that his diction is always unselfconscious: of course he had a most attentive ear for the varieties of
English poetic diction. Chatterton, whose memory is honoured
in the foundation of this lecture, was, as we know, both
honoured by Keats and admired as a poet by whom English
—poetic English—had been 'kept up'. When in 'Isabella'
Keats says that he writes to salute Boccaccio and 'thy gone
spirit greet', he is using, I think, a conscious Chattertonism;
and so also, perhaps, is the phrase 'husky barn' in a cancelled
line of the 'Ode to Autumn'. He refused his publisher's plea to
restrain the dolphins who 'bob their noses through the brine' in
Endymion, but allowed 'tip-top quietude' to dwindle into 'utmost
quietude'. By the time he came to revise, he was more confident
of Chatterton's English than of Hunt's, but here he did
his friend less than justice, for Hunt's preface to his own
poems—far less lofty and more empirical than Wordsworth's
famous document—shows an acute sense of how the spontaneous and 'animal' impulse might be brought back into the
diction of the poet who, in Hunt's phrase, 'knows his station',
and who would otherwise use the kind of dead language which
Wordsworth deplored.[12]

We cannot say of all poets that they are at their best when at
their most characteristic, that their excellence is inseparable
from their personal diction. It is true of Hardy, and it is perhaps
true of Keats. It is less true of Shelley than of any poet, and it is
certainly not true of Spenser or of Hopkins, who might be
thought to be enclosed within a poetic idiom of their own
creation. Perhaps because they have so obviously fashioned it
for themselves, their manner can be shed in favour of a fine

---

[12] Ibid. See especially Hunt's defence of his neologisms *swirl*, and *cored*, in the
excellent couplet:

> And so much knowledge of one's self there lies
> Cored, after all, in our complacencies.

Compare the many metaphors in which Keats uses the word *kernel.*
  Further evidence that Hunt's use of naïve neologisms was systematic turns up in a
letter of Byron to Thomas Moore (June 1818): 'I told him [Hunt] that I deemed *Rimini*
good poetry at bottom, disfigured only by a strange style. His answer was that his style
was on a system—or some such cant.'

simplicity that might have come from anywhere. It is the simplicity we meet in *The Faerie Queene* in lines like

> Thus do those lovers with sweet countervayle
> Each other of love's bitter fruit despoil.

Or in the fragment of Hopkins which begins

> To him who ever thought with love of me . . .

However impressive, this power of achieving a great and plain anonymity need not be taken as a touchstone. I comment on it in order to emphasize by contrast how indispensable Keats's personal idiom is. Unlike Wordsworth or Shelley he cannot cease to be immediately himself without losing his peculiar poethood. The early verses 'On Death' show what I have in mind; it is one of the few little pieces of its period which his more squeamish admirers can read without shuddering.

> Can death be sleep, when life is but a dream
>   And scenes of bliss pass as a phantom by?
> The transient pleasures as a vision seem,
>   And yet we think the greatest pain's to die.

Imitative no doubt, but with a simplicity that is rather beautiful, and yet because the thought has not Keats's own linguistic stamp it achieves no wide poetic dignity, it remains banal. But this is not banal—

> O to arrive each Monday morn from Ind!
> To land each Tuesday from the rich Levant!
> In little time a host of joys to bind,
> And keep our souls in one eternal pant!

It is *gemein*, but it is not banal. It has the true devotion of Keats in it.

Of course he can make other styles into his own, the Elizabethans above all, but they must *be* made his own: insubstantiality and nullity occur when he cannot work the change, when—to borrow his own phrase about Milton—what is life to another poet becomes death to him.[13] Even at its most

---

[13] An illuminating instance of failure in adaptation is 'Daisy's Song', where Keats takes the form and manner of a lyric by Blake, but gives it, most incongruously, a vulgar touch that is all his own.

unpropitious, *Endymion* is packed with borrowed life which has become Keats.

> There are who lord it o'er their fellow-men
> With most prevailing tinsel; who unpen
> Their baaing vanities, to browse away
> The comfortable green and juicy hay
> From human pastures; or, O torturing fact!
> Who, through an idiot blink, will see unpack'd
> Fire-branded foxes to sear up and singe
> Our gold and ripe-ear'd hopes.

This is apparently terrible, but let us compare it with the opening of the second *Hyperion*.

> Fanatics have their dreams, wherewith they weave
> A paradise for a sect; the savage too
> From forth the loftiest fashion of his sleep
> Guesses at heaven: pity these have not
> Trac'd upon vellum or wild Indian leaf
> The shadow of melodious utterance.
> But bare of laurel they live, dream and die;
> For Poesy alone can tell her dreams,
> With the fine spell of words alone can save
> Imagination from the sable charm
> And dumb enchantment.

The passage seems to be treading gingerly, with a precarious confidence, secured by a careful abstention from anything that may jar. We miss the deplorable rhymes which wrench the sense so nakedly in their direction, and yet which—like Byron's—in fact give a greater vigour and forcefulness of meaning to the *Endymion* passage than the opening of *Hyperion* can show. In the latter, Keats's greater caution seems to blur and weaken sense; his voice survives only in the thoughtful, colloquial note of—'Pity these have not . . .'; and the metaphors (*weave*, *spell*, *enchantment*) lie limply, and indeed decoratively, without pressing their conviction boisterously in upon us. Without gathering itself consciously together, the animation of the *Endymion* style can leap into the discovery of

> Innumerable mountains rise, and rise,
> Ambitious for the hallowing of thine eyes.

('Rise, and rise'—the rhyme takes the mountain range in its stride; and *ambitious* is a perfect example of Keats's power to make use of a grand word without reflecting on it, as unselfconsciously as he uses *baaing* or *comfortable*.) Or into a typically Keatsian argument:

> And, truly, I would rather be struck dumb
> Than speak against this ardent listlessness;
> For I have ever thought that it might bless
> The world with benefits unknowingly;
> As does the nightingale, upperched high,
> And cloistered among cool and bunched leaves—
> She sings but to her love, nor e'er conceives
> How tip-toe night holds back her dark-grey hood.
> Just so many love, although 'tis understood
> The mere commingling of passionate breath,
> Produce more than our searching witnesseth.

(The movement of that line—'the mere commingling of passionate breath' is as subtle as anything in Pope or Tennyson, but is given without pretension or pause; and the nightingale, in its characteristically awkward setting, is far more real than Clare's more graceful bird, 'lost in a wilderness of listening leaves'.) Or it may be into a passage like this—

> Straying about, yet cooped up in the den
> Of helpless discontent,—hurling my lance
> From place to place, and following at chance,
> At last, by hap, through some young trees it struck,
> And, plashing among bedded pebbles, stuck
> In the middle of a brook.

—where being young has all the force that it might have in Byron, together with a most un-Byronic sense of the *feel* of an event, the moment in the wood when the spear clattered into the stream. (Contrast this, or 'the sodden turfed dell' of the murder in 'Isabella', with the Claude landscape of *Hyperion*.) Or Keats may launch a *sententia*:

> But this is human life: the war, the deeds,
> The disappointment, the anxiety,
> Imagination's struggles, far and nigh,
> All human, bearing in themselves this good,

> That they are still the air, the subtle food,
> To make us feel existence and to show
> How quiet death is.

The passage rises into a greatness of generality and at once
presses onward; while the opening of the second *Hyperion* seems
to be feeling its way forward towards the plotted moment of a
great line, followed by an appropriate rest for appreciation:

> When this warm scribe, my hand, is in the grave.

It is moving, and impressive, but it is also in a damaging sense
aesthetic. We have seen it coming. Keats is no longer the
Squire, writing with 'ful devout corage', but a nineteenth-
century poet, nearly a Tennyson, feeling deeply and fashioning
a line out of the feeling; the pause between feeling and making
can be felt, and in the hush our sense of craftsmanship at work is
embarrassingly strong.

   Does it matter? Is this a philistine reaction, and should not I
just say I prefer the more immediate and emotional manner of
Endymion to that of *Hyperion*, as one might prefer *Maud* to *In
Memoriam*? I think, though, there is something of real critical
significance here. The wary, meticulous artistry which seems
natural to Arnold and Tennyson does indeed matter to Keats,
because it inhibits the play of his linguistic personality. *Hyperion*
is, so to speak, not *bad* enough, too full of hard-won decorum.
Keats distrusted art, because 'human nature' was finer as he
felt, but perhaps more because his nature was spontaneously
artful. The sad dilemma of his genius is that when he tries to
express reality he becomes abstract; when he turns towards the
discipline of art he becomes Parnassian. In *Hyperion* both things
occur and Keats knew it. He invited Wodehouse to mark in the
poem 'the false beauties proceeding from art and the true ones
from feeling'. It is a fatal distinction for his poetry and it should
be a meaningless one—the whole force of his language and
personality should make nonsense of it. But the Keats who
abandoned *Hyperion* because it had so much of Milton and 'the
artist's humour' in it, is the Keats who had come to make such a
distinction. He stifles his personality in order to make the
necessary calculations for the major philosophical poem,
the playing up, or playing down, of 'beauties' to enhance the
paragraphing and the overall effect. *Hyperion* thus becomes

the prototype of what might be called *romantic correctness*, the effect displayed in Saturn

> whose hoar locks
> Shone like the bubbling foam about a keel
> When the prow sweeps into a midnight cove . . .

or

> Proserpine return'd to her own fields
> Where the white heifers low

no less than in lines of Tennyson like

> And see the great Achilles whom we knew

or

> While Ilion like a mist rose into towers.

In 'Ulysses' and 'Tithonus' Tennyson perfects the model; portentous and yet truncated, it makes a kind of poem which seems more deviously intimate the more grandly generalized it is in style, and the more it appears to universalize the burden and the sorrow. It is ideally suited to Tennyson's genius. But is it suited to Keats?

> Then saw I a wan face
> Not pin'd with human sorrows, but bright blanch'd
> By an immortal sickness which kills not;
> It works a constant change, which happy death
> Can put no end to; deathwards progressing
> To no death was that visage; it had passed
> The lily and the snow; and beyond these
> I must not think now, though I saw that face—

In its admirable movement there is something withheld which makes us wonder if Keats has in fact anything to withhold, an impression not uncommon in Tennyson (we have it in 'A Vision of Sin'). Superb as Keats's passage is, our view as spectators is one of abdication, of great curtains rippling together. Very different from Moneta is the Niobe of *Endymion*.

> Perhaps, the trembling knee
> And frantic gape of lonely Niobe
> Poor lonely Niobe! When her lovely young
> Were dead and gone, and her caressing tongue
> Lay a lost thing upon her paly lip,

> And very, very deadliness did nip
> Her motherly cheeks.

The words here are 'unmisgiving' and alive (compare the potent word *gape* with *wan* and *blanch'd*). This is the real anguish of the human heart. It is typical of Keats that even the repetition of *very* and the loose feminism of *paly* in no way enfeeble the passage or add a note of hysteria. The contrast between caressing, with its firm sexual meaning, and the terrible disregard for itself of this face in torment, would be almost too painful, were it not that the intensity of the image 'causes all disagreeables to evaporate'. It is the same brief, almost unregarded intensity which marks Keats's vision of the brothers' activities in 'Isabella'—

> Half-ignorant, they turned an easy wheel

—and his expansion of the metaphor into brutal images of blood and suffering. It is the world's 'giant agony' in a graphically realized form, as meaningful as the glimpse Shakespeare gives us of the officer in *King Lear* who was ready to hang Cordelia—

> I cannot draw a cart, nor eat dried oats;
> If it be man's work, I'll do't.

These touches on the nerve are far more effective than a grave allegory of human suffering, but Keats's sense of guilt made him feel that one who was a true poet and no dreamer must prepare himself for a direct assault on 'the mystery'. He did not know, perhaps could not afford to know, that for him it had to be revealed indirectly, almost inadvertently, and that he was continually revealing it in this way. 'Isabella' struck him as a 'weak-sided' poem. But like *Endymion* it is as real as anything he wrote. And *Endymion* has as much life in it as *Don Juan* itself.

Byron thought otherwise, as we know, and in spite of himself Keats cared much what Byron thought. When in the recast *Hyperion* he made his frontal assault on the human condition he could not forbear—from the height of his new seriousness—a side-swipe in Dante's manner at those critics and 'careless hectorers in proud bad verse' who had dismissed him earlier as the 'drivelling' Keats.

> Tho' I breathe death with them it will be life
> To see them sprawl before me into graves.

202 JOHN BAYLEY

The notion of his lordship, for all his poise and *savoir-vivre*, tripped up and toppled into his own grave, is as gloatingly good as anything in *The Vision of Judgment*. 'Sprawl' is the old Keats: the bizarre picture expands into our mind's eye; but though he had the impulse to 'trounce Lord Byron' in a satire, he would have been ashamed to nurse it up for a long enough period, and become a 'self-worshipper' himself in the process. Satire is no more his forte than the grand manner. Though his vulgar native style often has the disconcerting force of good satiric writing (and we might remember that curiously Keatsian line in *Don Juan* about 'cooks in motion with their clean arms bare') it is precisely the element of the *gemein* which gives it its total modesty, and total lack of the keen but complacent self-appraisal which poised satire must have. The vulgarity which Keats's worldlier critics find hardest to stomach is the lack of this kind of self-awareness: no more than the Squire's does his poetry keep a sharp pleased eye on itself. And not only is Keats too full of the milk of human kindness to maintain the satiric appetite; he was going to drop the passage from *Hyperion* because in the context of the poem's intended seriousness, and select diminishment of effect, it would not do. He had lost the innocence which could include and enjoy so much. One of the reasons *The Cap and Bells* makes depressing reading is that he seems to be exposing and exploiting, with a kind of determined frivolity, the vigour and innocence with which he began, and which Hunt had inspired in him.[14] When he rejects honest vulgarity, and all that for him goes with it, he parts from a great deal. The evidence of this makes it perplexing to know what T. S. Eliot had in mind when he suggested that in the second *Hyperion* we see 'signs of a struggle towards unification of sensibility'. Does 'unification' here mean the disappearance of so much that makes sensibility in Keats's poetry so worth while?

Both the second *Hyperion* and *The Cap and Bells* show us, in their very different ways, Keats's growing awareness of, and distaste for, his poetical character. In one poem he seeks to evade it in a grave anonymity, in the other in a flippant cynicism. The former is a heroic but desolating attempt, and it

[14] e.g. stanza lxii, where Keats is parodying Hunt's style of narration.

might have led him to silence. For his disgust with the idea of
the writer carving out a principality for himself—as we say,
'Richardson's world', or 'a Browning character', or 'Trollope
country'—was on a typically heroic scale. 'Each of the moderns,' he notes, 'like an Elector of Hanover governs his petty
state.' His outburst against the storm in *Don Juan*, if correctly
reported by Severn, sounds oddly priggish to us, who find it
spirited enough; but Keats's revulsion was, I feel, against
Byron consciously making a good thing out of a new mode or
fashion of insight into human nature and human conduct. His
protest was against the growing pretension of the romantic
novelist, and it reminds us that Keats, for all his affinities with
Dickens or with Byron, could never have mustered the solipsistic assurance of such a novelist. He writes of the people at a
Scottish inn: 'I was extremely gratified to think, that if I had
pleasures they knew nothing of, they had also some into which I
could not possibly enter.' That is delightful and characteristic,
and all the more so from the emphasis with which he records it.
We might remember, too, how he noted for his sister the 'old
French emigrant with . . . his face full of political schemes' he
saw from his Hampstead window; and the curious respect with
which he observed the old woman at Belfast—'with a pipe in
her mouth and looking out with a round-eyed skinny-lidded
inanity, with a sort of horizontal idiotic movement of her
head. . . . What a thing would be a history of her life and
sensations!' But for all his sharpness of eye and pen he would
never have made anything out of it. He was (it was his own
highest term of approbation) too 'disinterested' to do so.

It is bitterly ironic that even the *gemein* goes bad on him when
he attempts to refine it to the standards of *Hyperion*. One of the
curiously intimate apprehensions he is so good at, touches that
seem to knit the innerness of the body with the imagination—
'ears, whose tips are glowing hot' or, 'eyes, shut softly up
alive'—is merely otiose here.

> I had no words to answer; for my tongue
> Useless, could find about its roofed home
> No syllable of a fit majesty
> To make rejoinder to Moneta's mourn.

In the gravely classic context, 'roofed home' is no more alive
than 'fleecy care' or 'finny tribe' would be. And the simile

> As when in theatres of crowded men
> Hubbub increases more they call out hush—

anticipates the fatuity of Arnold's in *Sohrab and Rustum*—'As some rich woman on a winter's morn.' That close and potent co-operation of the bad and the good which triumphs in 'Melancholy', 'The Nightingale', and the earlier narrative poems, is nullified in *Hyperion*, so that we merely shake our heads when Apollo wishes 'to flit into' a star, 'and make its silvery splendour pant with bliss'; and we sigh with relief when Keats cancelled his metamorphosis

> Into a hue more roseate than sweet pain
> Gives to a ravish'd nymph when her warm tears
> Gush luscious with no sob.

Compared with the sleepwalker's sureness with which he found the alterations in 'The Eve of St Agnes', there is no other word than tinkering for the changes Keats made between the two *Hyperions*. When he takes this kind of pains he becomes conventional, as if convention were an earnest of maturity. For T. S. Eliot and other critics the 'Ode to Psyche' is the finest of the odes, and Keats himself said it was the first poem 'over which I have taken even moderate pains'. But he is more at home with the linguistic innocence of the Elizabethans: the sheer efficiency of Milton and Dryden is not a happy model for him. The concluding stanza of the ode is indeed a *tour de force*, but not one of a Keatsian kind; it has the flat Augustan brio which we find in the description of the snake in *Lamia* (so like Pope's pheasant), and the landscapes of his imagination are formalized and parcelled out incongruously—Keats cannot inform the mixture with his own disconcerting truth.

> Yes, I will be thy priest and build a fane
>   In some untrodden region of my mind
> Where branched thoughts, new grown with pleasant pain—

We notice the lapse here as we might in Gray or Dryden, and again I take this as a sign that Keats is not fully himself. In the adroitness of the stanza the bad rhyme jars as it should not, and as a similar rhyme does not in the 'Sonnet to Homer'.

> Aye, on the shores of darkness there is light,
> And precipices show untrodden green;

> There is a budding morrow in midnight;
> There is a triple sight in blindness keen;

In both poems the adjective *untrodden* makes its distinguishing mark, but while it seems to draw the sonnet into a unique and intense locality, its power in the ode remains in the air. The sonnet earns the characteristic word, and moves us where the ode does not.

Keats's endings are worth a study in themselves. He *may* have been like Shakespeare in this respect: that he attached little importance to what he could do supremely and naturally well; this casualness (if it can be called that) fathers what we associate with Shakespearian greatness. 'The Nightingale', 'Autumn', and 'The Eve of St Agnes' 'slipped idly from him'; he does not bother with their 'imperfections', and they do not so much end as complete elsewhere their cycle of fruition, moving without disturbance into their season in our minds. This prolongation of his finest endings is in sharp contrast with the aggressive full stop of others. Keats's sincerity, his almost embarrassing tendency to mean what he says, is bothering (or at least has appeared to bother many critics and readers) at the conclusion of the 'Ode On A Grecian Urn', because it is put in the kind of poetic language which usually does *not* mean quite so intensely what it says. Compare 'Beauty is truth, truth beauty', with the line in *Endymion*—'I loved her to the very white of truth'—where the abstract word is brought home to us through the medium of the graphic kernel image. Phrases like 'the feel of not to feel it', 'a sort of oneness', 'one smallest pebble-bead of doubt', show how effectively and with what accuracy the Keatsian *gemein* can deal with propositions and ideas if it is allowed to do so in its own way, by means of the 'plump contrast' of sense. To generalize for Keats is not to be an idiot, but to run the risk of losing the necessary contact with his physical self.

The finality, as of a closing door, in the last couplet of 'The Grecian Urn', has affinities with the ending of *Lamia*.

> —no pulse, or breath they found,
> And, in its marriage robe, the heavy body wound.

We know from a letter of Wodehouse to Taylor, Keats's publisher, that Keats had difficulty in completing *Lamia*; that

he wished to end it even more abruptly by cutting off the last
twenty lines or so; and that—as Professor Garrod plausibly
suggested—he replied to the protests of his friend and publisher by telling them to finish it off as they wanted.[15] He valued
Lamia much more highly than his other two narrative poems,
and for the usual disquieting reason: he thought it had more
toughness and reality in it, and he had tried hard to put them
there. He wanted it to end with a flourish, a defiant full stop,
but—to adapt his own comment on poetry—we might say that
if a poem of his does not end as naturally as the leaves fall from a
tree it had better not end at all.

'The Eve of St Agnes' does end like the seasons and the
leaves; it is Keats's most moving ending to what I consider his
finest poem. Yet he insisted on altering the last lines 'to leave on
the reader a sense of pettish disgust'. (The account is Wodehouse's.) 'He says he likes that the poem should leave off with
this change of sentiment—it was what he aimed at, and was
glad to find from my objections to it that he had succeeded.'[16]

> Angela went off
> Twitch'd with the palsy; and with face deform
> The beadsman stiffened, 'twixt a sigh and laugh
> Ta'en sudden from his beads by one weak little cough.

We can only uphold Wodehouse's objection. But Keats felt that
this was more wry and worldly, less romantic and 'weak-sided'.
Was it a final gesture towards Byron and to the kind of
expectation in the reader which Keats felt that Byron had
created? Certainly Byron's most terrible gift was to dissolve the
selfhood of his victims, to make those under his spell feel that
reality was in him, not in themselves, and he made Keats feel it.
He made Keats want '*to write fine things which cannot be laughed at in
any way*'[17]—perhaps the most significant admission in his
letters. It was a desolating ambition for himself, though it
reveals an astonishingly shrewd insight into Byron's own social
and poetic obsession. It is like Keats to be dismissive of his
poem once written, but it is horribly unlike him to try to give it
an all-round reality, a Byronic sort of reality, by adding this
touch. And it is in marked contrast to the typically effortless

[15] *Keats' Poetical Works*, Introd., p. xxxv.
[16] Ibid., Introd., p. xl.
[17] My italics.

and natural relation which he had with romantic medievalism. 'They are not my fault', he says of the names in the poem, 'I did not search for them.' Mrs Radcliffe's world was native to him, Byron's was not.

None the less, the thread that obstinately though incongruously links the two poets is that of personality: and it is Keats's fate that the elements of greatness in him, of aspiration and virtue, all make against the personal actuality of his poetry, negate and extinguish it, are bent on passing it for 'a higher life'. In Byron these elements are in complete harmony with his personal style and show themselves through it. Keats is always in danger of losing himself, either to another kind of 'truth' or to his own ambition. His personality is not self-renewing—it is not ruthless and egocentric enough. A poet like Yeats or Byron can abandon to his following the attitudes which have served him—the energies of Lara, Childe Harold, even Don Juan —and yet remain even more richly and recognizably himself; but with Keats the processes of 'maturity' are those of real impoverishment and sacrifice, of muting and muffling. The realities of Calidore and Endymion, of Isabella and Porphyro, are disowned, together with the vocabulary and the sexual imagination that made them real. Reality *changes* for Keats, as it never does for Byron, and the eclipse of reality in his poetry is the eclipse of sex.

III

The most emphatic aspect of the *gemein* in Keats is, of course, the way he writes about sex. I do not think that any critic, not even Leigh Hunt, has found himself able to praise Keats's treatment of the subject, and I feel some qualms in attempting to do so now. But considering the general agreement that his poetry is full of sex, and the equally general agreement that he is a fine poet, this negative attitude is odd, to say the least. How does this side of Keats come to be so customarily dismissed—as indeed Keats himself was only too ready to dismiss it—with epithets like 'mawkish' and 'adolescent'? The critic's route of escape from the topic seems to be that Keats outgrew all that nonsense when he became full of flint and iron, or that it is in any case of little importance, something sloughed off in his finest poetry. Distrust of it unites the most dissimilar critics. It moves D. G. James to say that 'the most serious side of Keats does not emerge in *The Eve of St Agnes*';[18] it annoys Professor Blackstone so much that he curtly dismisses one of the most striking and characteristic passages of *Endymion* as 'hardly relevant to our purposes',[19] the purposes of thematic interpretation; Professor Muir takes refuge from it in the study of *Hyperion* as a political and spiritual allegory;[20] and Professor Garrod, debarred from that outlet by his own robust refusal to admit a growing maturity and reality in the later poems, fell back on the world of 'pure imaginative forms'[21] which Keats ideally inhabits.

Professor Garrod, indeed, disposed of the problem most honestly. He would not make the often implied contrast between the 'serious' and the sexual or 'adolescent' side of Keats, but he made another between Keats's supremacy in these 'pure imaginative forms', and his unfortunate 'relapses upon the real'. Imagination, he suggested, is as far removed from the erotic in Keats as can well be: the first produces his 'characteristic perfections', the second 'assails him with the old hunger and thirst for reality'. And with disastrous consequences.

> Let the mad poets say whate'er they please
> Of the sweets of Fairies, Peris, Goddesses,
> There is not such a treat among them all,
> Haunters of cavern, lake, and waterfall,
> As a real woman—

'That the same man', wrote Professor Garrod, 'could write like that, and elsewhere write poetry, we can only believe by finding it to be so.' This seems to me to go the root of the matter, and though I take the opposite view and find in these lines the most characteristic evidence of Keats's unique gift, Garrod's vigorous reaction does challenge us to decide what is good and bad in Keats, and why. 'Upon whatever page of the poetry there falls the shadow of a living woman,' he continues, 'it falls calamitously like an eclipse.' Again the emphasis is in the right place, though again my own feeling would be that when it is indeed a

[18] D. G. James, *The Romantic Comedy*.

[19] Bernard Blackstone, *The Consecrated Urn*. The passage in question is the lovemaking of Cynthia and Endymion in bk. ii.

[20] Op. cit., pp. 102 f.

[21] H. W. Garrod, *Keats*.

living woman that Keats writes of his poetry is never more real. Moneta and Mnemosyne are not real precisely because they are not there as women, in the sense that Cynthia, Lamia, Isabella, and Madeleine are; they have a function doubtless, a serious and symbolic function, but they do not exist, and it is this kind of existence, the existence that Keats can give to sexual fantasy, that is the kernel of his poetic achievement.

The 'Ode To Autumn' is usually considered his most perfect poem, the most free from any 'mawkish' or personal intrusion, and I suppose that Professor Garrod would not have considered the great personification of autumn there to be in any sense 'a living woman'. But in fact she surely is? The poem's weight and substance depend upon her sisterhood with those other ladies about whom the critics prefer to make no comment. Take the second line of the poem,

> Close bosom-friend of the maturing sun;

and the seventeenth,

> Or on a half-reap'd furrow sound asleep . . .

There is not only weight and perfection here but also the *gemein*, the warmly domestic. *Sound* asleep—the phrase expands and withdraws from the mythology of the classic seasons into the more intimate mythology of family and home. More perfect and more generalized as the phrases are, they are none the less cognate with the 'mistress' of the 'Ode To Melancholy', with her 'rich anger', 'peerless eyes', and the 'globed peonies' that are associated with her; with Lorenzo's Isabella, whose 'full shape did all his seeing fill'; with the Niobe of *Endymion* whom I have already mentioned, and with the picture of Cybele in that poem.

What the psychologists might make of this is both obvious and unimportant. The sexual psychology of Byron or Dostoevsky is clearly of the greatest possible significance to the critic of their work: there is no need to concern ourselves with that of Keats because it is in every sense so commonplace. Nor would it be relevant to dwell on the sexual reality of these figures if such a reality was all they possessed. The sensuous weight of Keats's language is evident enough, and its heavy condensation at these moments (like the boat in *Endymion* that 'dropped beneath the young couple's weight') also goes without saying. No, the real importance of such passages is their power of expansion and universalization. Keats is, I believe, unique among English poets in his power of generalizing the most personal and the most intimate sensuality back into a great and indeed an august idea of nature and life. It is a peculiarly romantic power: the Elizabethans, from whom he learned so much, do not have it. Keats can endow an intimate sensuality with the same power of expansion and suggestion with which Wordsworth, in 'The Leechgatherer' and elsewhere, endows his own spiritual and poetic predicament. In both cases we share in something that seems deeply and universally relevant. But unlike Wordsworth, Keats is not aware of the process, or aware of it only in the context of his feeling both antipathy and envy for Wordsworth's more conscious power of generalization. The irony with which we are by now so sadly familiar is that he assumed, as his critics have been ready to assume, that sex was for him a refuge, a cul-de-sac, a veritable chamber of maiden thought. His poetry shows otherwise: its power of expansion lay in the very 'mawk-ishness' which he felt he must grow out of. Sexual vulgarity is the matrix of a generalizing greatness.

'Perfection' in Keats is for this reason never a pure, elevated, separable affair. When his poetry is alive it is never 'perfect' in the sense in which Garrod observed that 'it is hard to conceive more perfect speech' than the first six lines of the 'Bright Star' sonnet, the remainder being 'in painfully inferior contrast'. The end couplet of a Shakespeare sonnet may be inferior to what precedes it in the sense Garrod had in mind, but this kind of perfection or inferiority just does not occur in Keats. The sonnet is a seamless whole, but it reverses the usual order of Keats's great effects; the expansion and the breadth are mani-fested at the opening, and in the conclusion we can see where they had their source. Professor Garrod felt the perfection began to 'waver' in the couplet:

> Or gazing on the new soft-fallen mask
> Of snow upon the mountains and the moors.

—significantly, because the image of the snow is marvellously balanced between the intimate and the spacious: in its erotic overtone 'the real woman' is beginning to appear.

In its small compass the 'Bright Star' sonnet has the same latent scope, the same promise of the illimitable, that we find in 'The Eve of St Agnes'. (Consider, for example, the significance in line six of the adjectives *pure*—Keats first wrote *cold*—and *human*. In themselves they contain two worlds.) Although Keats has no outstanding gift for verse narration, in the traditional sense his art holds the seed of that form which was to flower so conspicuously later in the century—the form of the short story. It is a form which demands for its highest success a deceptive slightness of setting combined with the utmost expansion of meaning, and, as I shall hope to show, we find these in 'The Eve of St Agnes' as we find them in a masterpiece like Joyce's story *The Dead*. How that characteristically romantic form, the allegory of spiritual quest and struggle, is as ill-suited to Keats as it is suited to Shelley, we have already seen: allegory sinks under the weight which Keats gives to his own apprehensions of intensity, but such moments are the life of the short-story form. I have already mentioned 'The Leechgatherer', and Wordsworth's poem has indeed this same quality, embodied in the place or person who provides for the narrator and hence for ourselves what Joyce called 'an epiphany'. It does not seem to me absurd to compare the leechgatherer, who is seen not only as a man but as a vision, as a creature of unknown age and provenance, with Keats's beadsman, or even with an apparition of similar intensity in *Endymion*, that of Cybele.

> Forth from a rugged arch, in the dusk below,
> Came mother Cybele! alone—alone—
> In sombre chariot . . . four maned lions hale
> The sluggish wheels; solemn their toothed maws,
> Their surly eyes brow-hidden, heavy paws
> Uplifted drowsily, and nervy tails
> Cowering their tawny brushes. Silent sails
> This shadowy queen athwart, and faints away
> In another gloomy arch

As well as being a Wordsworthian apparition the leechgatherer is a fully human figure (this gives the poem its force as a story) perhaps because Wordsworth here (and Keats habitually) combine with ease the intimate with the frankly literary or mythological, a mixture that, surprisingly, combines to make their visions like a portrait from life—perhaps life inheres in the very incongruity of the mixture? In stanza, spirit, and vocabulary, the leechgatherer joins with the world of Spenser, fully evident in such a phrase as 'the sable orbs of his yet vivid eyes'; and Keats can produce his Cybele as if in the garish background of the pantomimes he delighted in at Drury Lane, whisk her on as if with wires and away into the wings again.[22] Keats's essentially vulgar embrace of mythology (about which he became sensitive as the critics took care to assure him of its vulgarity) is triumphant in its eclectic and unselfconscious vigour: he is as familiar with his Andromeda in the *Endymion* chorus as with the bride in his Galloway Song. No lively use of mythology can come of an anxiety about good taste; Keats here is in the company of Chaucer and Shakespeare.

In the passage from *Lamia* which has been so much deplored, we can see a similar and splendid combination of the Keatsian *gemein* with a neo-classical vitality straight from Dryden. Dryden's worldliness is replaced by Keats's 'devout corage', but his energy is fused with it admirably in such lines as

> —a real woman, lineal indeed
> From Pyrrha's pebbles or old Adam's seed

or

> With no more awe than what her beauty gave,
> That, while it smote, still guaranteed to save.

This is not to say that *Lamia* is successful as a poem, as are—in their different ways—*Endymion* and 'The Eve of St Agnes'. Its failure is indeed best shown by the importance which we, and Keats, have to give to its 'meaning' (which yet neither he nor we can take seriously) and by the helplessness with which we find ourselves comparing its thematic tendencies—the fatal woman, the destructive infatuation, and so forth—with comparable themes in other poems. Failure in Keats, we might almost say, can be measured by the extent to which there seems

---

[22] That the pantomime was in Keats's head at this point comes out still more clearly a few lines later when Endymion has put

> Into his grasping hands a silken cord
> At which without a single impious word
> He swung upon it off into the gloom.

Keats afterwards substituted 'a large eagle' for the silken cord.

nothing for it but to appraise the significance which his themes might seem to have, particularly in relation to one another. Such an analysis is a sign of failure, though where *Lamia* is concerned of permissible failure, in our response to what he can best do.

IV

It is a measure of the success of 'The Eve of St Agnes' that if we respond to it we do not feel any need to make this kind of analysis. If we are determined to analyse we can call it another example of Keats's wish-fulfilment fantasy, pointing out what is certainly true, the way in which Madeleine's awakening,

> Her eyes were open, but she still beheld,
> Now wide awake, the vision of her sleep—

illustrates Keats's own deep yearning for the imagination to be like Adam's dream: 'he awoke and found it true'. But this is no more relevant than the description of the poem as 'an exquisitely coloured tapestry', 'a beautiful piece . . . which fences us elaborately from all infection of reality',[23] and so on. It is not a psychological conundrum with medieval trappings, like *Christabel*, or a picturesque labour of love of the past, like *The Lay of the Last Minstrel*, from which much of its material is taken. It is the most remarkable instance in romantic poetry of a poem based wholly upon literature and yet expanding wholly into life. Just as we are surprised, and yet wholly persuaded, by Wordsworth's literary vision of the leechgatherer in a line like 'the sable orbs of his yet vivid eyes', so it is a shock to find Keats's hero 'brushing the cobwebs with his lofty plume', but a shock that reminds us just how far from Mrs Radcliffe we have come; how completely viable, in any human setting, the vision has been made to be. In Keats, literature can become the most effective vehicle of reality.

The best insight into the true nature of the poem is also the earliest, that of Leigh Hunt. For me, Hunt is a wholly benign influence on Keats's poetic make-up, notwithstanding that Keats's own repudiation of him has been fervently echoed ever since, and I think him Keats's best critic as well. When he

[23] Garrod, *Keats*, op. cit.

remarks that Keats 'sympathised with the lowliest commonplace', we feel that this is the real bond between the two writers
and that it unites them with a third, whose sympathy with the
commonplace was indeed meticulous—James Joyce. Hunt not
only writes of 'the present palpable reality of *The Eve of St Agnes*',
as opposed to 'the less generally characteristic majesty of
Hyperion', but he also understands the nature of Keats's
language in the poem, and how its 'beauties', so far from being
merely luxuriant and richly coloured, have a penetrating and
revealing power that draws out to indefinite limits the
perspective of reality.

> Northward he turneth through a little door,
> And scarce three steps, ere Music's golden tongue
> Flatter'd to tears this aged man and poor . . .

Hunt has this to say of these lines about the Beadsman.

A true poet is by nature a metaphysician: he feels instinctively what
others get at by long searching. In this word *flattery* is the whole theory
of the secret of tears, which are the tributes, more or less worthy, of
self-pity to self-love. Whenever we shed tears we take pity on
ourselves, and we feel, if we do not consciously say so, that we deserve
to have the pity taken. In many cases the pity is just and the self-love
not to be construed unhandsomely.[24]

I suppose this might be felt to be a mere flight of critical
garrulity, typical of its period, and telling us more about Hunt
himself than about either the Beadsman or Keats's poetry. I
must admit to being both impressed and delighted by its
shrewd warmth—'more or less worthy' is particularly neat
—but the special interest of it for us is surely its close resemblance, as critical appraisal, to the way in which Coleridge,
Hazlitt, and Hunt himself, were recording at this time their
perceptions about Shakespeare. It is a type of criticism that
illuminates both authors but which would be lost on any other
Romantic poet; a type of insight whose value lies in exhibiting
and expatiating on a general truth implicit in a concentration of
artful language. A general truth, for it tells us nothing of Keats
himself, just as the similar perceptions of Coleridge and others
seemingly tell us nothing about Shakespeare. In the poetry of

---

[24] Leigh Hunt, *Imagination and Fancy, or Selections from the English Poets*.

Wordsworth or Byron there are concentrations of meaning which can be enlarged on so as to tell us much about those poets, and hence perhaps about the human situation, but they lack the anonymity which is so complete here, and to which Hunt unconsciously pays the greatest compliment he can by reflecting on a meaning as he would reflect on one in Shakespeare.

In showing the scope of the poem, these meanings that reveal themselves through the nature of Keats's language are even more important than the evident symbolic setting of warmth and cold, darkness and light, ecstasy and deprivation. As in most great imaginative works which we agree for convenience to call 'symbolic', the perspective of linguistic meaning humanizes and elaborates the more elementary and static significance of symbol: a phrase like 'bright dulness', for example, with which Keats describes the revelry in the castle, contributes as much to the epiphany of the story as the snow outside. As Hunt admiringly implies, it is by meanings of this sort that the Beadsman becomes a human being, and not a mere symbol of age and renunciation. And so it is with the other characters. Their individuality is all there in embryo, and it surrounds them with the freedom and the scope which would be a condition of further more detailed characterization. Madeleine herself is not 'what the woman is', in D. H. Lawrence's sense,[25] but a particular girl in a general situation, created from literature—the 'lap of legends old'—and from the intensity of Keats's vision of warmth and love in the dark night of human destiny. When

> She danc'd along with vague regardless eyes

we see her as we see Natasha and Jane Bennett, yet the brilliant stanzas open to reveal an impersonal glimpse into the divided nature of the dream of love, the simultaneous attraction and recoil.

> Innumerable of stains and splendid dyes,
> As are the tiger-moth's deep-damask'd wings;
> And in the midst, 'mong thousand heraldries,

[25] D. H. Lawrence, *Letters*, p. 198. (Lawrence is saying that he is not interested, as a novelist, in 'what the woman feels', but only in 'what the woman is'.)

And twilight saints and dim emblazonings,
A shielded scutcheon blush'd with blood of queens and kings.

Blush'd has a typically Keatsian weight; it universalizes the
erotic not only among the living but back into the past, calling
up the fears and desires that once warmed the dead. It concentrates Madeleine's livingness, as Porphyro's is concentrated in
'The carved angels, ever eager-eyed' who *'star'd,* where upon
their heads the cornice rests'. As well as being the perfect
oxymoron for the two sides of desire, *tiger-moth* has a similarly
uncontrolled metaphorical life: it reminds me of images of
attraction and pursuit in the 'warm darkness' of the later novels
of Henry James. The girl's impulse of withdrawal from this
dangerous world, into the old safety of sleep and childhood,
carries us too on the wings of metaphor.

> Flown, like a thought, until the morrow-day;
> Blissfully haven'd both from joy and pain;
> Clasp'd like a missal where swart Paynims pray;
> Blinded alike from sunshine and from rain,
> As though a rose should shut, and be a bud again.

Though stilled for now by the echo of *Venus and Adonis*—'Love
comforteth like sunshine after rain'—the words *clasp'd* and
blinded promise the struggle and tears, the necessary onset of
life, promise it, as it were, without speaking. The precision of
these words (in a stanza which has been called escapist and
sentimental) belongs not to Keats but to his story.

The distinction could be illustrated by comparing such
effects of universalized life, and sexual life in particular, in
Keats's poem with those in 'Le Cimetière marin'. There the
peremptory, indeed jaunty, precision of Valéry's language
(which in the sixteenth stanza, for example, strikes me as only
just pausing on the brink of a really disheartening and mechanical vulgarity)[26] remains with, and emphasizes, the presence of
the poet, and does not initiate the anonymous tale of humanity

---

[26] Les cris aigus des filles chatouillées,
Les yeux, les dents, les paupières mouillées,
Le sein charmant qui joue avec le feu,
Le sang qui brille aux lèvres qui se rendent,
Les derniers dons, les doigts qui les défendent,
Tout va sous terre et rentre dans le jeu!

that seems implicit in every word of 'The Eve of St Agnes'.
Keats thought the poet must 'die into life', and here he is indeed
'dying into' the life of his story, though it is very different from
his imagination of the process in the weighty symbolism of the
second *Hyperion*. It is perhaps in the nature of the true process
that he could not realize when it happened.

I will not continue to labour this significance of meaning, but
in view of the critics' deprecation, and Keats's own inevitable
modesty, I would emphasize how wholly dramatic is the
balance it makes between the particular and the general,
the real persons and the universalizing vision. Consider
Madeleine's simplicity of action, her apparently random
involvement in commonplace detail.

> Her falt'ring hand upon the balustrade,
> Old Angela was feeling for the stair,
> When Madeleine, St Agnes' charmed maid,
> Rose, like a mission'd spirit, unaware:
> With silver taper's light, and pious care,
> She turn'd, and down the aged gossip led
> To a safe level matting.

The last word drags a weight of the commonplace that is almost
sublime. It is a commonplace that gets into the heroine; her
kindness is immensely ordinary. She is the girl whose lover will
advise her to put on 'warm clothing' before they make the
escape; the girl whose destiny, whose womanhood and death,
are shown forth in the last stanza, a coda that seems to play
without a sound the chords of some majestic fictional ending.
'But though she was glad, he presently discovered that, beneath
her hood, she was in tears. It is to be feared that with the union
. . . she was about to enter, these were not the last she was
destined to shed.'[27]

> And they are gone: ay, ages long ago
> These lovers fled away into the storm . . .

The rumours of warmth and cold, the living and the dead, echo
backwards and forwards and vanish in darkness.

> Out went the taper as she hurried in;
> Its little smoke, in pallid moonshine, died.

[27] Henry James, *The Bostonians* (the concluding sentence).

It may be objected that a story cannot tell us so much of human life when it has day-dream and fantasy at its heart. But Keats was never more successful at realizing the interdependence of the two. The dreams of Madeleine and Porphyro are brought together; their fantasies coincide, but the pathos of their isolation is inseparable from the warmth of their meeting, is at one with the storm and the snow and the motionless figures in their icy hoods and mails.

> For on the midnight came a tempest fell.
> More sooth for that his close rejoinder flows
> Into her burning ear—and still the spell
> Unbroken guards her in serene repose.
> With her wild dream he mingled as a rose
> Marryeth its odour to a violet.
> Still, still she dreams—louder the frost wind blows
> Like Love's alarum pattering the sharp sleet
> Against the window-panes; St Agnes' moon hath set.

Well after the poem was written, and in a truculent and self-protective mood, Keats found it necessary to insist to his friend Wodehouse that the physical union of the lovers is described here. It is possible to wonder whether the imagination of the poem, as written, really bears him out? 'More sooth for that his close rejoinder flows'—it is this line, with its marvellous Keatsian concretion (*sooth* has a double meaning, echoing 'jellies soother than the creamy curd') which gives us the lovers' embrace. What follows—if Keats's own interpretation be insisted on—is figurative, and feebly so; and Keats's love-scenes are never figurative, nor is anything in the rest of the poem. If figurative, the lines are vulgar in a sense alien to Keats (we find it in Rossetti's *The House of Life*) and I suspect that the distaste for much of the poem which is apparently often felt nowadays, has its origin here.[28] Once again the influence of

---

[28] Cf. 'The Stealthy School of Criticism' (*Athenaeum*, (1871)), Rossetti's answer to Buchanan's attack on 'The Fleshly School of Poetry'. He tells us that in the sonnets (e.g. 'Love-Sweetness') 'all the passionate and just delights of the body are declared —somewhat figuratively it is true, but unmistakably—to be naught if not ennobled by the concurrence of the soul at all times'. The point is surely admirable (D. H. Lawrence himself would have whole-heartedly agreed with it) but the word *figuratively* goes a long way towards explaining the modern misunderstanding of, and antipathy for, the Victorian rendering of sex.

Byron, of a queasy compound of Byron and Keats, has a disastrous effect. Nothing is worse for Keats than the convention, already stirring in his time and tyrannical in our own, that the truth must be told, that it is 'weak-sided' and cowardly to leave anything out, especially anything so apparently important as this. But it is an illusory importance, for the intensity of the poem's imagination of love is conveyed by vision and not by fact; the relation of the lovers is imagined in terms of their wishes and their dreams.

The Dead seems to me an achievement very close to 'The Eve of St Agnes' in the nature and power of its vision: I should be tempted to call them the most remarkable, and in the broadest sense poetical, short stories in English. Joyce's mastery is of course entirely poised and self-conscious; the weight he gives to the commonplace is as elegant as in Keats it is instinctive, and yet the intensity of impersonal meaning in the language is as remarkable in the story as in the poem. Both have a ritual solidity of description, which somehow pledges that what one dreams and yearns for and regrets is as much a part of life as what one eats, that one's fantasies are as real as one's food. Joyce's dinner laid out is one for the dead to remember; his loving account of a Dublin musical party is the equivalent of Keats's tranced exploitation of the medieval and picturesque. The hero and heroine of *The Dead* dream of their past, which divides them as individuals and yet which in a strange and touching way also unites them and the others in a communion of living and a corresponding awareness of death. ' "I love to see the snow", said Aunt Julia sadly', a phrase which compresses the same meaning as the extinguished candle in 'The Eve of St Agnes'. Like the lovers, she is on her way to join the vast hosts of the dead. We cannot apprehend death, but we can perceive our relation to it here, with an intensity that does indeed, for the moment, 'make its disagreeables evaporate'. Both Joyce and Keats knew that what *is*, can and must be made beautiful by art, and Joyce's credo of the principle of beauty, even where it has not yet been imagined or apprehended, is an echo of Keats's own.[29]

[29] See *A Portrait of the Artist as a Young Man*, and *Critical Writings*, op. cit., p. 148. Also in the early essay 'Drama and Life' the para. (p. 43) beginning 'A yet more insidious claim is the claim for beauty'.

So far from its being 'elaborately fenced from all infection of reality', I have tried to show how 'The Eve of St Agnes' takes its place among moving and memorable fictions, and how its reality is of the same nature as theirs. It has supremely what Arnold called the power of natural interpretation, the power that 'calms and satisfies us as no other can'. Yet this phrase has its dangers, not much less so than Joyce's picture of 'the luminous silent stasis of aesthetic pleasure', for the point about the interpretative power is that it does *interpret*: the aesthetic diagnosis of art is irreproachable, but in concentrating on the end state it suggests—disastrously—that we can take a short cut. We can certainly agree that his poetry ultimately gives the rich calm of aesthetic satisfaction, but we must none the less beware of taking the aesthetic view of Keats. The Pre-Raphaelites did so, concentrating on his 'exquisite detail', and for them a line like 'My sleep had been embroidered with dim dreams' was the choicest example of his art. But it is the kind of line which, in Robert Bridges's phrase, 'displays its poetry rather than its meaning.'

Keats's poetry is in the meaning, and it is in a story which is filled with such meaning that he seems to me to achieve his masterpiece. But we must not forget that for him the poetry had to be in the meaning in a different and more direct sense, the sense in which for Wilfred Owen, a true descendant of Keats as Rossetti and the late romantics were not, the poetry of war could only be 'in the pity'. Owen's rich and Keatsian talent is in sharp contrast with the experience of war to which he felt that poetry must be offered up—'above all', he wrote, 'I am not concerned with poetry'. But his art transcended the use he wished to make of it, and became a majestic celebration of the eternity of man at war as well as a denunciation of the futility of war. 'Calm and satisfaction', 'the luminous stasis', cannot ultimately be kept out. His rich art has achieved a meaning much wider than the one required of it, and yet this greatness still depends on the urgency and simplicity of his purpose. There is a lesson in this for our reading of Keats.

Owen's poetry, like that of Keats, is inevitably on a grand scale—the scale of his feeling for those 'hearts grown great with shot'. It is this generosity, transcending the art of poetry, which antagonized Yeats, a firm believer in the need for a poet to be

master in his own house. But it does not need to express itself in
a conventionally 'grand' form, and I must admit to experien-
cing something of the same doubt about Owen's last and most
evidently impressive poem, 'Strange Meeting', that I feel about
the second *Hyperion*. It is a doubt which I hope takes the form of
humility, and in conclusion I should like to suggest that our
most disturbing apprehension of greatness in Keats (and, as an
illuminating parallel, in Owen) may be the singular kind of
uncertainty we have to feel about these poems, an uncertainty
which is not fully answered by the fact of untimely death.

For notwithstanding the conventional supremacy of the odes
(and they are really far less homogeneous, more typically
Keatsian than the convention implies), there is astonishingly
little general agreement about his best-known poems. Nothing
is more finally disconcerting about this most disconcerting of
our poets than our lack of·decision, and of accepted standards
of judgement, at moments when some sort of unanimity might
be expected. Is the passage from *The Fall of Hyperion* which I
have already quoted, and which ends with the comparison of
Moneta's eyes to 'the mild moon'

> Who comforts those she sees not, who knows not
> What eyes are upward cast.

—is such a passage, which Middleton Murry calls 'an
apprehension of an ultimate reality', and 'a wonderful symbol
of the unspeakable truth', the finest poetry or not? I have to
confess my sense of not knowing, and I can only hope that other
readers have experienced this peculiar kind of awed discom-
posure. It is certainly not just good poetry, and however
unaffirmed, our confidence in our own ability to tell the great
from the good in poetry is really pretty strong, but Keats upsets
it. That he does so seems to be not only because what I have had
to call 'badness' plays so strangely important a part in his total
meaning, and we look in vain for any trace of it here, but also
because here is the final proof that he has no poetic world of his
own, no aesthetic enclosure where he is a law unto himself, and
where we can recognize and appreciate at once his own special
kind of performance. His reality is not, after all, to be found in
one place. He does not 'know his station'. His power of loading

words with meaning is changed here into quite a different sort of potential, which remains enigmatic.

But one thing is certain—Keats could never have made the most of his genius. However good 'The Eve of St Agnes' may be—and I believe it to be his masterpiece—he could never have continued to write more poetic tales, or more odes, each richer and more full of satisfactions than the last. Nothing held him to the *mode*, as Shakespeare was held to the theatre, and whatever may appear to the contrary his lack of belief in writing poetry, just because he had the genius to write it, was fundamental. It has been argued that unless we believe in his emergent power to express what he so directly and deeply felt about 'suffering humanity', we degrade him to the status of a 'minor poet'.[30] No poet, perhaps, can be labelled minor who does not in some sense acquiesce in being so, and Keats did not, but—and this is the truth that must shape our last understanding of him—he did not acquiesce in the status of being a poet at all. We need not pretend that we have to place him as one.

[30] *John Keats: A Reassessment.* (Introductory note.)

9. TENNYSON'S METHODS OF COMPOSITION

BY CHRISTOPHER RICKS

IN 1931 Sir Charles Tennyson, the poet's grandson, published a volume of *Unpublished Early Poems* by Alfred Tennyson. A passage from Sir Charles's introduction provides my title and theme. Nobody has done more for Tennyson studies than he has; it is a pleasure to pay tribute to him in the month of his 87th birthday—and it is to be hoped that such a tribute may counter any accusation that what now needs to be said by way of preamble shows a lack of piety.

Our evidence for Tennyson's methods of composition is, of course, his manuscripts. They are scattered all over the world —from the Public Library in Adelaide, South Australia, to the University of Hawaii (what better home could there be for the manuscript of 'The Lotos-Eaters'?). The major collections are three. The Tennyson Research Centre at Lincoln has a superb collection of letters and biographical material, including Tennyson's library and those of his father and of his brother Charles. The Houghton Library at Harvard has a superb collection of poetical manuscripts—and so does Trinity College, Cambridge.

But the Trinity manuscripts are under interdiction: they may not be copied or quoted *in perpetuity*—restrictions dating from 1924, when they were presented by the poet's son, Hallam Lord Tennyson. It has to be conceded, reluctantly, that the wording of the restrictions is unambiguous; the college is not, in my opinion, misinterpreting the restrictions, nor are its librarians discourteous to scholars. Indeed, the arguments for maintaining the restrictions are real enough. Piety proclaims that the wishes of benefactors should be heeded—and shrewdness murmurs that otherwise potential benefactors will be scared away. During the furore in 1964 about Mrs Phyllis Grosskurth's excellent life of John Addington Symonds, the Librarian of

Indiana University married morality to expediency in a letter to *The Times Literary Supplement* (31 December 1964):

There is indeed a very real danger that executors of literary estates, or of political figures, will hesitate before depositing controversial material with institutions if testamentary and other stipulations are to be blithely ignored. . . .

The ethical point for custodians seems clear. Either respect the restrictions on use, or simply do not accept the material in the first place.

'Blithely ignored'—few librarians ever do anything blithely. Nevertheless the case for soberly setting aside (not blithely ignoring) the Trinity restrictions is a very strong one. For the fact is that both the present Lord Tennyson and Sir Charles wish the restrictions to be relaxed. The reasons: that Tennyson permitted his son Hallam to publish variants, and Hallam himself published poems from these manuscripts. That Tennyson would probably have destroyed the manuscripts if he had dreaded quotation. That, although Tennyson disliked variant readings, he also said: 'I like those old Variorum Classics—all the Notes make the Text look precious.'[1] By now Tennyson himself is a classic.

But the wishes of the poet's descendants are not being met. One consequence is that there can be no authoritative correction of the many errors in transcription which Hallam Tennyson himself made in publishing poems from these manuscripts. In 1913 he published a fragment about Semele,[2] which begins:

> I wish'd to see Him. Who may feel
> His light and love? He comes.

'Love' is an error; the manuscript clearly reads: 'Who may feel / His light and . . .'—but the correct reading may not be quoted. Since apparently no other manuscript of 'Semele' survives, an editor has either to perpetuate the error 'love', or to amend it without being able to cite his authority. In the circumstances, one is tempted to go in for crossword-clues: this is an evil setback.

[1] *Tennyson and His Friends*, ed. Hallam Tennyson (1911), p. 147.
[2] *The Works of Tennyson*, ed. Hallam Tennyson (1913), p. xxiv.

Again, it seems unlikely that Tennyson would really have preferred to see his poem 'Armageddon' printed in 1931 (and in my forthcoming edition) from the damaged Harvard manuscript (which has grave lacunae in the first nine lines), rather than permit the supply of the missing words from the Trinity manuscript of the poem. The Trinity manuscripts include many unpublished poems and fragments, as well as fascinating drafts of Tennyson's best poems and a manuscript of *In Memoriam* (this latter presented by Lady Simeon in 1897). Not only do the restrictions make a definitive edition impossible, they also put great obstacles in the way of any edition. A detailed scholarly examination of the manuscripts, which is *not* forbidden by the donor's conditions, is rendered almost impossible by the ban on copying anything from the manuscripts, even though such material would not be released but would be used solely to investigate the manuscripts themselves. As it is, anyone studying the Trinity manuscripts has to hope to hold in his head all of Tennyson's published and unpublished poetry. The restrictions even encourage silly scandal about what may lurk in such closely guarded manuscripts—dark talk, whether about Tennyson's love for Arthur Hallam or about his (apocryphal) skill at the *risqué* limerick.

So the simple rule, 'Either respect the restrictions on use, or simply do not accept the material in the first place', does not fit such a situation. For one thing, restrictions in perpetuity are altogether different from those which specify a lapse of time (say, to protect friends or relations). Should a college accept manuscripts on conditions which in fact constitute a permanent denial of the *raison d'être* of a college: free scholarly enquiry?

Nor do all reputable libraries concur with Trinity. The Bodleian has a manuscript of *Gareth and Lynette*, presented by Hallam Tennyson in 1922 on broadly the same conditions. A plea, supported by the family, has recently persuaded the library to relax the conditions. An optimistic letter then went to the University Library at Cambridge, where there is an important manuscript of *The Princess*, again with the same restrictions. Whereupon the Syndics of the Library decided that they had lately been rather remiss in enforcing the restrictions—henceforth the manuscript would be visible only in a glass case. My preamble does not wish to be shrill—it puts a case, and draws attention to some of the factors which still hinder Tennyson scholarship.

But is Tennyson criticism in any way affected by the obstacles to Tennyson scholarship? Yes, in so far as one of his major claims is simply that of craftsmanship. Whatever his limitations (in depth or range), his best poems are consummately made. And nothing can so sharpen understanding of what it is for a poem to be well made, as to study the processes by which it reached its final form. Why is that particular word so effective?—an answer may be discoverable in the other possibilities which the poet weighed but found wanting.

Few people now believe that the Victorians were 'complacent', and of all Tennyson's freedoms from complacency none is more striking than his refusal to rest content with his skill, to rest on his laurels. It is recorded that

A friend once expressed to Housman the hope that [his] paper on Swinburne might be published, and, on hearing that it was to be destroyed after his death, ventured to suggest that if Housman thought it bad he would already have destroyed it himself. 'I do not think it bad,' said Housman; 'I think it not good enough for me'.[3]

Tennyson would never have spoken with such witty hauteur, but his revisions show at its best the perfectionist's restlessness —the question always forming itself, not as 'Is this good?', but as 'Is this good enough?'

Many poets would have found no difficulty in resting satisfied with 'Tithon' (the early draft of 'Tithonus'), or with the 1830 version of 'Mariana'. There are very few occasions when Tennyson alters a passage for the worse, and such occasions are the result, not of faulty craftsmanship, but of timidity, a wish to retreat from a notion that might offend. There are two such cases in *In Memoriam*. In the first edition (1850), Tennyson wrote:

> But brooding on the dear one dead,
> And all he said of things divine,
> (And dear as sacramental wine
> To dying lips is all he said). . . .   (XXXVII.)

---

[3] A. S. F. Gow, *A. E. Housman: A Sketch* (1936), p. 21.

But *The Times* (28 November 1851) found this shocking: 'Can the writer satisfy his own conscience with respect to these verses? . . . For our part, we should consider no confession of regret too strong for the hardihood that indicated them.' The offending words were changed:

> (And dear to me as sacred wine
> To dying lips is all he said). . . .

That 'to me' introduces an enfeebling tone of doubt or of the apologetically personal; there is now a disconcerting swaying ('to me . . . to dying lips'). And Tennyson had meant what he had written: sacramental, not sacred—the emphasis was on a solemn ceremony not only sacred in itself but having the power to make sacred. Tennyson would have done better to brazen it out, to stand by his fiercely truthful hyperbole.

A similar thing happens with the pre-publication history of *In Memoriam*. In the first edition, section CXXIX ended:

> Strange friend, past, present, and to be,
>   Loved deeplier, darklier understood;
>   Behold I dream a dream of good
> And mingle all the world with thee.

Skilful writing, yet slightly swathed in the Tennysonian. 'Behold', 'dream a dream', 'mingle': these here have something of the plangent tremulousness which comes when Tennyson is writing with elegance rather than with energy. The lines perfectly fit Gerard Manley Hopkins's account of 'Parnassian verse', which he sketched out with particular application to Tennyson:

It can only be spoken by poets, but it is not in the highest sense poetry. . . . It is spoken *on and from the level* of a poet's mind, not, as in the other case, when the inspiration which is the gift of genius, raises him above himself. . . . Great men, poets I mean, have each their own dialect as it were of Parnassian, formed generally as they go on writing, and at last,—this is the point to be marked,—they can see things in this Parnassian way and describe them in this Parnassian tongue, without further effort of inspiration. In a poet's particular kind of Parnassian lies most of his style, of his manner, of his mannerism if you like.[4]

---

[4] *Further Letters*, ed. Claude Coller Abbott (2nd edn, 1956), pp. 216–17.

And, after quoting from 'Enoch Arden', Hopkins sums up: 'Now it is a mark of Parnassian that one could conceive oneself writing it if one were the poet.'

> Behold I dream a dream of good
> And mingle all the world with thee.

But if Tennyson is so remarkable at perfecting his own poetry, how is it that in the trial edition of *In Memoriam*, printed for his own use a few months before the first edition, this stanza is so much better? Because Tennyson became concerned, not to consummate his wording, but to retreat from a possibly offensive notion.

> Strange friend, past, present, and to be,
>   Loved deeplier, darklier understood;
>   Let me not lose my faith in good
> Lest I make less my love for thee.

No Parnassian, no Tennysonianisms, there. Instead, an austere confession that for Tennyson what counted supremely was not his faith in good but his love for Arthur Hallam. Because of the very mildness of tone, the effect is sharp to the point of paradox, and Tennyson, as he gazed at the trial edition, must suddenly have realized that he had virtually said: 'I could not love Honour so much, loved I not Hallam more.' It is not surprising, however unfortunate, that he replaced the lines with the ripe fluency of Parnassian verse. But these two changes for the worse are exceptions to the general rule. His wording was always considered; sometimes it was too considerate.

In 1931 Sir Charles drew attention to 'one curious characteristic of Tennyson's methods of composition' (p. x):

I have noted in these early poems a number of lines which the poet used again, often years afterwards, in quite different contexts, in his published work. It is known and has been remarked that Tennyson often stored observations and similes for long periods before finally working them into his poems, and this storage of actual lines from early compositions is a fresh illustration of the same tendency. The remarkable thing is that the lines, when finally taken from storage, fit so naturally and aptly into their new context that they are often among the best passages in the poems in which they are employed.

In what follows, I shall offer some new examples of such self-borrowing in Tennyson; my major concern is with Tennyson's poetic skill, but I want also to suggest that such self-borrowings are relevant to Tennyson's most impassioned subject: time. 'He was', said Humphry House[5] 'an Aeonian poet; one on whom the consciousness of time bore like a burden.' It was on the subject of time that Tennyson wrote those lines of his which are most likely to stand against time.

The point is implicit in a famous example of self-borrowing in Wordsworth. His sonnet 'Mutability' tells how the outward forms of truth

> drop like the tower sublime
> Of yesterday, which royally did wear
> His crown of weeds, but could not even sustain
> Some casual shout that broke the silent air,
> Or the unimaginable touch of Time.

Why is it moving to learn that the last line, 'the unimaginable touch of Time', had been part of a 'Fragment of a "Gothic" Tale' about thirty years earlier? Mainly because of the sureness of Wordsworth's sense of context, the life which here pours into the cliché 'the *touch* of Time'. But perhaps we are moved too by the poem's subject, 'Mutability', by the fact that despite mutability and the touch of time, for Wordsworth something important endured unchanging and still new: the line of poetry which he had written thirty years before.

Of course, the point is not, strictly, literary criticism; it is a point about biography, or methods of composition—it concerns the question why, of all the good lines which Wordsworth had available from his juvenilia, it should have been this one which later meant so much to him and which he was able to use so beautifully. In discussing Tennyson's self-borrowings, I shall point in passing to the frequency with which they concern time, and at the end try to bring together the implications of this.

Yet there is nothing which a poet can use which he cannot also abuse, and *Maud* provides important evidence that Tennyson's self-borrowings can lead to the heart of his failures as well as of his successes. As is well known, the germ of *Maud* was the poem

[5] *All in Due Time* (1955), p. 127.

'O! that 'twere possible', which Tennyson had written in 1833 or 1834, on the death of Arthur Hallam, and which he published in *The Tribute* in 1837. It was not until 1853 that he started seriously on *Maud*. It is not an accident that one reaches for an organic metaphor like 'germ' to describe the relationship of 'O! that 'twere possible' to the completed monodrama. What we find is not any change of context but the providing of a context. As originally published, 'O! that 'twere possible' had no dramatic or psychological setting; itself a cry, it cried out for one. That Tennyson was dissatisfied with it, is clear from his not including it in his volumes of 1842; by 1855, he had created its context.

Maud, then, shows the success of this method of composition, but it also shows us a failure. One section of *Maud* was bitterly ridiculed by many critics on publication, as falling far below the lyrical and psychological force of the rest: the song 'Go not, happy day' [I. xvii], which the hero exclaims in his love of Maud:

> Go not, happy day,
>   From the shining fields,
> Go not, happy day,
>   Till the maiden yields. . . .
> Pass the happy news,
>   Blush it thro' the West;
> Till the red man dance
>   By his red cedar-tree,
> And the red man's babe
>   Leap, beyond the sea.
> Blush from West to East,
>   Blush from East to West,
> Till the West is East,
>   Blush it thro' the West. . . .

And so on. The objection to this song is not to its happiness but to its being ill written: the graceless hyperbole which has the red man's babe leaping because of a love-match in England, and the cumbrous repetitions, uncharacteristically devoid of lyrical feeling.

There are indeed true moments of happiness in *Maud*—the section which follows this song ('I have led her home, my love, my only friend') is one of them. But 'Go not, happy day' is written in the wrong style; why does the hero fall into this nursery-rhyming? If we ask where we have met such a tone before, the answer is in some of the songs which Tennyson interpolated in the third edition of *The Princess* (1850). What has not been pointed out is that 'Go not, happy day' was originally one of the songs for *The Princess*;[6] Tennyson found no place for it there, and rather than waste it he made a place for it in *Maud* (made, not found). The tone resembles that of this song from *The Princess*:

> And blessings on the falling out
>   That all the more endears,
> When we fall out with those we love
>   And kiss again with tears![7]

The affinity is evident in the two poems which Tennyson published as 'Child-Songs' in 1880, but which he notes were originally for *The Princess*:

> Minnie and Winnie
>   Slept in a shell.
> Sleep, little ladies!
>   And they slept well.

But such a tone was not right for *Maud*—and we can now see why the red man's babe appeared. Not because of any aptness to *Maud* but because of *The Princess*. Almost all the intercalated songs include a baby; indeed, Tennyson added them expressly in order to emphasize the importance of the baby in the story of *The Princess*. But in transferring 'Go not, happy day', Tennyson was for once under the ill influence of his habit.[8]

For the habit at its best, we may turn to some of the finest lines he ever wrote, from perhaps his finest poem, 'Ulysses':

> To follow knowledge like a sinking star,
> Beyond the utmost bound of human thought.

In their context as Ulysses speaks (a context soaked in a consciousness of time):

---

[6] See the manuscript at the University Library, Cambridge.

[7] Self-borrowings lead to wheels within wheels. Tennyson dropped these four lines from *The Princess* in 1851, temporarily; the Harvard MS of *Maud* shows that he thought of using them in *Maud* at this time.

[8] The unevenness of 'The Sailor Boy' (1861) is explained, though not justified, by the fact that it too was originally a song for *The Princess*.

> Life piled on life
> Were all too little, and of one to me
> Little remains: but every hour is saved
> From that eternal silence, something more,
> A bringer of new things; and vile it were
> For some three suns to store and hoard myself,
> And this gray spirit yearning in desire
> To follow knowledge like a sinking star,
> Beyond the utmost bound of human thought.

In a Trinity notebook, these two lines form part of quite a different poem, 'Tiresias', which Tennyson did not complete and publish until 1885 but which he had begun at the same time as 'Ulysses': October 1833, the month in which he heard the news of Hallam's death. As published, 'Tiresias' begins:

> I wish I were as in the years of old,
> While yet the blessed daylight made itself
> Ruddy thro' both the roofs of sight, and woke
> These eyes, now dull, but then so keen to seek
> The meanings ambush'd under all they saw . . .

But in the Trinity manuscript, Tiresias had been in youth keen not 'to seek the meanings', but keen

> To follow knowledge like a sinking star,
> Beyond the utmost bound of human thought.

(Again, in 'Tiresias', the oppressive sense of time.) It is the context which triumphantly justifies Tennyson's decision as to where to use his resonant lines. What has a star to do with Tiresias? Whereas Ulysses is speaking to his mariners, and mariners do indeed watch and follow stars. And what had Tiresias to do with bounds and horizons? Whereas in his last voyage Ulysses yearns

> To sail beyond the sunset, and the baths
> Of all the western stars, until I die.

Again, notice how the contrast between Ulysses' aged frame and his burning spirit comes out in a juxtaposition absent from the context in 'Tiresias': the play of 'this gray spirit'[9] against the 'sinking star' (and of the 'suns' against the 'star'). All these

[9] Tennyson changed this from 'this old heart yet' (Kemble MS).

details bind the lines into their context, and so does the echo of
Dante in 'knowledge'. As Tennyson said, 'Ulysses' has as its
primary source the speech by Ulysses in Dante's *Inferno*, urging
his companions to their last voyage. Tennyson's 'knowledge'
calls up Dante's *canoscenza*. The difference between the use of
those two lines in 'Tiresias' and in 'Ulysses' is the difference
between talent and genius. It is Tennyson's sense of context
which releases all the energies of the lines.

The same is true of another of his great lines, again in a
context heavy with time: 'The phantom circle of a moaning
sea.' The scene is the last battle in *The Passing of Arthur*
(1869)—a scene likely to bring out the best in a poet whose
genius had shown itself more than forty years earlier in a poem
on Armageddon.

> Then rose the King and moved his host by night,
> And ever push'd Sir Modred, league by league,
> Back to the sunset bound of Lyonnesse—
> A land of old upheaven from the abyss
> By fire, to sink into the abyss again;
> Where fragments of forgotten peoples dwelt,
> And the long mountains ended in a coast
> Of ever-shifting sand, and far away
> The phantom circle of a moaning sea.

Could any location be more apt to 'this last, dim, weird battle
of the west'?—where the fighters are themselves phantoms in
the mist, where not only the sea is moaning, and where the life
of the king comes full circle?[10] And yet only a year before
(1868), Tennyson had printed, though not published, the line
as part of the last section of *The Lover's Tale*. In the trial edition,
which he suppressed once more, we hear of

> A dismal hostel in a dismal land,
> A world of reed and rush, and far away
> The phantom circle of a moaning sea.

How fortunate that Tennyson somehow knew not to waste the
line on such a context. Not, in fact, that he had created the line
for *The Lover's Tale* either. More than thirty years before, about

---

[10] Tennyson frequently used, in symbolic contexts, such words as circle, sphere, orb,
and round (all as verbs as well as nouns).

1833, it had formed the climax of his little poem describing Mablethorpe on the Lincolnshire coast. In 1850 he published these 'Lines', but without the second stanza which survives in a Trinity manuscript. The stanza may not be quoted, but it contains all but verbatim the line 'The phantom circle of a moaning sea'. In the fullness of time, Tennyson found for the line the right fullness of context.

For Tennyson, context often meant the mingling of a landscape with a mood. It was Arthur Hallam in August 1831 (*The Englishman's Magazine*) who praised Tennyson's 'vivid, picturesque delineation of objects, and the peculiar skill with which he holds all of them *fused*, to borrow a metaphor from science, in a medium of strong emotion'. The Harvard manuscript of *The Princess* includes these lines in its Prologue:

> Within, the sward
> Was kept like any lawn, but all about
> Large ivy suck'd the joinings of the stones,
> Beneath like knots of snakes.

No fusion, because that muscularity, that mood, answers to nothing in *The Princess*. In *The Marriage of Geraint*, Tennyson fuses description and mood, a mood haunted by time:

> And high above a piece of turret stair,
> Worn by the feet that now were silent, wound
> Bare to the sun, and monstrous ivy-stems
> Claspt the gray walls with hairy-fibred arms,
> And suck'd the joining of the stones, and look'd
> A knot, beneath, of snakes, aloft, a grove.

Sometimes such a gift for placing may crystallize into a discreet pun. We know from Hallam Tennyson's *Memoir*[11] that the following fragment was jotted down at Torquay:

> as the little thrift
> Trembles in perilous places o'er the deep.

But this jotting about the plant thrift was not used by Tennyson until he could engage with the other sense of thrift. His poem 'Sea Dreams' deals with his disastrous investing of all his funds in Dr Matthew Allen's wood-carving scheme:

[11] (1897), i. 465.

> Small were his gains, and hard his work; besides,
> Their slender household fortunes (for the man
> Had risk'd his little) like the little thrift,
> Trembled in perilous places o'er a deep . . .

At the other extreme from such a tiny instance of self-borrowing comes the incorporation *en bloc* of a whole passage of blank verse. Context here means pace—Tennyson is a master of pace. Who would have thought that the finest lines in the magnificent closing passage of *The Princess* were originally part of another poem written fifteen years before? The tempo, with its superb rallentando and its tranquil finality, is perfect:

> the walls
> Blacken'd about us, bats wheel'd, and owls whoop'd,
> And gradually the powers of the night,
> That range above the region of the wind,
> Deepening the courts of twilight broke them up
> Thro' all the silent spaces of the worlds,
> Beyond all thought into the Heaven of Heavens.
>
> Last little Lilia, rising quietly,
> Disrobed the glimmering statue of Sir Ralph
> From those rich silks, and home well-pleased we went.

Tempo depends here on time as well as timing. 'Last', 'quietly': the full potentialities of the lines emerge only in this context, as can be seen if we look back at them in *The Lover's Tale* of 1832, which Tennyson suppressed before publication:

> When thou and I, Cadrilla, thou and I
> Were borne about the bay or sitting gazed
> Till gradually the powers of the night
> That range above the region of the wind
> Deepening the courts of twilight, broke them up
> Thro' all the silent spaces of the worlds
> Beyond all thought, into the Heaven of Heavens.
> When thou and I, Cadrilla, thou and I
> Were moored by some low cavern, while without
> Through the long dark . . .

And so on, in a deft passage of Tennysonian verse. But those central lines needed to be something more than merely one among many memories; it was not till the end of *The Princess* that they found the placing which, as it were, they were made for.

A similar sense of what really constitutes the *end* of a poem informs Coleridge's great poem on time: 'Frost at Midnight'. Humphrey House[12] pointed out how finely Coleridge changed the ending; in the version of 1798 the poem had ended:

> Or whether the secret ministry of cold
> Shall hang them up in silent icicles,
> Quietly shining to the quiet moon,
> Like those, my babe! which ere tomorrow's warmth
> Have capp'd their sharp keen points with pendulous drops,
> Will catch thine eye, and with their novelty
> Suspend thy little soul; then make thee shout,
> And stretch and flutter from thy mother's arms
> As thou wouldst fly for very eagerness.

This, in House's words,

was a stopping rather than an end; for once the vista of new domestic detail was opened there was no reason why it should not be indefinitely followed, with increasing shapelessness. This was informal and conversational as family talk. The decision to stop at line 74 was one of the best artistic decisions Coleridge ever made. For not only is the present ending one of the finest pieces of short descriptive writing in the language, intricate and yet at the same time sparsely clear, compressing so much of the moods of various weather; but it also perfectly rounds the movement of the mind which has been the poem's theme:

> Therefore all seasons shall be sweet to thee,
> Whether the summer clothe the general earth
> With greenness, or the redbreast sit and sing
> Betwixt the tufts of snow on the bare branch
> Of mossy apple-tree, while the nigh thatch
> Smokes in the sun-thaw; whether the eave-drops fall
> Heard only in the trances of the blast,
> Or if the secret ministry of frost
> Shall hang them up in silent icicles,
> Quietly shining to the quiet Moon.

Tennyson's artistic decision was different in form but the same in intention—like Coleridge, he found an end rather than a stopping, and perfectly rounded the movement of *The Princess*.

[12] *Coleridge* (1953), pp. 82–3.

Such self-borrowings not only reveal Tennyson's sense of context and his preoccupation with time; they also underline the extreme rashness of the generalizations as to his development, the growth or decline of his powers. The little poem 'Poets and Critics' was not published till his posthumous volume of 1892, and its manner suggests that it encapsulates his long battling with the reviewers:

> Year will graze the heel of year,
> But seldom comes the poet here,
> And the Critic's rarer still.

Yet it was written sixty years before, and is Tennyson's reaction, not to a lifetime of reviewing, but to the reviews of his earliest volumes. And for Tennyson, year had indeed grazed the heel of year before he came to publish it.

It is the same with the honeymoon song that introduces the late poem 'The Ring', published in 1889, a song which must not be taken as evidence that his lyrical gift had astonishingly survived (or sadly declined) since it in fact dates from 1833.

> Shall not *my* love last,
> Moon, with you,
> For ten thousand years
> Old and new?

Love may last, as the poem itself had lasted—though this could be known to none but the poet and his immediate circle. The 'Ode on the Death of the Duke of Wellington' (1852) is imbued with a sense of the passing of an era:

> For tho' the Giant Ages heave the hill
> And break the shore, and evermore
> Make and break, and work their will . . .

But this vision of time was one which had come to Tennyson far back in time, twenty years before; it is the Soul, in a manuscript of *The Palace of Art*, who sees this vision:

> Yet saw she Earth laid open. Furthermore
> How the strong Ages had their will,
> A range of Giants breaking down the shore
> And heaving up the hill.

The convergence for Tennyson of self-borrowings and a preoccupation with time is implicit in two examples furnished by Sir Charles. The early unpublished poem 'An Idle Rhyme' provided a line for *In Memoriam* [XCV. 40]—the line is 'The deep pulsations of the world', which in *In Memoriam* goes on: 'Æonian music measuring out / The steps of Time.' And the early poem 'Sense and Conscience' provided a simile for *The Lover's Tale* —the simile ponders youth and age:

> Ev'n the dull-blooded poppy-stem, 'whose flower,
> Hued with the scarlet of a fierce sunrise,
> Like to the wild youth of an evil prince,
> Is without sweetness, but who crowns himself
> Above the naked poisons of his heart
> In his old age.'

Yet, as these examples bring out, this is not the case of an artist who has outlived his gift and who is forced to clutch at his unpublished juvenilia—rather as James Thurber, when blind and unable to draw, is said to have devised new captions for his old drawings. In Tennyson the habit was a lifelong one, as is well known from the composition of his first notably successful poem, 'Timbuctoo', with which he won the Chancellor's Gold Medal at Cambridge in 1829. For this, 'he patched up an old poem on "The Battle of Armageddon"'; in fact the Trinity manuscript shows that about 120 lines, or roughly half of 'Timbuctoo', was lifted whole from 'Armageddon'.[13] It is characteristic of Tennyson that he went on to borrow from 'Timbuctoo' itself; one of its lines turns up in *The Lover's Tale*, and two lines in the 'Ode to Memory'. What is also characteristic is the subject of these further self-borrowings: 'A center'd glory-circled memory', and 'the lordly music flowing from / The illimitable years'.

There is no breach between the young Tennyson and the old. His first political pronouncement as a peer was the poem 'Freedom', published in, and dated, 1884. Sir Charles has pointed out that its closing stanza was taken from the poem 'Hail Briton' which Tennyson had written but not published fifty years before. And it is not just the closing stanza which was taken over; the Trinity manuscripts make clear that much of

[13] *Memoir*, i. 46. For an account of the Trinity MS (which differs considerably from the 1931 text), see my note in *Modern Language Review* lxi (1966), 23–4.

'Freedom' was culled from political poems of 1832–3. The political viewpoint is altogether consistent.[14] Robert Frost wrote:

> I never dared be radical when young
> For fear it would make me conservative when old.

But Tennyson had no need of this 'Precaution'; when he wished to speak as a septuagenarian, he simply published at last the words which he had written in his twenties.

For Tennyson there was never a breach between the political and the personal. Yet when a man's son dies, and he writes a poem about the death, one would expect all of that poem at least to be newly created. When Tennyson's son Lionel died on his way home from India in 1886, Tennyson's funeral poem began (as Sir Charles has noted) with a stanza which he had written more than fifty years before in 'Hail Briton'. 'To the Marquis of Dufferin and Ava' thanks the Viceroy for all he had done for Lionel.

> At times our Britain cannot rest,
>   At times her steps are swift and rash;
>   She moving, at her girdle clash
> The golden keys of East and West.
>
> Not swift or rash, when late she lent
>   The sceptres of her West, her East,
>   To one, that ruling has increased
> Her greatness and her self-content.

And so through masterly transitions to personal thanks.

But if we look back fifty years, we see that in the earlier context 'East and West' was no more than a ringing description of the British Empire; it had none of the personal aptness here found for it. Dufferin had been Ambassador in Constantinople and Viceroy in India; Lionel Tennyson had died visiting India on his work for the India Office. And once again the lines seem to have risen to Tennyson's mind because of their sense of time, of an era. 'Not swift or rash'—the words may, without flippancy, be applied to the habit of composition itself.

---

[14] 'England and America in 1782' (published 1872) dates from 1832–4. Even 'Riflemen Form' (published 1859) was not a reaction to an immediate crisis, but dates from 1852; see my note in *Review of English Studies* NS XV (1964), 401–4. On 'Hail Briton', see M. J. Donahue, *Publications of the Modern Language Association of America* lxiv (1949), 385–416.

For Tennyson, there had never been an era's end so unforgettable as the French Revolution—from his first to his last poems, it preys upon his mind. In 'Hail Briton', he has eight lines on revolution and time; these eight lines[15] he transferred to *In Memoriam*, CXIII, where they became some of the noblest lines which he wrote in praise of Hallam, whose death had removed a man of great political promise:

> Should licensed boldness gather force,
>   Becoming, when the time has birth,
>   A lever to uplift the earth
> And roll it in another course,
>
> With many shocks that come and go,
>   With agonies, with energies,
>   With overthrowings, and with cries,
> And undulations to and fro.

The political and the personal are here truly joined, in the converging of self-borrowing and the sense of time.

The deep biographical roots of his self-borrowing (its being not a convenience but a cast of mind) are evident in the impulse to borrow from similar contexts.[16] Take these lines about time, from *The Princess*:

>   all the rich to-come
> Reels, as the golden Autumn woodland reels
> Athwart the smoke of burning weeds.

Tennyson created these lines from the conclusion to *In Memoriam*, which in the Lincoln manuscript includes this stanza:

> We pace the stubble bare of sheaves,
>   We watch the brimming river steal
>   And half the golden woodland reel
> Athwart the smoke of burning leaves.

When Tennyson's mind went back and rescued those lines he was not simply gleaning natural description, he was reaching to the context of ideal married love (itself golden and autumnal).

---

[15] They are in the Harvard MS but not the Heath MS.

[16] Sir Charles observes that *In Memoriam*, XCV. 54–5, incorporates two descriptive lines from 'In deep and solemn dreams'. It may be added that the latter too is an elegiac poem, and that the former is one of Tennyson's greatest evocations of 'Æonian music measuring out / The steps of Time'.

In *The Princess*, the lines go on to 'My bride, / My wife, my life'. In the manuscript of *In Memoriam*, they describe how the wedding-guests stroll through the countryside after the marriage of Tennyson's sister. The change from 'burning leaves' to 'burning weeds' is a fine one, in its slight unexpectedness, and in the way in which it transforms 'weeds' into part of the golden scene.

Only one of Tennyson's notable poems has self-borrowing at its very heart. 'Edwin Morris' is one of the best of Tennyson's 'English Idyls', a distillation of memory. The speaker remembers his rambles by the lake with the poet Edwin Morris and the curate Edward Bull, and how they used to talk about love. The speaker's own love-affair with Letty Hill came to nothing—he simply was not rich enough. Tennyson here did not so much indict as deprecate 'The rentroll Cupid of our rainy isles', and he hit precisely the right note, neither soft nor bitter. In the perfect conclusion of the poem, it is the word 'smoulders' which does full justice both to the landscape and to the erotic memory:

> long ago
> I have pardon'd little Letty; not indeed,
> It may be, for her own dear sake but this,
> She seems a part of those fresh days to me;
> For in the dust and drouth of London life
> She moves among my visions of the lake,
> While the prime swallow dips his wing, or then
> While the gold-lily blows, and overhead
> The light cloud smoulders on the summer crag.

Elsewhere in the poem, in the character of Edwin Morris the poet, Tennyson wrote one of his most lucid and attractive pieces of self-criticism; he stood back from his own 'Parnassian' mannerisms, and treated them with ironical affection. Into the mouth of Edwin, Tennyson puts the words of early Tennyson, self-borrowing but now with self-criticism. He did not just make up lines of plangent self-indulgence (they might have become too much like parodies), he quoted his young self.

> And once I ask'd him of his early life,
> And his first passion; and he answer'd me;
> And well his words became him: was he not
> A full-cell'd honeycomb of eloquence
> Stored from all flowers? Poet-like he spoke.

We should not miss the irony in 'poet-like' and 'well his words became him'; and the self-regarding simile ('a full-cell'd honeycomb of eloquence / Stored from all flowers') was an indulgence which Tennyson had permitted himself in an early draft of 'The Gardener's Daughter'.

Then Edwin speaks; of these ten lines, all but two are from the manuscripts of 'The Gardener's Daughter', so that if we feel the effect is sonorously Tennysonian, Tennyson would have agreed:

> 'My love for Nature and my love for her,
> Of different ages, like twin-sisters grew,
> [Twin-sisters differently beautiful.
> To some full music rose and sank the sun,]
> And some full music seem'd to move and change
> With all the varied changes of the dark,
> And either twilight and the day between;
> For daily hope fulfill'd, to rise again
> Revolving toward fulfilment, made it sweet
> To walk, to sit, to sleep, to wake, to breathe.'

As Parnassian verse (lovely, incidentally, in its feeling for time), this is exquisite. But by this date Tennyson was dissatisfied with the Parnassian.

For Edwin's second speech, too, Tennyson found no need to create plangencies; once again he culled them from drafts of 'The Gardener's Daughter'. So here too is self-quotation:

> 'I would have hid her needle in my heart,
> To save her little finger from a scratch
> No deeper than the skin: my ears could hear
> Her lightest breath; her least remark was worth
> The experience of the wise. I went and came;
> Her voice fled always thro' the summer land;
> I spoke her name alone.'

But the poet Edwin was not allowed to rest satisfied; in a remarkable passage of self-criticism, the speaker bridles at the mannerisms:

> Were not his words delicious, I a beast
> To take them as I did? but something jarr'd;
> Whether he spoke too largely; that there seem'd
> A touch of something false, some self-conceit,

Or over-smoothness: howsoe'er it was,
He scarcely hit my humour, and I said:
'Friend Edwin, do not think yourself alone
Of all men happy . . .'

The poem 'Edwin Morris' is one of Tennyson's best on the power of time (seen here by him confidently, not tragically); it is also a poem which has at its heart his perennial habit of self-quotation, used here with a different kind of awareness and with humour.

It seems important that so many of these self-borrowings have to do with time, but there are three counter-arguments. First, that there are dangers in even speaking of Tennyson's 'characteristic' preoccupation with time—everybody is pre-occupied with time, and literary critics are always fudging up 'characteristics' of an author or a period which are simply common to humanity. Second, that if most of Tennyson's poems *are* about time, it is hardly surprising or significant that most of his self-borrowings are also about time. Third, that 'time' is so elastic a concept that it is hard to imagine a poem which couldn't in some sense be claimed as 'about' time. Mr John Russell Brown has studied in Shakespeare's comedies the themes of love's wealth, love's truth, and love's order, but such words are hold-alls.

Yet it still seems that Tennyson writes about time with an unusual depth and imagination; that, even so, unexpectedly many of his self-borrowings are concerned with time; and that no far-fetched meaning has to be sought for 'time' in order to accommodate them. The habit of self-borrowing manifests both an awareness of, and a means of countering, time. It has the 'emotional importance' which Humphry House[17] brilliantly picked out in Tennyson's fascination with description:

Many of Tennyson's poems—*Maud* most notable among the longer ones—totter on the edge of madness. Constantly the one rallying-point in them as poems is the description of external things . . . In a number of poems he uses description as if it were in itself the final aim of poetic art . . . These descriptions . . . had for him a central emotional importance. They stabilised his mind in the contemplation of unending processes, and allayed the restlessness of the searching and journeying involved in his view of what poetry should do.

[17] *All in Due Time*, p. 129.

Does self-borrowing (a method of composition which became a means of composition) have for Tennyson a comparable function? The dangers of melancholia, even of madness, were not remote from Tennyson; in a world of unending flux, a world where all seemed ephemeral (even the works of the greatest poets), a world where personal identity was a mystery and often a burden, Tennyson found some rallying-point in the continuity of his own creativity. What helped to 'stabilize his mind' was the reassurance offered by his own past (as in his 'Passion of the Past'), and nothing was more reassuring in that past than the surviving, and still living, evidences of his powers. To revise a published poem was to show that the past was not done with, irrevocable, immutable. To quarry from his unpublished work was to show that the past was indeed a quarry, its geological obduracy the source of its riches. The threatening melancholia crystallizes in two lines in the poem 'Walking to the Mail' about the 'morbid devil in his blood':

> He lost the sense that handles daily life—
> That keeps us all in order more or less . . .

Is it just a coincidence that those lines too had originally been part of another poem ('The Gardener's Daughter')?

Tennyson's self-borrowings, then, seem to have the same emotional importance as his preoccupation with description. Just how important this continuity was to him can be seen from the Tennyson *Concordance*. Self-borrowing needs to be related not only to the word 'time' (over 300 times in the *Concordance*) or the favourite adjective 'slow', but also to his persistent need for the prefix 're-', itself a signal that the past still lives, can revive. 'The blossom that rebloom'd'; 'Remade the blood and changed the frame'; 'Rewaken with the dawning soul'; 'Remerging in the general Soul'; 'Can I but relive in sadness?'—there are innumerable examples.[18] For Tennyson, revision is truly a second vision.

It would be wrong, though, to imply that what is learnt from Tennyson's manuscripts is always solemn. A reminder of a different kind of creativity may be found in a *mot* by Browning, itself, as it happens, on time and endurance. Browning reports

[18] Notably: recommenced; regather; re-inspired; reissuing; re-listen; re-makes; remodel; re-orient; re-reiterated; re-risen; resmooth; resolder'd; retake; retaught; re-told; revisit.

Tennyson as saying '"This pair of dress boots is forty years old". We all looked at them, and I said it was good evidence of the immortality of the sole.'[19] The gap between 'soul' and 'sole' is ludicrously wide—but Tennyson himself had leapt it. The Trinity manuscript of 'Love thou thy land' shows that the final reading 'the soul of Discord' grew from the idea of the giant footprint of Discord, its sole.

Tennyson's self-borrowings go to the heart of his poetic skill and of his preoccupation with time. They also bring out the conflict which is often felt in reading Tennyson, the conflict between confidence in his extraordinary expertise and faint uneasiness about the extent to which the expertise is verbal or purely verbal. There is something strange about the predicament of a poet whose wife had continually to urge his friends to provide him with subjects or stories for poems. Yet the end-products are sheer Tennyson. The theme of 'Enoch Arden', of the long-lost traveller returning to his wife, is one that had haunted Tennyson; the Lotos-Eaters knew that if they returned to Ithaca they would come as ghosts to trouble joy, and *In Memoriam* (like the very early poem 'The Coach of Death') expresses the same fear. But the story of 'Enoch Arden' was given to Tennyson by his friend Thomas Woolner.

The oddity of Tennyson's sources is analogous to that of his style: how is it that such apparently dangerous habits so often resulted in something magnificently personal? Certainly the habit of self-borrowing leads to a central point: Tennyson's verbalism. The best criticism of Tennyson is by Walt Whitman:[20]

To me, Tennyson shows more than any poet I know (perhaps has been a warning to me) how much there is in finest verbalism. There is such a latent charm in mere words, cunning collocutions, and in the voice ringing them, which he has caught and brought out, beyond all others—as in the line, 'And hollow, hollow, hollow, all delight', in *The Passing of Arthur*.

It comes agreeably to hand that even that line, 'And hollow, hollow, hollow, all delight', had originally been groped for in a line which Tennyson rejected from 'Locksley Hall': 'hollow, hollow, hollow comfort'.

[19] 19 Mar. 1881; *William Allingham: A Diary*, ed. H. Allingham and D. Radford (1907), p. 311.   [20] 'A Word about Tennyson', *The Critic* (Jan. 1887).

10. THE FIRE I' THE FLINT: REFLECTIONS ON THE POETRY OF GERARD MANLEY HOPKINS

BY SEAMUS HEANEY

WHAT I have to say about Gerard Manley Hopkins springs from the slightly predatory curiosity of a poet interested in the creative processes of another poet. For years, much of the discussion of Hopkins's work had been a form of special pleading, a special pleading that began in Hopkins's own letters to his friends Robert Bridges and Canon Dixon, and was amplified in the writings of Bridges, F. R. Leavis, W. H. Gardner, and other commentators. Their criticism tends to begin at a point in Hopkins's own thought or sensibility, in his Catholicism, his notion of the incarnation, his philological passion, his aesthetic/philosophical vocabulary of inscape and instress, his metrical theories, and so on—it begins at a point beneath the poetry and the critical act then becomes a lever whose work it is to move the mass of the poetry through a distance of incomprehension, indifference, or hostility, into what these critics perceive to be its proper place, that is, as an inevitable and organic part of the structure of the English literary tradition. I assume that this work of leverage or persuasion has been successfully completed, and my critical instrument at this point will not be the lever but rather the tongs or the callipers. I want to cross a couple of ideas about poetry on each other, and hinge them in such a way as to take hold of and take some measure of the Hopkins *opus*. I want to approach him from the circumference of his art rather than from the centre of himself.

The title of the lecture is taken from a speech by the Poet in *Timon of Athens* where Shakespeare seems to be glossing the abundance and naturalness of his own art briefly and completely. The Poet has been murmuring to himself, composing on the tongue as Wordsworth and Yeats were prone to do years afterwards, to the consternation of Cumberland peasant and Coole Park house-guest alike, when the Painter, who is bringing a picture as a gift to Timon, addresses him:

> You are rapt, sir, in some work, some dedication
> To the great lord

to which the Poet replies:

> A thing slipp'd idly from me.
> Our poesy is as a gum which oozes
> From whence 'tis nourished: the fire i' the flint
> Shows not till it be struck; our gentle flame
> Provokes itself, and, like the current, flies
> Each bound it chafes.

Much could be said about this spawn of metaphor in which the four elements combine and coagulate by sleight of word, but I want to look at just one aspect, implicit in the very quick of the word 'slipp'd', which acts like a tuning fork for the music and movement of the whole piece. 'A thing slipp'd idly from me' —the poem is apparently dismissed as something let go or let fall almost accidentally; there is an understated tone to the phrase, an understatement artists are prone to when speaking about a finished work in order to protect the work's mystery and their own. Yet while the tone protects this mystery, and the immediate sense of 'slipp'd' makes light of the poem, behind the immediate sense lies a whole range of meanings and associations which insist on the poem as something nevertheless momentous in its occasion if momentary in its occurrence. Slip, after all, has also to do with unleashing energy; with propagation by separation from an original growth point; and (if one were to engage in special pleading) with the moment of arrival, words coming safely and fluently towards us out of the uncharted waters of the unconscious. All in all, what is accidental, energetic, and genetic in the poetic act is hinted at here in one syllable: the slipping is the slipping envisaged by Robert Frost when he declared that 'like a piece of ice on a hot stove the poem must ride on its own melting'. So the nonchalance of the Poet's tone is complicated by big—as in 'big with child'—implications in the word's ramifying meanings and associations.

And it is these ramifications which begin to spread and net in
the following lines:

> Our poesy is as a gum which oozes
> From whence 'tis nourished . . .

The slip has become the slip almost of mucus, the smoothness of
the verse insinuating a sense of natural release, the intimations
of propagation becoming explicit in the ooze and nurture of the
gum tree. And later, when 'our gentle flame provokes itself', the
stirrings of the flame are as involuntary as the sexual stirrings
which initiate growth and life itself; in fact, the flame is
something of an aura, the flicker at the edge of the ovum under
the microscope, a totally different kind of incandescence from
the frigid sparks out of stone with which it is explicitly
contrasted because, unlike this organic, oozy marshlight,

> the fire i' the flint
> Shows not till it be struck.

You may now have begun to see my drift, but I want you to be
patient while, like the current, I fly the bound I chafe. Or, to use
a subsequent speech of the Poet's on his own procedures:

> my free drift
> Halts not particularly, but moves itself
> In a wide sea of wax—

a wax which I hope to mould before the end of the lecture.

The kind of poetry in the speech I have just considered—
perhaps too particularly—is the kind of poetry which Eliot had
in mind when he spoke of the auditory imagination, that feeling
for word and syllable reaching down below the ordinary levels
of language, uniting the primitive and civilized associations
words have accrued. It is a poetry that offers a continuous
invitation into its echoes and recesses:

> Light thickens
> And the crow makes wing to the rooky wood;
> Good things of day begin to droop and drowse . . .

It is the kind of poetry symbolists wrote at the end of the
nineteenth century and poets with an aspiration towards symbolism required in the twentieth: 'A poem should be palpable
and mute . . . wordless / as the flight of birds . . . A poem should

not mean / but be'—the popularity of Archibald McLeish's poem is striking evidence of how current this view of poetry became.

To put it another way, the function of language in much modern poetry, and in much poetry admired by moderns, is to talk about itself to itself. The poem is a complex word, a linguistic exploration whose tracks melt as it maps its own progress. Whether they are defining poetry or writing it, the sense of poetry as ineluctably itself and not some other thing persists for modern poets. Here is Wallace Stevens defining it, in 'Adagia': 'Poetry creates a fictitious existence on an exquisite plane. This definition must vary as the plane varies, an exquisite plane being merely illustrative.' And here is T. S. Eliot writing it, on an exquisite plane, in 'Marina':

> Bowsprit cracked with ice and paint cracked with heat.
> I made this, I have forgotten
> And remember
> Between one June and another September.
> Made this unknown, half conscious, unknown, my own.
> The garboard strake leaks, the seams need caulking.
> This form, this face, this life
> Living to live in a world of time beyond me; let me
> Resign my life for this life, my speech for that unspoken,
> The awakened, lips parted, the hope, the new ships.

Now while this derives from a situation in Shakespeare's *Pericles*, knowledge of the derivation does not limit but liberates the scope of the poetry. For here we have 'de la musique avant toute chose'. The ear has incubated a cadence, a cadence which is to be found in the epigraph to the poem itself and which may well have constituted, in Valéry's terms, the poem's *donnée*:

> Quis hic locus, quae
> regio, quae mundi plaga?

Eliot himself has discussed all this in 'The Three Voices of Poetry' and C. K. Stead has followed the trail admirably in *The New Poetic*. The self conspires with the self and hatches not a plot but an image. The voice pays back into itself and argues nothing. 'It cannot be too strongly stated that a poem is not the expression of a feeling the poet had before he began to write',

Laforgue insisted with a bored wink to Eliot who took the tip
and affirmed:

It is the poet's business to be original . . . only so far as is absolutely
necessary for saying what he has to say; only so far as is dictated, not
by the idea—for there is no idea—but by the nature of that dark
embryo within him which gradually takes on the form and speech of a
poem.

And again, in another context:

He is going to all that trouble, not in order to communicate with
anyone, but to gain relief from acute discomfort. And when the words
are finally arranged in the right way . . . he may experience a moment
of exhaustion, of appeasement, of absolution, and of something very
near annihilation which is in itself indescribable.

The symbolist image of poetic creation, one might say, is the
unburdening of the indefinable through pangs that are indescribable, where the poem survives as the hieroglyph of a
numinous nativity. At any rate, from Shakespeare's ooze to
Eliot's dark embryo, we have a vision of poetic creation as a
feminine action, almost parthenogenetic, where it is the ovum
and its potential rather than the sperm and its penetration that
underlies their accounts of poetic origins. And out of this vision
of feminine action comes a language for poetry that tends to
brood and breed, crop and cluster, with a texture of echo
and implication, trawling the pool of the ear with a net of
associations.
     To take one final well-known example of the kind of work I
am thinking of:

> O rose, thou art sick!
> The invisible worm
> That flies in the night,
> In the howling storm,
>
> Has found out thy bed
> Of crimson joy:
> And his dark secret love
> Does thy life destroy.

These eight lines of Blake's are like four loaves and four fishes
that shoal and crumble as we try to consume their meaning. A
rose is a rose is a rose but not when it's sick. Then it becomes a

canker, a corruption, a tainted cosmos. The poem drops petal
after petal of suggestion without ever revealing its stripped
core: it is an open invitation into its meaning rather than an
assertion of it.

Now I wonder if we can say the same of this poem, also short,
also living off the life of its images:

Heaven–Haven
A nun takes the veil

I have desired to go
    Where springs not fail
To fields where flies no sharp and sided hail
    And a few lilies blow.

And I have asked to be
    Where no storms come,
Where the green swell is in the havens dumb
    And out of the swing of the sea.

In each case the verse lives by its music and suggestiveness, but
with one important difference: the suggestiveness here con-
denses on a stated theme, 'a nun takes the veil', and the
heaven–purity–cold idea equates with the haven–nunnery–
quiet images in a relationship that is essentially allegorical
rather than symbolic. The Hopkins poem is fretted rather than
fecund. In the Blake poem the rose might be a girl but it
remains a rose. Yet it is also a rose window, bloodshot with the
light of other possible meanings. The rose and the sickness are
not illustrative in the way the lilies and the haven are. In
'Heaven–Haven' it is the way things are exquisitely wrought,
the way a crystal is sharp and sided and knowable rather than
the way a rose is deep and unknowable that counts. Hopkins's
art here is the discovery of verbal equivalents, in mingling the
purity of images with the idea of a vow of chastity. The words
are crafted together more than they are coaxed out of one
another, and they are crafted in the service of an idea that precedes the poem, is independent of it and to which the poem is
perhaps ultimately subservient. So much for the dark embryo.
We are now in the realm of flint-spark rather than marshlight.
'Heaven–Haven' is consonantal fire struck by idea off language. The current of its idea does not fly the bound it chafes
but confines itself within delightful ornamental channels.

To take another comparison with a poet whose nervous apprehension of phenomena and ability to translate this nervous energy into phrases reminds us also of Hopkins: take this line by Keats, describing autumn as the season of fulfilment:

>Close bosom-friend of the maturing sun

and compare it with a Hopkins line that also realizes a sense of burgeoning and parturition, imagining Jesus in Mary's womb:

>Warm-laid grave of a womb-life grey.

Both lines rely on the amplitude of vowels for their dream of benign, blood-warm growth, but where Keats's vowels seem like nubs, buds off a single *uh* or *oo*, yeasty growths that are ready at any moment to relapse back into the original mother sound, Hopkins's are defined, held apart, and in relation to one another rather than in relation to the original nub: if they are full they are also faceted. Hopkins's consonants alliterate to maintain a design whereas Keats's release a flow. I am reminded of something T. S. Eliot wrote comparing Shakespeare and Ben Jonson. In Jonson, Eliot remarked, 'unconscious does not respond to unconscious; no swarms of inarticulate feelings are aroused. The immediate appeal of Jonson is to the mind; his emotional tone is not in the single verse but in the design of the whole.' We must say much the same of the Keats and Hopkins lines. Keats has the life of a swarm, fluent and merged; Hopkins has the design of the honeycomb, definite and loaded. In Keats, the rhythm is narcotic, in Hopkins it is a stimulant to the mind. Keats woos us to receive, Hopkins alerts us to perceive.

I think that what is true of this single Hopkins line is generally true of the kind of poetry he writes. For in spite of the astounding richness of his music and the mimetic power of his vocabulary, his use of language is disciplined by a philological and rhetorical passion. There is a conscious push of the deliberating intelligence, a siring strain rather than a birth-push in his poetic act. Like Jonson, he is *poeta doctus*; like Jonson's, his verse is 'rammed with life', butting ahead instead of hanging back into its own centre. As opposed to the symbolist poetic, it is concerned with statement instead of states of feeling. Indeed, at this point it is interesting to recall Ben Jonson's strictures on the Shakespearian fluency, rejecting linguistic mothering in favour

of rhetorical mastery. Jonson, you remember, was not impressed by the way Shakespeare's current flies each bound it
chafes:

I remember the players have often mentioned it as an honour to
Shakespeare that in his writing, whatsoever he penned, he never
blotted out line. My answer hath been, 'Would he had blotted a
thousand.'. . . He was, indeed, honest and of an open and free nature
wherein he flowed with that facility that sometime it was necessary he
should be stopped . . . His wit was in his own power: would the rule of
it had been so too.

Jonson believed that energy should not be slipped but kept
leashed. He values control, rule, revision, how things are fit,
how they are fitted. And the same is true of Hopkins: the rule of
his own 'wit' was Hopkins's study as both priest and poet. He
valued what he called 'the masculine powers' in poetry, the
presence of 'powerful and active thought'—it was typical that
when he realized his 'newrhythm' he had to schematize it into a
metric. The following extracts from a letter to Coventry
Patmore in which Hopkins discusses Keats are illuminating:

It is impossible not to feel with weariness how his verse is at every turn
abandoning itself to an unmanly and enervating luxury. It appears
too that he said something like 'O for a life of impressions rather than
thoughts' . . . Nevertheless, I feel and see in him the beginnings of
something opposite to this, of an interest in higher things, and of
powerful and active thought . . . His mind had, as it seems to me, the
distinctly masculine powers in abundance, his character the manly
virtues, but while he gave himself up to dreaming and self-indulgence,
of course, they were in abeyance . . . but . . . his genius would have
taken to an austere utterance in art. Reason, thought, what he did not
want to live by, would have asserted itself presently.

As is so often the case when a poet is diagnosing the condition of
another poet, Hopkins is here offering us something of a
self-portrait. The development he divined for Keats was one
which he had already undergone himself. For Hopkins, as a
schoolboy and undergraduate, had aspired to the life of sensations rather than thoughts, had luxuriated poetically and had
been touched by the gem-like flame of Walter Pater's influence
at Oxford. His masculine powers of powerful and active
thought were consciously developed, as consciously as his

theories of sprung rhythm and his private language of instress
and inscape: behind the one was a directed effort in Welsh and
classical versification, behind the other a scholastic appetite for
Scotism. We have only to look at his early poem 'A Vision of
Mermaids' to realize that when he spoke of 'an unmanly and
enervating luxury', he was speaking from experience.

> From their white waists a silver skirt was spread
> To mantle o'er the tail, such as is shed
> Around the Water Nymphs in fretted falls,
> At red Pompeii on medallion'd walls.
> A tainted fin on either shoulder hung;
> Their pansy-dark or bronzen locks were strung
> With coral, shells, thick-pearlèd cords, whateer
> The abysmal Ocean hoards of strange and rare.

This is gum oozing from whence 'tis nourished all right, from
that enervating, luxurious Keats whom the mature Hopkins
rounded on. In spite of the felicity of 'pansy-dark' and the
resonance of the fourth line, what we miss here is what Hopkins
described in his own mature poetry: 'But as air, melody, is what
strikes me most of all in music and design in painting, so design,
pattern or what I am in the habit of calling "inscape" is what
above all I aim at in poetry.' In fact, he might have been
speaking as his own ideal reader when he expressed his reaction
to the music of Henry Purcell:

> It is the forgèd feature finds me; it is the rehearsal
> Of own, of abrúpt sélf there so thrusts on, so throngs the ear.

In this earliest work there is no sense of the poetic emotion
distinguishing itself. His posture here is one of surrender to
experience whereas in his maturer work it is one of mastery, of
penetration. His own music thrusts and throngs and it is forged.
It is the way words strike off one another, the way they are
drilled, marched, and countermarched, rather than the way
they philander and linger among themselves, that constitutes
his proper music. Hopkins's sound and sense always aim to
complement each other in a perfectly filled-in outline: his
poems are closer to being verbal relief-work than to being a
receding, imploding vortex of symbol.

I wish to make one final comparison with another poet in
order to clarify this 'masculine' element in his approach. W. B.
Yeats is also a poet in whom we are offered the arched back of

English in place of its copious lap; and again in Yeats we are constantly aware of the intentness on structure, and the affirmative drive of thought running under the music, of which the music is the clear-tongued pealing. Like Hopkins, he was impatient of 'poetical literature, that is monotonous in its structure and effeminate in its insistence upon certain moments of strained lyricism' and he was possessed of 'the certainty that all the old writers, the masculine writers of the world, wrote to be spoken or to be sung, and in a later age to be read aloud for hearers who had to understand quickly or not at all'. These sentiments not only re-echo Hopkins's strictures upon Keats, but they also recall Hopkins's famous, impatient directions on how to get the best out of his work, for he too wrote to be spoken or to be sung: 'Take breath and read it with the ears, as I always wish to be read, and my verse becomes all right.' And in another context: 'Declaimed, the strange constructions would be dramatic and effective.' So I am setting up two modes and calling them masculine and feminine—but without the Victorian sexist overtones to be found in Hopkins's and Yeats's employment of the terms. In the masculine mode, the language functions as a form of address, of assertion or command, and the poetic effort has to do with conscious quelling and control of the materials, a labour of shaping; words are not music before they are anything else, nor are they drowsy from their slumber in the unconscious, but athletic, capable, displaying the muscle of sense. Whereas in the feminine mode the language functions more as evocation than as address, and the poetic effort is not so much a labour of design as it is an act of divination and revelation; words in the feminine mode behave with the lover's come hither instead of the athlete's display, they constitute a poetry that is delicious as texture before it is recognized as architectonic.

Yet Hopkins's poetry is immediately appealing or repellent, depending on the reader's taste, just because of its texture: is its immediate appeal not to the nervous system? It has worked its passage as modern rather than Victorian poetry not because it was published in 1918 but because, as Geoffrey Hartman has written,

I. A. Richards, William Empson, and F. R. Leavis championed Hopkins as the classic example of the modern poet. They agreed that his strength was immediately bound up with the immediacy of his relation to words: he seemed to fulfil the dream that poetry was language speaking about itself, language uttering complex words that were meanings *as* words.

He seemed, in other words, to possess those characteristics that I have made typical of the feminine mode; yet I still believe that he is essentially closer to the masculine, rhetorical mode.

Let us take a celebrated example of Hopkins's modern imagist technique—taking imagist in Pound's sense of 'that which presents an intellectual and emotional complex in a moment of time'. This is the famous fourth stanza of 'The Wreck of the Deutschland' where the protagonist has emerged from the experience, at once terrible and renovating, of Christ's sudden irruption into his life:

> I am soft sift
> In an hourglass—at the wall
> Fast, but mined with a motion, a drift,
> And it crowds and it combs to the fall;
> I steady as a water in a well, to a poise, to a pane,
> But roped with, always, all the way down from the tall
> Fells or flanks of the voel, a vein
> Of the gospel proffer, a pressure, a principle, Christ's gift.

Here Hopkins's procedures and eccentricities almost insist on being appreciated. His interest in dialect and archaism, in the use of the Welsh 'voel', meaning a small hill; his tendency to invert the functions of parts of speech, making 'proffer' a noun instead of a verb; and his incredible precision in making the gospel a 'proffer', with its suggestion of urgency and obligation to accept, so much more alive than 'offer'—all of this invites comment. As does the fact that 'proffer' alliterates with 'press-ure' and 'principle', three piston-strokes heightening the pressure down the line. Moreover, Hopkins's total possession of the silent contradictory motions of sand in the neck of an hour glass and water in the bowl of the hills, his completely exciting apprehension of these things in sound and sense allows one to comprehend easily what 'inscape' meant, and what he meant when he once wrote in his journal: 'I saw the inscape freshly, as if my eye were still growing.'

Now all this has the status of an imagist poem in its verbal life, but it has the status of analogy within the argument and

structure of the whole poem. It works like this. The streaming of
sand down the sides of the glass is faded into the downpour of
streams on the fells or flanks of a hill, and what had been at the
bottom a sinking becomes a source, because this downing
motion from above sustains, and rises as, a spring. So that
suddenly the downing motion of Christ, his dark descending,
becomes not something to make the soul sink in a quicksand of
terror but to steady and be sustained by descending graces
—Hopkins could well cry here, 'See where Christ's blood
streams in the firmament.' Once more, as in 'Heaven–Haven',
but in a much more complex manner, the whole figurative life of
the piece is analogous and diagrammatic; what is mimetic in
the words is completely guaranteed by what is theological
behind them, expressing the mystery of Christ's efficacy and
action in human life:

> Thou art lightning and love, I found it, a winter and warm;
>   Father and fondler of heart thou hast wrung:
> Hast thy dark descending and most art merciful then.

If one still needed convincing about how designed and
intended all this was, how it lives not only in its linguistic
elements but in the poet's pre-verbal intention and intellection,
one might compare it with another stanza of linguistic virtuosity, of considerable imaginative force, written by another
poet with a sacramental apprehension of the world. Dylan
Thomas's lines in 'The Force That Through The Green Fuse
Drives The Flower' also concern water and quicksand:

> The hand that swirls the water in the pool
> Stirs the quicksand; that ropes the blowing wind
> Hauls my shroud sail.
> And I am dumb to tell the hanging man
> How of my clay is made the hangman's lime.

This is much more the 'logic of imagination' than the 'logic of
concepts', more the yeasty burgeoning of images from a dark
embryo than the delighted and precise realization or incarnation of a mystery. It is not so much the word made flesh as the
flesh made word. If we ask the question, whose hand swirls the
quicksand, or who is the hanging man, we cannot and perhaps
should not expect a precise answer. It is not that kind of poem.

It is incantation, it deploys heraldic images—admittedly with excitement—but it does not aspire to spell an exact proposition. Whatever truth the poem proposes it is only coextensive with the poem itself.

Whereas 'The Wreck of the Deutschland', of course, is the utterance of Hopkins's whole reality, of his myth, if you like, and this reality or myth has been lived as the truth by generations before and since Hopkins. Yeats had to write his own holy book, *A Vision*, before he could embody its truths in poems, and those truths were finally 'a superhuman / Mirror-resembling dream', the creation of a Romantic fiat. But Hopkins's holy book was the New Testament, its commentary was the *Spiritual Exercises* of St Ignatius Loyola, its reality was in his own experience of conversion and vocation to the Jesuit rule. His intellect was not forced to choose between perfection of the life or of the work but was compelled to bring them into congruence.

I wish to suggest that Hopkins did indeed embody this congruence, that his understanding of the Christian mystery and the poetic mystery were structured in the same way; and in this respect, a remark by Ted Hughes in his Afterword to *A Choice of Shakespeare's Verse* is very pertinent. Hughes writes:

Poetic imagination is determined finally by the state of negotiation —in a person or in a people—between man and his idea of the Creator. This is natural enough, and everything else is naturally enough subordinate to it. How things are between man and his idea of the Divinity determines everything in his life, the quality and connectedness of every feeling and thought, and the meaning of every action.

Whether or not this holds generally, it is particularly true of Hopkins. His journals are scrupulous and slightly shocking evidence of the way his imagination was in constant, almost neurotic negotiation with his idea of the Creator, as on 24 September 1870 when he saw the Northern Lights and in the entry immediately following that:

At first I thought of silvery cloud until I saw that these were more luminous and did not dim the clearness of the stars in the Bear . . . This busy working of nature wholly independent of the earth and seeming to go on in a strain of time not reckoned by our reckoning of

days and years but simpler and as if correcting the preoccupation of
the world by being preoccupied with and appealing to and dated to
the day of judgement was like a new witness to God and filled me with
delightful fear.

Oct 20—Laus Deo—the river to-day and yesterday.

Again, the intimate negotiation was in progress—as abne-
gation—the previous year, in the entry beginning under 24
January 1869:

The elms have been in red bloom and yesterday (the 11th) I saw small
leaves on the brushwood at their roots. Some primroses out. But a
penance which I was doing from Jan. 25 to July 25 prevented my
seeing much that half-year.

But perhaps the most succinct and celebrated intimacy is his
remark about the bluebell: 'I know the beauty of Our Lord by
it.'

His relationship with the idea of the Divinity not only
determined the quality and connectedness of every feeling and
thought, but it underlay his poetic imagination and provided,
in Hughes's word, the groundplan of the poetic act as he
conceived it. For Hopkins, this act was closer to having fire
struck from him than it was to oozing gum; and the striking of
flame, 'the stroke dealt' from above is how he images God's
intervention in his life in 'The Wreck of the Deutschland'. God
appears in the opening stanza in powerful aspect, as much Thor
as Jehovah, ready to deal blows with his hammer:

> Thou mastering me
> God! Giver of breath and bread;
> World's strand, sway of the sea;
> Lord of living and dead;
> Thou hast bound bones and veins in me, fastened me flesh,
> And after it almost unmade, what with dread,
> Thy doing: and dost thou touch me afresh?
> Over again I feel thy finger and find thee.

This is a far more mature and demanding vision of the religious
vocation than that which we saw in 'Heaven–Haven': not quiet
retreat, not the religious life viewed from the outside but uttered
from the quick centre. The bronze notes of the verse only serve
to reinforce Hopkins's declaration to a bewildered Bridges:
'What refers to myself in the poem is all strictly and literally

true and did all occur; nothing is added for poetical padding.' It would be possible to read the first ten stanzas of the poem and relate the poetic mode, the psychological states, and the theological implications line by line, but I will confine myself to quotation and commentary relevant to my particular purpose.

Christ's storming of the soul is presented in images of lightning and fire:

> I did say yes
> O at lightning and lashed rod:
>
> .   .   .   .   .
>
> And the midriff astrain with leaning of, laced with fire of stress.

It is as if the 'sweep and hurl' fanned him into a glow, a glow which ignites his heart into a leaping flame of recognition and love:

> My heart, but you were dovewinged, I can tell,
>   Carrier-witted, I am bold to boast
> To flash from the flame to the flame then, tower from the grace
>   to the grace.

After this refining fire, he is soft sift that steadies and is sustained by the gospel proffer. He perceives Christ instressed in creation and stresses Christ's reality by imitation: stanzas v, vi, vii, and viii are an orthodox meditation on and affirmation of the mystery of Christ's incarnation, its redemptive effect on all nature and the consequent sacramental efficacy of natural phenomena. Then in stanza viii he returns to the moment of personal crisis, the realization of Christ in his own life, when 'the stress felt', 'the stroke dealt' bursts like a sloe on the tongue, 'brim, in a flash, full'. And there follows the clearest statement of the paradox of the religious vocation, of the Christian relationship with a master who demands all obedience from his creature in order that the creature may be perfectly himself:

> Thou art lightning and love, I found it, a winter and warm;
>   Father and fondler of heart thou hast wrung:
> Hast thy dark descending and most art merciful then.
>
>   With an anvil-ding
>   And with fire in him forge thy will
> Or rather, rather then, stealing as Spring
>   Through him, melt him but master him still.

This act of mastery is an act of love: the creature was 'trod' and now he is 'melted but mastered'. A sceptical critic might be forgiven, indeed, for thinking of Yeats's 'Leda and the Swan' rather than George Herbert's 'The Collar'.

But what I want to note is the striking correspondence between the imagery used to describe this central event in Hopkins's religious life and the central action in his life as a poet, that is, the experience of the poetic act itself. In each case a bolt from the blue, a fire that strikes, a masculine touch, initiates the action. The sonnet 'To R.B.' is worth quoting in full:

> The fine delight that fathers thought; the strong
> Spur, live and lancing like the blowpipe flame,
> Breathes once and, quenchèd faster than it came,
> Leaves yet the mind a mother of immortal song.
>
> Nine months she then, nay years, nine years she long
> Within her wears, bears, cares and combs the same:
> The widow of an insight lost she lives, with aim
> Now known and hand at work now never wrong.
>
> Sweet fire the sire of muse, my soul needs this;
> I want the one rapture of an inspiration.
> O then if in my lagging lines you miss
>
> The roll, the rise, the carol, the creation,
> My winter world, that scarcely breathes that bliss
> Now, yields you, with some sighs, our explanation.

Obviously Hopkins cannot escape, in this figure, the mothering function of his imagination, but what is important is that this is not in his case parthenogenetic but comes about through the union of distinct sexual elements, and the crucial element is the penetrative, masculine spur of flame, 'sweet fire the sire of muse'. The mastering God who came with lightning and lashed rod and 'the strong / Spur, live and lancing like the blowpipe flame', partake of the same nature. The fire in his heart only shows when it is struck.

There can be no more explicit illustration of the intercon- nectedness of Hopkins's poetic and religious vocations than his account of the origins of 'The Wreck of the Deutschland'. The passage from his letter to R. W. Dixon in October 1878 is well known but worth recalling at some length:

You ask, do I write verse myself. What I had written I burnt before I became a Jesuit and resolved to write no more, as not belonging to my profession, unless it were by the wish of my superiors; so for seven years I wrote nothing but two or three little presentation pieces which occasion called for. But when in the winter of '75 the Deutschland was wrecked in the mouth of the Thames and five Franciscan nuns, exiles from Germany, aboard of her were drowned I was affected by the account and happening to say so to my rector he said that he wished someone would write a poem on the subject. On this hint I set to work and, though my hand was out at first, produced one. I had long had haunting my ear the echo of a new rhythm which now I realized on paper . . . After writing this I held myself free to compose but cannot find it in my conscience to spend time upon it; so I have done little and shall do less.

Composition, in other words, was not just a matter of natural volition and personal appeasement but had to be a compliance with and an enactment of the will of God, and the will of God was the rule of his order, and the rule of his wit, in Jonson's term, was as much in the mastering grip of his rector as it was in the grip of his rhetoric. So much is explicit here, but implicit is the siring figure we find in his sonnet to Bridges. The new rhythm that was haunting his ear had the status of dark embryo, but it needed to be penetrated, fertilized by the dark descending will; the rector's suggestion had the status of an annunciation in what Stephen Dedalus, that other scholastic artist, called 'the virgin womb of the imagination'.

Moreover, since Hopkins's poems were conceived as the crossing of masculine strain on feminine potential, it is natural that they are most fully achieved when siring vision is most rapturously united with a sensuous apprehension of natural life. United, and not simply in attendance upon each other. The sonnet 'Spring', for example, while being a delightful piece of inscaping, with its

> thrush
> Through the echoing timber does so rinse and wring
> The ear, it strikes like lightnings to hear him sing,

is nevertheless structurally a broken arch, with an octave of description aspiring towards a conjunction with a sestet of doctrine. Doctrine and description only hold hands, as it were, in 'Spring', but in 'The Windhover' they are in intense communion, the spirit holding intercourse (the Wordsworthian locution is entirely appropriate) with beauty. In fact, 'The Windhover' is an extended mime of the process described in the sonnet to Bridges, an anatomy of the moment of inspiration and illumination, when the blowpipe flame of delight and insight lances the sensibility:

> I caught this morning morning's minion, king-
>   dom of daylight's dauphin, dapple-dawn-drawn Falcon,
>   in his riding
>   Of the rolling level underneath him steady air, and striding
> High there, how he rung upon the rein of a wimpling wing
> In his ecstasy!

The octave of the sonnet constitutes 'the fine delight that fathers thought' and the thought is delivered in the moment of appeasement—'the achieve of, the mastery of the thing'. There follows the much interpreted sestet where Hopkins's imagination is luminously determined by his idea of the Creator, 'with aim / Now known and hand at work now never wrong'. Human perfection in the Christian sphere is not just a matter of dealing out physical being, or of flashing 'honour . . . off exploit', as in the case of the animal and secular worlds: all the panoply of such mastery must be downed when Christ is master, must buckle under the 'anvil ding' and be tempered to a new brilliance. The final lines do indeed vault into the consciousness with the lift of symbol, and yet, despite the gleam and deliquescence and intense sufficiency of the verbal art, they are still intent on telling a truth independent of themselves, that the fire in the flint of nature shows not till it be struck, and that nature's 'bonniest . . . her clearest selvèd spark / Man' is only completely selved and achieved in a selfless imitation of Christ. And this conclusion is not rhetoric in the pejorative sense, not the will doing the work of the imagination: not a mustered hurrah for asceticism in face of full-blooded exultation, but a whole man's 'wincing and singing':

> No wonder of it: shéer plód makes plough down sillion
> Shine, and blue-bleak embers, ah my dear,
>   Fall, gall themselves, and gash gold-vermillion.

When I settled on 'the fire i' the flint' as the dark embryo for this lecture, I wanted to explore my notion that the artist's idea of the artistic act, conscious or unconscious, affected certain intrinsic qualities of the artefact. I hope I have clarified my sense of the artistic act in Hopkins as a masculine forging rather than a feminine incubation, with a consequent intentness rather than allure in his style. His idea of the Creator himself as father and fondler is central to the mastering, design-making rhetoric and fondling of detail in his work. And just as Christ's mastering descent into the soul is an act of love, a treading and a melting, so the poetic act itself is a love-act initiated by the masculine spur of delight. But Hopkins was no doubt aware that even the act of love could be read as a faithful imitation of Christ, a sign of grace, in so far as the Church fathers perceived the sign of the cross in the cross and splay of a man and woman in their ecstasy.

11. KIPLING'S MAGIC ART
BY JACQUELINE S. BRATTON

IN 'The Song of the Banjo' Kipling gives that instrument a voice, and it speaks of

> . . . tunes that mean so much to you alone—
> Common tunes that make you choke and blow your nose—
> Vulgar tunes that bring the laugh that brings the groan—
> I can rip your very heartstrings out with those.[1]

The poet admired the banjo, and respected its power. It spoke, he claimed, with the wisdom of the centuries; and much of his own poetry is set to its tunes. They are an embarrassment to his critics. The first Chatterton lecturer on Kipling, Professor Andrew Rutherford, bravely avowed his boyish pleasure in some of the 'simple, unsophisticated' poems; less confident critics have approached Kipling with elaborate caution, for fear of the banjo tunes: only 'the good Kipling' is respectable reading for the critically mature.[2] But it is not stories like 'Mary Postgate' that contain, it seems to me, the kernel of Kipling's art; rather it is the vulgar ditties, laden, like the potent cheap tunes which are interwoven with our lives, with quite illegitimate emotional power. If one is to understand his art and his aims, it must be through an understanding of the uncritical, emotional responses which he deliberately sought to call up.

Just as the banjo tunes are charged with emotions which belong to the situations they recall, rather than to their independent power, so many of Kipling's verses are inextricably embedded in frameworks of circumstance which add to their significance. Each framework is personal, and 'means so much to you alone'; but it is also public, and forms a bond with those

---

[1] 'Song of the Banjo', 1894, quoted from *The Definitive Edition of Rudyard Kipling's Verse* (London, 1940), p. 98.
[2] See Andrew Rutherford, 'Some Aspects of Kipling's Verse', *The Proceedings of the British Academy* li (London, 1965), 378; and the discussion of critical attitudes in Elliot L. Gilbert, *The Good Kipling* (Ohio, 1971), pp. 3–13.

to whom, we discover, it is also significant. The voice of the
Radio Uncle who read the *Just So Stories* to me has a special
place in the hearts of thousands of others of my generation. It is
not simply that many of Kipling's pieces belong to that adolescent world where we are always reading things for the first
time, and so linking them emotionally with whatever mountain, hill, or stream was first illuminated for us by their
visionary gleam; rather that the verses appeal on a primitive
poetic level, at which each poem's delivery, its circumstances,
purposes, and concomitant rituals are as important as its
content. Kipling deliberately sought in much of his poetry to
evoke this aspect of the enjoyment of verse—its connection, as
he felt, with other aspects of life. Poetically used words were his
tools for intensifying and dignifying the emotional experience of
everyday life, and leaving each of his readers to return to his
own life with a new idea of its importance and its shape.

   This is, as T. S. Eliot pointed out, a magical conception of the
use of art.[3] Eliot cited R. G. Collingwood's definition: 'A
magical art is an art which is representative and therefore
evocative of emotion, and evokes of set purpose some emotions
rather than others to discharge them into the affairs of practical
life.' Collingwood further defined the effect of magic as 'the
exact opposite of a catharsis' intended to 'develop and conserve
morale' because the 'emotions aroused by magical acts are not
discharged by those acts'.[4] He gave Kipling's art as an instance, and added further generic examples: all military music,
hymnody, and those poems in which the subject-matter is
propaganda and is held to be more important than the manner
of writing. T. S. Eliot did not feel that this notion of art was
sufficient to cover all aspects of Kipling's work; and some of the
corollaries which Collingwood offers as consequent upon the
definition do not relate to Kipling's methods and achievements.
Collingwood was of the opinion that magic could only become
'true art' in the hands of an artificer by whom the artistic and
the magical motives, the interest in perfecting the creation
itself, and in its emotional effectiveness for a particular task,
were not felt to be distinct, and that this state of mind has been

---

[3] T. S. Eliot, *A Choice of Kipling's Verse* (London, 1941), Introduction, p. 20 n. 2.
[4] R. G. Collingwood, *The Principles of Art* (Oxford, 1938), pp. 66–9.

impossible since the Middle Ages. But to present Kipling, the craft-obsessive mason and maker of tribal lays, as a post-medieval magical writer to whom the 'goodness or badness' of a poem 'has little, if any, connexion with its efficacy in its own proper work' is to miss the point of his magic. I would like to examine, therefore, the magical methods, as well as the magical motives, of Kipling's verses, and attempt to explore his verse and his ideas about it by means of the notion of the magical power of words.

Kipling himself did not say much about the springs of art; what ideas he did articulate have been felt to be inadequate to the analysis of his stories, especially the later, denser examples; but they chime well with a magical view of his verse. In *Something of Myself*[5] he speaks throughout of his sense that his artistic life was controlled from outside; he begins by 'ascribing all good fortune to Allah the Dispenser of Events' and later attributes all good work to 'the peremptory motions of my Daemon', which caused him to produce stories so nearly vicariously, as it were, that when he looked at them and at his success, he felt ' "Lord ha' mercy on me, this is none of I." ' In the course of some few stories and poems he elaborates upon this idea: the best-known example is 'Wireless',[6] the story in which a consumptive chemist's assistant, of most homely and modern aspect, becomes, when drugged, a receiver through some accidental cosmic sympathy for certain lines of Keats which are drifting about the ether struggling to get themselves expressed. Through the juxtaposition with experiments with wireless Kipling implies that poetry is like radio, 'the Power —our unknown Power—kicking and fighting to be let loose . . . There she goes—kick—kick—kick into space.' The magic, it seems, rests in the words themselves, and has in this case very little to do with the poet and his personality or motives. It is a version of the inspirational theory of poetry, as Kipling's choice of a Romantic poet indicates and the narrator's pronouncement later in the story underlines: he says (in the slightly pontificat-ing tone that many of Kipling's literary narrators adopt) that we must 'Remember that in all the millions permitted there are

[5] London, 1937, pp. 1, 113, 78.
[6] *Traffics and Discoveries*, 1904, *Sussex Edition*, vii. 215–43.

no more than five—five little lines—of which one can say:
"These are the pure Magic. These are the clear Vision."' They
are, you will recall, the fragment of Keats the chemist is
struggling to get right:

> Charm'd magic casements, opening on the foam
> Of perilous seas, in faery lands forlorn

and a snatch of 'Kubla Khan':

> A savage place! as holy and enchanted
> As e'er beneath a waning moon was haunted
> By woman wailing for her demon-lover.

They are quintessential Romantic lines, appealing to the
supernatural as a source of creativity.

In verses about the creative process Kipling offers a variation
on Romance as the root and object of poetry. It becomes 'the
Boy-god' who inspires engineers driving steam-trains as he
inspired cavemen tipping arrow heads and sailors trimming
sails, all of them looking back the while and mourning his
passing; it is the identity of purpose that unites a cockney singer
with 'Omer smiting his blooming lyre and which conversely
sets apart Ung the artist and his father from their clients who
cannot see the pictures waiting to be made.[7] It is a man's appeal
to some force outside himself, to vision, history, and idealism.
One notices that the extension of the idea immediately takes in
not only other arts, but also activities which are not artistic in
their nature—Kipling perceives a continuum of human activities which all have their own versions of the combination of
inspiration and craftsmanship. Everything from civil adminis-
tration to cooking is a magical gift, and its possessor is dignified
and justified by his painstaking practice of it. The writer, then,
is gifted with words; they are the Magic; his is the obligation to
work it.

Collingwood specifies in his definition of the magical artist
that it is important for his artifact to be representational: since
it is created not for its intrinsic beauty, but for the emotional
effect it will have, the only vital requirement for success is that

---

[7] 'The King', 1894, *Definitive Edition*, pp. 376–7; 'When 'Omer Smote 'Is Bloomin'
Lyre', *Definitive Edition*, p. 351; 'The Story of Ung', *Definitive edition*, pp. 345–8.

its meaning and purpose should be clearly articulated.[8] At first blush this seems to fit much of Kipling's verse. It is often said that his poems are simpler than his stories, and have fewer levels of meaning; that they can be taken in at first reading and offer no further reverberations or complexities. This, indeed, was the basis of that critical view of his work which dismissed the verse as good bad poetry or not poetry at all but mere balladeering.[9] But it is not what Kipling understood by the magical power of verse. He did indeed intend to write for those who would use his verses 'to develop and conserve morale', to raise their emotions to be discharged in action; but he sought, therefore, for ways of using words not simply, to deliver a message to the greatest number of active persons, but covertly, obliquely, magically, as a charm, to put spells on them. They listened to the story he told, and responded not to its superficial meaning alone, but to its tone. The effect of words lay for him in their irrational potency; and in shaping the obvious and simple phrase, understood by all, to the tune that would work on the hearer on an irrational level.

Kipling's way of working on verse confirms the primacy in the imaginative process of the inarticulate pattern: he would take up a tune, picking it out of the air or asking another person for a suggestion, and work the words out of himself to its cadences, which he would alter as he worked to suit his purpose. The selection of the patterning tune would be at random not, I think, because it was irrelevant, as some critics have implied,[10] but because it was the *donnée*, the Daemon-given element—the most important element of all. To see the connections between the original poem and Kipling's one must consider their irrational levels. Sometimes Kipling plays off the tonal and the articulated statements in ironic counterpoint; but more often, more characteristically, the words become incantations whose force is generated chiefly by their stress, their repetition, and the tonal values they acquire. In *Captains Courageous* there is a scene in which the uses of song are made

[8] Collingwood, op. cit., pp. 68–9.

[9] See, for instance, George Orwell's essay 'Rudyard Kipling', 1942, *Collected Essays*, ed. S. Orwell and I. Angus, 4 vols (London, 1968), ii. 184–97, 194, and T. S. Eliot's use of the term 'ballad-maker', op. cit., p. 6.

[10] See Charles Carrington, *Rudyard Kipling, His Life and Work* (London, 1955), p. 356.

plain.[11] The boy Harvey, who is being educated by his contact with the simple working life, listens to a fo'c'sle sing-song. After a ballad with 'an old-fashioned creaky tune' and a beautiful chorus which 'made Harvey almost weep, though he could not tell why', the black Scottish cook sings, and the effect is 'much worse . . . he struck into a tune that was like something very bad but sure to happen whatever you did. After a little he sang, in an unknown tongue . . . the tune crooned and moaned on, like lee surf in a blind fog, until it ended with a wail.' It is, he says, the song of Fin M'Coul. They are overwhelmed. Then the ship's boy sings, and is reproved for approaching in his song taboo words, the last verse being 'a Jonah'. Suddenly the black Celt is moved to prophecy and second sight. A complex of magical notions surrounds the singing of sailors' songs; they are potent words, influencing the success of the trip as well as the spirits of the crew, and equally potent when only their tune is understood.

The appropriateness of this apparently very primitive version of the poetic use of words to Kipling's chosen audiences need not be laboured. Moved by his Daemon and by his convictions to address poetry to those ignorant of its sophisticated languages, to children, for example, and to soldiers, he was obliged to rely heavily upon the understanding which can be derived from comprehending only the tone of voice in which the language is spoken. In exploring the magical qualities of Kipling's verse I shall accordingly begin with the verses in which this restriction is most powerful, his poems for or about 'the people', the soldier songs with their reliance upon popular forms, and his writing for children or adolescents, where he resorts to a use of words inspired by childish story-telling and play. The techniques developed in these special writings were carried over into the 'mixed form' of stories and poems which marks the apex of his achievement, and they became tools for subtle and complex purposes.

There are several stories which hinge upon the irrational power of words used by popular singers or by children. 'The Village that Voted the Earth was Flat'[12] is based upon the

---

[11] *Captains Courageous*, 1897, *Sussex Edition*, xx. 67–74.
[12] *A Diversity of Creatures*, 1917, *Sussex Edition*, ix. 163–214.

premiss that a song, conceived and delivered in the music-hall, could affect all England profoundly and one village permanently. The punishment of universal derision is visited upon the cruel and greedy village through the power of illusion: in a fake crusade they are persuaded to vote that the earth is flat; and then it is driven home by the song that is made about them. This ditty, deliberately banal, and deteriorating into guttural belches and delirious howls, is composed in Kipling's own manner, by modelling upon an existing song, '"Nuts in May" with variations'; but its power is compulsive, even frightening. It is launched in music-hall and cinema, and then 'the thing roared and pulverised and swept beyond eyesight all by itself —all by itself' until it finally prostrates the House of Commons:

Then, without distinction of Party, fear of constituents, desire for office, or hope of emolument, the House sang at the tops and at the bottoms of their voices, swaying their stale bodies and epileptically beating with their swelled feet. They sang 'The Village that voted the *Earth* was flat': first because they wanted to, and secondly—which is the terror of that song—because they could not stop.

There is an instance of words chanted and sung to precipitate action amongst another, perhaps less rational group, Stalky and Co's schoolmates, in 'The United Idolaters'.[13] They delight in words: 'As the Studies brought back brackets and pictures for their walls, so did they bring back odds and ends of speech—theatre, opera, and music-hall gags—from the great holiday world.' These fragments act as jokes, and also talismanically, the possession and use of jargon being, for Kipling especially, a sign of the potent inner ring. In this story a craze for *Uncle Remus* sweeps the school, and nonsense chants pass from boy to boy. Eventually the stirring effect of the words issues in action, rival quasi-religious allegiances grow up, some supporting Brer Terrapin and others the Tar Baby, and 'House by House, when the news spread, dropped its doings, and followed the Mysteries—not without song . . . Some say . . . that the introits of the respective creeds ("Ingle—go—jang" —"Ti—yi—Tungalee!") carried in themselves the seeds of dissent.' Battle ensues, and as a result of the destructive orgy,

---

[13] *Debits and Credits*, 1926, but in the *Sussex Edition* included in *Stalky and Co.*, xvii. 193–216.

exhilarating and cathartic to the boys, a practical purgation follows: a misfit temporary master, who does not understand the Coll., is forced to leave.

Kipling's version of effective poetry for the people, rather than for literary critics, has many sources. The most obvious is the London music-hall. Kipling's acquaintance with the halls, in so far as it influenced his writing, seems to have been brief but intense. In the autumn of 1889 he moved to lodgings in Villiers Street, and plunged into the life of the metropolis. Already a sought-after new writer, he held himself aloof from literary circles, and deliberately sought to know England at the level of the streets. In *Something of Myself* he recorded the three-month involvement with the music-hall opposite his lodgings, Gatti's-under-the-Arches, where he 'listened to the observed and compelling songs of the Lion and Mammoth Comiques, and the shriller strains—but equally "observed"— of the Bessies and Bellas'. The experience of 'the smoke, the roar, and the good-fellowship of relaxed humanity at Gatti's "set" the scheme for a certain sort of song'.[14] The songs were the *Barrack-room Ballads*, based on his observation of soldiers in India and of the Guardsmen who frequented Gatti's, and filtered through the attitudes of the 'elderly but upright bar-maid' he took with him to the hall. In 'My Great and Only',[15] which is more contemporary evidence of these events, since it was one of the sketches he sent back to his Indian newspaper from his English visit, he expatiated more fully on his explora-tion of 'the diversions of heathendom' as exemplified by the London music-hall. In his sketch he claimed to have written a music-hall song, and to have had it performed with great success by a Comique singer. There are various unlikely or discrepant details in both these accounts. He does not say, for instance, how a barmaid came to have free time to accompany him regularly to evening performances in the music-hall; and while he apparently gives convincing detail of his meeting the singer, through advertisements for songs in the theatrical press, it is not explained how the man came to be performing, at that

[14] Op. cit., pp. 80–1.
[15] *The Civil and Military Gazette* (Lahore, Jan. 1890), reprinted in *Abaft the Funnel* (New York, 1909), *Sussex Edition*, xxix. 259–67.

moment, at Gatti's. If the writing and performance of Kipling's music-hall song is a fiction, however, it is only the more interesting; for the story is in that case a fantasy of success in a kind, one may presume, that he coveted for himself, at a period when literary recognition was coming to him very freely already.

Kipling clearly knew much about the hall. Many details of 'My Great and Only' fit exactly with the events at Gatti's in these months. It seems very likely that there was, as he claims, a singer with whom he became friendly. They were friendly people, and susceptible to admiration and cigars. It may have been Leo Dryden, who was the singer who delivered the song that in the sketch Kipling says was a rival to his own composition. It was called 'Shopmates', a parody of a tragic ballad called 'Shipmates', and itself, according to Kipling, 'a priceless ballad' of 'grim tragedy, lighted with lurid humour'. It is more likely that his acquaintance was James Fawn, who appeared at Gatti's on the same bill as Dryden for the week beginning 11 November and stayed after him until the Christmas change of bill on 23 December. Fawn was a versatile comic singer, who began with convivial and character songs—the less 'swell' end of the Comique range—and moved on in later years to be an old-fashioned red-nose comic. In these months he was involved in a successful court action to protect his most famous song, 'Ask a P'liceman', from performance by another singer in a pantomime. This may have suggested Kipling's ironic remark that he was taught about property rights in songs by the singer he befriended, who stole his from him. The current topic of debate in music-hall circles was the issue of 'protected' material, as Kipling mentions in the sketch; he also says there that his song borrowed the chorus of a 'protected' piece, which seems to make it less likely that his song was performed freely, as he suggests.

In 'My Great and Only' snatches of Kipling's song are given, and another verse from it is introduced, as being sung by Ortheris, at the end of the story 'Love o' Women',[16] where it serves as a last facet in the framing of a grisly incident. It is clearly the forerunner of the *Barrack-room Ballads*; but it is not so

[16] *Many Inventions*, 1893, *Sussex Edition*, v. 359–92.

clear that Fawn would have sung it. Its resemblance to his songs is more apparent than real. The differences emerge when it is set beside the song which I take to be its inspiration, which Fawn did sing in the autumn of 1889. This was called 'The Soldier', and was written by E. W. Rogers and published by R. Maynard in 1890. Rogers was a successful song-writer, who worked for Marie Lloyd and George Robey as well as Fawn, producing among other things 'The Lambeth Walk'. Kipling knew 'The Soldier'; he quoted, or rather rewrote, the most significant verse of it in relation to his own piece in 'The Army of a Dream', a story published in 1904.[17] 'The Soldier' has six verses and a chorus which varies, as that of Kipling's music-hall song does, with each repetition. Rogers's song, however, follows the usual pattern of the music-hall character study and takes up a new, unrelated aspect of its subject for each verse. This practice had a practical use, in that a song going badly could be cut or stopped at any point. Kipling had noticed the structure; he says that his song consisted of a chorus plus 'four elementary truths'. It is clear, though, from the portions given, that its story was one indivisible whole. While the song Fawn sang presented in turn various soldiers from a militiaman to General Gordon, Kipling's tells the story of a guardsman's rejection by an undercook, and his subsequent wooing of a housemaid. It has a punchline ('An'. . . she can't foot the bill') which really only makes sense in relation to the convention about soldiers' sponging on women which is enunciated in the other song:

> Who is it mashes the country nurse? The soldier!
> Who is it borrows the lady's purse? The soldier!
> Getting it toddles towards the bar
> Orders a drink and a big cigar,
> Hands it back quietly, and says ta! ta! the soldier!

This is the stanza improved upon in 'The Army of a Dream'.

> 'Oo is it mashes the country nurse?
> The Guardsman!
> 'Oo is it takes the lydy's purse?
> The Guardsman!

---

[17] *Traffics and Discoveries*, 1904, *Sussex Edition*, vii. 245–305.

Calls for a drink, and a mild cigar,
Batters a sovereign down on the bar,
Collars the change and says 'Ta-ta!'
The Guardsman!

The description of the gallery at Gatti's, when he thought they 'would never let go of the long-drawn howl on "Soldier"' could easily refer to their response to Fawn singing Rogers's song. The piece is a typical music-hall character sketch; it is superficially completely explicit, simple, and repetitious, while the complexity of the audience's response to the character presented is accommodated by juxtaposition. The listeners are invited in each verse in turn to recognize a different aspect of the soldier: his laughable conceit in his ludicrous uniform, his humanity in enjoying a good tune and a good drink, his culpable unscrupulousness with women; finally a contrast is made between the despicable fake soldier, the militiaman, and the real one, whom 'we must admire'. Crosscurrents are added by the mentioning of well-known names, Kassassin, Roberts. Kipling rejects this broad sweep of reference. His soldier resembles a broadside ballad hero, the protagonist of a drama of pride and passion on a humble level. The refrain he borrowed, 'And that's what the girl told the soldier', suggests the series of innuendoes it no doubt originally accompanied; but the pattern of the chorus he adds to it owes more to older popular tradition, and accommodates a much more compressed, economical, and powerful use of words than in the real song Fawn sang:

Oh, think o' my song when you're gowin' it strong,
And your boots are too little to 'old yer,
And don't try for things that are out of your reach,
And that's what the Girl told the Soldier,
Soldier! Soldier!
That's what the girl told the soldier.

The whole piece, pulled together by the repetition of descriptive lines in the first and last verses which no music-hall writer could have produced—'At the back o' the Knightsbridge Barricks / When the fog's a-gatherin' dim'—has an art which far outstrips E. W. Rogers.

What Kipling really admired, I feel, was not the songs, though he repeatedly said they were 'works of art',[18] but their presentation, and their audiences' response. Their effect upon the people was magical; its potential at a time when poetry seemed to be shrinking in upon itself and appealing to fewer and fewer readers, was unlimited. At the end of 'My Great and Only' he invoked the 'mighty intellect' who would one day 'rise up from Bermondsey, Battersea, or Bow . . . coarse, but clear-sighted, hard but infinitely and tenderly humorous, speaking the People's tongue . . . and telling them in swinging, urging, ringing verse what it is that their inarticulate lips would express'. Here, and again in 'The Village that Voted the Earth was Flat', he described the triumphant reception of the potent song. As the Comique began, the poet clutched his pot of beer, and hoped for the presence of heavy-booted guardsmen. At the first verse he fancied he 'could catch a responsive hoof-beat in the gallery . . . Then came the chorus and the borrowed refrain. It took—it went home with a crisp click.' They joined in the chorus, with a howl, and were 'hooked . . . With each verse the chorus grew louder'; and at the final repetition, 'as a wave gathers to the curl-over, singer and sung-to filled their chests and hove the chorus, through the quivering roof—horns and basses drowned and lost in the flood—to the beach-like boom of beating feet'. The potent animality of the images is very noticeable.

The song in 'The Village that Voted the Earth was Flat' is sung by a woman clearly modelled on Nellie Farren, whom Kipling saw in burlesque at the Gaiety, and admired for her

---

[18] See his correspondence about the music-halls, and especially the song 'Ka-foozle-um', published in J. B. Booth, *The Days We Knew* (London, 1943), pp. 29–35. The extant printed version of 'Ka-foozle-um' is by S. Oxon, printed in 1865, and is a jocular tale of the wooing of a Turkish maiden by a Jew of whom her father disapproves and whom he eventually murders; its humour is reminiscent of W. S. Gilbert. The tune seems to have been popular with the writers of burlesques. Lewis S. Winstock, in his article 'Rudyard Kipling and Army Music', *Kipling Journal* (June 1971), 5–12, mentions that it has now become an obscene song, 'The Harlot of Jerusalem', and speculates as to what versions Kipling knew; the apparent nonsense word 'ka-foozle-um' seems to have had overtones of brotheldom as early as 1825, when scene vii of *The Life of an Actor*, performed at the Adelphi, took place 'Outside of Mrs Cafooslem's Boarding House'.

boyish charm, but also, it seems clear, for the devotion which she inspired in the gallery boys:[19]

She swept into that song with the full orchestra. It devastated the habitable earth for the next six months. Imagine, then, what its rage and pulse must have been at the incandescent hour of its birth! She only gave the chorus once. At the end of the second verse, 'Are you *with* me, boys?' she cried, and the house tore it clean away from her . . . It was delirium. Then she picked up the Gubby dancers and led them in a clattering improvised lockstep thrice round the stage till her last kick sent her diamond-hilted shoe catherine-wheeling to the electrolier. I saw the forest of hands raised to catch it, heard the roaring and stamping pass through hurricanes to full typhoon; heard the song, pinned down by the faithful double-basses as the bull-dog pins down the bellowing bull, overbear even those; till at last the curtain fell . . . Still the song, through all those whitewashed walls, shook the reinforced concrete of the Trefoil as steam pile-drivers shake the flanks of a dock.

Notice the insistence upon sub-human, but immensely powerful, expression. The power with words to move masses of people to physical demonstration was the art Kipling wished to learn from the music-hall.

A further important aspect of that magic is also contained in these scenes. The worker of the spell is the performer; the writer feels his power in private, safe even from the awareness of his existence amongst those whom he moves. 'Dal, the woman singer, is vulnerable, being as overwhelmed in emotion as her audience, and can only whisper her gratitude huskily; but Kipling, safe in the knowledge that 'They do not call for authors on these occasions' felt that whatever joy might be sent him, the

---

[19] See the account of her following in W. Macqueen-Pope, *Nights of Gladness* (London, 1956), pp. 143–4. They ran as a bodyguard every night by her carriage, and welcomed her back from tours with huge banners emblazoned 'The Boys Welcome Their Nellie'. The impresario Bat in this story seems to owe something to the Gaiety manager George Edwardes. In a bad poem addressed 'To Lyde of the Music Halls' ('A Recantation', *Definitive Edition*, pp. 369–70) about Marie Lloyd, invoking her by the extraordinary title of 'Singer to Children!' he again stressed the power and consequent obligations of the popular singer:

> Yet they who use the Word assigned,
> To hearten and make whole,
> Not less than Gods have served mankind,
> Though vultures rend their soul.

success of his music-hall song gave him perfect felicity, an utter happiness which fame greater than Shakespeare's could not surpass. As the lines of the song mutated in the instant oral tradition of the drunken music-hall audience under his window that night, he murmured to himself, ' "I have found my Destiny" '. If none of it really happened, such an invention is even more striking than the recording of feeling supercharged by the heat of the moment. The desire for self-effacement has often been observed in Kipling's poems: it is, of course, the whole burden of his epitaph; and it issued first in conjunction with the desire to express and call out strong emotion, in the character-song formula of the *Barrack-room Ballads*. The occasion on which he actually attained the sort of overwhelming success which he describes so ecstatically here was to come later, with 'The Absent-Minded Beggar'. He certainly enjoyed the popularity which the song (and pockets full of tobacco) gave him with the troops in South Africa, but he hardly felt the piece was his own. He gave its profits to the fund for the troops, and for some time he left it out of his collected verse; the remark that he would shoot the man who wrote it, if it were not suicide, is often taken to mean that he was ashamed of its 'elements of direct appeal', its open sentimentality, and backhanded aggressiveness.[20] I think it more likely that it is a rather coy reference to his disowning of the song, coupled with the ambivalence he always shows towards great popular success. There is a tantalizing mystery for him in the compulsive tune which thrusts itself on the attention long after conscious critical faculties have rejected it in wearied revulsion. In 'The Absent-Minded Beggar' he created that self-activating artifact, and in reality, as in the fantasy of 'My Great and Only', 'Builded better than he knew'. His disclaimer has the same force as the last line of the earlier piece, which dismisses his success: 'and the same, they say, is a Vulgarity!'

The *Barrack-room Ballads*, however, have more about them than that. In them the music-hall strain is tonally dominant; but like all his ballads, they draw formal and verbal elements from many other kinds of popular poetry. Poets of the people, in 1889, wrote not only for the halls, but also for the newspapers

---

[20] See *Something of Myself*, pp. 150–1.

and magazines and the drawing-room; for the schoolchild and reciter, as well as for the variety artist. Kipling felt their verse too partook of the magical, in that it affected large audiences of unliterary persons, and evoked emotion closely concerned with action, issuing in practical results within the communities for which it was written. In *Captains Courageous* the fishing community, gathered together for its memorial day, is moved by a recitation by an 'actress from Philadelphia', whose 'wonderful voice took hold of the people by their heartstrings'[21] despite the inferiority of the port of Brixham as she describes it to their own town. The Victorian popular poets drew upon sources of which Kipling too was aware, and to which he could turn directly, in older popular verse: upon folk-song and oral ballads, broadsides and chapbooks, hymns, and the post-Romantic tradition of narrative verse on patriotic, historical, and nationalistic subjects which was fathered by Scott and Macaulay. A ballad like 'Danny Deever' welds together Rossetti's 'Sister Helen' and an obscene army song; 'The Widow's Party' takes the highly serious ballad of 'Edward, Edward', familiar still from the Romantic versions of Percy and Scott, and treats it as a writer for the broadsides or the early music-hall would, undercutting it by rendering it in comic cockney. 'Snarleyow', under a name from Marryat, couples a stanza shaped like that of a comic ballad by W. S. Gilbert ('Etiquette', for example) with a music-hall chorus of downbeat cynicism, to tell a story George Sims would have made tear-jerking and Kipling makes tragic. The elements of all nineteenth-century ballad making can be traced in the collection, with additions from sources which supply rhythm, without any words at all, like the tramp of feet on a route march or the rather different beat of parade-ground drill. In rendering the character song of Tommy Atkins, inspired by the Indian Army, James Fawn, and the gallery at Gatti's, Kipling brought batteries of verbal magic from many sources to bear upon the model and the audience, and his spell was hugely successful.

The first of the *Barrack-room Ballads* were published by W. E. Henley, in the magazine he wielded as a weapon in his struggle with Aestheticism. Soldierly poems were very much to his

[21] Op. cit., p. 193.

purpose. He also edited such poems into 'a book of verse for boys', *Lyra heroica*, in 1892. He thought it the first such collection, but it was anticipated by several popular poets and editors of books of recitations, including Frederick Langbridge who, in the autumn of 1889 as Kipling studied humanity in the streets of London, was editing *Ballads of the Brave: Poems of Chivalry, Enterprise, and Constancy*, to be 'a good Boys-Poetry-Book'. He was in turn inspired by William Cox Bennett, who had aspired to the creation of a history of England in verse, for the inspiration of the working classes and the young, in 1868. These are clearly magical uses of poetry, following Collingwood's definition, intended to inspire emotions to be discharged into the business of life. Kipling was the inheritor of these ambitions, and indeed partook more fully than he would have liked to think of the drive to convert and educate which came down to the late Victorian Empire-builders from their Evangelical parents. Accordingly he felt that children, like uneducated adults, were fit audience for his spell-binding; and just as his music-hall-inspired poems for the soldier drew upon all aspects of nineteenth-century popular poetry, so he brought the resources of a craft much wider than that of the average versifier of history to bear upon the educative task. In 1911 Kipling cooperated with C. R. L. Fletcher in producing a history book with interspersed verses; but his best historical/educative poems accompany his own fictional writing for children. In the Mowgli stories, *Kim*, and most clearly in *Puck of Pook's Hill* and *Rewards and Fairies*, one may see the full scope of his mixed form of story and songs, where the verses contribute at levels beyond or below or alongside the rational, augmenting or modifying the pattern of the narrative with magical reinforcements.

In his earlier writing for children the education aimed at was moral, and only in a very general sense historical. He sought, through the stories and verse of *The Jungle Books*,[22] to evoke the child's sense of the possibility of belonging to a society with a character, aims, and organization transcending but also protectively encompassing the individual. The Law is set out, and illustrated; dissent of various kinds is voiced, and accommodated or suppressed; and emotional acceptance, the internaliz-

---

[22] 1894 and 1895; *Sussex Edition*, vol. xii.

ing of the sanctions enforcing social control, is encouraged, all through the use of verses beside or within the narratives.

The basic attraction of the Mowgli stories is the transformation of domestic realities—mother and father and brothers, and uncles and other adult teachers—by the exotic settings of Mowgli's jungle, which makes both the exotic accessible and safer, and the everyday more exciting and important. The pleasurable juxtaposition begins on the first page: the chapter heading to 'Mowgli's Brothers' is a quite alien and exciting section of something called 'Night-song in the Jungle'. The verse is high and mysterious, about 'the hour of pride and power'; the first sentence of the story is domestic, half-comic, about scratching and yawning and spreading out the paws 'to get rid of the sleepy feeling in their tips'. Wolves are humanized and made familiar; their jungle law, the moral ordering of the universe which accommodates both wolves and little boys, when they obey it, has been mentioned and is to be demonstrated.

The use of incantation and repetition, and of words of power and ritual, is pervasive in the stories; Mowgli repeatedly saves himself by the Master-Words of the Jungle, repeated in all the right languages. The Law Baloo teaches is couched in eminently chantable verse, which he, and his pupils real as well as fictional, deliver in 'a sort of sing-song', and learn from it their part. Conversely in the story of 'Kaa's Hunting' the Bandar-log have their song, expressing the philosophy which leads to their horribly ignoble death, and demonstrates their social worthlessness. But the impulse of Mowgli to selfish and careless play, which he must learn is wrong, is shared by the child reader. At the end of the tale, after punishment and forgiveness, the story is flipped upwards, indeed almost undercut, by the addition of the text of the monkeys' song, which delights by its verbal energy, irony, and invention: 'Here we sit in a branchy row . . . Then join our leaping lines that scumfish through the pines . . .' It is offered to be enjoyed, and now that we have learned by the story to see through its attractions, we can also enjoy our superiority to its enticements.

There is a related effect in 'Rikki-Tikki-Tavi', where the vanity and empty-headedness of the taylor-bird are mocked and criticized throughout the story, as he wastes time making a series of premature or unhelpful songs instead of assisting in the fight against the cobras. At the end, though, his chant in honour of Rikki-Tikki-Tavi is given:

> Who hath delivered us, who?
> Tell me his nest and his name.
> Rikki, the valiant, the true,
> Tikki, with eyeballs of flame,
> Rik-tikki-tikki, the ivory-fangèd,
>   the hunter with eyeballs of flame.

This combines a joke for the adult reader of the story, in that it is a parody of Swinburne, a good example of the excited poet foolishly singing for the victories of others, with a comic–heroic praising of the mongoose which is very satisfying to the child listener or reader as a contrast to the modesty he shows himself at the end of the tale.

A rather different use of the division between layers of the story which the juxtaposition of narrative and verse can give is the climactic use of 'Mowgli's Song', at the end of 'Tiger! Tiger!' The tale has demonstrated Mowgli's , the individual's, essential separateness: having learnt the Law of the Jungle, which admits him to the society of the disciplined and truly adult, he has made the painful discovery that others do not keep the Law, and so no ideal community exists; he has gained only his selfhood, and the society of a few equal individuals. Adherence to the Law under this disillusion is the hardest moral lesson to learn, especially where duty is taught entirely, as it is here, in terms of society, without relating it to a superhuman power which offers future justification. Mowgli passes the test, and triumphs over his enemies, and departs laconically at the end of the story into the grown-up world which he has entered through his ordeal. The reader, however, is presumed not to have arrived yet at this transition; and so after the tale, his emotions of angry triumph, and pain and grief for Mowgli's sufferings, are given expression in a verse. 'Mowgli's Song' is the song of the younger self, the reader; in strange, unrhymed verse 'that came up into his throat all by itself' it voices the reader's protest, and asks the unanswerable question as to why the world is so hard, and ends with 'My heart is heavy with the things that I do not understand'.

The combination of song and story in this way is not pursued in the following books: *Captains Courageous* uses songs integrated with the narrative, as do some stories in *The Day's Work*: 'The Brushwood Boy', for example, has a music-hall song sung by the troops and a sort of children's song to the piano used to reveal the possessors of a common dreamworld to each other, suggesting again a magical idea of the sources and powers of poetry. In *Kim* deliberately riddling use is made of snatches of verse for chapter headings: it is not so much that their relevance to the story is obscure, rather that they set the incidents or emotions of the chapters they head into quite other contexts, and deliberately jolt the attention of the reader away from the immediacy of the tale. They stress the fictional nature of the story: it is capable of expression, they suggest, in other terms, the incidents are not uniquely real but related to art and archetypes often expressed differently. They appear to be snatches from longer poems. These were then later completed, but it was important at their first use that they were not recognizable, so that they seize the attention and suggest the existence of other tales unread. Poetry is felt, as in 'Wireless', to have a life of its own, only occasionally and intermittently accessible to the reader, through the poet, and for him equally impossible to command, dependent upon the revelations of his Daemon. Their effect upon the story is like that of an epic simile; they relate the aspect of the story which they isolate to other worlds, enlarging and at the same time distancing the narrative, controlling focus and perspective. Their expression in rhythms and vocabulary so remote from those of the story is deliberately unsettling.

In the *Just So Stories*[23] the intercutting of different modes is even stranger; it arose out of the circumstances of oral narration, and is uncomfortable for the reader who has only the printed page. There is a pervasive sense of the private language and the shared joke. This is felt most obviously in the contrasting styles of the stories, which are in a heavily stylized, poetic language, and of the commentary accompanying the pictures, which attempts to reproduce the factual simplicities and unexpected twists of conversation with small children. Responses to

[23] 1902; *Sussex Edition*, vol. xiii.

questions Kipling's own children asked are incorporated, and
attempts are made to extend the shared jokes to other children.
In his book the verses, which were completed after the stories,
are broadly of two kinds. Some, like the mouth-filling sing-song
of Old Man Kangaroo, are poems for children to chant, using
words for their amusing qualities of sound. Others take up the
implicit relationship between the adult and the child to whom
he tells the fantastical tales and bring their domestic life into
focus. An example is 'When the cabin portholes are dark and
green', the vignette from the life of a travelling family which
appears at the end of the story of 'How the Whale Got its
Throat'. This domestication of the story by the verse can have a
moralizing effect, as in 'The Camel's Hump', where the fun of
chanting and the relation of the story to the world of the nursery
combine to drive home the moral point:

> Kiddies and grown-ups too-oo-oo,
> If we haven't enough to do-oo-oo,
> We get the hump—
> Cameelious hump—
> The hump that is black and blue!

Kipling's affection for his daughter which prompted the book
is most openly expressed in the verses; in the intimate and
tender poems which he attaches to the stories of Taffimai he
combines the expression of his personal feeling with a humour
and ingenuity which also please the child reader.[24] These
poems move decisively towards the kind of writing for children
that he was to develop in the Puck stories. They have the
primitive poetic satisfaction of delightful rhymes: 'racial talks
and such' / 'gay shell torques and such', 'Broadstonebrook' /
'come and look'. They extend the world already introduced in
their stories, and without the explicitness of narrative they
make available a complex of feeling that attaches to that world
for Kipling. His sense of the transience of childhood is con-
nected in the poems to the loss of past times, and the child,
unable to conceive of either idea herself, is put in touch with
both through simple images of the natural world and by the

[24] We have the testimony of several readers, including Rosemary Sutcliff ('Rudyard
Kipling', Three Bodley Head Monographs (London, 1968), pp. 95–6) that children
are aware of the depth of love expressed in the Taffimai stories.

connection which is made to the particular, mortal, but end-
lessly recurring love of father and daughter.

> There runs a road by Merrow Down—
> A grassy track to-day it is—
> An hour out of Guildford town,
> Above the river Wey it is.
>
> Here, when they heard the horse-bells ring,
> The ancient Britons dressed and rode
> To watch the dark Phoenicians bring
> Their goods along the Western Road . . .
>
> But long and long before that time
> (When bison used to roam on it)
> Did Taffy and her Daddy climb
> That down, and had their home on it . . .
>
> Of all the tribe of Tegumai
> Who cut that figure, none remain,—
> On Merrow Down the cuckoos cry—
> The silence and the sun remain.
>
> But as the faithful years return
> And hearts unwounded sing again,
> Comes Taffy dancing through the fern
> To lead the Surrey spring again.

In these verses one also feels Kipling's ability to convey the
sense of history as something real, of which the child reader or
listener is a part;[25] but the flowering of this is in *Puck of Pook's
Hill*[26] and *Rewards and Fairies*.[27] The former was unequivocally
meant for tales told to children, with his own, now old enough
to be introduced to less fabulous histories, as its first audience.
In *Something of Myself*[28] he wrote of *Rewards and Fairies* as stories
which 'had to be read by children, before people realised that
they were meant for grown-ups' and it is in that volume that he
takes the next step in his use of poems, working 'the material in
three or four overlaid tints and textures', which took the mixed
form away from the writing for children which had inspired it to
become the major medium of his mature work. The crosscurrents between the poems and the various levels of the stories

---

[25] See Rosemary Sutcliff, 'Kipling for Children', *Kipling Journal* (Dec. 1965), 25–8:
'history is something to do with oneself'.

[26] 1906; *Sussex Edition*, vol. xiv.

[27] 1910; *Sussex Edition*, vol. xv.

[28] *Something of Myself*, p. 190.

came to serve as a means of holding together the parts of his audience, and satisfying them at different levels of comprehension, intellectual and emotional. The poems for children had always had this function in some ways. In *Puck of Pook's Hill* he worked to spread the significance of the stories through the various effects of narrative and verse, and so bring home the awareness that history affects everybody's life, and that the child is involved in, and may begin to approach emotionally, processes beyond comprehension on a rational level. With linked verses and tales Kipling impresses the linkedness of all things.

The techniques already developed in writing for children are taken further. The shift of point of view, so that the verse voices the attitude of someone who has been seen only incidentally in the story, is carried over from *The Jungle Books* into the 'Pict Song' which concludes the story of 'The Winged Hats'. It is used with a new seriousness. The awareness that political and imperial struggles, with which the story involves us, are felt quite differently by the subject peoples in the background and underfoot is an important insight, dramatized and made available by the verses. Other juxtapositions have an effect more like the chapter headings in *Kim*, in that the poems, surprising the reader by their difference of tone from the stories they accompany, make him aware of the same set of ideas or circumstances existing in different contexts. An example is the 'Smuggler's Song' which concludes 'Hal o' the Draft', which not only shifts the focus of our sympathy from Hal and the king's agent to the smugglers they have outwitted, but also makes us perceive the smuggling as outliving the richly Elizabethan setting of the story, and occurring in Georgian times. Hal's recognition of the ballad Dan sings, and his interest in new objects in modern England that he can make use of in his own art, have already made clear a vital continuity of human interests and occupations. It gives life to the history that Dan can't be bothered with when it comes as a lesson.

The humanizing of the lessons of history makes them, of course, less clear cut, and so on other occasions the stories are summed up and their import made more explicit in the verses. At the end of the series of Saxon and Norman stories in *Puck of Pook's Hill* the runes of prophecy on Weland's sword, which have been seen to be fulfilled, are given as a magical verse, and

the reader perceives the continuity of the events thus epitomized. The verses are used to simplify or make concrete the
message of the story more often in *Rewards and Fairies*, where
they are used by Kipling in his effort to make complex stories of
adult activities comprehensible to the child reader. 'If' is
placed as a summary of the qualities needed and exemplified in
the political manœuvres discussed in the American tales, in the
midst of which it appears; after 'Simple Simon', the layered and
elliptical tale of the dedication of Francis Drake, refracted
through Cattiwow's struggle to shift the log and Simon's
devotion to his friend and his untimely iron ships, the essentials
of Drake's character and its making are summed up in a very
simple form in 'Frankie's Trade', an appropriate sea shanty.
The story of St Wilfrid and his priest and the conversion of the
heathen Meon, which handles ideas about faith and allegiance
and diplomatic relationships, is simplified but also deepened
and affirmed in the verses at the beginning and end. 'Eddi's
Service' shows Eddi the priest in a more Christian and saintly
light than he appears in the story; and 'Song of the Red
War-boat' voices the heathen's devotion to his leader which is
overborne and perhaps subsumed by the Christian's service to
his God.

There is a very wide range of form and tone in these poems,
reflecting the variety of their functions. Ballads and shanties are
appropriate to the settings of some stories, and they are suitable
to the purposes of incantation and epitome; in other places the
need is for a poem which will elevate or dignify, supplying ritual
weight rather than working rhythms to stories which break
down 'history' into tales of individual lives for the sake of the
child's response. In these tales the lesson to be learnt is
important in general terms, and its relation to a system of belief
and behaviour to which they too owe allegiance needs to be
solemnly understood. This is the governing motive of the books:
Kipling's belief in history and the importance of place, continuity, and tradition, in moulding people to their destiny and
duty. It is expressed in the songs of Puck and Sir Richard, and
'A Tree Song', all voicing love for England; in Thorkild's song
of love for his native shore; in the dialect verses praising Sussex
called 'A Three Part Song', and in 'A British–Roman Song',
rising to the climactic 'Children's Song' at the end of *Puck of*

Pook's Hill, when Dan and Una and the readers are supposed to find their own voices to add to the songs of praise. Love of country thus approached through history necessarily involves, as in the work of Sir Walter Scott, a sense of mortality, of the loss of past times and the transience of one's own; and 'Cities and Thrones and Powers', perhaps the best poem of the earlier volume, captures the poignancy which is so important in the intensity of the emotions involved:

> Cities and Thrones and Powers
> Stand in Time's eye,
> Almost as long as flowers,
> Which daily die:
> But, as new buds put forth
> To glad new men,
> Out of the spent and unconsidered Earth,
> The Cities rise again.

This is placed at the beginning of the long story of Rome's doomed Empire, and is laden with rhythmic suggestion of that fall. But the story begins by shifting the mood abruptly and ironically to a matter-of-fact and homely level: 'Dan had come to grief over his Latin.' This is a tonal effect developed from the juxtaposition of domestic and exotic in the *Just So Stories*; here it serves both to bring home the relevance of the tale to the reader, and to relieve him of some of the awe and solemnity of the subjects handled by giving a familiar point of reference. A similar effect opens 'A Doctor of Medicine', a grim story about the plague with Culpepper as its ironically treated hero; there the opening is a hymn about astrology, set, I think, to the tune of 'Immortal, Invisible, God only wise', which depends bathetically to the opening of the tale: 'They were playing hide-and-seek with bicycle lamps after tea.'

The reverse of this effect is seen when Kipling uses a much more complex poetic form than that of the hymn to add intensity of feeling unavailable to the child reader on an explicit narrative level. The story of the 'Marklake Witches', for instance, has overtones which Dan and Una do not grasp. The reader is admitted to some of them with the author's help over the fictional children's heads, but there are levels which only adults familiar with matters of prejudice and ignorance will infer. All the weight of sadness in the tale is, though, conveyed in 'The Way Through the Woods', in a poetic image of limitation and loss available to all readers through the sound of the poem:

> They shut the way through the woods
> Seventy years ago.
> Weather and rain have undone it again,
> But now you would never know
> There was once a road through the woods
> Before they planted the trees.
> It is underneath coppice and heath,
> And the thin anemones.
> Only the keeper sees
> That, where the ring-dove broods,
> And the badgers roll at ease,
> There was once a road through the woods.

The shifts between the high and the homely are much more complex than in the earlier books, especially when the group of poems and stories is a long one. *Puck of Pook's Hill* begins with such a series. We have the mysterious 'Harp Song of the Danish Women', and then the story descends to the cockleshell boat the children sail in the stream. Their vessel is dignified by their imaginations, until the tale moves, by the teasing contrast made between their scraps of modern science and his medieval hardihood, to Sir Richard's real voyage. It ends in further jokes. Then Thorkild's sea shanty strikes a heroic note, but the ensuing story plunges into corrupt power politics; the whole is resolved by the gnomic runes on Weland's sword. By the time Kipling had followed this method through to the end of the second book, his loading of the stories with allegories and allusions had rendered the connections quite obscure on a conscious level to any but an enquiring critical eye. 'The Tree of Justice' contrives to connect a ballad about poachers and fairies, Old Hobden, the children's dormouse, the keeper's gallows, the mad King Harold and the bitter jester Rahere, thieving gypsies, and an enigmatic carol about the cycles of the world. It is quite possible, however, that the child who had followed and learned by Kipling's method through the two volumes might respond to the final song on a level of intuitive appreciation as acute as any.

For my final point is that Kipling believed in the power of art,

and especially of poetry, to influence the imagination beyond
the level of consciousness, with a magical, irrational, effect,
which he pursues. Throughout these stories literature is used as
a link with the past, as one of the most powerful bonds between
people, an epitome of tradition and a potent weapon for it. The
stories make this explicit, while the poems seek to wield the
book itself in that way, to cast its spell upon the reader. An
extended example is the first Roman tale, 'A Centurion of the
Thirtieth'. It begins with the potent 'Cities and Thrones and
Powers', and shifts for its locating, homely note to learning
Latin. This is a meaningless chore to Dan at the beginning of
the tale; but the *Lays of Ancient Rome* are stimulating, and the
game Una plays from them leads to her contact with the ancient
Roman Parnesius. He, ironically, has never been taught the
history of his own people. He has, however, a living faith, which
he expresses in his hymn to Mithras, in Latin which to the
children has 'deep, splendid-sounding words' (in the story of St
Wilfrid, too, they respond to the tunes of Latin chant, deeply
stirred by the *Dies irae*). The story closes with 'A British–
Roman Song' in an English metre derived from a classical one,
and the next tale, leading straight on, opens with a new Lay of
Ancient Rome, a jaunty marching song for the legions whose
theme in fact foreshadows the doom of the Empire. Thus the
songs within the stories are potent in themselves, incantations
and evocations, and learning is done through emotional responses to them, leading to the understanding of them on other
levels.

This, then, is what poetry was for Kipling. He used and
explored its irrational, magical powers, hoping to intensify and
enlighten by directing the most primitive of our responses to
words. His ballads, chants, and incantations are not falsely
naïve, not a rejection of complexity and subtlety in poetry;
rather they are the strong essences of a literary craft most subtle
in its methods. To approach the deeper springs of motive and
character he used verse, as Dan and Una innocently use the
words of *A Midsummer Night's Dream*, conjuring up Puck, who
leads them through songs and stories to the possession of
their heritage. Kipling's poems conjure up people, who lead
his readers to understand others and themselves, and the
emotional language that we have in common.

12. W. B. YEATS: POET AND CRANK

BY LAURENCE LERNER

I

I HAVE chosen to talk about the poetry of Yeats this evening for three reasons. The first, and in a sense the most important, is that I like it so much. We are often told that Yeats is the greatest English poet of this century, and to me this grey commonplace is continually coming to life in the form of the unforgettable lines that haunt all modern readers of poetry. Yeats is the man who, in imagining country-house life as a fountain, wrote of the fountain that

> (It) rains down life until the basin spills,
> And mounts more dizzy high the more it rains
> As though to choose whatever shape it wills
> And never stoop to a mechanical
> Or servile shape, at others' beck and call.

These lines could be about his own poetry, choosing its shape to fit the strangeness of his experiences, the recklessness of his passions—never at the beck and call of tight metre or mechanical patterns, yet always magnificent in form. Yeats is the man who, in telling us that you cannot learn creative writing as you learn philology, put it in these two perfect and arrogant lines:

> Nor is there singing school, but studying
> Monuments of its own magnificence.

He is the poet whose terse violent love-lyrics burn with a blend of Blake, of the metaphysicals, and of his own crude hatred of old age and bodily decrepitude; the old man who concludes a dialogue of he and she by making her say

> I offer to love's play
> My dark declivities.

I can hardly hope to describe why Yeats seems to me the most eloquent, the most ecstatic, and the most splendid of modern poets; and I shall not try to—or not directly. The power and beauty of his poetry is a reason for reading it, for thinking about it, and learning it by heart—but for talking about it? I realize, as I reflect, that my second reason is, in another sense, more important. This is that the poetry of Yeats raises with peculiar and agonizing neatness a central critical problem, perhaps *the* central problem in the criticism of poetry: the relation between the value of a poem and the value of its subject-matter. I can state this problem quite simply, though I cannot (alas) answer it simply. How is it that the greatest poet of the century, a poet of wisdom and understanding of the heart, a sage as well as a singer—how is it that he expounded in his poems such absurd, such eccentric, such utterly crackpot ideas?

II

Everyone knows that Yeats had a taste for queer religions, for theosophy, Rosicrucianism, the Order of the Golden Dawn, alchemy; that he attended seances, encouraged and studied the automatic writing of his wife, studied Plotinus, Cornelius Agrippa, Madame Blavatsky; and in the end wrote out his whole intricate system in his book *A Vision*. Further, that he continually incorporated into his poetry the fruits of these studies, even wrote some poems to illustrate points in his system. It seems to me astonishing that poetry as great as Yeats's should have emerged from all this; but it has not astonished everyone. It will not, for instance, astonish those who take the occult seriously and regard *A Vision* as a great book; and I would like first of all to say something to them. Mr F. A. C. Wilson and Mr Cleanth Brooks have been among the most influential of those who have made this claim: Mr Wilson is more interested in the tradition, Mr Brooks in *A Vision* proper, but they agree in their willingness to move behind the poetry for further illumination.

Now in discussing their case, I must admit to one initial disadvantage. I have struggled hard with *A Vision*, but I find it unreadable. I mean that literally—I cannot read the book because I cannot find it coherent, cannot find enough to tie one page to those that went before: reading it is simply not a continuous experience. The aim of *A Vision* seems to be to set forth a psychology and a theory of history. Both these are represented by means of a symbolism drawn from the twenty-eight phases of the moon. There are two phases when (according to the psychology) human life is impossible, so we have twenty-six psychological types and presumably (this is not specified) twenty-eight historical phases in our era. My first puzzle is to know why these two systems have both been described in the same terms. I am assured by Mr Brooks that 'the phase of an age does not determine the phase of men living in that age', but I am not told, either by him or by Yeats, whether you *tend* to be born in your own phase—and if so, what significance attaches to those who are not; if not, why the terminology is the same. I can discover no resemblance between (let us say) 'the approach of solitude bringing with it an ever-increasing struggle with that which opposes solitude—sensuality, greed, ambition, physical curiosity in all its species—[and] philosophy return[ing] driving dogma out'—this is phase 14 of our Christian era—and the obsessed man of phase 14 in the psychology, whose true Mask is Oblivion, his false Mask Malignity, his true Creative Mind Vehemence, his false Creative Mind Opinionated Will, his Body of Fate None except Monotony, his Will Obsessed. Actually, it's not quite clear if that first description was of phase 13 or phase 14, but when we look at phase 13 of the psychology, we find no greater resemblance there. Will, Mask, Creative Mind, Body of Fate. These are the four faculties into which Yeats analyses and classifies personality. Will and Mask are antithetical, Creative Mind and Body of Fate (which seem to mean thought and its object) are primary. Innumerable diagrams, some quite complicated, show the relations of these faculties to one another and their place on the Great Wheel. Compare this scheme for a moment with another modern system, another mythology for explaining the mind and its workings—the Freudian terminology of id, ego, and superego, with its dynamisms of projection and introjection, reaction formation, repression, resistance, wish-fulfilment . . . The Freudian system is at least as complicated as Yeats's, but every item in it was pressed upon its author by the evidence, was devised in slow and patient response to what Freud was discovering about dreams and neurotic behaviour.

In contrast, what strikes us about Yeats's system is how arbitrary it all is. What do you *do* when your Creative Mind is Transformatory, or your Body of Fate has the character of Tumult, or of Absorption? What have Shakespeare, Balzac, and Napoleon in common that makes them the examples of phase 20? or (an even odder grouping) Cardinal Newman, Luther, Calvin, George Herbert, and A.E., the examples of phase 25? I look in Mr Cleanth Brooks's enthusiastic essay on *A Vision* to find the answers to such questions, and am told that the book contains 'the finest rhythmic prose written in English since that of Sir Thomas Browne'! When a shrewd or lively touch of observation crops up in the character sketches (and how rare this is), it seems totally independent of the system it is illustrating. The illuminating concept of the anti-self, about which Yeats had written so well in *Per amica silentia lunae*, developing a theory of artistic creation remarkably like Freud's, has been swamped and spun and disintegrated by the revolutions of the gyres and the lists of faculties.

When we turn to the section on history, with its discussion of the Great Year and the two ways of dividing it into phases, we are no better off. I will not linger on this part of *A Vision* except to say that it has, at any rate, one charm—the disarming frankness with which Yeats admits that he does not know what he's talking about. 'Of what followed from phase 17 to phase 21 [I can say] almost nothing, for I have no knowledge of the time', he writes; and even more revealing is this: 'Then follows, as always must in the last quarter, heterogeneous art; hesitation amid architectural forms, some book tells me.' Notice the order: it must have happened, because the system said so—what then does it matter what the book was which he opened to make sure that it did happen?

Now what are we to do, confronted with all this poppycock? Treat it with the contempt it deserves? How can we do that, when it is by the greatest of modern poets? If he took it seriously, should not we? But did he take it seriously? Yeats had a good deal to say about what we should think of his system: the trouble is he had too much to say, not all of it consistent. At one time he tells us that all symbolic art should arise out of a real belief; at another he hears the spirits who 'dictated' *A Vision* telling him that they have only come to give him metaphors for

poetry, or blames himself for being fool enough to write half a
dozen poems unintelligible without some part of his doctrine.
There is no reason why we should take much notice of any of
these remarks: Yeats was as full of blarney as any Irishman. We
have to make up our own minds about his ideas, and work out
our own answer to the question, how could such ideas give rise
to such poetry?

There are two easy answers to this question, which I shall
mention only to dismiss, since they do not solve the problem,
they abolish it. One is that the poetry is no good anyway: for Mr
Yvor Winters, who maintains this, there is no problem. I shall
not pause to refute him: I hope my occasional quotations from
Yeats will do that unaided. The other is that there is no
connexion between the ideas and the greatness of the poetry.
Now since the poems are about the very things dealt with in
A Vision—the cycle of history, Byzantium, the phases of the
moon, the Hunchback, and the Saint—you can only maintain
this by denying any connexion between the subjects of the
poems and their greatness. You have to say that it does not
matter what a poem means, as long as it sounds beautiful.
This view offends me as much as it would have offended Yeats:
I care about, and I intend to discuss, the meaning of his
poetry.

Clearly we have got to say that these crackpot ideas, when
they are turned into poetry, are able somehow to slough off their
eccentricity, to take on a form that bestows on them, or restores
to them, a wisdom and seriousness they had lacked. In a sense,
of course, this problem is not peculiar to Yeats: is it not the old
problem of the unbeliever's appreciation of religious poetry?
Not altogether: in this case the problem is sharper and more
awkward. For the unbeliever who responds to holy sonnets or
devout hymns does at least take Christianity seriously: he must,
or he could not respond. You may reject all Christian beliefs,
but unless you think that the experiences they describe in the
believer are real experiences, which you might share, the poems
will not speak to you. Two classes of reader are debarred from
responding to religious poetry: the devout Christian who holds,
with Dr Johnson, that 'man, admitted to implore the mercy of
his Creator, and plead the merits of his Redeemer, is already in
a higher state than poetry can confer', and the happy atheist

who finds that talk of sin, repentance, expiation, and conversion is a language he does not understand, about experiences he cannot conceive. Both classes are rare enough not to matter; but when it comes to *A Vision* I find myself (and I know I am not alone in this) very much in the position of that happy atheist. But when I turn to the poems—well, let us look at one, and one of the most famous.

> Turning and turning in the widening gyre
> The falcon cannot hear the falconer;
> Things fall apart; the centre cannot hold;
> Mere anarchy is loosed upon the world,
> The blood-dimmed tide is loosed, and everywhere
> The ceremony of innocence is drowned;
> The best lack all conviction, while the worst
> Are full of passionate intensity.
>
> Surely some revelation is at hand;
> Surely the Second Coming is at hand.
> The Second Coming! Hardly are those words out
> When a vast image out of *Spiritus Mundi*
> Troubles my sight: somewhere in sands of the desert
> A shape with lion body and the head of a man,
> A gaze blank and pitiless as the sun,
> Is moving its slow thighs, while all about it
> Reel shadows of the indignant desert birds.
> The darkness drops again; but now I know
> That twenty centuries of stony sleep
> Were vexed to nightmare by a rocking cradle,
> And what rough beast, its hour come round at last,
> Slouches towards Bethlehem to be born?

Now the first thing to say is what you must all have felt, listening to the poem: it's impossible to make fun of *this*. We are in another world, now, hearing the true voice of prophecy: solemn, mysterious, terrifying. It's true that this is a poem about Yeats's theory of history, that there is a long note by Yeats himself explaining it—or rather, not explaining it. The Great Year which began with the advent of Christianity is running out, we are in a phase of violence, our civilization is on a widening gyre and will be replaced by one which will spring 'as in a lightning flash' from the contrary, narrowing gyre.

But who cares about all this? In the first place, Yeats has

trimmed his system to make the poem. *A Vision* tells us that we entered phase 23 in 1927—it's still five phases too early to say 'its hour come round at last'. More important, what is this violence? Surely it is the violence of the world we know: the best do, alas, so often lack all conviction, the worst *are* full of passionate intensity. This opening stanza matters so much because, wherever Yeats got the idea from, it is *true*; and its power comes from itself—from the slow unleashing of its image of a flood, the growing sense of terror in rhythm and metaphor. As we repeat the poem over and over, only the opening image of the falcon remains puzzling, and perhaps this is the poem's weakness; yet without knowing that hawk and falcon are Yeats's images for the human intellect (and you could find that out from other poems), without speculating that the falconer is God, losing control of man, or the heart, losing control of the mind (for, of course, the interpreters do not agree)—without any of this we can feel, can't we, how just an image it is for the sense of growing chaos, or loss of control, that is the subject of the poem?

The strange image of the second stanza—the 'shape with lion body and the head of a man'—has a variety of origins —some biblical, some from Yeats's more esoteric reading. But what matters for Yeats as he writes the poem is the origin that lies behind them all, the collective unconscious, the *spiritus mundi* (or *anima mundi*, as he more usually calls it), the 'great memory passing on from generation to generation'. And the poem tells us that this is where the image comes from: we cannot ask for fairer treatment than that. Now if such a theory is true, of a collective storehouse of symbols, then we can say that no intellectual assent is needed by the reader before he re-sponds. I used the phrase 'collective unconscious', but I did not mean to imply any assent to the Jungian doctrine that goes by that name. A Freudian will explain the universality of symbols by the common element in individual personal development, not by any *supra*-personal pool of memory; someone else may explain them as the product of centuries of accumulating speculation about memory and the world soul—and a Jungian if he is consistent must grant that both these, and indeed the total sceptic, should be just as responsive as he is to these symbols. This is why scholarship and theories of the *anima mundi*

are such odd, such unnecessary companions: if the images
work, surely they do not select only believers to work on. You do
not even have to realize that any particular image is symbolic
for it to work on you. For a long time, before I had read Yeats's
prose or his commentators, I thought *spiritus mundi* must be an
old book where Yeats had found the image. I know better now,
but I also know that I did not appreciate the poem any the less
for this. If any of you have made the same mistake, do not
worry. Why would such a book seem important to Yeats? Only
because it embodied some very old and universal symbols
whose power he would recognize, symbols that belong in the
general storehouse of images. Or sound as if they would belong
in it, if it existed (which, for poetical purposes, is the same
thing).

   And the second coming itself? No historian takes historical
cycles very seriously nowadays, certainly not in the detailed
form Yeats gave them. But what we must take seriously is our
impulse to see recurrences and phases in history: not the
system, but the urge towards formulating it. And it is to this
urge that this poem speaks, for it is about the violence, the
distress, that forces us towards the wild speculation of the end.
The poem ends not on an assertion, but on a shock. An
ambiguous shock, too. Are we being told that the new era will
be one of violence, contrasting with the two thousand years of
Christian love; or are we being given a shocking suggestion
about the true nature, or at least the true effect, of Christianity?
I do not see how we can fail to take it, at least partly, as the
second; and I do not care what unpublished notes a critic digs
up to tell us that Yeats meant, or claimed to mean, only the first.
This is a great poem because it exploits and offends the fears
and the prejudices we all have.

   That is why I think 'The Second Coming', though it is
written to illustrate the system, has a meaning and a power
almost completely independent of it. So has 'Leda and the
Swan'. The annunciation that founded Greece, and began the
cycle immediately before Christianity, was made to Leda: her
swan corresponds to Mary's dove. This sonnet is meant to
describe the first movement of that Great Wheel. But all you
have to know is the story of Troy, and that Leda gave birth to
Helen.

A shudder in the loins engenders there
The broken wall, the burning roof and tower
And Agamemnon dead.

These wonderful lines are not about the Great Wheel. They show, opening out from Leda's violent personal drama, a famous event still in the future then, though long in the past for us; their excitement comes from the fame and antiquity of that event, not from its place in any cycle of twenty-eight phases.

I will choose one more example. In 1885 a brahmin visited Dublin as representative of the Theosophical Society. Yeats asked him if he believed in prayer, and was told:

No, one should say before sleeping 'I have lived many lives, I have been a slave and a prince. Many a beloved has sat upon my knees, and I have sat upon the knees of many a beloved. Everything that has been shall be again.'

Many years later, Yeats turned this into his poem 'Mohini Chatterjee':

I asked if I should pray,
But the Brahmin said,
'Pray for nothing, say
Every night in bed,
"I have been a king,
I have been a slave,
Nor is there anything,
Fool, rascal, knave,
That I have not been,
And yet upon my breast
A myriad heads have lain."'

That he might set at rest
A boy's turbulent days
Mohini Chatterjee
Spoke these, or words like these.
I add in commentary,
'Old lovers yet may have
All that time denied—
Grave is heaped on grave
That they be satisfied—
Over the blackened earth
The old troops parade,

> Birth is heaped on birth
> That such cannonade
> May thunder time away,
> Birth-hour and death-hour meet,
> Or, as great sages say,
> Men dance on deathless feet.'

We can notice, to begin with, that the poem does not assert that the doctrine of reincarnation is true. It is asserted by the brahmin, and 'in commentary' the poet adds his reaction. What he gives us is an account of what it feels like to believe in it, or perhaps simply to be attracted by it—an account of what human attitudes and wishes it expresses.

Above all, there is the wish to glory in human achievement. Man's great enemy, the one enemy he cannot defeat, is time; therefore the supreme assertion of the human spirit is to fight time.

> I have been a king,
> I have been a slave,
> Nor is there anything,
> Fool, rascal, knave,
> That I have not been.

What is the name of this emotion? Pride, surely—even arrogance, if we can purge that word of all distasteful associations. It is a common emotion in Yeats—even the rhythm is found in other poems:

> I choose upstanding men
> That climb the streams until
> The fountain leap, and at dawn
> Drop their cast at the side
> Of dripping stone; I declare
> They shall inherit my pride . . .

The need we feel for reincarnation is a need that human achievement shall not be crushed. As an example, as the supreme example, Yeats mentions love, our greatest achievement, and the one most subject to time. The brahmin offered a way to believe that the great lovers would get a chance to build their love into a lasting monument: as lasting as the carving of the old Chinamen in 'Lapis Lazuli', another symbol of man 'thundering time away'.

And some of the images of 'Mohini Chatterjee' go further
than reincarnation:

> Over the blackened earth
> The old troops parade.

This wonderful and obstinate image—what is it an image of?
Perhaps the continuing individual life, but perhaps also the
tread of the generations, the mere persistence of man. And the
last couplet

> Or, as great sages say,
> Men dance on deathless feet

seems as proud of the sages as of the dance itself: proud of the
creation of the image, of the conception man has devised to
describe (perhaps even to persuade himself of) the brahmin's
doctrine. In short, this is a poem about man's indomitable
spirit. I can think of no doctrine in which I disbelieve with more
confidence than in reincarnation, yet I should have been proud
to have written this poem, and I would not have wanted to write
it any different.

I have tried to show how Yeats's system, when turned into
poetry, widens its significance and sheds its eccentricities: how
the symbols, freeing themselves from an arbitrary and detailed
magical meaning, become no more (and no less!) than the great
universal symbols of the poetic tradition. The universal quality
of these symbols—moon, tower, darkness, great year, or
Babylonian starlight—is after all embedded in the language
itself. Out of half-forgotten doctrine and repeated powerful use,
these images have acquired a power deeper and wider than the
particular meaning that any occult system can throw on them
(though the occult has contributed its mite, no doubt, to such
wider power). This is the power that is available only to Yeats
the poet, not at all to Yeats the crank.

III

I will not linger more on this because I want to use what time I
have left to say the things about Yeats's poetry that need
nothing but the poetry to say. I said when I began that I had
three reasons for talking about Yeats; and though I have left so
little time for it, the third is really the most important reason of

all. My second reason raised an issue that is central for the criticism of poetry: my third raises one that is central for discussing the poetry of Yeats. When you read Yeats's poetry, purely as poetry, what is it about? Is it about anything coherent? Did he write a lot of individual poems merely, or did he create a poetic world?

I am sure he did: as coherent and valuable a world as any modern poet. It's true that his poems occasionally contradict one another: total consistency is an appalling virtue. In particular, he varies between the joyous view that 'everything we look upon is blest', and the bleak view that love is a consolation in a world

> [Where] the crime of being born
> Blackens all our lot.

But a lot of what may look like inconsistency is simply the evidence of the ceaseless dialogue that he held with himself. More than once he held the dialogue out loud and explicitly, most notably in his 'Dialogue of Self and Soul'. I believe that this poem lies at the very centre of Yeats's work. If I was forced to name his best single poem I'd be tempted to choose it; if I had to name the most typical of his best poems, the one with most repercussions in his other work, I'd choose it without hesitation. It is in two parts, and I'd like to read the first with you (the Dialogue proper) as carefully as time permits.

The Soul begins, exhorting to withdrawal, solitude, study (study of Plotinus, perhaps, or of *A Vision*).

> I summon to the winding ancient stair;
> Set all your mind upon the steep ascent,
> Upon the broken, crumbling battlement,
> Upon the breathless, starlit air,
> Upon the star that marks the hidden pole;
> Fix every wandering thought upon
> That quarter where all thought is done:
> Who can distinguish darkness from the soul?

'Wandering' had been a favourite romantic adjective of the early, undisciplined Yeats, where hair strays and stars wander the sky. Now such fancies are to be kept sternly in order: *set all your mind* upon the steep ascent. Only the last line of the stanza seems puzzling: 'Who can distinguish darkness from the soul?'

It suggests to us how total is the austerity, the withdrawal from common life, that is being urged; and by the end of the poem its significance will have become clearer.

Then comes one of those touches of genius that never fail Yeats. The Self does not even answer. So absorbed is the Self in living, so uninterested in withdrawal and in pure thought, that it stares at the blade on its knees, too fascinated to do more than murmur to itself:

> The consecrated blade upon my knees
> Is Sato's ancient blade, still as it was,
> Still razor-keen, still like a looking glass
> Unspotted by the centuries;
> That flowering, silken old embroidery, torn
> From some court lady's dress and round
> The ancient scabbard bound and wound,
> Can, tattered, still protect, faded adorn.

The Self does not even say that the sword is a symbol: the Soul does that, in a moment. It was, as a matter of fact, a real sword, given to Yeats by a Japanese admirer; and the intricate, meditative lines about it make it seem real to us, and the memories real that it calls up.

Soul speaks again:

> Why should the imagination of a man
> Long past his prime remember things that are
> Emblematical of love and war?
> Think of ancestral night that can,
> If but imagination scorn the earth
> And intellect its wandering
> To this and that and t'other thing,
> Deliver from the crime of death and birth.

Perhaps Soul's tone is pitying as well as scornful in the beginning, shaking his head sadly as he says 'Why should the imagination of a man . . .' But scorn imposes itself, and the contemptuous word 'wandering' appears again, this time more contemptuously still. Then in the last line, with its fierce opening verb like a loud chord, scorn transforms itself to dignity and massive movement:

> Deliver from the crime of death and birth.

The Self is still staring at the sword:

> Montashigi, third of his family, fashioned it
> Five hundred years ago, about it lie
> Flowers from I know not what embroidery—
> Heart's purple, and all these I set
> For emblems of the day against the tower
> Emblematical of the night,
> And claim as by a soldier's right
> A charter to commit the crime once more.

I picture the Self looking slowly up during this stanza, as his lines slowly turn into a reply to the Soul: looking up and perhaps raising the sword as he announces, with a completely decisive rhythm,

> and all these I set
> For emblems of the day against the tower.

Taking over the Soul's metaphor of a crime, Self glories in it: he is as firm and as fierce as Soul was in the last stanza. Of course he will go on committing the crime: for

> Over the blackened earth
> The old troops parade.

And then, in its final proud verse, the Soul announces its own defeat. Where does its winding stair lead to? To a state of contemplation in which the senses will be suspended, personality will no longer exist:

> Such fullness in that quarter overflows
> And falls into the basin of the mind
> That man is stricken deaf and dumb and blind,
> For intellect no longer knows
> *Is* from the *Ought*, or *Knower* from the *Known*—
> That is to say, ascends to Heaven;
> Only the dead can be forgiven;
> But when I think of that my tongue's a stone.

Why does the Soul feel itself undone by the consummation it seeks? I suppose because it is not offering a religious dogma or religious hope. Detached from the body, the Soul may have no existence, or none worth having: so the path of withdrawal, the ascent to the tower, is one which you destroy yourself by following. When the Soul has ascended to Heaven, no one can distinguish it from darkness.

Why is this such a great poem? For one thing, because
neither of the speakers is a puppet. The Soul was not put up
simply to be knocked down, it offers what Yeats had given
many years of his life to. If you read the essays that Yeats
collected under the title *The Cutting of an Agate*, you can see the
theme of this dialogue beginning to take shape. You can see him
losing some of his old confidence in essences, in 'mysterious
wisdom won by toil', and gaining a new wish for a 'delight in the
whole man—blood, imagination, intellect, running together'.
This is a contrast that runs right through the later Yeats, and
takes many forms. It is the contrast between the musician and
the orator, between 'the way of the bird until common eyes have
lost us' and that of the market cart, between the learned man
and the girl who goes to school to her mirror only, between the
Soul and the Self. Partly, it is the contrast between the Bishop
and Crazy Jane. The Self represents the totality of living,
accepts 'the frog-spawn of a blind man's ditch'; the Soul
chooses—abstracts—from life one thing, usually one intellectual thing, and pursues that only. What the Soul stands for we
may therefore name abstraction.

This theme, of abstraction versus the fullness of living, ties in
very naturally with the other great theme of the later Yeats, his
hatred of old age. Here is the opening section of 'The Tower':

> What shall I do with this absurdity—
> O heart, O troubled heart—this caricature,
> Decrepit age that has been tied to me
> As to a dog's tail?
>   Never had I more
> Excited, passionate, fantastical
> Imagination, nor an ear and eye
> That more expected the impossible—
> No, not in boyhood when with rod and fly,
> Or the humbler worm, I climbed Ben Bulben's back
> And had the livelong summer day to spend.
> It seems that I must bid the Muse go pack,
> Choose Plato and Plotinus for a friend
> Until imagination, ear and eye,
> Can be content with argument and deal
> In abstract things; or be derided by
> A sort of battered kettle at the heel.

The contrast here is between philosophy and fishing. Philosophy is done sitting at a desk; it is done with the intellect only; it is abstract. Fishing is a bodily activity, it is done by the whole man, it is done by young men, the young men of the third section of the poem:

> I leave both faith and pride
> To young upstanding men
> Climbing the mountain-side,
> That under bursting dawn
> They may drop a fly.

Yeats is a poet. Poetry is like philosophy in that it is a 'sedentary trade'; but it is also like fishing, for it is not abstract, it demands the whole man. But fishing is for the young, and the bitterness of this verse results from the conflict between what the poet wants and what would be appropriate to his age. It is this which gives such withering force to the image of the kettle when it reappears at the end, or such contempt to

> It seems that I must bid the Muse go pack,
> Choose Plato and Plotinus for a friend

(and how fortunate for Yeats that these two symbols of abstract thought begin with such a scornfully plosive sound as pl). What Troilus said of love, Yeats is here saying of age: 'This is the monstrosity in love, lady, that the will is infinite and the execution confined, that the desire is boundless and the act a slave to limit.' Proudly and querulously Yeats says, over and over, that he will not accept his limits, that he will not give up the Muse, his lust, the boundlessness of his desire: he will not be an old scarecrow, a 'tattered coat upon a stick'.

There are other forms of abstraction besides study. To abstract is to take one thing only from life's complexity:

> Hearts with one purpose alone
> Through summer and winter seem
> Enchanted to a stone
> To trouble the living stream.

These are the hearts of the men of 1916, the leaders of the Easter Rising, who wrung a reluctant tribute from Yeats—his poem 'Easter 1916'. This poem tells how the men were transformed under the spell of violence, how they 'resigned their parts in the casual comedy' of everyday living, how a terrible beauty was born, a beauty that the poem celebrates. But in the middle of this hymn Yeats put a section that tells of the price they paid for their greatness. It is by far the best thing in the poem:

> Hearts with one purpose alone
> Through summer and winter seem
> Enchanted to a stone
> To trouble the living stream.
> The horse that comes from the road,
> The rider, the birds that range
> From cloud to tumbling cloud,
> Minute by minute they change;
> A shadow of cloud on the stream
> Changes minute by minute;
> A horse-hoof slides on the brim,
> And a horse plashes within it;
> The long-legged moorhens dive,
> And hens to moor-cocks call;
> Minute by minute they live:
> The stone's in the midst of all.

The stone is the symbol of the dedicated man, the man who sacrifices himself for political action and by his narrowness, his intensity, becomes 'a bitter, an abstract thing'. Even in this poem, the finest tribute that Yeats ever paid such men, he puts a picture of their limitations right in the centre: the stone is surrounded by the restlessness and variety of life. Nothing in 'Easter 1916' is so moving as this varied and subtle evocation of change, movement, and process, the rhythms and the rhymes shifting delicately to mirror the elusive life that washes against the stone. And when the section is over, the next, before moving to its conclusion of praise, lingers a moment to remind us bluntly how very limiting it is to call something a stone.

> Too long a sacrifice
> Can make a stone of the heart.

The stone ceases to be an image and becomes a mere idiom, so that there shall be no mistake.

But there is one form of abstraction that Yeats does defend: this is art. Art too is out of living, it too is something frozen, something motionless, even (like the golden nightingale Yeats loved to refer to) something dead. But when the artist abstracts, he does so on a paradoxical principle: he is in search of just that essence which makes life full, rich, and changing. He seeks the very quality that Plato and Plotinus miss. This, I take it, is the theme of 'Sailing to Byzantium' (Yeats's 'Ode on a Grecian Urn'). Because he is old he must withdraw from nature, from the mackerel-crowded seas, from the welter of living that belongs to the young. It is now the turn of Soul: but in this poem Soul has a new function—not to climb the winding stair, but to sing. Its function now is to celebrate the Self. The figures on Keats's Grecian Urn were likewise frozen in a moment of change, and remain as permanent symbols of the most transient thing we know, youthful love. This underlying paradox gives such power to Keats's cry 'More happy love . . .

> . . . For ever panting and for ever young'

and to Yeats's golden nightingale, that has been gathered 'into the artifice of eternity', and yet sings

> Of what is past, or passing, or to come.

'Sailing to Byzantium' is a poem about art. Yeats wrote poem after poem in praise of art, and some of them are his finest. The very first poem in his first volume says 'words alone are certain good'; and though he learned to understand more and more fully what this meant, and what difficulties it implied, he never forsook the theme, or ceased to believe in words. In old age he praised art as the one form of abstraction that did not involve a rejection of the salmon-falls, the young men fishing, the pride like that of the morn. And all through his life he praised it for another reason that widens beyond a theory of art, and becomes a philosophy of living.

   Let us divide theories of art, crudely, into two: those that stress the artistic experience itself, and those that stress its consequences. If you value art because it brings wisdom and understanding, because it broadens the sympathies and stimulates the imagination, because it leads to the love of God, or the dictatorship of the proletariat, or a sharpening of the moral sensibilities, your theory of art can, in general, be called didactic. If, on the other hand, you value it because the actual experience of hearing the Ninth Symphony or reading the odes

of Keats is uniquely precious, and would be worth having even
if it left no trace, even if you dropped down dead the next
moment, if you dislike talk about the moral and social importance of art because that seems to come from those to whom the
poems themselves do not matter enough, then your theory of art
can, in general, be called aesthetic. Crude as this distinction is,
it is not too crude for Yeats: for all his life he belonged quite
firmly to the second camp. He was always impatient of
attempts to put art to the service of something else; and because
it is mainly the early Yeats we think of as an aesthete, I will
illustrate with one of his last poems. I should like to read you the
first part of 'Lapis Lazuli':

> I have heard that hysterical women say
> They are sick of the palette and fiddle-bow,
> Of poets that are always gay,
> For everybody knows or else should know
> That if nothing drastic is done
> Aeroplane and Zeppelin will come out,
> Pitch like King Billy bomb-balls in
> Until the town lie beaten flat.
>
> All perform their tragic play,
> There struts Hamlet, there is Lear,
> That's Ophelia, that Cordelia;
> Yet they, should the last scene be there,
> The great stage curtain about to drop,
> If worthy their prominent part in the play,
> Do not break up their lines to weep.
> They know that Hamlet and Lear are gay;
> Gaiety transfiguring all that dread.
> All men have aimed at, found and lost;
> Black out; Heaven blazing into the head:
> Tragedy wrought to its uttermost.
> Though Hamlet rambles and Lear rages
> And all the drop-scenes drop at once
> Upon a hundred thousand stages,
> It cannot grow by an inch or an ounce.

This poem was written in the thirties, the great decade of
political art; and I take it that the hysterical women of the first
stanza are those for whom art is a luxury which, at times like
these, must yield to politics: because the world is in a mess, we

shall have no more poems, or at any rate none that do not aim to cure the mess.

Yeats was never one to deny that the world was in a mess: just before this poem comes 'The Gyres', with its terrible vision of how 'irrational streams of blood are staining earth'. What he denied was that art should aim to cure it. Art was not to be beautiful by ignoring suffering and turning its back on the real world: that had been the fault of his early poetry. But, having faced that world, it was to use it as material for tragedy. The artist should feel the troubles of his time as intensely as the actor must feel the sufferings of Lear; but if he feels them with an intensity that deflects him into a didactic purpose, he is like an actor who 'breaks up his lines to weep'. The poet builds his poem out of his feelings of compassion and urgency, but he does not sacrifice the poem to them. To make the point Yeats chose the most tendentious word he could to describe the experience of watching, or creating, a tragedy; and to shock the hysterical women, he called it gaiety. The true artist, worthy of his part, the true musician, of the 'accomplished fingers', do not run away from the mess the world is in, but they do turn it into a beauty that is gay. Many years before he had made the same point even more wildly, through the mouth of one of his many personae, Tom O'Roughley. Tom is talking of personal, not public sorrow, and so perhaps shocks us even more:

> And if my dearest friend were dead
> I'd dance a measure on his grave

(which was just what Yeats was doing, in that volume, in the very next poem in fact, to his friend Robert Gregory).

'Lapiz Lazuli' states, then, that art offers an experience to be taken for its own sake only: that out of tragedy comes tragic joy. It is not only art that offers this. I suggested that this was a theory of art that widens into a way of living. To lose oneself in an experience so fully that one no longer cares about the consequences is to live as fully as possible: to respond in this way to art, is a type of responding in such a way to all experience. I will therefore quote, as a parallel 'Lapis Lazuli', a poem that is not about art at all; and I will end with this poem, for the very good reason that my time is up. I am glad to end on this theme, and on this poem. On this theme, because on the whole I am not of Yeats's camp on this matter. I believe in literature that does care about its consequences, and my admiration for those poems that state Yeats's aesthetic view is therefore wrung from me by the sheer splendour of the poems themselves. To confess to this admiration is, to me, the finest tribute I can pay Yeats the poet; and I can see that it is, in a sense though not a fatal sense, to yield to his position. And I am glad to end with this poem—'An Irish Airman foresees his Death'—for a whole lot of reasons. It was written near the middle of Yeats's career, and it resembles both his early and his late work: it is therefore an illustration of what I have been assuming through most of this talk, the continuity between the early and the late Yeats. It describes a delight that has many parallels, among them the pleasure I take in Yeats's poetry. And—if I may finish on the note of simple praise on which I began—it is one of my favourite poems:

> I know that I shall meet my fate
> Somewhere among the clouds above;
> Those that I fight I do not hate,
> Those that I guard I do not love;
> My country is Kiltartan Cross,
> My countrymen Kiltartan's poor,
> No likely end could bring them loss
> Or leave them happier than before.
> Nor law, nor duty bade me fight,
> Nor public men, nor cheering crowds,
> A lonely impulse of delight
> Drove to this tumult in the clouds;
> I balanced all, brought all to mind,
> The years to come seemed waste of breath,
> A waste of breath the years behind
> In balance with this life, this death.

13. KEITH DOUGLAS: A POET OF THE SECOND WORLD WAR

BY G. S. FRASER

My first words this evening should be to thank the Council of the British Academy for the great honour it has done me in asking me to deliver the second annual Chatterton Lecture, on the Meyerstein Foundation, and to explain the considerations which guided me in my choice of a subject. The conditions of Meyerstein's bequest are very generous. There is to be an annual lecture, by a critic who on accepting the invitation to lecture has not yet completed his fortieth year; and the lecturer can talk about any English poet at all, so long as the poet is no longer living. Nevertheless, such a posthumous generosity as Meyerstein's does, it seems to me, impose an almost personal gratitude on its beneficiaries; there is no harm, at least, in trying to devise the sort of lecture that Meyerstein might himself have enjoyed listening to. I never met him; but from friends of mine, much younger than himself, who knew him well, I have learned that one of his most striking characteristics was his interest in youthful poetic promise. Indeed, Chatterton, after whom these lectures are named, and of whom Meyerstein wrote the definitive biography, is the very type of the young poet of almost incalculable promise, cut down like a flower. Keith Castellain Douglas, who is my subject today, had a rather longer span of life than Chatterton. He was killed in action twelve years ago, three days after the beginning of the invasion of Normandy, at the age of 24. I feel that Meyerstein, if he were with us, would enjoy listening to an account of such a young man, who did fine things, and who might have done finer things still if he had lived longer, more than listening to the most scholarly account of, say, the later poems of William Wordsworth.

There is, however, another, and in this case a rather ironic, reason why Keith Douglas seems to me to be a peculiarly appropriate subject for a Chatterton Lecture. Chatterton is a

symbolic figure, an emblem of unfulfilled renown, in a double
sense. We have all heard of him; and few of us have really read
him. He lives in our imaginations as a legend; he lives in
Wordsworth's great lines from 'Resolution and Independence',

> I thought of Chatterton, the marvellous boy,
> The sleepless soul that perished in his pride . . .

He does not live for us, in the same way, in his own lines. He
had, of course, no lines of his own so great as these two of
Wordsworth's; but it is not only that, it is that we hesitate to
look into his works lest, after being moved by the drama of his
life, we should find them profoundly disappointing. Keith
Douglas's life was not a tragic life like Chatterton's; it was a full,
happy, and adventurous life, though cut short violently and
early. Yet there is a real sense in which Douglas's life, like
Chatterton's, might stand between us and his poems.

Douglas is remembered today (if, indeed, the English general
reader remembers him with any vividness at all) as a war poet.
He is remembered as one of three young English poets of great
promise and early fame—the other two were Alun Lewis and
Sidney Keyes—who all perished in the Second World War.
Now, the attitude of the English public to war poets is an odd
one. Poetry is what the English do best, but it is only, I think, in
wartime that they remember that; it is only in wartime that they
clamour for new poetry, that they ask, 'Where are the new
young poets?', that they buy eagerly volumes and anthologies
and periodicals devoted to new verse. Good young English
poets, during a war, are published easily; so, I am afraid, are
other young poets who are not so good; and in fact the sense of
exile, the novelty of a foreign scene, the stress of action do,
during a war, stir many young men into trying to express
themselves in verse who, in quieter times, would never think of
themselves as poets. And, in fact, so long as a war continues, so
long as many of our young people are overseas, we find that we
can read poetry by young men in the forces, even if it is not quite
successful poetry, with sympathy. At the least, it will have a
documentary interest; it will have the interest of an exile's letter
home. That documentary and sentimental interest, alas, soon
fades, once a war is over; and with it there tends to fade,
however unfairly, our interest in the more genuine poetry which

a war had produced. How often, today, do we open the works of Alun Lewis or Sidney Keyes? And yet, during the last world war, critics were right to praise them.

From the point of view of his post-war reputation, moreover, Keith Douglas was unfortunate in the time of his death; he ought to have died a year or two earlier. He was killed, as I have said, in Normandy in 1944. He had not yet published a volume, though some of his earlier poems had been published, along with some of the early poems of J. C. Hall and Norman Nicholson, in a kind of three-man anthology, *Selected Poems*, in 1943. But he was known mainly by what he had published in periodicals and war-time anthologies; and anthologies soon go out of print, periodicals are soon mislaid. It was not till 1947 that Douglas's prose book, *Alamein to Zem Zem*, was published, with some of his war-poems (sometimes in inaccurate texts) at the end. It was not till 1951 that Douglas's old Oxford acquaintance John Waller and myself were able (at the request of the late Richard March) to produce a careful and correct text of Douglas's *Collected Poems*, arranged in reverse chronological order. The poems, by that time, had no longer the impact of news; they had not yet acquired the impact of history.

It is true that, in 1951, Keith Douglas's *Collected Poems* were well received; Mr Ronald Bottrall, I remember, wrote a particularly perceptive review in the *New Statesman*. Yet they appeared in an unfortunate year. The year 1951 marked something like a watershed between two movements in contemporary English poetry. The prevailing mood among the younger poets of the 1940s, or at least among a fairly coherent group of them, was what was often called the mood of neo-romanticism. It was a mood that owed a great deal to poets like Dylan Thomas and Mr George Barker; it is carried on today by a poet like Mr W. S. Graham. It was a mood that preferred evocation to description, images to statements, feeling to thought, colour, one might say, to line. It was a mood, also, to which Keith Douglas had almost nothing to offer. I remember a typical new romantic poet of the 1940s, Mr Tom Scott, telling me that he found Douglas's poetry hard, cold, and dry. Since 1951, indeed, a whole new school of young poets has come into notice that does share Douglas's ideals of precise and disciplined statement in verse: I am thinking of poets like Mr Philip Larkin, Miss

Elizabeth Jennings, Mr Philip Oakes, Mr Kingsley Amis, Mr Gordon Wharton, Mr Bernard Bergonzi, Mr John Wain. But these new young poets do not share Douglas's temperament. Their attitude to life is more negatively ironical than his, or at least more constrained and more hesitant. For in a sense, though not in the cant sense of the 1940s, Douglas *was* a romantic poet.

Keith Douglas's mother—and it is a great pleasure and honour for me, and I am sure for all of us, that she is able to be present with us this evening—wrote to me the other day, reminding me of an excellent short statement, called 'On the Nature of Poetry' which Douglas, in 1940, contributed to *Augury*, an Oxford miscellany of prose and verse of which he was one of the editors. It is worth quoting in full. It was written, we must remember, by a boy of 20; and the qualities that come out in it are, I think, not only Douglas's simplicity and sincerity, his remarkable lack of undergraduate pose, but also his penetration. It might be a statement by a very mature man. It owes, I think, here and there, just a little to Croce:

Poetry is like a man, whom thinking you know all his movements and appearance you will presently come upon in such a posture that for a moment you can hardly believe it a position of the limbs you know. So thinking you have set bounds to the nature of poetry, you shall as soon discover something outside your bounds which they should evidently contain.

The expression 'bad poetry' is meaningless: critics still use it, forgetting that bad poetry is not poetry at all.

Nor can prose and poetry be compared any more than pictures and pencils: the one is instrument and the other art. Poetry may be written in prose or verse, or spoken extempore.

For it is anything expressed in words, which appeals to the emotions either in presenting an image or picture to move them; or by the music of words affecting them through the senses; or in stating some truth whose eternal quality exacts the same reverence as eternity itself.

In its nature poetry is sincere and simple.

Writing which is poetry must say what the writer has himself to say, not what he has observed others to say with effect, nor what he thinks will impress others because it impressed him hearing it. Nor must he waste any more words over it than a mathematician; every word must work for its keep, in prose, blank verse, or rhyme.

And poetry is to be judged not by what the poet has tried to say; only by what he has said.

These aphorisms seem to me to be true; and perhaps Keith Douglas's criticism of many of the new romantic poets of the 1940s might have been that they wanted to be judged by what they had tried to say, not by what they had said, that they did not make words work hard enough for their keep. His criticism of our immediate contemporaries, the poets of the 'New Movement' of the 1940s, might be perhaps that they are not sincere and simple enough; that they too often say what they have observed others to say with effect, or what they think will impress their hearers because it impressed them hearing it. That would apply, for instance, to the many attempts by young poets in the last few years to imitate Mr Empson's attitudes and catch his tone. Thinking as he did about poetry, Keith Douglas could obviously belong, in the strict sense, to no 'school'. And when I say that he was essentially a romantic poet, I am referring not to his formal ideals about poetry, but to his personal temperament.

Thus, Douglas's attitude to war was, though humane and deeply compassionate, a heroic attitude. It had nothing in common with the humanitarian, pacifist attitudes of contemporaries of his like Nicholas Moore or Alex Comfort or Douglas's friend John Hall. He was a good soldier, and in a sense he enjoyed his war. He enjoyed, at least, the exercise of the will in action. He was an officer, and an efficient officer, who enjoyed the company of his fellow officers, and accepted and enjoyed the responsibility that went with his rank. In that, among our poets of the last war, he was almost unique; Alun Lewis and Sidney Keyes were both also officers, and conscientious ones, but neither of them was a natural soldier in the sense that Keith Douglas was. And much more typically the soldier–writer of the last war tended to be, like myself, the sergeant-major's nightmare: the long-haired private, who could not keep step, who not only looked like a bloody poet, but turned out in the end to be one: a great nuisance to his superiors generally till he could be parked in an office with a typewriter. Douglas, on the other hand, was physically and temperamentally adapted to war. It was a rough game that he was good at playing. Again, he was a very intelligent man, as these aphorisms on poetry prove, but not a man, I think, who had much use for intellectual chatter. The two or three times I personally met him, I do not remember our exchanging a word on any abstract topic. Whatever else he may have pined for during the war years, it will not have been evening parties in Chelsea.

Douglas, in fact, was a cavalier. Riding was almost his favourite sport, and in war he thought of his tank as if it were a horse. There is a poem, written at Enfidaville, in Tunisia, in 1943, which gives us, I think, some leading clues to his temperament. I shall read it in full:

ARISTOCRATS
'I think I am becoming a God'

The noble horse with courage in his eye
clean in the bone, looks up at a shellburst:
away fly the images of the shires
but he puts the pipe back in his mouth.

Peter was unfortunately killed by an 88;
it took his leg away, he died in the ambulance,
I saw him crawling on the sand; he said
It's most unfair, they've shot my foot off.

How can I live among this gentle
obsolescent breed of heroes, and not weep?
Unicorns, almost,
for they are falling into two legends
in which their stupidity and chivalry
are celebrated. Each, fool and hero, will be an immortal.

The plains were their cricket pitch
and in the mountains the tremendous drop fences
brought down some of the runners. Here then
under the stones and earth they dispose themselves,
I think with their famous unconcern.
It is not gunfire I hear but a hunting horn.

In that fine last line, as Sir John Waller remarks in his notes to the *Collected Poems*, there is an echo of Roncesvalles. And the aristocratic morality, evoked in this poem, was the morality to which in the depths of his nature Keith Douglas was most profoundly drawn. He was an aloof, gay, and passionate man. He loved risk. The state of the world, and perhaps the nature of man, and perhaps his own nature in its depths, filled him with profound sadness; nevertheless, for him the sadness of human existence was a kind of destiny that had to be bravely and lovingly embraced. He was as far as can be from a nagging or carping attitude to life. And this partly explains the obscurity of his present reputation. The new poetry of the last five years has in itself many virtues of reticence and control; but it does not express, in its spirit, precisely these generous, aristocratic virtues.   .

Keith Douglas was born in 1920, in Tunbridge Wells. When he was 8, his father left his mother, and the boy never saw him again. Thus he acquired very early that earnest and sometimes rather anxious sense of responsibility that is found often, for instance, in the eldest sons of widows. At 11, he entered Christ's Hospital on the Nomination Examination, and from then on was able to pay for his education through scholarships. He took an active part in sports and amateur theatricals at Christ's Hospital, and also did well at lessons, though the headmaster thought him lazy. Already, as a schoolboy, he was writing very accomplished verses, and at 16 sold a poem to Mr Geoffrey Grigson for *New Verse*—a hard nut to crack. He made many friends at Christ's Hospital, though he also seems to have been considered, especially by some of the masters, rather 'difficult'. In 1938 he went up on a scholarship to Merton College, Oxford, to read English, and was lucky enough to have Mr Edmund Blunden assigned to him as tutor. He soon became one of the best known of undergraduate poets. The years just before the last World War, and just after its beginning, were, in fact, rather a good period for Oxford poetry: Douglas's contemporaries included Sidney Keyes, John Heath-Stubbs, John Short, and J. C. Hall. John Waller, another Oxford poet of the period, and the future editor of Douglas's *Collected Poems*, published some of Douglas's best early work in his wartime Oxford magazine, *Kingdom Come*. Douglas at one time was editor of *Cherwell* and helped to prepare for Basil Blackwell the undergraduate miscellany *Augury*, from which I quoted his aphorisms about poetry. He was one of the poets included in the anthology *Eight Oxford Poets*. His years at Oxford seem to have been happy and successful. He made lots of friends, many of them women. The exotic beauty of four of these is commemorated in an unfinished fragment, of which this is one version:

TO KAISTIN YINGCHENG OLGA MILENA
> Women of four countries
> the four phials full of essences
> of green England, legendary China,
> deep Europe and Arabic Spain, a
> finer four poisons for the five senses
> than any in medieval inventories.
>
> In giving you this I
> return the wine to the grape
> return the plant her juices
> for what each creature uses
> by chemistry will seep
> back to the source or die . . .

Douglas had early joined the Oxford OTC, partly for the sake of the free riding it offered, and thus he was liable for service on the outbreak of war. He was not, in fact, called up till fairly late in 1940. He trained in various places in Great Britain and in June 1941 was posted to the Middle East, transferred to the Notts Sherwood Rangers Yeomanry, but seconded to a staff job at base. He disliked this, and on the eve of El Alamein ran away to rejoin his old regiment, who welcomed him. He fought with them in a Crusader tank from El Alamein to Wadi Zem Zem in Tunisia, continuously, except for one interval of hospitalization and convalescence in Palestine, after he had been blown up by a land-mine. He kept a diary, and the book he made out of it, *Alamein to Zem Zem*, is probably one of the very few accounts, indeed, of fighting in the Second World War likely to rank, as literature, with classics of the First World War like Sir Herbert Read's *In Retreat*, the war chapters in Mr Robert Graves's *Good-Bye to All That*, or Mr Siegfried Sassoon's *Memoirs of a Fox-Hunting Man* and *Memoirs of an Infantry Officer*. The book has two great qualities: visual immediacy, and an almost frightening emotional detachment.

I observed [Douglas says] these battles partly as an exhibition—that is to say, I went through them like a little child in a factory—a child sees the brightness and efficiency of steel machines and endless belts slopping round and round, without knowing or caring what it is all there for. When I could order my thoughts I looked for something more significant than appearances; I still look, I cannot avoid it, for something decorative, poetic, or dramatic.

The qualities of Douglas's prose in *Alamein to Zem Zem*—the brutal vividness of presentation, combined with an apparent almost icy detachment—are to be found, of course, in even greater concentration, in the poems he wrote in the Western Desert and during periods of leave in Cairo or convalescence in Palestine. These he published almost as soon as he had written them, sending many of them on airgraphs to M. J. Tambimuttu's *Poetry London*, giving others to his friends Bernard Spencer and Lawrence Durrell to put into the excellent magazine they were bringing out in Cairo, *Personal Landscape*. At the end of 1943 Douglas was posted home to train for the invasion of Europe. And with that posting the history of his career, as a poet, really comes to an end. His last completed poem is called 'On a Return from Egypt'. I shall read it to you later; it expresses very beautifully both a clear premonition of death, and a bitterness at the foreknowledge that he will not be allowed to survive, to write the poems he might have written:

> And all my endeavours are unlucky explorers
> come back, abandoning the expedition;
> the specimens, the lilies of ambition
> still spring in their climate, still unpicked:
> but time, time is all I lacked
> to find them as the great collectors before me.

This premonition did not affect his outward cheerfulness; Tambimuttu, one of his closest friends and warmest admirers, tells us of Douglas's gaiety when he dropped into the offices of *Poetry London*, the pleasure he took in riding in Hyde Park. Douglas was killed in Normandy on 9 June 1944. Shortly before his death he had managed to get some information from behind the enemy lines, and for this he was mentioned in dispatches. In an obituary article, in *Poetry London*, on Douglas, Tambimuttu wrote:

I can say without any hesitation that Douglas's view of life and his actions were the most sound and realistic that any man of our generation can come to. He accepted the greatest gifts of this life and lived with passionate sincerity. His conclusions about life in action are the most mature any poet has arrived at in this war . . . Douglas lived the poetry he believed in.

I want now to consider Keith Douglas's poems. And here I am confronted with a difficulty. If he were a very famous poet, much of whose work I could rely on most of you having read, I could simply allude to poems familiar to you, and make observations and judgements on these, illustrated by occasional quotations. But he is not a very famous poet; and the obvious alternative would seem to be to take rather a few poems, perhaps only three or four, out of his quite large output—140 pages of poetry *is* quite a large output for a man of 24—and to read these aloud, and go into them in some detail. But, on the other hand, can the examination of three or four poems, however carefully chosen, give us a proper notion of any poet's range? Fortunately, some sort of compromise is, I think, possible. Douglas's poems fall into a number of distinct groups, and any later group is always more interesting and important than the group that immediately precedes it. The poems that he wrote at school are mainly important in that they show us a boy patiently learning his craft. The poems that he wrote at Oxford have more depth and subtlety, but they have something in common—both in their charm, and in their occasional weakness—with all undergraduate poetry. They are very 'literary' poems. In the poems which Douglas wrote during his period of military training in England, we begin to feel that he is biting deeper into experience; or that experience is biting deeper into him. Finally, the poems written in the Middle East are, of course, Douglas's most important achievement. If we take these groups in turn, we shall get a fairly accurate picture of his development.

There is, however, one more group still: the group of poems Douglas was never able to finish. The most important of these is a poem, or a set of frustrated beginnings of a poem, called 'Bête Noire'. This, as it stands, is not anything achieved. It is a succession of hopeless attempts to grapple with an intractable subject, the subject of what Douglas called, in conversation and in letters, 'the beast on my back'. It is the subject of what any of us colloquially might call 'the black dog on my back': or in more ambitious language, it is the subject of what Freudian psychologists call, or used to call, the Death-Wish and Jungian psychologists call the Shadow. I imagine a Jungian psychologist would say that Douglas was very much aware of his Shadow, in a sense at times almost obsessed with it, but that he had never properly accepted it, or come to terms with it, and that therefore, in spite of the impression he gave of being far more mature than his years, he was not, when he died, yet a fully integrated personality. There was, as it were, a crucial and painful experience still to come, of which he had a kind of poetic premonition. The Shadow, in more homely terms than those of the psychologists, is the sudden awareness, which can be a blinding and shattering one, of all the nastiness, all the ulterior self-centredness, in our own motives and in those of others. To accept the Shadow is, in Christian language, to accept the possibility of damnation and the reality of Original Sin. The Shadow, if we try to suppress our latent awareness of it—most people of a liberal morality and of progressive views try to do this, most of the time—can, as it were, irrupt upon us. And the moment of its irruption is the moment when we feel not only that we have never loved anybody properly, but that nobody has ever loved us, that love is a lie.

If you have read, for instance, either of Mr Philip Toynbee's two excellent experimental novels, *Tea with Mrs Goodman* and *The Garden to the Sea*, you will agree with me that the character, or the archetype, Charley, in both of them, who sneers and jeers at everybody, who distrusts the sincerity of every vow and the purity of every motive, is an excellent personification of the Shadow. He is horrible; yet he is an irreducible element in each of us with which we have to come to terms if we ever wish to become whole beings. If we do come to terms with him, recognize him as having a function, he ceases to be the Devil, and becomes something manageable and even comic, say, Mr Punch. Douglas, I think, found it excessively difficult to come to terms with his Shadow just because he was such an unusually good man. He had high principles, and he always acted on his principles. As a boy, his first thought was of what he owed to his mother; as a young man, of what he owed to his country. His personal interests he had concentrated on high and wholesome things, on love, and poetry, and comradeship, and adventure. So it seemed to him inexplicable, I suppose, that he should have these black despairing moods. What had he done to deserve them? He had certainly never shirked any duty or danger, he was incapable of a mean act, and yet his black beast was liable to pounce upon him at the most unexpected moments, like the sense of guilt of a very bad, or the sense of inadequacy of a very weak, man. On his bad days, it could spoil everything:

> It's his day.
> Don't kiss me. Don't put your arm round
> And touch the beast on my back.

Had Douglas survived, given this obsession with the Shadow, and given also the strain under which he had laboured as a fighting soldier and the iron self-control which he had always exercised, given the roaring guns and the dead men and the buckled tanks in the Western Desert, I think that, a few years after the war, he might have had a bad breakdown. He would have emerged from that breakdown, I imagine, having come to terms with the Shadow, and with a new depth as a poet. 'Bête Noire', as I say, is an unfinished poem, a failure; but in its light, or against its darkness, all Douglas's other poems must be read.

I shall be fairly brief about the poems Douglas wrote while still a schoolboy. In a schoolboy's poems one does not look for originality of thought or feeling. One looks for adroitness in handling words, for signs that the handling of rhythms, the shaping of phrases, gives a young poet pleasure. Here is the poem which Douglas at 16 sold to *New Verse*, a short poem which says nothing very much, but says it very agreeably:

DEJECTION

> Yesterday travellers in summer's country,
> Tonight the sprinkled moon and ravenous sky
> Say, we have reached the boundary. The autumn clothes
> Are on; Death is the season and we the living
> Are hailed by the solitary to join their regiment,
> To leave the sea and the horses and march away
> Endlessly. The spheres speak with persuasive voices.
> Only tomorrow like a seagull hovers and calls
> Shrieks through the mist and scatters the pools of stars.
> The windows will be open and hearts behind them.

The Oxford poems, written between 1938 and 1940, deserve, of course, much more attention. There are about thirty of them. They show, as contrasted with the school poems, a growing range and suppleness. But most of them are still very much what I would call 'literary' poems and also still very much 'occasional' poems. There is about them, occasionally, a slightly self-indulgent melancholy and a youthful romantic morbidity. One of the best of them, 'Leukothea', is about a beautiful dead woman. Her beauty was so supernatural that the poet imagines it has resisted corruption in the ground. A bad dream disillusions him:

> So all these years I have lived securely. I knew
> I had only to uncover you
> to see how the careful earth would have kept
> all as it was, untouched. I trusted the ground.
> I knew the worm and the beetle would go by
> and never dare batten on your beauty.
>
> Last night I dreamed and found my trust betrayed
> only the little bones and the great bones disarrayed.

That is good partly because it is so beautifully phrased, but good partly also because, I think, one finds oneself, half consciously, reading into it a meaning far deeper than the fantastical surface meaning. One thinks of the parable, in the Bible, of the buried talent. One thinks of people who fling themselves, from some practical compulsion, into the thick of the world, but dream always of reaching a stage when they can afford to cultivate some gift, to pursue some vision, which meant much in their boyhood, and then, when they have their chance, find that the vision has faded, the gift has decayed. It is Yeats's theme in a shorter, sharper, more completely bitter poem:

> Toil and grow rich,
> What's that but to lie
> With a foul witch
> And after, drained dry,
> To be brought
> To the chamber where
> Lies one long sought
> With despair?

'Leukothea', however, is rather exceptional. More typically, Douglas's Oxford poems express a mood which most generations of undergraduates must have felt, and Douglas's own generation, waiting to go to war, particularly poignantly. There is the sense of magical years, soon passing, but for that reason to be treasured all the more highly; there is the special sense of the magic of Oxford as a place:

> This then is the city of young men, of beginning,
> ideas, trials, pardonable follies,
> the lightness, seriousness, and sorrow of youth . . .

Already, however, towards the end of Douglas's Oxford period, his concept of poetry was becoming more mature. He was trying to say more, and to friends who had liked his early lyrical smoothness it seemed that the new style he was developing was a rather harsh and rough one. Answering such a criticism from his friend John Hall, Keith Douglas, when a soldier, wrote:

In my early poems I wrote lyrically, as an innocent, because I was an innocent; I have (not surprisingly) fallen from that particular grace since then. I had begun to change during my second year at Oxford. T. S. Eliot wrote to me when I first joined the Army, that I appeared to have finished with one form of writing and to be progressing towards another, which he did not think I had mastered. I knew this to be true without his saying it.

The nature of the change in style, and the degree of the progress towards mastery, can be seen in two poems, the two most successful ones, out of the comparatively small batch which Douglas wrote during his period of military training in England. One of these, called 'The Prisoner', is addressed to a Chinese girl called Cheng. There is in it a new depth, a new intimacy, a new painfulness:

> Today, Cheng, I touched your face
> with two fingers, as a gesture of love;
> for I can never prove enough
> by sight or sense your strange grace,
>
> but mothwise my hands return
> to your fair cheek, as luminous
> as a lamp in a paper house,
> and touch, to teach love and learn.
>
> I think a hundred years are gone
> that so, like gods, we'd occupy.
> But alas, Cheng, I cannot tell why,
> today I touched a mask stretched on the stone

> person of death. There was the urge
> to break the bright flesh and emerge
> from the ambitious cruel bone.

The other important poem of this training period, 'Time Eating', might be described as metaphysical. This, like 'The Prisoner', gives us a hint about some of the deep sources of Douglas's *bête noire* obsession:

> Ravenous Time has flowers for his food
> In Autumn, yet can cleverly make good
> each petal: devours animals and men,
> but for ten dead he can create ten.
>
> If you enquire how secretly you've come
> to mansize from the smallness of a stone
> it will appear his effort made you rise
> so gradually to your proper size.
>
> But as he makes he eats; the very part
> where he began, even the elusive heart,
> Time's ruminative tongue will wash
> and slow juice masticate all flesh.
>
> That volatile huge intestine holds
> material and abstract in its folds:
> thought and ambition melt and even the world
> will alter, in that catholic belly curled.
>
> But Time, who ate my love, you cannot make
> such another; you who can remake
> the lizard's tail and the bright snakeskin
> cannot, cannot. That you gobbled in
> too quick, and though you brought me from a boy
> you can make no more of me, only destroy.

Nothing in Douglas's earlier writing had led us to anticipate the melancholy gusto, here, of his metaphysical wit:

> That volatile huge intestine holds
> material and abstract in its folds:
> thought and ambition melt and even the world
> will alter, in that catholic belly curled.

There is something of the passionate ingenuity of Donne in these four lines, combined with something of the eloquent directness of Dryden.

During the period of his army training in England, Douglas began, therefore, as it were, to reconnoitre himself in depth. But his main reputation will probably rest on the best of the thirty or so poems which he wrote while on active service in the Middle East. These are uneven; there are, in almost all of them, if we compare them to his Oxford poems, certain technical roughnesses, of which Douglas was quite conscious. For he is not seeking merely as in 'The Prisoner' and 'Time Eating' to probe new and painful depths of personal feeling, but to absorb into his verse raw material which might, of its very nature, seem intractable to poetry. 'Cairo Jag', for instance, which I shall now read to you, will remain, to anybody who served in the Middle East during the last war, a vivid piece of documentation. It brings it all back, so to say. But is it, in the ordinary sense, a *poem*, is its painfulness resolved? Do its images merely pile up brutally or do they work, in the end, into some large reconciling pattern? It is a marginal case among Douglas's poems: certainly very memorable, but not certainly very good. I leave you to judge:

> Shall I get drunk or cut myself a piece of cake,
> a pasty Syrian with a few words of English
> or the Turk who says she is a princess—she dances
> apparently by levitation? Or Marcelle, Parisienne
> always preoccupied with her dull dead lover:
> she has all the photographs and his letters
> tied in a bundle and stamped *Décédé* in mauve ink.
> All this takes place in a stink of jasmin.
>
> But there are the streets dedicated to sleep
> stenches and sour smells, the sour cries
> do not disturb their application to slumber
> all day, scattered on the pavement like rags
> afflicted with fatalism and hashish. The women
> offering their children brown-paper breasts
> dry and twisted, elongated like the skull,
> Holbein's signature. But this stained white town
> is something in accordance with mundane conventions—
> Marcelle drops her Gallic airs and tragedy
> suddenly shrieks in Arabic about the fare
> with the cabman, links herself so
> with the somnambulists and legless beggars:
> it is all one, all as you have heard.

But by a day's travelling you reach a new world
the vegetation is of iron
dead tanks, gun barrels split like celery
the metal brambles have no flowers or berries
and there are all sorts of manure, you can imagine
the dead themselves, their boots, clothes and possessions
clinging to the ground, a man with no head
has a packet of chocolate and a souvenir of Tripoli.

So it was. And the only moral comment Douglas allows himself to make in the poem is that so it was:

it is all one, all as you have heard . . .

And, when we have read the poem carefully, we realize that he means by that not only that it is all one in Cairo, that the shrieking Marcelle is at one with the shrieking cabman and the legless beggars, the squalor is universal, but also that it is all one between Cairo and the desert: moral death and disorder match physical death and disorder; Marcelle's photographs and letters of her dull dead lover exactly match the dead soldier's packet of chocolate and souvenir from Tripoli, are as futile, and pathetic, and meaningless, and ultimately enraging. It is the kind of poem which Pope or Dryden would have written in neatly antithetic heroic couplets, Cairo in one line, the desert in the next. Douglas leaves it as a jumble, giving us one clue that will enable us to sort it out for ourselves. We *can* sort it out, but we still wonder if it is a good poem; it is, at least, a very bold and original experiment.

It is interesting to contrast 'Cairo Jag' with the poem that immediately precedes it in Douglas's *Collected Poems*, 'Behaviour of Fish in an Egyptian Tea Garden'. During the Middle East it was Cairo which focused all Douglas's negative emotions, which made a satirist of him. But 'Cairo Jag' fails, if it does fail, because it lacks that 'coolness at the centre' which Saintsbury noted as the mark of a great satirist like Dryden; it is too near hysteria. 'Behaviour of Fish in an Egyptian Tea Garden' is urbane, detached, even gay in tone. A single metaphor is brilliantly sustained, and in sustaining it Douglas can bring to bear all his powers of visual fantasy. Yet the effect is more properly satirical, more damaging to its object, than that of 'Cairo Jag':

As a white stone draws down the fish
she on the seafloor of the afternoon
draws down men's glances and their cruel wish
for love. Slyly red lip on the spoon

slips in a morsel of ice-cream; her hands
white as a milky stone, white submarine
fronds, sink with spread fingers, lean
along the table, carmined at the ends.

A cotton magnate, an important fish
with great eyepouches and a golden mouth
through the frail reefs of furniture swims out
and idling, suspended, stays to watch.

A crustacean old man clamped to his chair
sits coldly near her and might see
her charms through fissures where the eyes should be
or else his teeth are parted in a stare.

Captain of leave, a lean dark mackerel,
lies in the offing; turns himself and looks
through currents of sound. The flat-eyed flatfish sucks
on a straw, staring from its repose, laxly.

And gallants in shoals swim up and lag,
circling and passing near the white attraction;
sometimes pausing, opening a conversation;
fish pause so to nibble or tug.

Now the ice-cream is finished, is
paid for. The fish swim off on business
and she sits alone at the table, a white stone
useless except to a collector, a rich man.

One has no doubts that *that* is a good poem.

But Douglas's temperament was not that of the satirist; it was, as I have said, a romantic temperament, in its ardour, though without that passion for self-deception, that indignant refusal to see things as they are, which we sometimes associate with the idea of romanticism. In the desert, he could still find release, in poetry, for the positive ardour of his mind. He need not merely be a satirist. He could address his Muse, partly as a lost, cruel mistress, partly as the moon:

> I listen to the desert wind
> that will not blow her from my mind;
> the stars will not put down a hand,
> the moon's ignorant of my wound

moving negligently across
by clouds and cruel tracts of space
as in my brain my nights and days
moves the reflection of her face.

Skims like a bird my sleepless eye
the sands who at this hour deny
the violent heat they have by day
as she denies her former way:

all the elements agree
with her, to have no sympathy
for my tactless misery
as wonderful and hard as she.

O turn in the dark bed again
and give to him what once was mine
and I'll turn as you turn
and kiss my swarthy mistress pain.

One is very often aware of Douglas's reading—one is aware, there, of how well he knew Wyatt:

as she denies her former way—

without ever feeling that he is writing pastiche.

I earlier this evening read to you one of Douglas's poems of action, 'Aristocrats'. It was not a mere poem of action, but a poem in praise of chivalry. He is never merely a descriptive poet: and his best poem of action, 'Vergissmeinicht', is like the earlier 'The Prisoner' essentially a poem about love and death:

Three weeks gone and the combatants gone,
returning over the nightmare ground
we found the place again, and found
the soldier sprawling in the sun.

The frowning barrel of his gun
overshadowing. As we came on
that day, he hit my tank with one
like the entry of a demon.

Look. Here in the gunpit spoil
the dishonoured picture of his girl
who has put: *Steffi. Vergissmeinicht*
in a copybook gothic script.

> We see him almost with content
> abased, and seeming to have paid
> and mocked at by his own equipment
> that's hard and good when he's decayed.
>
> But she would weep to see to-day
> how on his skin the swart flies move;
> the dust upon the paper eye
> and the burst stomach like a cave.
>
> For here the lover and killer are mingled
> who had one body and one heart.
> And death who had the soldier singled
> has done the lover mortal hurt.

Always look in a poem like that, which moves you, and which might seem to move you merely by its material, by what it rawly presents, for the handling. Douglas, I think, never wrote a more skilful poem than this; or one in which his skill is more modestly subdued to the total effect he is aiming at. What gives us the effect, for instance, in the first stanza, of the tanks lumbering bumpily and relentlessly on, is a kind of wheeling motion in the stanza itself, repetitions and a concealed rhyme:

> Three weeks *gone* and the combatants *gone*,
> returning over the nightmare *ground*
> we *found* the place again, and *found*
> the soldier sprawling in the sun . . .

What saves the stanza about the dead soldier's appearance from being merely repellent is, again, the deliberate formality of the syntax and the choice of a literary adjective—'the swart flies', not 'the black flies', and an objective precision of statement, without emotional commentary, that gives an effect of icy pity:

> But she would weep to see to-day
> how on his skin the swart flies move;
> the dust upon the paper eye
> and the burst stomach like a cave.

And in the last stanza the effect of aesthetic distance, of the whole experience being held in control, is clinched by the eighteenth-century antithesis:

> And death who had *the soldier* singled
> has done *the lover* mortal hurt.

I shall not attempt to 'place' Douglas as a poet: I think that four or five of the poems I have read to you this evening would have to be considered very seriously indeed by any anthologist attempting to produce a representative selection of the best poems, written by the younger English poets, over the past twenty-five years; and I think it would be hard, among poems by younger poets of the 1950s, which have attracted much attention in the last few years, to match these four or five poems. But what is specially and sadly interesting about Douglas is the sense that his development was continuous and steady; the sense that, if he had been spared—he would be now in his middle thirties, if he were alive—he might well be, today, the dominating figure of his generation and a wholesome and inspiring influence on younger men. He had courage, passion, and generosity. These are three qualities that our age generally needs. I said, earlier, that I would read to you his last completed poem. In it, he foresaw his death; in it, he sighed for the flowers that he would not now pick; it makes a better peroration to this lecture than any possible prose sentences of mine:

ON A RETURN FROM EGYPT

> To stand here in the wings of Europe
> disheartened, I have come away
> from the sick land where in the sun lay
> the gentle sloe-eyed murderers
> of themselves, exquisites under a curse;
> here to exercise my depleted fury.
>
> For the heart is a coal, growing colder
> when jewelled cerulean seas change
> into grey rocks, grey water-fringe,
> sea and sky altering like a cloth
> till colour and sheen are gone both:
> cold is an opiate of the soldier.
>
> And all my endeavours are unlucky explorers
> come back, abandoning the expedition;
> the specimens, the lilies of ambition
> still spring in their climate, still unpicked:
> but time, time is all I lacked
> to find them, as the great collectors before me.

The next month, then, is a window
and with a crash I'll split the glass.
Behind it stands one I must kiss,
person of love or death,
a person or a wraith,
I fear what I shall find.

INDEX

Persius, influenced Donne 28, 31
Person, H. A., on commonplace
books 19
Petrarch, *Africa* 109–10; *De viris
illustribus* 109; influenced later writers
33, 42–3, 45, 68
Petronius, on food 96
Phalaris, Bentley on his *Epistles* 81
Philips, Ambrose, poems parodied 132
Pindar, influenced Gray 155–6
Pinto, Vivian de Sola, on Rochester 61
Pope, Alexander, satirist 81, 88, 95, 99,
104; compared with other poets 149,
204, 328; helped Wycherley 111;
influenced by Horace 149
the *Dunciad*: 'Pope and Dulness' by
Emrys Jones 105–39; compared
with, and influenced by other
writers 106, 108–12, 121–4, 126–
7, 133–4, 136–9
works other than the *Dunciad*: *The
Rape of the Lock* 107, 115–18, 135;
other works 85, 109, 121, 132–5,
139
Pre-Raphaelites *see* Rossetti, D. G.
Purcell, Henry, and Hopkins 254
Puttenham, George, *Art of English Poetry*
2–3; on Skelton 2, 20–1

Quarles, Francis, imitated by Rochester
66–7

Rabelais, influenced and influenced by
other writers 109–10, 112; translation
109
Radcliffe, Mrs Ann, compared with
Keats 207, 213
Ralegh, Sir Walter, compared with other
poets 44, 73
Ramsay, Robert Lee, on Skelton 17
Restoration poetry 68–71, 78, 114,
122–4
Reynolds, John Hamilton, and Keats
190
Richardson, Samuel, *Clarissa* 108
Rochester, Earl of *see* Wilmot, John
Rogers, E. W., song-writer 274–5
Rojas, Fernando de, influenced Donne
33
Romantic literature 149, 152, 184–5,
188, 190, 192, 214, 267–8, 279
Rome, compared with London 24, 28–9
Rossetti, D. G., and Pre-Raphaelites,

influenced Kipling 279; and Keats
218, 220
Ruskin, John, on Scott as a poet 160
Rutherford, Andrew, on Kipling 265

Sandys, George, his version of
Metamorphoses 137–8
Scott, Tom, on Douglas 314
Scott, Sir Walter, influenced and
influenced by other writers 171, 174,
279
Waverley Novels, particularly ballads,
songs and poetry: 'The Poetry of
the Early Waverley Novels', by
Claire Lamont 160–83; *The
Antiquary* 160, 161 ('Elspeth'),
168–70, 180–1; *The Bride of
Lammermoor* 160, 176–80; *Guy
Mannering* 163–4, 171, 174 ('Meg
Merrilies'); *The Heart of Midlothian*
162–3 ('Madge Wildfire'), 170–6,
182 ('Madge Wildfire'); *Waverley*
163–8, 171 ('Davie Gellatly')
Scriblerus Club 82, 108, 132
Seneca, and Apicius 100; imitated by
Rochester 68
Settle, Elkanah, in Pope's *Dunciad* 135
Shadwell, Thomas, on virtuosi 82
Shakespeare, William, compared with
Rochester 56–7, 71; Gray on 156;
influenced later writers 31–3, 35, 50,
146, 171 ('Ophelia'), 249; Jonson on
252–3; and Keats 187–90, 193, 201,
205, 210, 212, 216 (*Venus and Adonis*),
222; nineteenth-century critics on
214–15; quotation from applied to
poems of Hopkins 246–8, 250, 263;
and Skelton 14; Troilus on love 306
Sheffield, John, Earl of Mulgrave, duel
with Rochester 63
Shelley, P. B., compared with other
poets 185, 195–6, 211
Short, John, poet 318
Sidney, Sir Philip, compared with
Rochester 68–9
Skelton, John: 'Skelton', by John
Holloway 1–22; attacked Wolsey 15,
19–20; Caxton on 3–4; compared with
other poets esp. Chaucer 3, 5–14, 17–
21; influenced by Latin poets 15–16;
metre 9–10, 16–18; Puttenham on 2,
20–1; used proverbial sayings 14–17,
21